THE

W O R K S

Of the late INGENIOUS.

Mr. GEORGE FARQUHAR:

Containing all his

POEMS, LETTERS,

ESSAYS AND COMEDIES.

In Two VOLUMES.

VOL. I.

The TENTH EDITION. Corrected from the Errors of former Impressions. To which are added some MEMOIRS of the Author, never before Publish'd.

LONDON:

Printed for JOHN RIVINGTON, W. JOHNSTON, S. CROWDER, T. CASLON, T. LOWNDES, W. NICOLL, S. BLADON, C. CORBET, and R. BALDWIN.

MDCCLXXII.

MEMOIRS

OF

Mr. GEORGE FARQUHAR.

MR. *FARQUHAR*, an ingenious comic Writer and Poet, was the Son of a Clergyman in *Ireland*, and born at *Londonderry* in the Year 1678. There he received the Rudiments of Education, and discovered a Genius early devoted to the Muses. When he was very young, he gave Specimens of his Poetry; and discovered a Force of Thinking, and Turn of Expression, much beyond his Years. His Parents, having a numerous Issue, could bestow on him no other Fortune than a liberal and polite Education; therefore, when he was qualified for the University, he was sent to *Trinity College* in *Dublin*. This was in the Year 1694. He made great Progress in his Studies, and acquired a considerable Reputation: but his gay and volatile Disposition could not long relish the Gravity and Retirement of a College-life; and therefore, soon quitting it, he betook himself to the Diversions of the Stage, and got admitted into the Company of the *Dublin* Theatre. He had the Advantage of a good Person, and was well received as an Actor, though his Voice was somewhat weak: For which he was resolved to continue on the Stage, till something better should offer. But his Resolution was soon broken by an Accident, whereby he was near turning a feigned Tragedy into a real one: for being to play the Part of *Guyomar*, who kills *Vasquez*, in Mr. *Dryden*'s *Indian Emperor*, and forgetting to exchange his Sword for a Foil, in the Engagement he wounded his brother Tragedian, who represented *Vasquez*, very dangerously; and tho' the wound did not prove mortal, yet Mr. *Farquhar* was so shock'd at it, that he determined never to appear on the Stage any more.

Soon

Soon after this, Mr. *Farquhar*, who had now no I[
ducement to remain at *Dublin*, went to *London*. Aft
his Arrival there, which was in the Year 1696, the c
lebrated Actor and his Friend Mr. *Wilks*, ceased not
follicit him, till he had prevailed with him to write
Play. *Wilks*, knowing his Humour and Abilities, a
fured him, that he was confidered by all in a muc
higher Light than he had yet fhewn himfelf in ; and th
he was much fitter to furnifh Compofitions for tl
Stage, than to echo thofe of other Poets upon it ; but b
was more fuftantially invited by a genteel Accommod:
tion, which fuffered him to exercife his Genius at h
Leifure ; for the Earl of *Orrery*, who was a Patron a
well as Mafter of Letters, conferred a Lieutenant's Com
miffion upon him in his own Regiment in *Ireland*, whic
Mr. *Farquhar* held feveral Years, and behaved himfel
well as an Officer, giving feveral Proofs both of Cou
rage and Conduct. In the Year 1698, his firft Comedy
called *Love and a Bottle*, appeared upon the Stage
and for its fprightly Dialogue and bufy Scenes wa
well received by the Audience, tho' *Wilks* had n
Part in it. It may not be amifs to remember, that th
Year after the celebrated Mrs. *Oldfield* was, partly upo
his Judgment and Recommendation, admitted on th
Theatre ; fhe then being fixteen Years of Age.

In the Beginning of the Year 1700, he brought hi
Conftant Couple, or, *Trip to the Jubilee*, upon the Stage
it being then a Jubilee Year at *Rome*, when ▓▓▓▓▓lot:
of all Countries made their Trip thither, to ▓▓▓▓▓
and Trinkets for the Convenience of their Soul▓▓▓ Bo
dies. In the Character of Sir *Harry Wildair*, our Au
thor drew fo gay and airy a Figure, fo fuited to *Wilks*
Talents, and fo animated by his Gefture and Vivacity o
Spirit, that the Player gained almoft as much Reputa
tion as the Poet. Towards the latter End of this Year
we meet with Mr. *Farquhar* in *Holland*, probably upor
his military Duty ; from whence he has given a very fa
cetious Defcription of thofe Places and People, in Two
of his Letters dated from the *Brill* and from *Leyden*
And in a third, dated from the *Hague*, he very humou
roufly relates how merry he was there at a Treat made
by the Earl of *Weftmorland*, while not only himfelf, but
						King

King *William,* and others of his Subjects, were detained there by a violent Storm. There is also among his Poems, an ingenious Copy of Verses to his Mistress upon the same Subject; which Mistress is supposed to have been Mrs. *Oldfield:* For that Lady was often heard to speak afterwards of many agreeable Hours she had spent in Captain *Farquhar's* Company. In the Beginning of 1701, he was a Spectator, if not a Mourner, at Mr. *Dryden's* Funeral; but the Description he has made of it in one of his Letters is not much calculated to inspire Sorrow.

Mr. *Farquhar,* encouraged by the prodigious Success of his last Play, made a Continuation of it in the same Year 1701, in his Comedy called *Sir Harry Wildair,* or, *The-Sequel of the Trip to the Jubilee;* in which Mrs. *Oldfield* received as much Reputation, and was as greatly admired in her Part, as *Wilks* was in his. In 1702, he published his Miscellanies, or, Collection of Poems, Letters, and Essays, which contain a variety of humourous and pleasant Sallies of Fancy. It is said, that some of the Letters were published from Copies returned him, at the Request of Mrs. *Oldfield.* There is at the End of them an Essay, which is called, *A Discourse upon Comedy, in Reference to the English Stage.* There is one among the Letters, which he calls *The Picture,* containing a Description and Character of himself, which begins thus: *My Outside is neither better nor worse than my Creator made it, and the Piece being made by so great an Artist, 'twere Presumption to say there were many Strokes amiss. I have a Body qualified to answer all the Ends of its Creation, and that's sufficient. As to the Mind, which in most Men wears as many Changes as their Body, so in me 'tis generally dressed like my Person in black. In short, my Constitution is very splenetic and very amorous; both which I endeavour to hide, lest the former should offend others, and the latter incommode myself: And my Reason is so vigilant in restraining those two Failings, that I am taken for an easy-natured Man by my own Sex, and an ill-natured Clown by yours.—I have very little Estate, but what lies under the Circumference of my Hat; and should I by Misfortune come to lose my Head, I should not be worth a Groat. But I ought to thank Providence, that I can by three Hours Study live*

A 3

one-

*one-and-twenty, with Satisfaction to myself; and contr.
to the Maintenance of more Families, than some who t
Thousands a Year.* This, though not all, is enough
a Specimen.

In the Year 1703, came out another diverting Com
of his, called *The Inconstant*, or, *The Way to win h*
But now plain *English* Productions, with nothing
good Sense, natural Humour, and Wit to recomm
them, began to give way to *Italian* and *French* Ope
the airy Entertainments of Dancing and Singing, w.
conveyed no Instruction, awakened no generous Paf
nor filled the Breast with any thing great and mai
and therefore this Comedy was received more co
than the former, tho' not at all inferior to then
Merit. Mr. *Farquhar* was married this Year, and
was at first reported, to a great Fortune; which in
he expected, but was miserably disappointed. The I
had fallen in love with him, and so violent was her
sion, that she resolved to have him at any Rate; an
she knew he was too much dissipated in Life to fa
love, or to think of Matrimony, unless Advantage
annexed to it, she first caused a Report to be sprea
her being a great Fortune, and then had given hir
understand, that she was in love with him. *Farq*
married her; and what is pretty extraordinary, the
he found himself deceived, his Circumstances em
rassed, and his Family increasing, he never upbra
her for the Cheat, but behaved to her with all the
licacy and Tenderness of an indulgent Husband.

Very early in the Year 1704, a Farce called
Stage Coach, in the Composition of which he was joi
concerned with another, made its first Appearance,
was well received. His next Comedy, named *The T*
Rivals, was play'd in 1705. In 1706 was acted
Comedy, called *The Recruiting Officer*. He dedicate
to all Friends round the Wrekin, a noted Hill near *Shr*
bury, where he had been to recruit for his Comp;
and where, from his Observations on Country Life,
Manner that Serjeants inveigle Clowns to inlist, anc
Behaviour of the Officers towards the Milk-maids
Country Wenches, whom they seldom fail of deba
ing, he collected Matter sufficient to build a Con

upon; in which he was fo fuccefsful, that even now
that Comedy fails not to bring full Houfes. His laft
Comedy was *The Beaux's Stratagem*, of which he did not
live to enjoy the full Succefs. He was unhappily op-
preffed with fome Debts; and this obliged him to make
Application to a certain Courtier, who had formerly
given him many Profeffions of Friendfhip. His pretended Patron advifed him to convert his Commiffion
into the Money he wanted, and pledged his Honour,
that in a fhort Time he would provide him another.
This Circumftance appearing favourable, and unable to
bear the Thoughts of Want, he fold his Commiffion:
But when he renewed his Application, and reprefented
his diftreffed Situation, his noble Patron had forgot his
Promife, or rather perhaps had never refolved to fulfil
it. This diftracting Difappointment fo prey'd upon our
Author, that it carried him off this worldly Theatre,
while his laft Play was acting in the Height of its Succefs, at that of *Drury-lane*. His Death happened in
1707, before he was 30 Years of Age. His friend Mr.
Wilks was very kind to his two Daughters, and propofed
to his Brother Managers, who readily came into it, to
give each of them a Benefit, to put them out to Mantua-
makers.

The Author of the *Mufes Mercury,* or *Monthly Mifcellany,*
for *May* 1707, has the following Paffage. *All that love
Comedy will be forry to hear of the Death of Mr.* Farquhar,
*whofe two laft Plays had fomething in them truly humorous and
diverting. It is true, the Critics will not allow any Part of
them to be regular; but Mr.* Farquhar *had a genius for
Comedy, of which one may fay, that it was rather above Rules
than below them. His Conduct, though not artful, was fur-
prifing; his Characters, though not great, were juft; his
Humour, though low, diverting; his Dialogue, though loofe
and incorrect, gay and agreeable; and his Wit, though not
fuper-abundant, pleafant. In fhort his Plays have, upon the
whole, a certain Air of Novelty and Mirth, every Time they
are reprefented; and fuch as love to laugh at the Theatre
will probably mifs him more than they now imagine.* He
feems to have been a Man of Genius, rather fprightly
than great, rather flowery than folid. His Comedies
are diverting, becaufe his Characters are natural, and

A 4   fuch

fuch as we frequently meet with; but he has ufed no
Art in drawing them, nor does there appear any Force
of Thinking, or deep Penetration into Nature, in any of
his Performances; but rather a fuperficial View, pleafant
enough to the Eye, tho' capable of leaving no great
Impreffion on the Mind. He had, it muft be allowed,
a lively Imagination; but then it was not capable of
any great Compafs. He had Wit too; but it was of
fuch a Kind, that it rather loft than gained by being
dwelt upon: and it is certainly true, that his Comedies
in general owe their Succefs as much to the Player as to
any thing intrinfically excellent in themfelves.

However, if the Sale of Books be any Proof of their
Merit, there is Reafon enough to think well of Mr.
Farquhar; for the Eighth Edition of his Works, containing all his Poems, Effays, and Comedies, publifhed
in his Life-time, was printed in *London*, in 2 vols. 12mo.
in the Year 1742.

T O

TO THE

R E A D E R.

SIR,

*I*N *this Collection of Letters, it is but reasonable that you should have one among the rest ; and tho' I may want the Honour of your Acquaintance, yet be assur'd, there is no Person in the World more willing to oblige you than your humble Servant. I have heard such a Character of your Honour, your Wit, your Judgment, your Learning, and your Candour, that I am in a perfect Rapture to think how happy I shall be in your Hands.*

It was a good ancient Custom with our Forefathers, to begin their Prefaces with Kind Reader. *I would have reviv'd that Fashion with all my Heart, and call'd you* Courteous, *or* Gentle Reader, *as you very well deserve ; but I thought the Stile a little too obsolete for a Book that I design'd should be a Beau. For you must understand, Sir, that this Gentleman is Span new from Top to Toe, talks of every Thing but Religion, admires himself very much, and his greatest Ambition is to please the Ladies. But to finish his Character, he is perfectly civil to every Body he meets, and with a more particular and profound Respect does he run to kiss your Hands.*

He is none of those Bully-books that come bluff into the World, with Damme, Reader, *you're a Blockhead if you don't commend me.* No, no, Sir———*If you like him, why you have all the Sense that he thought you had*———*If you dislike him, you have more Sense than he was aware of, that's all.*

Besides all this, he has more Manners than to come among Gentlemen with his Taylor's Bill in his Hand, and to entertain the Company with a long Preface or Inventory to his Equipments ; as such a Thing cost so much, and such a Thing is worth so much, the Work of such a Part is excellent, the

A 5 *Fashion*

Fashion from Paris, *and the* Taylor *a* Frenchman; *you muſt pardon him for that,* Sir: *If you like the Suit, taking it all together, approve his Fancy, and allow it becomes him, he's your very humble Servant.*

Moreover, Sir, *I wou'd have you to know, that this Gentleman is of ſome Circumſtance and Condition, and has not been engag'd in the Shifts that ſome late Sparks are put to for their Habiliments, who ferrit all the Wit-brokers in Town, taking up from ſeveral Places, and ſtrut in a ſecond-hand Finery, patch'd up of the Scraps and Remnants of the eminent* Men of the Age. *For I muſt tell you,* Sir, *tho' his Cloaths be but plain, yet they are his own, taken up handſomely at one Place, where he may have Credit for as much more, when theſe are worn out.*

And now, dear Sir, *let me intreat you to receive him with the uſual Forms of Civility; if you be a Courtier, you will ſhew your Breeding; receive him with a ſincere Smile, ſwear to do him all the Service you can, and you will certainly keep your Word——as you us'd to do. From the City he expects more than an ordinary Reception, becauſe he is become one of their Honourable Society; he is bound to his Bookſeller, and ten to one may ſerve ſeven Years in his Shop, if the Town don't club to purchaſe his Freedom; he expects good Quarter from the Wits and Critics, becauſe he ſets up for neither; beſides, he has ſcatter'd ſome little Nonſenſe here and there, that they might not be diſappointed of their Prey. But his greateſt Concern is for his Entertainment with the Ladies, reſolv'd however not to complain, thinking it a greater Honour to fall a Sacrifice to the Reſentment of the Fair, than to live by the Approbation of Men. Tho' he has ſome Grounds for a more moderate Fate at their Hands, becauſe a great Part of the Work was firſt deſign'd for one of that Sex, without any farther Conſideration of pleaſing the World; and the Beauties of the Book, if there be any, were brought from a Lady's Cabinet to the Preſs; and if it can but from the Preſs get back again into the Ladies Cloſets, there may it reſt, and Peace be with it.*

Now, Sir, *as we met good Friends, pray let us part ſo; I hate quarrelling mortally, and eſpecially with a Perſon of your preſent Character and Condition; and as you like my Epiſtolary Stile, we ſhall ſettle a farther Correſpondence.*

On

On the Death of General Schomberg, *kill'd*
at the Boyn.

A PINDARICK.

I.

WHAT difmal Damp has overfpread the
War?
The Victor gives more than the Conquer'd
fears:
The Streams of Blood are loft in Floods of
Tears,
And Victory with drooping Wings comes flagging
from afar.

II.

The *Britiſh* Lion roars
Along the fatal Shores;
Th' *Ibernian* Harp in mournful Strains,
Mixt with the *Eccho* of the Flood, complains:
Round whofe reflecting Banks the grieving Voice,
Shakes with a trembling Noife,
As if afraid to tell
How the Great, Martial, Godlike *Schomberg* fell.

III.

Gods! How he ftood,
All terrible in Blood,
Stopping the Torrent of his Foes, and Current of the
He, *Mofes* like, with Sword inftead of Wand,   (Flood.
This redder Sea of Gore cou'd ftrait command;
But not, like *Mofes*, to fecure his Flight,
But Spite of Waves and Tides, to meet and fight.

IV.

he labouring Guns oppos'd his Paffage o'er
   With Throws tormented on the Shore,
Of which delivered, they ftart back and roar,
As frighted as the Monfter which they bore.
The furious Offspring fwath'd in curling Smoak,
   And wrapt in Bands of Fire,
   Hot with its Parent's fulph'rous Ire,
And wing'd with Death, flies hiffing to the Stroke.

V.

   Like fome great rugged Tow'r,
   The ancient Seat of Pow'r,
Bending with Age its venerable Halls,
With old and craggy Wrinkles on its Walls,
The Neighbour's Terror whilft it ftands, and Ruin when
   Thus mighty *Schomberg* fell —   (it falls.
   Spreading wide Ruins o'er the Ground,
With Defolation all around,
   Crufhing with deftructive Weight
   The Foes that undermine his feat;
Whilft *Victory*, that always fpread
Her tow'ring Pinions o'er his Army's Head,
Making his Banner ftill her Lure,
Like *Marius*'s Vultures, to make Conqueft fure,
Seeing the fpacious Downfal fo bemoan'd,
Perch'd on the Ruins, clapt her Wings, and groan'd.

VI.

Thus * *Ifrael*'s Hero 'twixt the Pillars fat,
The *Ne plus ultra* of his Fate;
Thefe *Columns* which upheld his Name,
   Much longer by their Fall,
Than thofe erected ftrong and tall,
The ftanding Limits of *Alcides*'s Fame,
   He fat depriv'd of Sight,
Like a black rolling Cloud involv'd in Night,
Conceiving *Thunder* in its fwelling Womb,
Big with furpizing Fate, and rufhing Doom:
No Flafh the fudden Bolt muft here difclofe:
The Lightning of his Eyes extinguifh'd by his Foes.

* *Sampfon.*

His

His Foes induftrious in their juggling Fate,
 Him flavifhly enchain'd we fee,
  To what muft fet him free,
And them his cheated Keepers captivate.
He fhook his Chains with fuch a Noife,
 The trembling Rout,
  Amidft their Joys,
  Gaz'd all about,
And heard the real *Sampfon* in the Voice:
 They faw him too, 'twas *Sampfon* all,
 Who by his Thundring Fall
 Gave the loud dread Alarm,
Dragging a Train of Vengeance by each *Giant* Arm,
Their chilling Fears did fuch Amazement frame,
They feem'd all ftiff and dead before the Ruin came:
The Ruin! only fuch unto his Foes;
From thence his glorious Monument arofe;
But *Time*'s corroding Teeth, in fpite of Stone,
Has eat thro' all, and even the very Ruin's gone:
But *Schomberg*'s Monument fhall ne'er decay,
 The gliding *Boys*
 Time never can disjoin,
Nor on its Floods impofe his Laws;
They flide, untouch'd, from his devouring Jaws,
And always running, yet muft ever ftay.

VII.

Hark! how the *Trumpets* hollow Clangors found!
The Army has receiv'd an univerfal Wound:
 The Death of *Schomberg* hung
 On every fault'ring Tongue,
 Whilft pallid Grief did place
A fympathizing Death in every Soldier's Face:
 But hold, ye mighty Chiefs,
 Sufpend your needlefs Griefs,
And let victorious Joy your Arms adorn;
 The mighty Warrior's *Ghoft*,
 Upon the *Stygian* Coaft,
Your Sorrows, more than his own Fate, does mourn.
 He fcorns to be lamented fo,
Moving in ftately *Triumph* to the Shades below.
Behold the Sprites that lately felt the Blow

          Of

Of his commanding warlike Arm,
They fhivering all ftart wide, and even more fleeting
  As if that powerful Hand,   [grow;
That cou'd their groffer Shapes alive command,
Had Power to diffolve their airy Form.

VIII.

Then let not funeral Plaints his Trophies wrong,
Let Spoils and Pageants march his Hearfe along,
And fhout his *Conclamatum* in Triumphal Song.
All baleful *Cyprus* muft be here deny'd,
But Laurel Wreaths fix in their blooming Pride;
For as he conquer'd living, fo he conqu'ring dy'd.

Written on Orinda's *Poems lent to a* Lady, *in Imitation of* Ovid.

ME *Damon* fends his amorous Caufe to plead,
   Orinda muft for *Damond interaede:*
Me has he chofe to move your angry Mind,
Me the foft Fav'rite of the fofter Kind.
Me has he chofe your rigorous Breaft to move,
He knows my Force in Poetry and Love.
Me has he chofe to tell his anxious Pain;
Read me, and read the Paffion of the Swain.
Whatever Power of Love my Lines can fhow,
It falls far fhort of what he feels for you:
Where'er *Orinda* melts in moving Strains,
Think, *Cælia,* think that *Damon* thus complains:
Whene'er I grieve, think *Damon* grieves for you,
Pity the Swain that does fo humbly fue:
This *Damon* begs, *Orinda* begs it too.

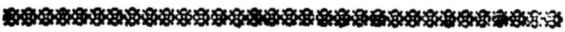

To the ingenious Lady, *Author of the* Fatal Friendfhip, *defign'd for a Recommendatory Copy to her Play.*

LET others call the facred Nine to aid
   Their moving Thoughts, in moving Numbers laid;
Invoke the fiery *God,* with all the Throng,
That ancient Bards implor'd to guide their Song;
                    Whilft

Whilſt I for nobler Inſpiration ſue,
Scorning their weaker Helps, invoking you.
You, who alone have Pow'r our Thoughts to raiſe,
And wing our Fancy to attempt your Praiſe,
Nought but your charming Beauty can diſpenſe
A Flame ſufficient to deſcribe your Senſe.
Whilſt ſo much Beauty in your Form is ſhown,
No Pen on Earth can reach it but your own.
Go on then, *Daphne*, *Phœbus* will purſue,
His chaſter Fires are all enjoy'd by you;
You are his fairer Nymph, you bear his Laurel too.
Go on, thou Champion for thy Sex deſign'd,
And prove the Muſes are of Female Kind;
Let diſtant Nations *Engliſh* Beauties prize,
As much for Charms of Wit, as Pow'r of Eyes:
Your moving Scenes the raviſh'd Audience drew,
Raptures we felt, as when your Eyes we view;
Such Arts were us'd to mix our Hopes and Fears,
You made Grief pleaſing, and we ſmil'd in Tears.
Thus Lovers view a Miſtreſs's Diſdain,
And love to look, tho' ſure to look in Pain.
Th' Effects of labour'd Art your Work reveals,
Yet a ſuperior Art that Art conceals.
Here Nature gains, tho' naked, thus diſplay'd;
Like Beauty, moſt adorn'd, when leaſt array'd.
Go on then, doubly arm'd, to conquer Men;
Phœbus his Harp and Bow, you boaſt your Eyes and Pen.
All to the firſt without Reluctance yield,
But your victorious Pen has forc'd the Field.

❋❋❋❋❋❋❋❋❋❋❋❋❋❋❋❋❋❋❋❋❋❋❋❋❋❋❋

An Epigram on the Riding-Houſe in Dublin, *made into a Chapel.*

A Chapel of the Riding-Houſe is made;
We thus once more ſee *Chriſt* in Manger laid;
Where ſtill we find the Jockey Trade ſupply'd,
The *Layman* bridled, and the *Clergy* ride.

To a Lady, being detain'd from visiting her by a Storm.

SO poor *Leander* view'd the *Sestian* Shore,
Whilst Winds and Waves oppos'd his Passage o'er;
More moist with Tears, because by Floods restrain'd,
Than in these Floods had he his Wish obtain'd;
So drown'd yet burnt within, upon the Banks he
    lean'd;
Lean'd, begging Calms; and as he begging lay,
Implor'd with Sighs the Winds, with Tears the Sea.
One wou'd have thought by all these Mixtures sent,
To raise a second greater Storm he meant.
Just so whilst kept from you by Storms I weep;
The Winds my Sighs, my Tears augment the Deep;
With flowing Eyes I view the distant Side,
The Space that parts us doth myself divide.
Here's only left the poor external Part,
Whilst you, where'er you move, possefs my Heart.
Depriv'd of Love, and your blest Sight, I die,
Whilst you the first, and Storms the last deny.

The Lover's Night.

THE Night's black Curtain o'er the World was
    spread,
And all Mankind lay Emblems of the Dead;
A deep and awful Silence, void of Light,
With dusky Wings sat brooding o'er the Night:
The rolling Orbs mov'd slow from East to West,
With Harmony that lull'd the World to Rest;
The Moon withdrawn, the oozy Floods lay dead,
The very influence of the Moon was fled;
Some twinkling Stars, that thro' the Clouds did peep,
Seeming to wink as if they wanted Sleep;
All Nature hush'd, as when dissolv'd and laid
In silent *Chaos* ere the World was made;
Only the Beating of the Lover's Breast
Made Noise enough, to keep his Eyes from Rest;
His little World, not like the greater, lay,
In loudest Tumults of disorder'd Day;

His

His Sun of Beauty shone to light his Breast,
With all its various Toils and Labours prest;
The Sea of Passions in his working Soul,
Rais'd by the Tempests of his Sighs, did roll
In tow'ring Floods, to overwhelm the whole;
Those Tyrants of the Mind, vain Hope and Fear,
That still by Turns usurp an Empire there,
Now raising Man on high, then plunging in Despair.
Thus *Damon* lies, his Grief no Rest affords,
'Till swelling full, it thus burst out in Words.
Oh! I could curse all Woman-kind but one,
And yet my Griefs proceed from her alone;
Was not our Paradise by Woman lost?
But in this Woman still we find it most.
Hell's greatest Curse a Woman, if unkind,
Yet Heav'ns great Blessing, if she loves, we find.
Oh! if she lov'd, no God the Bliss cou'd tell,
She wou'd be Heav'n itself, were she not so much Hell,
Thus our chief Joys with most Allays are curst,
And our best Things, when once corrupted, worst.
But Heav'n is just; ourselves the Idols fram'd,
And are for such vain Worship justly damn'd.
Thus the poor Lover argu'd with his Fate;
Æmylia's Charms now did his Love create,
That Love repuls'd, now prompted him to hate.
Sometimes his Arms wou'd cross his Bosom rest,
Hugging her lovely Image printed on his Breast;
Where flattering Painter Fancy shew'd his Art,
In charming Draughts, his Pencil *Cupid's* Dart;
The Shadow drawn so lively did appear,
As made him think the real Substance there;
Then was he blest, all Rapture stunn'd with Joy,
Excess of Pleasure did his Bliss destroy;
He thought her naked, soft, and yielding Waste,
Within his pressing Arms lay folded fast;
Nay, by the Gods, she really there was plac'd:
Else how cou'd Pleasure to such Raptures flow?
Th' Effect was real.——Then the Cause was so.
What more can most substantial Pleasure boast,
Than Joy when present, Memory when past?
Then Bliss is real which the Fancy frames,
Or these call'd real Joys, are only Dreams.

The

The Brill, August the 10th, 1700, *New Stile.*

Dear S A M,

TO give you a fhort Journal of my fhort Voyage,
on *Wednefday* I got to *Harwich* about Four in
the Afternoon, and alighted at one of the cleaneft, beft
furnifh'd *Inns* in the Kingdom; my Warrant for the
Packet-boat coft me *Half a Piece*, and to the Officers
for not executing their Duty, *Half a Crown*. This
Place, like moft Sea-Ports, we found extravagantly
dear; but to eafe that Inconvenience, we were advis'd
to get aboard by Eleven at Night. Here I met a Gentleman, whofe Company I was very happy in, though
extremely concern'd for the Occafion of his Voyage,
which was an Exprefs to the King of the Duke of
Gloucefter's Death. This was the firft News I had of
this public Lofs, which I had not much Time to reflect upon, being fo nearly touch'd on the Score of my
private Concern by a violent Storm that immediately
came upon us: You may guefs at our Circumftances,
when I affure you, that our greateft Comfort was the
Lightning, that fhew'd the Seamen their Bufinefs, which
otherwife they muft have grop'd for; all Intercourfe of
Speech being broken off by the Loudnefs of the Thunder.
We had fuch warm Work, that I fometimes allowed it a
juft Thought, that Satan fhould be entitled *Prince of
the Air*; and again, why the Devil fhould command
the Artillery of Heaven I could not fo well comprehend. I fupported myfelf with the Thought, that
Providence had no defign upon me, but that this Tu-
mult of the Elements was their Manner of expreffing
their Grief for the Lofs of his *Highnefs*; or that they
were angry at Mr. L———r for bringing fuch un-
welcome News into their Dominions, and for making a
Property of them to fpread it abroad. By this Kind of
Poetical Philofophy I bore up pretty well under my Apprehenfions, tho' never worfe prepared for Death, I muft
confefs; for I think I had never fo much Money about
me at a Time. We had fome Ladies aboard that were
fo extremely fick, that they often wifh'd for Death, but
were

mnably afraid of being drown'd. But as the
e fays, *Sorrow may laft for a Night, but Joy cometh
erning*; the Weather clear'd up with the Day,
d turn'd Wefterly, and in a few Hours, I was
> fay, we faw *England* out of Sight. All *Thurf-*
had a frefh Gale and cold Chickens; our Wine
out at a ftrange Rate; for our Stomachs ebb'd
v'd like the Element. On *Friday* Morning we
ie Coaft of *Holland*, a ftiff Gale, and the Sea
h. I was mightily pleafed to view the Con-
you may be fure; but as I ftood upon the *Peep*
; its firft Appearance with my *Perfpective*, I had
Rebuke for my Curiofity by a great Sea, that
Fore and *Aft*, that I was feafon'd for a *Dutchman*
ately. Whether this be a Compliment of Salu-
fually paid to Strangers, or that the *Batavian*
ards took me for a Spy upon their Frontiers, I
ave the Skipper to determine. In fhort, by
; of a ftaunch Ship, and the Influence of a ftaunch
in Favour of the *Old Bailey Bar*, we got over
at the *Maefe*; and the *Dutch* Wave has clear'd
-fight of an Error that we *Britons* are very fond
the *Thames* is the fineft River in the Univerfe;
.n affure you, *Sam*, that the *Rhine* is as much
it, as a *Pair of Oars* before a *Sculler*, let all the
between *Chelfea* and *Richmond* argue never fo
the contrary; tho' in one Sort of *Traffick* upon
t of the *Thames* we exceed the whole World,
· the Quantity and Cheapnefs of the Commo-
nd I believe the Store-houfe for this Kind of
ncluding the *Play-houfe* and the *Rofe*, may con-
th moft *Marts* in *Europe*.
Day at Eleven we landed at the *Brill*, and
ave a fmall Tafte of this *Republick*, that makes
Noife in the World.——My Fancy, in refpect
ctation, has generally been fo fruitful, that the
Part of my Hopes has frequently ended in
intments; and I have feldom found Things
> to anfwer the *Idea* that I have ufually fram'd
Excellence; but here I muft confefs the Rea-
:eds the Shadow, and I am pleas'd once in my
find a Thing that can afford me fubftantial
Pleafure

Pleasure in the Enjoyment. I have read much of this Place, fancy'd more, yet all falls short of what I see.

At my first Entrance into this Town, I made one Discovery, which I believe has hitherto escap'd most Travellers, *viz.* That the *Dutch* are the greatest *Beaux* in the World, only with this Difference from the Gentleman at *White's*, that their Finery is much more noble and substantial ; I never knew the fairest, finest, full-bottom Wig, most nicely fixt on the most beautiful Block in the Side Box, look half so genteel as a *Dutch* Canal with a stately Row of flourishing Trees on each Side, and some Twenty beautiful Bridges laid a-cross it, within Sixty or Seventy Paces one of another. I never knew a Valet, and a Barber with Razors, Tweezers, Perfumes, and Washes, work half so hard upon a Gentleman's Face, that design'd a Conquest on a Birth-Night, as I have seen a lusty *Dutch* Woman with a Mop and warm Water scrub the Marbles and Tiles before the Door, till she had scour'd them brighter than any Fop's Complexion in the Universe. No First-rate Beau with us, drawn by his Six before and Six behind, lolling luxuriously in his Coach, appears half so gallant as a jolly *Skipper* at the Stern of his Barge, with a fur'd Cap like Rays about his Head, the Helm in his Hand, and his Pipe in his Mouth, with Liberty seated in One *Whisker*, and Property in t'other ; and in this Splendor making the *Tour* of half a Dozen fine Cities in a Day, without either Qualm of the Spleen or Twinge of the Gout. Such a Person I take for a Beau of the first Magnitude, who scorning to be lugg'd by Beasts as Fellows are to *Tyburn*, can harness the Winds and Waves for his Equipage ; and improving on the Works of Providence, make the universal Elements (Air and Water) submit to his private Composition of Advantage and Diversion. To see the Wind work in his Sails, and play with his Pendants, must certainly afford more substantial and pure Satisfaction, than the Wince of a Horse, or the Crack of a Coach-whip.

In short, dear *Sam*, I am not so bigotted to Domestic Customs, as not to approve what is admirable here : and you must pardon me, that I have thrown up the Prejudices of Nativity with my Beef and Pudding as I

came

came over ; and 'tis no fmall Part of my prefent
Wonder, why we fhould call the *Dutch* a flovenly Sort
of People, fince to the Eye, which muft determine that
Circumftance, they are much more gaudy than that
Nation we fo mimic and admire, and with this Advantage, that they are gay without Levity, and fine
beyond Foppery. Why we fhould mention the *Dutch*
with Contempt, and the *French* with Admiration, is a
fevere Satire upon the *Englifh* Judgment, when the
Bravery of the Former attract the Admiration of Men,
and the Pageantry of the Latter draw only the Eyes of
Women : But our *Englifh* Ladies are fo very fine, that
we are very willing to pleafe them, and thus are drawn
into this unreafonable Prejudice ; but we ought to take
care, that by being thus particular Slaves to our refpective *Miftreffes*, we be'nt drawn at laft into univerfal
Bondage to a *Mafter.* The *French* have taken no fmall
Pains of late Years to render themfelves agreeable ;
they treat us like a Miftrefs, do every Thing that they
fancy will pleafe us, till they bring us at laft to act
whatfoever fhall pleafe them. But this is no news ;
and I think it a little improper to tell you an *Englifh*
Story from a Place where you may expect fome foreign
Entertainment. I have no more to fay at prefent, but
that I am juft going for *Rotterdam*, and departing from
a *Scotch* Houfe here, where nothing of that Country is
to be found but the Landlord ; for the Rooms are a
Paradife for Cleanlinefs, but the Hoft is a Rogue for
his Reckoning. I have got fuch a Heap of Silver out
of a Piftole, as upon a handfome Counter might give
Credit to a Banker ; and I can affure you, that while I
have a Brother to that Piftole left, you fhall not fee

Your Friend and Servant.

Leyden,

Leyden, October, 15, 17(

Dear S A M,

THE ufual Excufe of Gentlemen abroad for ne
lecting their Friends at home is, that new S
of different Objects continually entertaining us w
Changes of Admiration, the Ideas of our old Acquain
ance are by Degrees worn out by the Acceffion of t
new; but this kind of Forgetfulnefs were too fever(
Charge upon the Merit of my Friends and my ou
Gratitude, both which I will chufe to maintain; a
I leave it to your Charity to make me an Excufe i
my Silence. The Truth is, I have had a very tedic
Fit of Sicknefs, which had almoft fent your Friend
longer Journey than he was willing to undertake
prefent; but now being pretty well recovered, I c
only inform you in general, that every Day fupri2
me with fome agreeable Object or other; and I fi
very much to my Wonder, that the Accounts I have h
of this Country are very different from the Obfervatio
that may be made upon the Place. Some general R
marks there are indifputably certain, as that nothi
can parallel the *Dutch* Induftry, but the Luxury
England; and that the Money laid out in the Taverns
London, in purchafing Difeafes, would victual the whc
United Provinces very plentifully at their wholfor
Courfe of Diet; that the Standing Army maintain'd
the *Dutch* for their Security againft a foreign For(
are not half fo expenfive as the Fifty thoufand Lawy(
kept up by our civil Factions in *England*, for no oth
Ufe but to fet us continually by the Ears; People, li
the *Jews*, that are tolerated in all Governments for t
Intereft of the Public, while their main Drift is to e
rich themfelves, and who by their Gettings and Cu
ning have brought their Riches and Practice into
Proverb. The Lawyers here put the Queftion onl
Whether the Thing be lawful? and upon Applicati(
to the Statutes the Controverfy is immediately d
termined. But our Cafuifts at *Weftminfter* difpute n
fo much upon the Legality of the Caufe, as upon tl

Lett

etter of the Law, and make more Cavils on the
leaning of the Words that fhould determine Juftice,
ian upon the Equity of the Allegations contended for
y the Parties ; and the Bulk of our Laws have loaded
iftice fo heavily, that 'tis become a Burden to the
eople, who in Regard of their Sufferings in this Kind
iould borrow an Appellation from Phyfic, and be
all'd *Patients* rather than *Clients*.

Another Thing worth Confideration, in Refpect of
he Laws in *Holland*, is this: None but honeft Men
nake Eftates by their Practice; for the fiding with the
nrong Party brings the Lawyer into Contempt, and
ays him under a fevere Reprehenfion, either of Ig-
iorance in his Bufinefs, or Knavery to the People:
ience it comes to pafs, that Injuftice, not finding a
Patron to fupport its Caufe, is forc'd to remove to a
neighbouring Country, where the wrong Side was never
known to make its Affertor blufh; where the Eloquence
of S——rs and the Impudence of S——n are plaufible
Pretences for patronizing Injuftice and abufing the
Client : But there are Bravoes in all Parts of the World,
that will take Money for cutting of Throats, whether
there be Grounds or not for the Refentment.

So much for the Law, now for the Gofpel, *Sam.*
I think *Holland* may contend for the Catholic Church
with any Part in *Europe*, becaufe it is more univerfal
in its Religion than any Country in the Univerfe.
'Tis a pleafant Thing to fee *Chriftians, Mahometans,
Jews, Proteftants, Papifts, Armenians* and *Greeks*, fwarm-
ing together like a Hive of Bees, without One Sting
of Devotion to hurt one another; they all agree about
the Bufinefs of this Life, becaufe a Community in
Trade is the Intereft they drive at; and they never
joftle in the Way to the Life to come, becaufe every
one takes a different Road. One great Caufe of this fo
amicable a Correfpondence and Agreement, is, that
only the Laity of thefe Profeffions compofe the Mixture; here are no Ingredients of Prieftcraft to four the
Compofition; Pulpits indeed they have, but not like
Hudibras's Ecclefiaftic Drums, that are continually
beating up for Volunteers, to the alarming the whole
Nation. Here is no Intereft of Sects to be manag'd

under

under the Cloak of gaining Profelytes to the '
nor ftrengthning of Parties by Pretence of reclain
Souls ; every Shepherd is content with his own
and *Mufti, Levite, Pope* and *Prefbiter*, are all Ch:
in this, that they live in Unity and Concord.

'Tis a ftrange Thing, *Sam*, that among us,
can't agree the whole Week, becaufe they go di
Ways upon *Sundays :* This is to make the Lord's
Sower of Diffenfion, and Religion (which is call
Bond of Peace) to be the Brand of Difcord and
buftion : But we have fome Preackers that think
felves infpir'd with the Spirit, when they are
poffefs'd by the Devil ; the Fervency of whbfe
difmiffes Congregations with Heats and Heart-bu
of Spirit, and blows up the Coals on the Altar
their Neighbour's Houfes on Fire ; the Efficacy
Pulpit is fufficiently fhewn in the Practice of the
gregations. No People in the World are fo 1
notional Principles of Faith ; and to what Purpo
following Inftance will fhew you. Two Gentlei
my Acquaintance, one a devout Hearer at *Covent*
den Church, and the other a violent Zealot for]
Burgefs's Meeting, met one Evening at *Tom's*
Houfe, and wou'd adjourn to the *Fleece Tavern*,
courfe upon fome Point of Doctrine managed that
by their refpective Minifters. The Drawer brou:
a Bottle of new *French*, and the Diffenter intr(
Predeftination : After two or three hearty Glaffe
Difpute grew pretty warm, and the Quotations
Fathers and the Texts of Scripture made fuch a
that two Wenches, that ufually ply upon thofe :
over-hearing the Buftle, took them for a couple
vites, and fo made account to bolt in upon 'em, a
their Mackarel ; the Fervency of the Argumen
prefently abated upon the Appearance of the L
and a Topick of a more familiar Nature affum'd
both being pretty well convinc'd of their Oppo
Fire and Fancy, the Whores were difmifs'd, and
deftination re-affum'd ; the Argument grew warm
the Difputants grew fuddled : In fhort, they dil
themfelves ftark drunk, drew their Swords to deci(
Controverfy ; and had not one Mr. *Fern* come in,

ds that Predeſtination had not ſent one to the
ınd t'other to the Gallows. But they parted
at laſt, and ſaid one to t'other, *I am ſorry at my
lear Friend, that you won't go to Heaven my Way*;
away he reel'd to a Bawdy-houſe. Now the
f the Fable is this : If the Divines, inſtead of
peculative Theology, had preach'd that Day a
ng Sermon againſt Drunkenneſs and Fornication,
bable that the *Faith* of theſe Gentlemen had been
ıe leſs fortify'd, and their *good Works* much more
'd.

I beg your Pardon for this Digreſſion ; I was
to ſay that, excepting a few general Remarks,
f which I have mention'd, the Accounts we have
People are very lame, and ſometimes exactly op-
o the Truth : I ſhall mention one or two Particu-
ıt I found very obvious.

have a Notion in *England* that the *Dutch* are very
Drunkards ; whether this Aſperſion ariſes from
People's confounding the *High-Dutch* with the
or that there is a Sottiſhneſs in their Miens and
lexions, I can't determine ; but this I can aſſure
hat the Report is as falſe, as ſhou'd I aver, that
ople in *London* are the moſt chaſte and ſober Gen-
ı in the World. 'Tis true, indeed, they will take
oping Glaſs of Brandy, but that is only what is
tely neceſſary to moderate the Moiſture and Cold-
f their Conſtitution, and us'd in ſuch Quantity by
eaner Sort only, who living continually in the
ː, muſt require an Allowance to fortify themſelves
ſ the Chilneſs of their Habitations ; for you muſt
that whole Families, Men, Women and Children,
ontinually in Boats. and have no more Tenement
y-land than a *Thames* Salmon ; but notwithſtand-
ıis incumbent Neceſſity of their taking a Cup of
ːreature, I never have ſeen, ſince I came into this
try, but one *Dutchman* drunk ; and altho' his Im-
ıence was no more than is naturally incident to any
in his Condition, yet the whole Boatful of People,
ıe Number of ſixty Perſons, ſhew'd the greateſt
ſion imaginable to his Circumſtances, except two
ıreé jolly *Engliſhmen* that made very good Sport with

his Humour; and had not we, with some *French* Gentlemen, protected his Carcase, his Countrymen wou'd have sous'd him in the Canal very heartily for his Debauch.

As the laborious Life of the inferior Sort requires an exhilerating Glafs, so the same Neceffity, both as to Time and Charge, secures them from Excefs : As for their Gentry, they are indeed sociable in their own Houfes; but were it not for Strangers, all Places of Public Entertainment muft confequently fall ; which is the greateft Argument imaginable for the Sobriety and Temperance of a People ; whereas 'tis very well known, that if the very Taverns in *London*, with Seven or Eight handfome Churches, and One or Two of our Inns of Court, (all which we could well enough fpare) were but handfomely feated on the Banks of a River, they would make a Figure with some of the moft remarkable Cities in *Europe*. This indeed is a noble Argument of the Riches of *England* ; but whether our Luxury fprung from Plenty, or the Temperance of *Holland*, the Effect of Neceffity, be the happier State, is a Queftion that I want Leifure now to determine.

Another Account we have current among us, that there are no Beggars in *Holland* ; that they are very careful in employing the Poor. That their Manufactures require a great many Hands is moft certain, but ocular Demonftration is too ftrong a Proof againft all this Induftry ; and I am apt to believe, that the Order of Mendicants is of a very late Inftitution, elfe fo vifible a Falfity cou'd never have put this Trick upon Travellers. Whether their late expenfive Wars have ruin'd more People than their Manufactures can employ, or that the Poverty of the *Spaniards* in the Neighbouring *Netherlands*, have by degrees infected the meaner Sort, I fhan't be pofitive ; but nothing is more certain, than that a well-difpos'd Chriftian may find as many Objects of Charity here as in any Part of *England*, if we may judge of their Wants by the Fervency of their Cries.

I do believe that the Charity of the *Dutch* is no great Encouragement to Beggars ; which is the Reafon (I conceive) why the Poor flock all to the Highways and

Trad-

outs, where the Opportunity is good for Appli-
o Strangers.

thefe, and fome other fuch-like Particulars, I
t a Matter of Speculation, how the Generality
Englifh Nation, being fo near Neighbours to
ite, fhou'd be fo very fhort in the Knowledge of
nners and Conftitution of this People ; but this
prefume to proceed upon the following Ac-

of our *Englifh* that vifit this Place, are either
Gentlemen that come abroad to travel, or Mer-
that make a fhort Trip upon their own private
ns.

the ufual Way with the firft of thefe to take
! en paffant, either going or coming ; and being
ul Sparks, are fo fond of the Finery at *Paris*,
elicacy of *Rome*, that they han't Leifure, forfooth,
ell upon the Solidity of this Place. *France* and
e their Provinces, and *Holland* their Inn upon
oad ; they lie for a Night, and away the next
ng.

y can tell you, perhaps, that the *Dutch* Manner
velling is very commodious ; that the *Hague* is a
Village, *Amfterdam* a fine City, and that the
are a Parcel of heavy, dull, unconverfible
ires, and fo they leave them. Nothing can relifh
f old *England* than this peremptory Declaration. I
willingly underftand how Gentlemen can make
Eftimate of the Wit and Ingenuity of a People,
they don't ftay to make one Acquaintance in the
ry, nor can fpeak one Syllable of their Language.
ft of our young Nobility and Gentry travel under
lition of *French* Governors, who, however honeft
ir Intentions of ferving their Pupils, are never-
full of their *Moy-Meme*; and from the Prejudices
th and Education, like all other People, are moft
ible to the Manners, Language, Drefs and Beir of their own Nation: and though perfectly
, perhaps, in the Accomplifhments that compofe
we call a fine Gentleman, yet 'tis probable they
all fhort in thofe Qualifications that are abfolutely
ary to an *Englifhman*, in refpect of the Intereft of

B 2   his

his Country, and of thefe I take the *Dutch* Language to
be none of the moft trivial. For at the prefent Juncture,
which renders it not only ours, but the Intereft of
Europe, that we fhould be well with thefe People, it
were not unneceffary that our Amity fhould be linked
with private Friendfhips and Correfpondence, as by
public Leagues and Alliances. An Inftance of which
is very vifible to our Prejudice in the Habitudes and
Familiarity contracted by our young Gentlemen at
Paris, which, without all Difpute, is one great Reafon
for the Influence retain'd by that Court, not only over
our Fafhions and Behaviour, but which is extenfive
alfo to Matters of more weighty Confequence, including
even our Councils, Laws and Government.

The fecond Sort of People that make a Turn into
this Country, are our Merchants, whofe Speculations
are limited by a few Particulars, their Affairs not ex-
tending to the Policies of State, nor the Humours of
the People, they are fatisfied to mind their Bufinefs
only, and to underftand the Encouragement of Trade,
the Prices and Cuftoms upon Goods, the Value of
Stock, and the Rates of Exchange : Their Converfation
lies chiefly between the Store-houfe and the Broad-fide,
and that in one or two Cities at moft, where their
Corefpondents are refident. So that all the Account we
muft expect from thefe Perfons, muft only relate to
their Trade in general, or to fome particular Branch
of it, which is univerfally underftood already through
the Intercourfe of our Dealing, and neither fo improving to our Polity, nor fatisfactory to the Curious.
But even among their Encouragments of Trade fo univerfally known and admir'd, as the advantageous Situation of their Country, their natural Propenfity to
Navigation, the Lownefs of their Impofts, *&c.* yet by
an odd Accident I came to underftand one Policy in
their Trading Conftitution, which I have never hitherto
met with in any verbal or written Account whatfoever.
The Matter was thus in all its Circumftances.

One Day upon the *Exchange* at *Rotterdam*, I cafually
met a Gentleman, who fome time ago lived one of the
moft confiderable Merchants in *Ireland*, and about
fome four Years fince, by great Loffes at Sea, was
                                                      forc'd

fly his Country in a very mean Condition. I
in mind of his Misfortunes by a Favour he
ferr'd upon me of a Bottle of Claret and a
ongue, at launching of a new ship that he had
Dublin; which Vessel (Bottom and Goods all
was unfortunately loft the very firft Voyage.
tleman feem'd very fenfible of his Misfortunes,
ıl told me, That he ftill had a glafs of Wine
ngue at my Service, if I would come and fee
is Houfe that Evening. I made him a Vifit,
ℸ to my no fmall Surprize, an handfome Houfe,
rnifh'd, excellent Meat, and as good *Burgandy*
oy'd the Heart of Man. I took the Freedom
ı Merchant how a Bankrupt fhou'd come by all
Anfwer to which he gave me the following Ac-
his Affairs.

utch, Sir, (faid he) have a Law, that whatever
t in any Part of *Europe,* who has had any con-
Traffic with this Country, whofe Honefty is
by his former Accounts, and can prove by
Teftimony, that his Loffes and Misfortunes
chargeable upon his Ignorance nor Extrava-
ut purely thofe of unfortunate Chance, above
of human Prevention; that then fuch a Mer-
ıy repair to them, have the Freedom of any
in the State, have a Supply of whatever
e is willing to take up out of the Public Re-
pon the bare Security of his Induftry and In-
and all this upon the Current Intereft, which
above Four *per Cent.*

nt to this (continu'd the Gentleman) my Qua-
for this Credit being fufficiently teftify'd, I
here two Thoufand Pounds Sterling, and in
s have gain'd Fifty *per Cent.* So that by God's
·, and my own diligent Endeavours, I queftion
n a few Years I fhall be able to fhew my Face
editors, return to my Country, and there live
·o.

ıre two Points remarkable enough: A cha-
ıɛ̃tion to relieve diftrefs'd Strangers, and a
f State for the Intereft of the Republic, which
ʳ foon difcover by repeating the Conditions.

His Honefty muft be manifeft from his former Accoun
his Sufficiency in Bufinefs apparent from his precede
Manner of Dealing, his Misfortunes fuch as were abo
human Prevention, as by Storms, Pirates or the lik
but above all, he muft have fome confiderable Traf
with this Country; there's the Clincher, the *Utile*, t
greateft Encouragement imaginable for all Foreigne
to traffic with this Nation, and for the moft ingenio
Traders, who are not always the moft fortunate,
feek a Refidence among them : and what a Life a
Vigour thefe two Circumftances may add to the Tra
of a Nation, the flourifhing Condition of this People
the moft fufficient Witnefs.

Now, *Sam*, I have tir'd you moft certainly, for I a
weary myfelf, and we are feldom the fooneft tir'd wi
our own : The Gravity of my Stile you muft impute
the Air of the Country, and the Length of my Letter
a very rainy Day that has kept me within ; and to c
cufe the Matter it fhall coft you nothing, for I fent
by a Gentleman who can affure you that what I he
faid is true. I fhall at leaft conclude with a Tru
that I am,

Dear S I R, Yours, &

⟨ornamental divider⟩

An Epilogue *fpoken by Mr.* Wilks, *at his firft A
pearance upon the* Englifh *Stage.*

AS a poor Stranger wreck'd upon the Coaft,
    With Fear and Wonder views the Dangers paft
So I with dreadful Apprehenfions ftand,
And thank thofe Pow'rs that brought me fafe to Lan
With Joy I view the fmiling Country o'er,
And find, kind Heav'ns ! an hofpitable Shore.
'Tis *England* ———— This your Charities declare,
But more the Charms of *Britifh* Beauties there ;
Beauties that celebrate this Ifle afar,
They by their Smiles, as much as you by War ;
True-Love, true Honour, here I can't fail to play,
Such lively Patterns you before me lay.

V

: Offence, tho' not from Cenfure free,
diftant Ifle too kind to me;
with Favours I was forc'd away,
I wou'd not accept what I cou'd never pay.
[cou'd pleafe; but there my Fame muft end,
1er none muft come to boaft, but mend.
ement muft be great, fince here I find
s, Examples, and my Mafters kind.

XXXXXXXXXXXXXXXXXXXXXXXXXX

ilogue *on the propos'd Union of the two Houfes.*

W all the World's ta'en up with State Affairs,
Some wifhing Peace, fome calling out for Wars.
sewike fit we fhou'd inform the Age,
ire the prefent Politics o'th' Stage:
ifferent States, ambitious both, and bold,
e-born Souls; the New Houfe and the Old,
mg contended, and made ftout Effays,
fhou'd be Monarch, abfolute in Plays,
as the Battle held with bloody Strife,
many ranting Heroes loft their Life;
h their Enmity, that e'en the Slain
quer Death, rife up and fight again.
'rom the Gallery, Box, the Pit and all,
dience look'd, and fhook its awful Head,
ing to fee fo many Thoufands fall,
n look'd pale to fee us look fo red.
ce of Numbers, and Poetic Spell,
rais'd the ancient Heroes too from Hell,
1 our Troops; and on this bloody Field,
feen great *Cæfar* fight, great *Pompey* yield.
ims of Treafure too we did advance,
w fome mercenary Troops from *France*;
ooted Rogues, who when they got their Pay,
o their Heels——*Alons*——and run away.
ou have feen great *Philip*'s conqu'ring Son,
1 twelve Years did the whole World o'er-run;
as he fought, and found a harder Job
t One Play-houfe, than fubdue the Globe:

All

All this from Emulation for the Bays,.
You lik'd the Conteſt, and beſtow'd your Praiſe :
But now (as buſy Heads love ſomething new)
They would propoſe an *Union*—Oh, *Mort dieu.*
If it be ſo, let *Cæſar* hide his Head,
And fight no more for Glory, but for Bread.
Let *Alexander* mourn, as once before,
Becauſe no Worlds are left to conquer more.
But if we may judge ſmall from greater things,
The preſent Times may ſhew what *Union* brings,
You feel the Danger of *United Kings.*
If we grow one, then Slav'ry muſt enſue
To Poets, Players, and, my Friends, to you.
For to one Houſe confin'd, you then muſt praiſe
Both curſed Actors, and confounded Plays.
Then leave us as we are, and next advance
Bravely to break the Tye 'twixt *Spain* and *France.*

❊❊❊❊❊❊❊❊   ❊❊❊❊❊❊❊❊❊❊

On the Death of a Lady's Sparrow, in imitation
Catullus for his Leſbia's.

MOurn all ye Muſes, mourn ye Nymphs and Lov
Mourn all ye Woods, mourn all ye Trees ;
Weep all ye Streams, ye Foreſts fade and mourn, (Grov
Your well-lov'd Bird muſt ne'er again return.
Let the dull Air ne'er be ſerene again,
Let all the Winds with loudeſt Sighs complain.
The once bleſt Winds, whilſt they cou'd bear away
His charming Notes, and with his Feathers play.
How ſhall I grieve, or how bewail his Death ?
None fit to ſing, that wants his tuneful Breath :
Like the melodious Swan prepar'd to die,
He ſhou'd himſelf have ſung his Elegy.
Ye winged Choriſters, come here and ſing,
Lament his Death ; ſweet Flow'rs and Bloſſoms bring,
To ſtrew his Grave with Beauties of the Spring.
Sweet was his Voice, well were his Notes belov'd,
His careful Miſtreſs with his Tunes he mov'd ;
Oft has he ſung upon the Flow'ry Plain,
But ne'er, alaſs ! like wretched me, in vain.

. her alone the pretty Bird wou'd fly,
to the Fair, and in her Bofom lie;
ofom, fairer than the Silver Sky:
did the Wanton play, and there was bleft,
ere alone he made his downy Neft;
r Difcourfe to him he underftood,
indly anfwer'd with what Voice he cou'd.
her Head oft wou'd he flutt'ring move,
pread a living Canopy above;
houfand pretty things fhew'd his officious Love.
fhe walk'd, when fhe began to fing,
her own Breath he fann'd her from his Wing;
would he pluck the Daifies here and there,
o her Hands the blufhing Prefents bear.
Woods he fcorn'd, and chofe with her to dwell,
ingers did all Boughs by far excel.
nged Chorifters, come here and fing,
his Death; fweet Flow'rs and Bloffoms bring,
w his Grave with Beauties of the Spring.
! he's gone, his pleafing Sports muft ceafe;
one, alas! and now no more can pleafe;
his Voice, and ftill his ftiff'ning Wing,
'er again muft to his Miftrefs fing.
s deep Grave by mournful *Cupid* made,
lf clofe by in a fad Pofture laid,
ing his Golden Arrow, late his Spade.
d his Grave let circling *Fairies* play,
the whole Night, and fcarce depart by Day.
l things grieve, *Selinda's* Sparrow's gone;
's Sparrow, fo belov'd alone.
m the tender Virgin mourns and cries,
r dear Sparrow fhe laments and fighs,
to be bury'd there, whene'er fhe dies.
hall the winged Choir flock here and fing,
her Death, fweet Flow'rs and Bloffoms bring,
w her Grave with Beauties of the Spring.

On the *Death of the late* Queen.

Whilst Heav'n with Envy on the Earth look'd do
Saw us unworthy of the Royal Pair,
And justly claim'd *Maria* as its own,
Yet kindly left the Glorious *William* here:
The Heav'n and Earth alike do in the Blessings sha
He makes the Earth, She Heav'n our great Allies:
And tho' we mourn, she for our Comfort dies;
Nor need we fear the rash presumptuous Foe,
While She's our Saint above, and he our King belo

A S O N G.

I.

Tell me, *Aurelia*, tell me pray,
How long must *Damon* sue;
Prefix the Time, and I'll obey,
With Patience wait the happy Day
That make me sure of you.

II.

The Sails of Time my Sighs shall blow,
And make the Minutes glide;
My Tears shall make the Current flow,
And swell the hasting Tide.

III.

The wings of Love shall fly so fast,
My Hopes mount so sublime,
The Wings of Love shall make more haste,
Than the swift Wings of Time.

The *Affignation.* A SONG.

I.

'HE Minute's paft appointed by my Fair.
  The Minute's fled
  And leaves me dead
 Anguifh and Defpair.

II.

latter'd Hopes their Flight did make
ith the appointed Hour ;
: can the Minutes paft o'ertake,
d nought my Hopes reftore.

III.

: your Plaints, and make no Moan,
ou fad repining Swain ;
ugh the fleeting Hour be gone,
e Place does ftill remain.

IV.

Place remains, and fhe may make
nends for all your Pain ;
Prefence can paft Time o'ertake,
r Love your Hopes regain.

X X X X X X X X X X X X X X X X X X X X X X X X X X X X X

An Epigram.

NS vitam panis, nobis dans gaudia vinum,
Omnia dans aurum, funt pretiofa nimis :
mmunt bonum eft, at res eft flebilis altra
ns, eft communis famina ubique, nibil.

In Englifh *thus,*

Ature's chief Gifts unequally are carv'd ;
  It furfeits fome, while many more are ftarv'd.
3read, her Wine, her Gold, and what before
Common Good, is now made Private Store :
ng that's Good we have among us Common,
J enjoy the Common Ill——A Woman.

*To a Gentleman that had his Pocket picked of a W
and some Gold by a Mistress.*

A Burlesque Letter.

I'M forry, *Sam*, thou'rt fuch a Ninny
  To let a Wench rob thee of Guinea.
And thus to fpend and lofe your Cobbs,
By lavifh op'ning both your Fobbs.
You're fairly fobb'd to let her get all,
Both one and alfo t'other Metal.
Your Work was on a pretty Score,
You dug the Mine, fhe found the Ore,
The Devil take the cunning Whore.
You flily laid her down to reft her,
And on the Bed fhe found a Tefter.
Your Watch too, *Sam*, (Thefe Men of Power
Muft lie with Doxies by the Hour)
A Minute's Time did that command;
Then her's, it feems, was Minute Hand.
She wound you up to her own Liking,
Then ftole the Watch while your were ftriking:
Then think not, Sir, that you're undone;
What's wound fo high, muft next run down:
In revelling Time, you thought no Sin
To play a Game at *In and In.*
I wonder tho' you did not win for't,
Since that you were fo fairly in for't:
But what deftroy'd you in a Trice,
She held the *Box*, you fhook the Dice:
The Devil was in the Dice then furely,
To lofe when you plaid fo fecurely,
And *Three* to *One* was lay'd fo purely.
But what's the worft of all Mifhaps,
You dread, they fay, fome After-claps:
If that be fo, my deareft *Sammy*,
You'll curfe, and bid the Devil damn ye:
The Fruits of *Wild Oats*, which you fcatter,
Is nothing elfe but *Barley Water.*
The Seed-time's good, you know my Meaning,
But, faith, the Harveft's only gleaning.

Take Heart howe'er, 'tis my Defire,
You will revive, the P——x expire ;
Then rife like *Phænix* from the Fire.
The Metal's ftronger that's well folder'd,
And Beef keeps fweeter once 'tis powder'd :
So farewel, *Sam*, and may you ne'er want
Such a true faithful humble Servant.

May *the Fourth, from* Temple Inner,
The Poft's going out, I in to Dinner.

Gray's Inn, Wednefday.

'TIS a Prefumption to imagine, that you have thought my Letters worth the keeping, and yet a greater Prefumption to expect you fhou'd now return them, if you have kept them fo long ; but I hope the Defign will partly excufe my Requeft : I have promis'd to equip a Friend with a few Letters to help out a Collection for the Prefs, and there are none I dare fooner expofe to the World than thofe to you, becaufe your Merit may warrant their Sincerity, and becaufe your Ladyfhip was pleas'd to commend them : This makes me imagine, Madam, that they have ftill fecur'd a Place in your Cabinet, tho' the unworthy Author cou'd merit no Room in your Heart ; whence I may infer, that they may be as acceptable to you in Print as in my Manufcript ; but if you have a Mind to fecure Trophies of fo poor a Conqueft, I fhall be proud to return them as foon as ever they are tranfcrib'd ; for which I now pawn my Word and Honour, as fincerely as I once did the Heart of,

MADAM,

Your moft humble Servant.

Tuefday

Tuesday Morning, one St
on, and t'other off.

I Have had your Letter, Madam, and all that I
derstand by it is, that your Hand is as great a
dle as your Face; and 'tis as difficult to find out
Senfe in your Characters, as to know your Beau
your Mask: but I have at laft conquer'd the Mai
head of your Writing, as I hope one Day I fhall th
your Perfon; and am fure you han't lost your Virgi
if the Lines in your Complexion be half fo crooke
thofe in your Letters. I return your Complimer
Advice in the fame Number of Particulars that you
pleas'd to fend me. Firft, If you are not handfome
ver fhew a Face that may frighten away that Adr
which your Wit has engaged. Secondly, Never
lieve what a Gentleman fpeaks to you in a Mafk:
while the Ladies wear double Faces, 'tis but Juftice
our Words fhould bear a double Meaning.———L
You muft never advife a Man againft wandring, if yo
fign to be his Guide. You tell me of fwearing
known Lye: I don't remember, Madam, that I
fwore I lov'd you; tho' I muft confefs that a little I
in a half Mourning Mantua and a deep Mourning C
plexion, has run in my Head fo much fince M
Night, that I'm afraid fhe will foon get in my He
But now, Madam, hear my Misfortune.

The angry Fates, and dire Stage-Coach,
Upon my Liberty incroach,
To bear me hence with many a Jog,
From thee my charming dear Incog.
Unhappy Wretch! at once who feels
O'erturns of Hack and Fortune's Wheels.

This is my Epitaph, Madam, for now I'm a
Man; and the Stage-Coach may moft properly be ca
my Hearfe, bearing the Corps only of deceas'd F——
for his Soul is left with you, whom he loves above
Womankind; by whom you may judge of the He
of his Paffion, for he cares not one Farthing for y
whole Sex, as I hope to be faved.

Thur

Thurſday 11 *o'Clock.*

peep is Child's Play, and 'tis Time for a Man to
be tir'd of it. I went Yeſterday to *Bedlam* upon
mad Aſſignation, ſtay'd till Seven like a Fool, to
t one, who, unleſs ſhe were mad, wou'd never
. I begin to believe that they are only Wiſe that
ere, and we Poſſeſs'd that put them in; they at
have this Advantage over us Lunatics at Liberty,
hey find Pleaſure in their Frenzy, and we a Tor-
in our Reaſon. I was ſo tir'd with walking there
g, that I could not bear the Fatigue of putting off
loaths, but ſat up all Night at the Tavern; ſo that
Letter is but juſt come to my Hand, when, like
: *Prettyman,* I have one Boot on and the t'other off.
and Honour have a ſtrong Battle, but here comes
riend to claim my Engagement, ſo Love is put to
out, and away for *Eſſex* immediately; but a Word
vice before we part. Pray conſider, Madam, whe-
our good or ill Stars have uſually the moſt Aſcen-
over your Inclinations, and accordingly proſecute
Intentions of correſponding with me or not; wou'd
e advis'd by me, you wou'd let it alone; for by
[neaſineſs that my ſmall Converſe has already rais'd
:, I gueſs at the greater Diſturbance of being far-
:xpos'd to your Charms, unleſs I may hope for
:hing which my Vanity is too weak to enſure. For-
1as always been my Adverſary; and I may con-
.that Woman, who is much of her Nature, may
e the ſame Way; but if you prove as blind as ſhe,
1ay, perhaps, love me as much as ſhe hates me. My
le Service to your two Siſter Fairies, and ſo the
. take you all.

If you will anſwer this——you may.

Eſſex,

Essex, Friday Morn.

I Have been on Horseback, Madam, all this Mor
which has so discompos'd my Hand and Head,
I can hardly think or write Sense ; the Posture of
Affairs is a little extraordinary in some other Parts a
me ; for my Saddle was very uneasy. The Hare we hu
put me in Mind of a Mistress, which we must g;
after with Hazard of breaking our Necks, and aft
our Pains, the Puss may prove a Witch at the Long
I have had no Female in my Company since I left
Town, or any Thing of your Sex to entertain me :
your *Essex* Women, like your *Essex* Calves, are
Butchers Meat ; and if I must cater for myself,
mend me to a Pit Partridge, which comes pretty cl
and where I may have my Choice of a whole Cc
How well I love this Kind of Meat you may g
when I assure you, that I have purely fed upon
Idea ever since, which has stuck as close to me as
Shirt ; which by the Way I han't shifted since I
into the Country ; for clean Linen is not so modish
as a Lover might require. I receiv'd just now an
pertinent Piece of Banter from an angry Fair ; she
I pawn'd my Soul to the Devil for the great Succe
my Play. But her Ladyship is thus angry, becau
would not pawn my Body to the Devil for another
of Play, of which I presume the Lady to be a very
petent Judge ; I shall disappoint her now, as forme
for I will set her raging mad with the Calmness o
Answer : Besides, Madam, there is nothing can pu
out of Humour, that comes by that Post which b
a Line from you ; tho' I must tell you in
, that I begin to have but a mean Opinion of
r ; for were it in the least parallel to your Wi
of your other Conquests wou'd raise your
g any Correspondence with a Person, whose
is his Indifference.

Gray's Inn, Wednesday Morning.

THE Arguments made use of last Night for still
keeping on your Mask, I endeavour'd to refute
with Reason; but that proving ineffectual, I'll try the
force of Rhime, and send you the Heads of our Chat
in a Poetical Dialogue between You and I.

You.

Thus Images are veil'd which you adore :
Your Ignorance does raise your Zeal the more.

I.

All Image-Worship for false Zeal is held;
False Idols ought indeed to be conceal'd.

You.

Thus Oracles of old were still receiv'd,
The more ambiguous, still the more believ'd.

I.

But Oracles of old were seldom true ;
The Devil was in 'em——sure he's not in you.

You.

Thus masqu'd in Mysteries does the Godhead stand,
The more obscure, the greater his Command.

I.

The Godhead's hidden Power wou'd soon be past,
Did we not hope to see his Face at last.

You.

You are my Slave already, Sir, you know,
To shew more Charms wou'd but increase your Woe ; }
I scorn an Insult to a conquer'd Foe.

I.

I am your Slave, 'tis true ; but still you see
All Slaves by Nature struggle to be free.
But if you wou'd secure the stubborn Prize,
Add to your Wit the Fetters of your Eyes ;
Then pleas'd with Thraldom would I kiss my Chain,
And ne'er think more of Liberty again.

Sunday,

I Came, I faw, and was conquer'd; never had M
more to fay, yet can I fay nothing; where oth
go to fave their Souls, there have I loft mine; but I h
that Divinity, which has the jufteft Title to its Serv
has received it; but I will endeavour to fufpend th
Raptures for a Moment, and talk calmly.

Nothing upon Earth, Madam, can charm bey
your Wit, but your Beauty; after this, not to love y
would proclaim me a Fool; and to fay I did, whe
thought otherwife, would pronounce me a Knave:
any Body call'd me either, I fhould refent it; and if y
but think me either, I fhall break my Heart. You ha
already, Madam, feen enough of me to create a Lik
or an Averfion; your Senfe is above your Sex, then
your Proceeding be fo likewife, and tell me pla
what I have to hope for. Were I to confult my Me
my Humility would chide any Shadow of Hope; b
after a Sight of fuch a Face, whofe whole Compofiti
is a Smile of Good-nature, why fhould I be fo unju
to fufpect you of Cruelty: Let me either live in Lo
and be happy, or retire again to my Defart to check
Vanity that drew me thence; but let me beg to rece
my Sentence from your own Mouth, that I may he
you fpeak, and fee you look at the fame Time; th
let me be unfortunate if I can.

If you are not the Lady in Mourning
that fat upon my Right Hand at
Church, you may go to the Devil,
for I'm fure you're a Witch.

❖❖❖❖❖❖❖❖❖❖§❖§❖❖❖❖❖❖❖❖❖

Madam,

I F I ha'n't begun thrice to write, and as often thrown
away my Pen, may I never take it up again; my
Head and my Heart have been at Cuffs about you thefe
two long Hours——Says my Head, You're a Coxcomb

fo

r troubling your Noddle with a Lady, whofe Beauty
as much above your Pretenfions, as your Merit is be-
w her Love.   Then anfwers my Heart, Good Mr.
head, you're a Blockhead; I know Mr. F———r's
ferit better than you; as for your Part, I know you
b be as whimfical as the Devil, and changing with
pery new Notion that offers; but for my Share, I am
fat, and can ftick to my Opinion of a Lady's Merit for
per; and if the Fair She can fecure an Intereft in me,
Monfieur Head, you may go whiftle.   Come, come,
anfwer'd my Head) you, Mr. Heart, are always leading
his Gentleman into fome Inconvenience or other; was
t not you that firft entic'd him to talk to this Lady?
Your damn'd confounded Warmth made him like this
Lady, and your bufy Impertinence has made him write
b her; your leaping and fkipping difturbs his Sleep by
Night, and his good humour by Day: In fhort, Sir, I
will hear no more on't: I am Head, and I will be
obey'd————————You lie, Sir, reply'd my Heart,
(being very angry) I am Head in Matters of Love, and
if you don't give your Confent, you fhall be forc'd;
for I am fure that in this Cafe all the Members will be
on my Side.   What fay you, Gentlemen Hands? Oh
(fay the Hands) we would not forego the tickling Pleafure of touching a delicious white, foft Skin for the
World.————Well, what fay you, Mr. Tongue?
Zounds, fays the Linguift, there is more Extafy in
fpeaking three foft Words of Mr. Heart's fuggefting,
than whole Orations of Signior Head's; fo I am for the
Lady, and here's my honeft Neighbour Lips will ftick
to't. By the fweet Power of Kiffes, that we will, (reply'd
the Lips,) and prefently fome other worthy Members
ftanding up for the Heart, they laid violent Hands *(ne-
mine contradicente)* upon poor Head, and knock'd out his
brains. So now, Madam, behold me as perfect a Lover
as any in *Chriftendom,* my Heart purely dictating every
Word I fay; the little Rebel throws itfelf into your
Power, and if you don't fupport it in the Caufe it has
taken up for your Sake, think what will be the Condition of the Headlefs and Heartlefs

Farquhar.

Monday.

Monday, Twelve o'Clock at Night.

GIVE me Leave to call you, dear Madam, and te
you that I am now ſtepping into Bed, and that
ſpeak with as much Sincerity as if I were ſtepping in
my Grave : Sleep is ſo great an Emblem of Death, th
my Words ought to be as real, as if I were ſure ne
to awaken ; then may I never again be bleſt with t
Light of the Sun, and the Joys of *Wedneſday,* if you a
not as dear to me as my Hopes of waking in Health t
morrow Morning ; your Charms lead me, my Inclin
tions prompt me, and my Reaſon confirms me,

M A D A M,

Your Faithful, and

Humble Serva

*My humble Service to the Lady,
who muſt be chief Mediator
for my Happineſs.*

Madam,

IN order to your Ladyſhip's Command, I have ſe
you my Thoughts upon your two weighty Maxi
of amorous Policy——*If we fly, they purſue,* and *E
joyment quenches Love :* But I ſhall run a greater Haza
of your Diſpleaſure by my Obedience, than I ſhould t
the Neglect of your Commands ; theſe Subjects leadi
me into more Gravity, than is well conſiſtent with r
own Inclinations, or the Peruſal of a fair Lady. B
to the Buſineſs.

To examine rightly how far theſe Female Maxi
are in Force, we muſt diſpoſe Mankind into a Diviſio
which I think hitherto has eſcap'd the *Logicians;* to w
the Men of Idleneſs, and Men of Buſineſs. Under t
firſt Branch of which Diſtinction is reducible a gre
Sh

re of the World, and especially that which composes
Character of what we call the *Beau Monde*; for to
ke them all of a Piece, we must give them a *French*
me too.

The Practice of these Gentlemen, I must confess, has
ne a great Way to pass these Maxims for authentic,
d have sufficiently authoriz'd the Ladies to stick so
mly to their Principles; but wou'd they consider a
tle upon what a scurvy Foundation these Topics are
ounded, they would damn the Doctrine for the Sake
the Adorers.

These idle Gentlemen (begging their Pardon for so
miliar an Epithet) shou'd shew the Ladies what a
ifference there is between modish Intriguing and true
ove; for these Sparks make Intriguing their Business,
d Love only their Diversion. They visit their
istress as they go to the Park, because it is the Mode;
d continue to sollicit her Favour, not thro' the Im-
ulse of Passion, but because they have nothing else to
b. Some other Motives there are to engage these
arks in the Pursuit of a fair Lady; as, for Instance,
on the Survey of his Rent-Roll the Lover finds two
three Thousand a Year still unmortgag'd, sends
wn immediately to his Steward to screw up his Te-
ats to due Payments, and concludes with *Money con-
ers all Things:* A potent Proverb I must confess, to
ck his Resolution. But here consider, Madam, what
is that pursues you; not the Gentleman, but Fidlers,
asquerades, Jewellers, Glovers, Milleners, hir'd Po-
s, with the confus'd Equipage of all their respective
rades; the Devil a Dart of Love is in the whole
undle, no more than there is in the Straw and Oats
at keep a Horse for *Newmarket*; here are only two
easts to be back'd, one for Pleasure, and t'other for
rofit; I will feed one for the Plate, and pamper the
her for my own Riding.

A second Life to his Pursuit is his Vanity; the Beau
ving receiv'd a Repulse over Night, steps to his Glass
the Morning, and surveying his charming Shape,
'eath, (says he) *why should I despair of Success? Blood,
m as pretty a Fellow as another, but I think my Calves
e a little of the largest. Ah, that's it, she did not like my*
Dress

Dress Yesterday————*Here, Boy, reach my blue Coat, I'll tie my Cravat with a double Knot To-day, and wear the Buckles of my Garters behind.* Thus while his foppish Fancy can invent any particular Change or Whimsey in his Dress, his Hopes are nourish'd by an abusive Presumption, that the Ladies are smitten by such *Bagatel* Impertinence. Here indeed, Madam, the first Maxim, *If we fly, they pursue,* is in Force, but upon scurvy Terms; for the Continuation of such a Coxcomb's Address is the greatest Sat're upon the Sex; and a Woman of true Sense, rather than be plagu'd with such a Follower, if there were no other Way, should give him her Person to be quit of his Company; for here I dare be sworn your second Maxim will hold, that *Enjoyment quenches Love:* For these Gentlemen love as they hunt, for Diversion, as I said before; and no sooner is one Hare snapt up, but they beat about for another. Besides, Madam, 'tis but a modest Presumption that these Men of Pleasure and Idleness must have an Ingredient of the Fool in their Composition, which cannot relish the true and lasting Beauties of a fine Woman; they cannot make a true Estimate of her Sense, her Constancy, her several little kind and endearing Offices, which can only engage the Affections of a Man that truly understands their Value.

This brings into my Consideration how far these Maxims may be applicable to your corresponding with the latter Part of the Distinction, which I call'd the Men of Business; by which I understand Men of Sense, Learning and Experience, and call them Men of Business, because I wou'd exclude a Parcel of flashy, noisy, rhiming, atheistical Gentlemen, who arrogate to themselves the Title of Wit and Sense, for no other Cause but the Abuse of it: Such must be rank'd with the first Sort of Lovers, for they are the idlest of Mankind; neither do I confine the Character of a Man of Business to the Law, the Church, the Court, Trade, or any particular Employment: I intend it a farther Latitude, and inclusive of all those, who deriding the Fop, and detesting the Debauchee, have laid down to themselves some certain Scheme of Study, in any lawful Art or

Science,

Science, for the Benefit of the Public, or their own private Improvement.

Upon this Foundation we may rationally conclude the Actions of such Men to flow directly from the Operations of their Reason. But here, Madam, without Doubt, the Ladies will interrupt me——*Hold, Sir,* (say they) *we absolutely deny that Love and Reason are consistent;* from which it follows, that your Men of Business have no Business here.

I am very sorry, Madam, in the first Place, that the Qualification which must recommend a Man to a fair Lady, must debase him so near the Level of a Brute, and deprive him of that divine Stamp by which he is distinguish'd from the Beasts of the Field. What an Affront is this to your Sex, that one must no sooner begin to admire a Woman, but he must cease to be a Man; and that the Glory which a Lady receives by the Plurality of her Adorers, should depend only upon the Esteem of so many irrational Creatures! No, no, Madam, I am too much a Courtier to let this vulgar Calumny and severe Reflection upon your Sex pass unexamined.

I shall therefore make bold to say, that this very Opinion touching the Inconsistency of Love with Reason, has cost the fair Sex more Tears, and has subjected Men to more Curses, than the worst Circumstances of Falshood and Perjury; for depending upon this Principle of the Ladies, the greatest Rascals have appear'd the most passionate Lovers, because the greatest Knaves make the best Fools, and the most usual Cloak for natural Villany, is an artificial Simplicity.

But granting such Follies and Absurdities to be the Results of a real Passion, such Love ought not to gain one Grain the more Weight in the Balance of true Sense; for if the Lover be a Fool, this Extravagance is but what is natural to his Temper, and exposes itself as wildly in the Effects of his other ordinary Passions, as in Anger, Fear, Joy, Grief, and the like, and must not properly be call'd the Strength of his Love, but the Weakness of his Reason; and the same Pitch of Passion that may make a *Wittall* appear Lunatic, would scarcely be discernible in a *Dorimant*. But if the Force

of

Love raife a Man of true Senfe to the Pitch of playing
the Fool, 'tis then, if not more ridiculous, at leaſt
much more dangerous in the Confequence; for be
affur'd, Madam, that the Bent of his Defire muſt be
too violent to laſt long, and when once it begins to
decline, 'twill prove as violent in the Fall as in the
Rife; and the conftant Refult of a fober Reflection, is
the Hatred and Deteftation of any Thing that had made
him guilty of Extravagance, and debas'd him below
the Dignity of his Reafon; and there is no Medium in
this Cafe between the extravagant Lover and the inveterate Enemy.

But begging your Ladyfhip's Pardon for this Digref-
fion, I fhall return to my Man of Bufinefs, and fee
how far your Principle, *If we fly, they purfue,* is applicable to a Perfon of this Character.

To the Examination of this Point, 'twill not be
amifs to confider the feveral Paces and Proceedings of
fuch a Lover in his Amour. A Man of Bufinefs and
Study has his Thoughts too round and compact within
himfelf, to have his Fancy fallying out upon the Appearance of every Beauty that his daily Converfation
may throw in his Way; but if once it lights upon that
Fair, which can roufe him from his Indifference, raifing
a Pleafure in his Eyes when fhe's prefent, and an Un-
eafinefs in his Heart in her Abfence, 'tis no Impru-
dence to indulge the Thought. Love (he confiders) is
a Bleffing; and fince it depends fo much upon a Sympathy of Natures, why may'nt I expect that the fair
Creature, who has rais'd fuch Emotions in me, may in
Time, perhaps, be brought to have a mutual Concern
upon her? The Happinefs that I may expect from her
Love, if her other Qualities be proportionable to her
Beauty, will infinitely reward the Pains of my enquir-
ing into her Life and Converfation. Here is the Foundation of Love fairly laid; and now the Gentleman goes
to work upon the Structure: He firft enquires into the
Lady's Character, but that as a Man of Senfe ough
io do, without trufting the Malice of fome that may be
her Enemies, nor yet confulting the Partiality of her
Friends. His Reafon may make a tolerable good Balance between both; and if perhaps fome Slip in her
Conduct

ft has made the Scale of her Accufation the heavieft,
fome Grains of Love to throw into the other to
rpoife it. His next Bufinefs is to gain Admittance
Company; here he may find a thoufand Beauties
nent, or as many Failings perhaps to deftroy, his
; and to his Examination he muft refer his Judg-
ipon the different Characters he might have heard
before; for no reafonable Man will peremptorily
de from the Mouth of Common Fame; 'tis a no-
Liar, and generally in Extremes. If he believes
ie Lady's Prejudice, he may wrong her Innocence
:drefs; and if he trufts flying Report in her Favour,
y be impos'd upon himfelf: For the Vulgar (by
I mean the Lac'd Coat as well as the Hobnail)
enter into the nice Secrets of Female Behaviour;
>metimes miftake Levity for Freedom, ill Humour
avity, Noife and Tattle for Wit and Senfe: Some-
they change Hands, and call an Air of good Breed-
iquetry; they brand Affability and Good-nature with
me of Loofenefs; and, in fhort, there can be no fuch
as a Woman in their Eftimate, all muft be Angels,
Devils. Now my Lover fhall find out all thefe Di-
>ns; he fhall, in Spite of Female Diffimulation,
to the very Bottom, and difcover the leaft Paint
:he Mind, as he does that upon the Face. Having
the Lady's Temper conformable to his own, or be-
leaft affur'd, that he can frame his own Humour
are with her's; having known her Senfe and Under-
ig fufficient for a prudent Conduct, at leaft pliable
d Advice, he ftands fix'd in his Refolution, and
'd upon his Affection.
is the beautiful Edifice of Love is gradually and
rais'd, whereof Reafon is ftill the Corner-ftone;
ce the trifling Pomp of a Fop's Preparation, which,
Lord Mayor's Pageant, is built in a Night, glitters,
gaz'd at for a Day; and the next dwindles into no-
The Building thus finifh'd, the next Bufinefs is
ite the Fair Gueft; 'tis impoffible to confine the
of his Addrefs to any particular Obfervation, bethey may be fo diverfify'd by the Circumftances of
>ver, the Accidents of Time, Place, or according
ie Humours and Inclinations in the Lady's Temper,

L. I.   C   which

which laft have always prov'd the moft effectual M
of gaining a Heart. If the Lady's Difpofition be in
able to Gaiety, he makes the Mufes fpeak a good V
for him; he can difpenfe in an Evening with a very
Play, to have the Pleafure of acting the Lover him
nay, he can comply fo far, as to commend a very
thing, if his Miftrefs is pleas'd to approve it; he can
a Turn in the *Mall* with his Hat off, tho' the Weathe
very cold, and join with her in railing at my Lord S
a-one, or Miftrefs Such-a-one, tho' perhaps he un
ftands the Quarrel to be no more than a Pique, or a J
of Malice. If the Lady's Temper be more grave and
date, he can fit an Hour or two condemning the Vic
the Town, and extolling the Pleafures of a Country I
nay, fometimes perhaps he may have a Fling at the
vernment, and be a little Jacobitifh to pleafe her; he
wait on her to Church, and hear a Levite thump, J
and Nonfenfe out of a Pulpit Cufhion for an Hour,
call it an excellent Sermon, to humour her Approbati
with a thoufand other little foolifh Fancies, which
caufe they are not very hurtful in themfelves, and
Cuftom has brought them into Play, muft be borne u
upon this Occafion; and when all is done, Cerem
looks as decently in Love, as in Religion; and a Cle
in an Intrigue makes as aukward a Figure as a Quake
Church. Our Lover therefore writes, vifits, fighs,
clares his Paffion with all Demonftrations of Submif
and Sincerity; all which is often repeated to fave
Lady's Modefty, and to footh a little pleafing Vanity
cident to the Female Sex of feeing themfelves admi
He is fatisfy'd alfo that the World fhou'd know it,
fubmits to the Cenfure of a whining Coxcomb, to fav
the Lady's yielding by the plaufible Excufe of a h
Siege; but if after all this he finds his Pretenfions to
Purpofe, your Maxim, Madam, *If we fly*, &c. will
be of Force to detain him longer; he has the fa
Thread of Reafon to guide him out of the Labyri
that led him in; he has not perhaps the fame Supports
his Hope, that every glittering Spark with a Coach u
Six can pretend; but were his Fortune ever fo confide
ble, he wou'd not affront the Lady's Honour, nor
own Judgment, fo far as to fuppofe her of a mercen
Temp

Temper; neither can he imagine that the charming Fair, whose Sense he has so much admir'd, shou'd be captivated with the tying of his Cravat, or the Fancy of his Snuff-Box. No, no, he is rather convinc'd, that there is something disagreeable to the Lady in his Person, Behaviour, or Conversation, which being a Defect of Nature, or Education, he must patiently submit to, without cutting his Throat; and he's the more willing to take up with his Failings, because Time may perhaps produce some other Lady, that may value him upon these very Circumstances that made the first disdain him; so that in Spite of your celebrated Maxim, he betakes himself to his Business, has the Manners to free the Lady from his Impertinence, and the Prudence to disengage himself of the Trouble. Neither is he much distress'd to withdraw his Affections; for as the Prospect of Happiness was the first Foundation of his Love, so the Progress of his Passion must have been hourish'd with Favours to keep it alive, and as naturally without this Fuel will the Fire go out of itself.

I have already, Madam, so far transgressed the Bounds of a *Billet-doux*, that I am afraid to meddle with your second Maxim : But give me a Moment's Patience, Madam, and I'll make quick Work with—*Enjoyment quenches Love :* One Simile, Madam, and I take my Leave. What a strange and unaccountable Madness wou'd it appear in a Subject of *England*, a Gentleman that enjoys Peace and Plenty, Ease and Luxury; if he, discontented with his happy State, shou'd raise a Combustion in his Country, turn ambitious Rebel, make a Party against his Prince, and by Force and Treachery lay hold upon the Government, and all this for the bare Pleasure of being called King. I can assure you, Madam, did the Pleasures of a Monarch consist in nothing more than being plac'd in a Throne, with a Crown upon his Head, and the Scepter in his Hands, we should have the upstart Prince use his Government as a Fool does a fair Lady after Enjoyment ; he wou'd soon be cloy'd with his Desire, and uneasy till he got quit of it. But if our *Noll* understood the Policy of Government, the many Glories that attend a Crown, the Pomp of Dependencies, the Sweets of absolute Power, with the many Delights and Joys that attend his Royalty, he would maintain his Station to the last Drop of Blood.

This is eafily applicable to a Man of Senfe gaining the Crown of Beauty; he can judge of the Charms of his Pof-feffion, and values Enjoyment only as the Title to his greater Pleafures : There are a thoufand Cupids attending the Throne of Love, all which have their feveral pretty Offices and ferviceable Duties to exhilerate their Mafter's Joy, and contribute to his conftant Diverfion, if he but underftands how to employ them.

How far, Madam, I have recommended to you the Ad-dreffes of an ingenious Man, I dare not determine; but I am afraid I have faid fo much againft the Paffion of Fools, that I have ruin'd my own Intereft; tho' you can't reckon me among the idle Part of Men, being fo happily employed this Morning by the Commands of fo fair a Lady.

Your Ladyfhip's moft humble Servant.

+-+

Friday Night, 11 *o'Cleck.*

IF you find no more Reft from your Thoughts in Bed than I do, I cou'd wifh you, Madam, to be always there, for there I am moft in Love. I went to the Play this Evening, and the Mufic rais'd my Soul to fuch a Pitch of Paffion, that I was almoft mad with Melancholy. I flew thence to *Spring-Garden,* where with envious Eyes I faw every Man pick up his Mate, whilft I alone walked like folitary *Adam* before the Creation of his *Eve;* but the Place was no Paradife to me; nothing I found enter-taining but the Nightingale, which methought in fweet Notes, like your own, pronounc'd the Name of my Dear *Penelope.*——*As the Fool thinketh, the Bell clinketh.* From hence I retir'd to the Tavern, where methought the fhin-ing Glafs reprefented your fair Perfon, and the fparkling Wine within it, look'd like your lively Wit and Spirit; I met my dear Miftrefs in every thing, and I propofe prefently to fee her in a lively Dream, fince the laft thing

I do,

, is to kifs her dear Letter, clafp her charming Idea
y Arms, and fo fall faft afleep.

My Morning Songs, my Ev'ning Pray'rs,
My Daily Mufings, Nightly Cares.
                                    Adieu.

✕✕✕✕✕✕✕✕✕✕✕✕✕✕✕✕✕✕✕✕✕✕✕✕✕

Ere am I drinking, Madam, at the Sign of the
Globe; and it fhall go hard but I make the Voy-
of old Sir *Drake* by to-morrow Morning : We have
:fh Gale and a round Sea ; for here is very good Com-
r and excellent Wine ; From the Orb in the Sign, I
ftep to the Globe of the Moon, thence make the Tour
ll the Planets, and fix in the Conftellation of *Venus.*
fee, Madam, I am elevated already. Here's a Gen-
an tho', who fwears he loves his Miftrefs better than
mine, but if I don't make him fo drunk that he fhall
orge his Opinion, may I never drink your Health
n; the generous Wine fcorns to lie upon a Traitor's
ach, 'tis Poifon to him that profanes Society by be-
a Rogue in his Cups. I wifh, dear Madam, with all
Heart that you faw me in my prefent Circumftances,
wou'd certainly fall in Love with me, for I am not
:lf; I am now the pleafanteft foolifh Fellow that ever
'd a Lady's Heart, and a Glafs or two more will fill
with fuch Variety of Impertinence, that I cannot fail
afs for agreeable. You, Drawer, bring me a Plate of
——Ha ! How the Wine whizzes upon my Heart;
d is forging his Love-Darts in my Belly———— Ice,
Dog, Ice——The Son of a Whore has brought me
hovies. Well ! This is a vexatious World. I wifh
re fairly out of it, and happy in Heaven, I mean your
Arms ; which is the conftant Prayer of your Humble
ant, Drunk or Sober.

defign To-morrow in the Afternoon to beg your Pardon for
he ill Manners of my Debauch ; and make myfelf as great
t Emperor, by inviting your Ladyfhip to the Entertainment
ioclefian.

IN purſuance to your Order, Madam, I have ſent ye here inclos'd my Picture; and I challenge *Vandike* o *Kneller* to draw more to the Life. You are the firſt Perſon that ever had it; and if I had not ſome Thought that the Subſtance would fall to your Share, I would no part with my Likeneſs. I hope the Colours will neve fade, tho' you may give me ſome Hints where to men the Features, having ſo much Power to correct the Life.

The Picture.

MY Outſide is neither better nor worſe than m Creator made it, and the Piece being drawn by ſ great an Artiſt, 'twere Preſumption to ſay there wer many Strokes amiſs. I have a Body qualify'd to anſwe all the Ends of its Creation, and that's ſufficient.

As to the Mind, which in moſt Men wears as man Changes as their Body, ſo in me 'tis generally dreſt lik my Perſon in black. Melancholy is its every Day Ap parel; and it has hitherto found few Holidays to make 1 change its Clothes. In ſhort, my Conſtitution is ver Splenetic, and yet very amorous; both which I en deavour to hide, leſt the former ſhould offend other and that the latter might incommode myſelf. And t Reaſon is ſo vigilant in reſtraining theſe two Faiting that I am taken for an eaſy-natur'd Man with my ow Sex, and an ill-natur'd Clown by yours.

'Tis true, I am very ſparing in my Praiſes and Com pliments to a Lady, out of a Fear that they may affec myſelf more than her. For the Idols that we worſhi are generally of our own making; and though wiſe Men may not ſpeak what they think, yet Truth ma catch them on t'other Hand, and make them thin what they ſpeak. But moſt of all am I cautiou of promiſing, eſpecially upon that weighty Article o Conſtancy, becauſe, in the firſt Place, I have neve try'd the Strength of it in my own Experience; and ſecondly, I ſuppoſe a Man can no more engage for hi Conſtancy than for his Health, ſince I believe they bot equally depend upon a certain Conſtitution of Body and how far, and how frequently, that may be liable t
Alteration

Alteration, especially in Affairs of Love, let the more judicious determine.

But so far a Man may promise, that if he find not his Passion grounded on a false Foundation, and that he have a Continuance of the same Sincerity, Truth and Love to engage him; that then his Reason, his Honour, and his Gratitude, may prove too strong for all Changes of Temper and Inclination.

I am a very great Epicure, for which Reason I hate all Pleasure that is purchas'd by Excess of Pain. I am quite different from the Opinion of Men that value what is dearly bought; long Expectation makes the Blessing always less to me, for by often thinking of the future Joy, I make the Idea of it familiar to me, and so I lose the great Transport of Surprize; 'tis keeping the Springs of Desire so long upon the Rack, till at last they grow loose and enervate: Besides, any one of a creative Fancy, by a Duration of Thoughts, will be apt to frame too great an Idea of the Object, and so make the greater Part of his Hopes end in a Disappointment.

I am seldom troubled with what the World calls Airs and Caprices; and I think it an Idiot's Excuse for a foolish Action, to say 'twas my Humour. I hate all little malicious Tricks of vexing People for Trifles, or using them with frightful Stories, malicious Lies, stealing Lap-dogs, tearing Fans, breaking China, or the like: I can't relish the Jest that vexes another in earnest: in short, if ever I do a wilful Injury, it must be a very great one.

I am often melancholy, but seldom angry; for which reason I can be severe in my Resentment, without injuring myself: I think it the worst Office to my Nature, to make myself uneasy for what another should be punish'd.

I am easily deceiv'd, but then I never fail at last to find out the Cheat; my Love of Pleasure and Sedateness makes me very secure, and the same Reason makes me very diligent when I am alarm'd.

I have so natural a Propensity to Ease, that I cannot fearfully fix to my Study, which bears not a Pleasure in

the

the Application, which makes me inclinable to Poetry above any thing else.

I have very little Estate, but what lies under the Circumference of my Hat; and should I by Mischance come to lose my Head, I should not be worth a Groat; but I ought to thank Providence that I can by three Hours Study live one and twenty with Satisfaction to myself, and contribute to the Maintenance of more Families, than some who have Thousands a Year.

I have something in my outward Behaviour, which gives Strangers a worse Opinion of me than I deserve; but I am more than recompens'd by the Opinion of my Acquaintance, which is as much above my Desert.

I have many Acquaintances, very few Intimates, but no Friend, I mean in the old Romantic Way; I have no Secret so weighty, but what I can bear in my own Breast; nor any Duels to fight, but what I may engage in without a Second; nor can I love after the old Romantic Discipline. I would have my Passion, if not led, yet at least waited on by my Reason: and the greatest Proof of my Affection that a Lady must expect, is this: I would run any Hazard to make us both happy, but would not for any transitory Pleasure make either of us miserable.'

If ever, Madam, you come to know the Life of this Piece, as well as he that drew it, you will conclude that I need not subscribe the Name to the Picture.

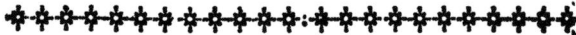

WELL! Mrs. *V*—— and my charming *Penelope* are to lie together to-night; what wou'd I give to be a Mouse (God bless us) behind the Hangings to hear the Chat. You don't know, Madam, but my Genius, which always attends you, may overhear your Discourse; therefore not one Word of *George*. I'm resolv'd to have a Friend to lie with me to-night, that I may quit scores with you; and it shall go hard but I prove as kind to my Companion, as you are to yours; though I must confess, that I had rather be in Mrs. *V*———'s Place, with

with all the little Pillows about me, or in that of Monfieur *Adonis* upon the Chair.

> *My Rival is a Dog of Parts,*
> *That captivates the Ladies Hearts;*
> *And yet by* Jove *(I scorn to forge)*
> Adonis *self must yield to* George.
> *I am a Dog as well as he,*
> *Can fawn upon a Lady's Knee;*
> *My Ears as long, and I can bark,*
> *To guard my Mistress in the Dark:*
> *I han't four Legs, that's no hard Sentence,*
> *For I can paw and scrape Acquaintance.*
> *I am a Dog that admires you,*
> *And I'm a Dog if this ben't true;*
> *And if* Adonis *does outrival me,*
> *Then I'm a greater Son of a Bitch than he.*
> *Reach my Waistcoat——but ne'er trouble it,*
> *I am already a Dog in a Doublet.*

Was ever such a poetical puppy seen? But when my Mistress is sick, 'tis then *Dog-days* with me, tho' tis but a Cur's Trick, I must confess; but I would be content to bark at this Rate all my Life, so that I might hunt away all Rats and Mice from my fair Angel, whose fearful Temper is the only Mark of Mortality about her. The Remembrance of the Water-Rat last Night has inspir'd me with the following Lines.

> *Fair* Rosamond *did little think*
> *Her Crystal Pond should turn a Sink,*
> *To harbour Vermin that might swim,*
> *And frighten Beauties from the Brim.*
> *Henceforth, detested Pond, no more*
> *Shall Beauties crown your verdant Shore;*
> *Your Waves so fam'd for am'rous League,*
> *Are now turn'd Ratsbane to Intrigue.*

Now good Morrow, my fair Creature, and let me know how you are recover'd from your Fright.

WHY

WHY should I write to my dearest *Penelope*, when I only trouble her with reading what she won't believe? I have told my Passion, my Eyes have spoke it, my Tongue pronounc'd it, and my Pen declar'd it; I have sigh'd it, swore it, and subscrib'd it; now my Heart is full of you, my Head raves of you, and my Hand writes to you, but all in vain. If you think me a Dissembler, use me generously like a Villain, and discard me for ever; but if you will be so just to my Passion, as to believe it sincere, tell me so, and make me happy; 'tis but Justice, Madam, to do one or t'other.

Your Indisposition last Night, when I left you, put me into such Disorder, that not finding a Coach, I miss'd my Way, and never minded whither I wander'd, 'till I found myself close by *Tyburn*. When blind Love guides, who can forbear going astray? Instead of laughing at myself, I fell to pitying poor Mr. F——r, who, whilst he rov'd abroad among your whole Sex, was never out of his Way, and now by a single She was led to the Gallows. From the Thoughts of Hanging, I naturally enter'd upon those of Matrimony: I consider'd how many Gentlemen have taken a handsome Swing, to avoid some inward Disquiets; then why shou'd not I hazard the Noose, to ease me of my Torment? Then I consider'd, whether I shou'd send for the Ordinary of *Newgate*, or the Parson of St. *Anne*'s; but considering myself better prepar'd for dying in a fair Lady's Arms, than on the three legg'd Tree, I was the most inclinable to the Parish-Priest: Besides, if I dy'd in a fair Lady's Arms, I shou'd be sure of Christian Burial at last, and shou'd have the most beautiful Tomb in the Universe. You may imagine, Madam, that these Thoughts of Mortality were very melancholy; but who cou'd avoid the Thoughts of Death when you were sick? And if your Health be not dearer to me than my own, may the next News I hear be your Death, which would be as great a Hell, as your Life and Welfare is a Heaven to the most amorous of his Sex.

Pray let me know in a Line, whether you are better or worse, whether I am Honest or a Knave, and whether I shall live or die.

I can

I Can no more let a Day pafs without feeing or writing to my dear *Penelope*, than I can flip a Minute without thinking of her. I know nobody can lay a jufter Claim to the Account of my Hours, than fhe who has fo indifputable a Title, to my Service; and I can no more keep the Difcovery of my Faults from you, than from my own Confcience, becaufe you compofe fo great a Part of my Devotion. Let me therefore confefs to my deareft Angel, how laft Night I faunter'd to the *Fountain*, where fome Friends waited for me; one of 'em was a Parfon, who preaches over any Thing but his Glafs: Had not his Company and *Sunday* Night fanctify'd the Debauch, I fhou'd be very fit for Repentance this Morning; the fearching Wine has fprung the Rheumatifm in my Right Hand, my Head akes, my Stomach pukes, I dream'd all this Morning of Fire, and wak'd in a Flame: To compleat my Mifery, I muft let you know all this, and make you angry with me. I defign tho' this Afternoon to repair to St. *Anne*'s Prayers, to beg Abfolution of my Creator and my Miftrefs; if both prove merciful, I'll put on the Refolution of amending my Life, to fit me for the Joys of Heaven and you.

Dear Madam,

NOW I write with my aking Hand the Dictates of my aking Heart; my Body and my Soul are of a Piece; both uneafy for Want of my dear *Penelope*. Excufe me, Madam, for troubling you with my Diftemper; but my Hand is fo ill, that it can write nothing elfe, becaufe it can go no farther.

MIsfortunes always lay hold on me, when I forfake my Love, or fall fhort of my Duty; your Coach was full, and Mr. C——r was vanifh'd, fo I had no Pretence left to avoid fome fober Friends, that wou'd haul me into a Cellar to drink Cyder; a dark, chilly, con-

founded

founded Hole, fit only for Treafon and Tobacco. Beir
warm with the Throng of the Playhoufe, I unadvifed
threw off my Wig; the Rawnefs of this curfed Plac
with the Coldnefs of our Tipple, has feiz'd upon me
violently, that I'm afraid I fhan't recover it in a Tric
I have got fuch a Pain in my Jaws, that I fha'nt be ab
to eat a Bit: So now, Madam, I muft either live up
Love or ftarve. For Heaven's Sake then, dear Madar
fend me a little Subfiftence; let not a hungry Wret
perifh for want of an Alms: Your Charity, for t
Lord's Sake. Kind Words is all I crave; and the m
uncharitable Prelate will afford a Beggar his Bleffing.
Pity my Condition, Fair Charmer, I have got a Co
without, and a Fire within, Love and Cyder do not agre
fo I'll have no more Cellars. If you don't fend n
fome Comfort in my Afflictions, expect to have a No
to this *Purpofe*——Be pleas'd to accompany the Cor
of an unfortunate Lover, who dy'd of an aching Cho
and a broken Heart.

XXXXXXXXX✦X✦X✦XXXXXXXXX)

YOUR Verfes, Madam, I have read, fcan'd an
consider'd over and over; I muft ftill complain
the Difficulty of your Characters; but your Senfe is lil
a rich Mine, hard to come at, but when found, an in
nite Treafure, I wou'd anfwer you in Verfe, but for t
Reafon that follows.

Of all the fpecious Wiles and formal Arts,
Us'd by our young intriguing Men of Parts,
None can their Ignorance in Love exprefs,
So much as whining Words in fawning Verfe,
The Nymph, whofe fofter Breaft foft Numbers gain, ⎫
Muft have a Soul celeftially ferene, ⎬
Seraphically bright, and fparkling as her Mien. ⎭
But Women now that Character difown,
They are all Mortal, very Mortal grown.
By Verfe was Beauty's Empire firft ordain'd,
And ftubborn Man to Love by Verfe was chain'd.
Verfe gave to Love his Quiver and his Bow,
Nay, e'en from Verfe he had his Godbead too.

And now ungrateful Beauty scorns that Aid,
By which its greatest Triumphs first were made :
A sordid Blockhead, with an empty Skull,
Shall have Access, because his Pocket's full.
Curse on thee, Gold—why, Charmer, tell me why
Shou'd that which buys a Horse, bright Beauty buy?
O cou'd I find (grant Heav'n that once I may).
A Nymph fair, kind, poetical and gay ;
Whose Love shou'd blaze, unsully'd, and divine,
Lighted at first by the bright Lamp of mine ;
Free as a Mistress, faithful as a Wife,
And one that lov'd a Fiddle as her Life ;
Free from all sordid Ends, from Int'rest free,
For my own Sake affecting only me.
What a blest Union shou'd our Souls combine ?
I her's alone, and she be only mine.
Free gen'rous Favours shou'd our Flames express,
I'd write for Love, and she shou'd love for Verse,
In deathless Numbers shou'd my fair one shine,
Her Love, her Charms shou'd blazon every Line,
And the whole Page be like herself, Divine.
Not Sacharissa's self, great Waller's Fair,
Shou'd for an endless Name with mine compare ;
My Lines should run so high, the World shou'd see
I sung of her, and she inspired me.
Vain are thy Wishes, wretched Damon, vain,
Thy Verse can only serve thee to complain :
Wealth makes the Bargain, Love's become a Trade,
Blind Love is now by blinder Fortune led.
Who then wou'd sing, or sacred Numbers boast,
Since Love, the just Reward of Verse, is lost ?
Of the soft Sex why were the Muses made,
If in soft Love they can't afford us Aid ?
No, Cupid, no, you have deceiv'd too long,
My Muse and Love have ever done me wrong ;
Farewel, ungrateful Love, farewel, ungrateful Song.

You see, Madam, that my Rhyme has argu'd me out of Love; but I'm violently suspicious that my Reason will convince me, that I am still as much your Captive as ever; for I have the greatest Inclination in the Word to intreat the Favour of meeting your Ladyship in the *Park*
To-

To-morrow by Six. If you tarry till Seven, you may find me at the End of the Lover's Walk, hanging upon one of the Trees, which will be the readiest Way, for aught I see, to bring our Amour to a Conclusion. I am an impudent Fellow; that's to prevent your Reflection upon my presuming to appoint you a Place of Assignation.

IF any Thing should come to your Hands, Madam, that I writ last Night, I humbly beg that you wou'd pardon its Impertinence; for I was so fuddled, that I hardly remember whether I writ or not. You'll think perhaps that my Excuse needs as much an Apology as my Fault; but you ought to forgive me, when I assure you, that I shall never forgive myself. I have vow'd this Morning never to taste Wine, till I can recover that Opportunity of seeing you, that Wine made me lose. I went to the *Royal Exchange* at Two, and stay'd in the City till Twelve at Night; I din'd with Mr. *B——x*, who (by the Way) is a pretty Gentleman, but has a confounded Wife; such Stories have I heard of her Persecution, and his Long-suffering, that he deserves to go to Heaven, and she to Hell for sending him; and so much for a Citizen's Wife. I come now from Mr. *Dryden's* Funeral, where we had an Ode in *Horace* sung, instead of *David's* Psalms; whence you may find, that we don't think a Poet worth Christian Burial. The Pomp of the Ceremony was a Kind of Rhapsody, and fitter, I think, for *Hudibras* than him, because the Cavalcade was mostly Burlesque; but he was an extraordinary Man, and bury'd after an extraordinary Fashion; for I do believe there was never such another Burial seen. The Oration indeed was great and ingenious, worthy the Subject, and like the Author, whose Prescriptions can restore the Living, and his Pen embalm the Dead. And so much for Mr. *Dryden*, whose Burial was the same with his Life; Variety, and not of a Piece. The Quality and Mob, Farce and Heroics; the Sublime and Ridicule mixt in a Piece, great *Cleopatra* in a Hackney-Coach.

And

now, Woman, to the application of it is, &c. over,
... it is also more ... that neither V... on perfect Man,
nor a Woman, from the imperfections ... it ...
a better one V... it ... ...
... ... beauty make ... love make ... ...
... ... V... ... ... Return, V...
... Gratitude, that ... ...
beauty immortal. Now, Woman, if your beauty
... V... ... ...
I will have no V... unless I love it ... ...
... ...
... Infant ... all the Worms in the ... and
... Power ... ... one Feature ... ... Face,
... ... I am not now a Man, I married Years
... I am now, I ... ... And ... ...
... My ... ...
... ...
... ... upon me.

... Strange ... ... Declaration of your un-
... Thoughts of me, and cast a Damp upon my
that ... ... Melancholy or Rage:
prove the latter, ... then I shall destroy myself
... Way; in the Fervency of my Passion, and
... of Coldness, which has alarm'd Part of the
To be accus'd of Coldness and Neglect is——
say no more upon that Subject, 'tis too warm;
touch it, will set me in a Blaze. I remember
... of my Uneasiness t'other Day, and I remem-
Cause was repeated last Night; and, in short,
by a thousand ... that make me mad; and
... ... me a Time of telling me
... me Leave to tell you,
... 'twill give me Cause
... you, tho' at the same
... Expression. Now, Ma-
... I han't clos'd my Eyes

H 5

Hague, October 23, *New Stile*

THIS is the second Post, dear Madam, since I have heard from you, which makes me apprehensive that you are not well, or that you have forgot the Person whose Health and Welfare so intirely depends upon yours. I am proud to say, that all my Words, my Letters, and Endeavours, have unfeignedly run upon the Strain of the most real Passion that ever possest the Breast of Man; and if, after all this, they should all prove vain, I leave you to judge how poor an Opinion I shou'd have of my Understanding, which must be a very mortifying Thought for a Person who is very unwilling to pass for a Fool. 'Tis true, I have laid out all the little Sense I had in your Service, and if it should be cast away, I should turn Bankrupt in my Understanding, and run stark mad upon the Loss. For God's Sake, Madam, let me know what I have to trust to, that I may once more set up for a Man of some Parts, or else run away from my Senses as fast as I can; my Thoughts begin to be very severe Creditors, and I am perfectly tir'd of their Company. The King came hither last Night about Eleven from *Loo*; and if the Weather prove fair, designs for *England* next *Wednesday*. Providence has design'd my staying so long, out of its great Mercy to secure me from the Violence of a terrible Storm, which has lasted here this Fortnight past, to that Degree, that *Holland* is no more at present than a great leaky Man of War, tossing on the Ocean, and Mariners are forc'd to pump Night and Day to keep the Vessel above Water. I can assure you, without a Jest, that the Cellars and Canals have frequent Communication, and happy is he that can lodge in a Garret: There are Fellows planted on all the Steeples, with a considerable Reward to him that can make the first Land, tho' they had more Need to look out for a Rainbow; for without that I shall believe that God Almighty, in his Articles with *Noah* after the Flood, has excluded the *Dutch* out of the Treaty. I have transcrib'd your Letter to my Lord A——k, and will consult with Captain L———ce about your Affairs, whether it be proper to mention Matters now, or defer it till we come over: My Lord W'est——s

treate

treated us Yefterday with a Pot of *Englifh* Venifon fent him by his Mother.   But never was poor Buck fo devour'd by hungry Hounds ; we hunted him down with excellent *Burgundy*——Could this Place afford us good Toafts as it does Wine, 'twere a Paradife.   But we made fhift to call you all over, every Beauty in *London*, from the D——fs of *G*——*n* to Mrs. *B*——*le* ; and when we got drunk, we toafted the *Dutch* Ladies ; and by the Time we got thro' the whole Affembly, we were grown as dull and fottifh as if we had lain with them.   You muft pardon my Breeding, Madam, and confider where I am ; but I do blufh a little, and can't fay a Word more, but that I am,

M A D A M,

Your faithful and moft humble Servant.

I Receiv'd your Letter, Madam, with the ftrange Relation of your being robb'd : I can't tell whether my Grief or Amazement was greateft ; it fufpended the Pain of the Rheumatifm for fome Hours, tho' I gain'd little by that, for it only gave Place to a greater.   All the Confolation I can afford in your Sorrow, is, that you have a Companion in your Afflictions that fympathizes in every Particular of your Grief.   I confider myfelf a Lady robb'd of my fine Things, ftripp'd of my beft Clothes, and, what is worfe, of all my pretty Trinkets, that have coft me fome Years in purchafing.   Tho' this be the greateft Misfortune a fine Lady can fuftain, yet I am ftill more troubled at the Manner of the Action, than at the Greatnefs of my Lofs, that in a Houfe fo well peopled as mine, in an Hour fo early, when all the World was awake, that all my good Stars fhould then be afleep, is very provoking.

By this, Madam, you may judge whether my Heart be not tun'd to the very fame Notes of Sorrow with yours ; and as I have the fame Reafons for my Grief, fo perhaps fhall agree with your Ladyfhip as to the Thoughts which may afford you moft Confolation.

Religion

Religion teaches me, that nothing in this World is pro
perly our own, but borrow'd; and since I am oblig'd
resign even my very Life without murmuring, when
that lent it is pleas'd to recal it, why should I repine
parting with Things of so much less Importance? But
comfort myself after a more worldly Manner, I consi
that my Clothes had been worn out in a Year or tw
that my fine Things had been out of Fashion in a Year
two more; so that I have only lost the Use of th
Things which four or five Years wou'd have robb'd m
of without breaking a Lock, or opening a Window. B
sides, another Thing which gives me no small Comfor
is a Reflection on the Mercies of Providence in Matt
of greater Moment, as in Relation to my Life, my H
nour, &c. one Instance of which is pretty fresh in m
Memory. I recollect that some few Months ago I was
a foreign Country, far from my Relations to comfort m
or Friends to assist me; a Stranger to the Place, mor
the Language; like a Child among Savage Beasts; I ha
no Companion but a Brute more savage than they, wh
betray'd me into the Hands of a Villain, that wou'd ha
ruin'd me past Redemption, had not Providence sent
Gentleman to my Rescue, who is now at *Richmond* dyi
for Love of me. This Deliverance, I think, may ma
sufficient Amends for the present Loss.

Now, Madam, that I have guess'd at your Though
upon the Matter, give me Leave to present you with m
own Sentiments upon this Affair. And in the first Plac
I think that if the Rogues had stripp'd you of all that yo
enjoy in the World, even the white Covering to your fa
Nakedness, I wou'd catch you in my Arms before an
Duchess in *Christendom* set out in Brocade and Jewels.

I think, Secondly, that a Lady without a Husband li
very much expos'd to all Abuses from the rude World
that the Weakness of their Constitution is a sufficie
Proof, that their Maker design'd Man for their Guard
Now if a Lady will neglect the Protection which Provi
dence has design'd her, when there is one that begs i
very earnestly, and has so long sollicited for the Honou
of the Place; 'tis but just, I think, that she meet wit
some small Rubs to mind her of her Insufficiency. I know
Madam, that your Ladyship has a very good and worth
                                        Gentlema

...an very near you, one who is both a Friend and
...to you; but yet a Husband is still the best *Guard-*
..., and there are some Privileges annex'd to his
...which would make Rogues more cautious how they
...your Bed-Chamber. In the third Place, Madam,
...Leave to ask you one Question: Don't you think
...ief that robb'd you to be a very barbarous Fellow?
...uld you not be very severe upon him, if he were
...Most certainly you would. Then what must I
...f a Person that has robb'd me of a Jewel much
...ecious than any they have taken from you, I mean,
...e and Quiet? A little Thief has stole my Heart
...ny very Breast; the Loss of which has cost me
...ghs and Uneasiness than all the Wealth in the
...could have done. I have pursu'd this charming
...from Place to Place, from Town to Country, from
...m to Kingdom, yet all in vain——I beg you now,
..., to consider this, and be not too severe upon the
...ogues, tho' they should be taken.
...is the first Service my Hand has done me since I
...dw; and were not the Air too piercing for me to
...abroad after so much Bleeding, I would have
...all this personally; but happen what will, three
...Days shall be the utmost Confinement I can lay
...y Desire of waiting on you; and that you have
...long releas'd from my Company, you are more
...n to the Force of my Illness, than the Strength of
...olution, which is always too weak to encounter
...ion of,

MADAM,

Your most sincere and humble Servant.

:::

...w,

...s a sad Misfortune to begin a Letter with an
...m; but when my Love is cross'd, 'tis no Won-
...t my Writing should be revers'd. I would beg
...rdon for the other Offences of this Nature which

I have

I have examined, but that I have so little Reason
judge favourably of your Mercy; tho' I can assure y
Madam, that I shall never excuse myself my own Share
the Trouble, no more than I can pardon myself the V
nity of attempting your Charms, so much above the Rea
of my Pretensions, and which are reserv'd for some mo
worthy Admirer. If there be that Man upon Earth th
can merit your Esteem, I pity him; for an Obligation t
great for a Return, must to any generous Soul be very u
easy, tho' still I envy his Misery.

May you be as happy, Madam, in the Enjoyment
your Desires, as I am miserable in the Disappointment
mine; and as the greatest Blessing of your Life, may th
Person you admire love you as sincerely and as passionat
ly, as he whom you scorn.

✺✺✺✺✺✺✺✺✺✺✺✺✺✺✺✺✺

A

DISCOURSE

UPON

COMEDY,

In Reference to the

ENGLISH STAGE.

In a LETTER to a Friend.

WITH Submission, Sir, my Performance in
the Practical Part of Poetry, is no sufficient
Warrant for your pressing me in the Specula-
have no Foundation for a *Legislator*; and the two
little *Plays* I have wr... are cast carelesly into
ld, without any D... ...rface, because I was
...earn... Law... ...ve in Defence of a
...pliment go farther
ne, Sir,
...age in
... nor
which
...azard,

Hazard, not Study, brings into my Head, without
preliminary *Method* or *Cogitation*.

Among the many Difadvantages attending Poe
none feems to bear a greater Weight, than that fo
fet up for Judges, when fo very few underftand a T
of the Matter. Moft of our other Arts and Scie
bear an awful Diftance in their Profpect, or with a
and glittering Varnifh dazzle the Eyes of the
fighted Vulgar: The *Divine* ftands wrapt up in his C
of Myfteries, and the amufed *Laity* muft pay Tithes
Veneration to be kept in Obfcurity, grounding
Hopes of future Knowledge on a competent Stock
prefent Ignorance; (in the greater Part of the Chri
World this is plain.) With what Deference and R
nation does the bubbled *Client* commit his Pew and C
into the Clutches of the *Law*, where Affurance b
Juftice by *Prefcription*, and the wrong Side is never kn
to make its *Patron* blufh. *Phyfic* and *Logic* are ftro
fortified by their impregnable Terms of Art, and
Mathematician lies fo cunningly intrench'd within his
and *Circles*, that none but thofe of their Party dare
into their puzzling Defigns.

Thus the Generality of Mankind is held at a ga
Diftance, whofe Ignorance not prefuming perhaps
open Applaufe, is yet fatisfy'd to pay a blind Vener
to the very Faults of what they don't underftand.

Poetry alone, and chiefly the *Drama*, lies open to
Infults of all Pretenders; fhe was one of Nature's el
Offsprings, whence by her Birthright, and plain S
plicity, fhe pleads a genuine Likenefs to her Moth
born in the Innocence of Time, fhe provided not ag
the Affaults of fucceeding Ages; and, depending
gether on the generous End of her Invention, negl
thofe fecret Supports and ferpentine Devices us'd by
ther Arts, that wind themfelves into Practice for
fubtle and politic Defigns: Naked fhe came into
World, and 'tis to be fear'd, like its Profeffors, will
naked out.

'Tis a wonderful thing, that moft Men feem to ha
great Veneration for *Poetry*, yet will hardly allow
vourable Word to any Piece of it that they meet:
your *Virtuofoes* in Friendfhip, that are fo ravifh'd with
notic

nal Nicety of the Virtue, that they can find no Per-
orth their intimate Acquaintance.   The Favour of
whipt at School for *Martial's Epigrams*, or *Ovid's*
rs, is sufficient Privilege for turning *Pedagogue*, and
g all their Successors; and it would seem, by the
of their Correction, that the Ends of the Rod were
n their Buttocks.   The Scholar calls upon us for
ums and *Oeconomy*; the Courtier cries out for *Wit*,
Purity of Stile; the Citizen for *Humour* and *Ridicule*;
Divines threaten us for Immodesty; and the Ladies
have an Intrigue.   Now here are a Multitude of
cs whereof the twentieth Person only has read *One*
, and yet every one is a Critic after his own Way;
is, such a Play is best, because I like it.   A very fair Argument, methinks, to prove the Excellence of
y, and to which an Author wou'd be very unwilling
ppeal for his Success! Yet such is the unfortunate
: of Dramatic Poetry, that it must submit to such
;ments; and by the Censure or Approbation of such
ety, it must either stand or fall.   But what *Salve*,
: Redress for this Inconvenience? Why, without all
ute, an Author must endeavour to pleasure that Part
he Audience, who can lay the best Claim to a judi-
s and impartial Reflexion.   But before he begins,
him well consider to what Division that Claim does
t properly belong.   The Scholar will be very angry
ie for making that the Subject of a Question, which
elf-evident without any Dispute; for, says he, who
pretend to understand Poetry better than we, who
e read *Homer*, *Virgil*, *Horace*, *Ovid*, &c. at the Uni-
sity? What Knowledge can out-strip ours that is found-
upon the Criticisms of *Aristotle*, *Scaliger*, *Vossius*, and
like? We are the better Sort, and therefore may claim
: as a due Compliment to our Learning! and if a
:t can please us, who are the nice and severe Cri-
s, he cannot fail to bring in the rest of an inferior
uk.

I should be very proud to own my Veneration for Learn-
g, and to acknowledge any Compliment due to the
:ter Sort upon that Foundation; but I am afraid the
arning of the better Sort is not confin'd to College
adies; for there is such a Thing as Reason without Syl-
logism,

logism, Knowledge without *Aristotle*, and Languages
sides *Greek* and *Latin :* We shall likewise find in the Co
and City several Degrees, superior to those at Commen
ment.   From all which I must beg the Scholar's Pard
for not paying him the Compliment of the better Se
(as he calls it ;) and in the next Place enquire into
Validity of his Title from his Knowledge of *Critici*
and the Course of his Studies.

I must first beg one Favour of the Graduate ——— {
here is a Pit full of *Covent-Garden* Gentlemen, a Gall
full of Cits, a hundred Ladies of Court-Education, a
about two hundred Footmen of nice Morality, who h
ing been unmercifully teaz'd with a Parcel of fooli
impertinent, irregular Plays all this last Winter, make
their humble Request, that you wou'd oblige them w
a Comedy of your own making, which they don't qu
tion will give them Entertainment.   O, Sir, replies
Square-Cap, I have long commiserated the Condition
the *English* Audience, that has been forc'd to take up w
such wretched Stuff, as lately has crowded the Stag
your *Jubilees* and your *Foppingtons,* and such irregu
Impertinence, that no Man of Sense cou'd bear the l
rusal of 'em.   I have long intended, out of pure Pi
to the Stage, to write a perfect Piece of this Natur
and now, since I am honour'd by the Commands.
so many, my Intentions shall immediately be put
Practice.

So to work he goes ; old *Aristotle, Scaliger,* with the
Commentators, are lugg'd down from the high She
and the Moths are dislodg'd from the Tenement of Yea
Horace, Vossius, Heinsius, Hedelin, Rapin, with some ha
dozen more, are thumb'd and tofs'd about, to teach
Gentlemen, forsooth, to write a Comedy ; and here
he furnish'd with *Unity of Action, Continuity of A*
Extent of Time, Preparation of Incidents, Episodes, N
ration, Deliberations, Didactics, Pathetics, Monologues,
gures, Intervals, Catastrophes, Choruses, Scenes, Machin
Decorations, &c. a Stock sufficient to set up any Moun
bank in *Christendom :* And if our new Author would t
an Opportunity of reading a Lecture upon the Play
these Terms, by the Help of a *Zany* and a Joint-stool,
Scenes might go off as well as the Doctor's Packet

b

e Misfortune of it is, he fcorns all Application to
ulgar, and will pleafe the better Sort, as he calls
m. Purfuant therefore to his Philofophical Dic-
he firft chufes a fingle Plot, becaufe moft agree-
) the Regularity of Criticifm ; no matter whether it
: Bufinefs enough for Diverfion or Surprize. He
not for the World introduce a Song or Dance, be-
his Play muft be one intire Action, We muft ex-
o variety of incidents, becaufe the Exactnefs of his
Hours won't give him Time for their Preparation.
Jnity of Place admits no Variety of Painting and
:ct, by which Mifchance perhaps we fhall lofe the
ood Scenes in the Play. But no matter for that ;
lay is a regular Play ; this Play has been examin'd
pprov'd by fuch and fuch Gentlemen, who are
h Critics, and Mafters of Art ; and this Play I
ave acted. Look'e, Mr. *Rich*, you may venture to
t a hundred and fifty Pounds for dreffing this Play,
was written by a great Scholar, and Fellow of a
;e.
:n a grave dogmatical Prologue is fpoken, to in-
the Audience what fhould pleafe them ; that this
ias a new and different Cut from the Farce they fee
Day ; that this Author writes after the Manner of
ncients, and here is a Piece according to the Model
: *Athenian Drama*. Very well! This goes off *Hum*,
fo, fo. Then the Players go to work on a Piece
d knotty Stuff, where they can no more fhew their
:han a Carpenter can upon a Piece of Steel. Here
Lamp and the Scholar in every Line, but not a Syl-
of the Poet ; here is elaborate Language, founding
:ts, Flights of Words that ftrike the Clouds, whilft
)or Senfe lags after, like the Lanthorn in the Tail
Kite, which appears only like a Star, while the
th of the Player's Lungs has Strength to bear it up
Air.
: the Audience, willing perhaps to difcover his an-
Model, and the *Athenian Drama*, are attentive to
rft Act or two ; but not finding a true Genius of
/, nor the natural Air of free Converfation, with-
iy regard to his Regularity, they betake themfelves
er Work : Not meeting the Diverfion they expected

L. I.　　　　　D　　　　　on

on the Stage, they shift for themselves in the Pit, if
one turns about to his Neighbour in a Mask, and fo
fault of Entertainment now, they strike up for mo
verting Scenes when the Play is done: And tho' the
be regular as *Aristotle*, and modeft as Mr. *Collier*
wifh, yet it promotes more Lewdnefs in the Confequ
and procures more effectually for Intrigue, that
Rover, *Libertine*, or *Old Bachelor* whatfoever. A
comes the *Epilogue*, which pleafes the Audience very
becaufe it fends them away, and terminates the F
the Poet; the *Patentees* rail at him, the Players
him, the Town damns him, and he may bury his
in *Paul's*, for not a Bookfeller about it will put
Print.

This familiar Account, Sir, I would not have
charge to my Invention, for there are Precedents fi
ent in the World to warrant it in every Particular.
Town has been often difappointed in thofe Critical I
and fome Gentlemen, that have been admir'd in thei
culative Remarks, have been ridicul'd in the Pr
All the Authorities, all the Rules of Antiquity
prov'd too weak to fupport the Theatre, whilft o
who have difpens'd with the Critics, and taken a
tude in the *Oeconomy* of their Plays, have been the
Supporters of the Stage, and the Ornament of the D
This is fo vifibly true, that I need bring in no Inft
to enforce it; but you fay, Sir, 'tis a Paradox tha
often puzzled your Underftanding, and you lay
Commands upon me to folve it, if I can.

Look'e, Sir, to add a Value to my Complaifanc to
I muft tell you in the firft Place, that I run as g
Hazard in nibbling at this *Paradox* of *Poetry*, as *I*
did by touching *Tranfubftantiation*; 'tis a Myftery the
World has fweetly flept in fo long, that they take it
ill to be waken'd; efpecially being difturb'd of
Reft, when there is no Bufinefs to be done. But I
that *Bellarmine* was once as *Orthodox* as *Ariftotle*;
fince the *German Doctor* has made a fhift to hew
the *Cardinal*, I will have a tug with *ipfe dixit*, tho'
for't.

But in the firft Place I muft beg you, Sir, to lay
your fuperftitious Veneration for Antiquity, and the
Expre

ions on that Score ; that the prefent Age is illite-
their Tafte is vitiated ; that we live in the Decay
ie, and the Dotage of the World is fall'n to our
———'Tis a Miftake, Sir ; the World was never
ftive or youthful, and true downright Senfe was
more univerfal than at this very Day ; 'tis neither
l to one Nation in the World, nor to one Party of
; 'tis remarkable in *England*, as well as *France*,
od genuine Reafon is nourifh'd as well by the Cold
dkland, as by the Warmth of *Italy* ; 'tis neither ab-
l the Court with the late Reigns, nor expell'd the
/ith the Play-houfe Bills ; you may find it in the
Jury at *Hicks's Hall*, and upon the Bench fometimes
the Juftices ; then why fhould we be hamper'd fo
Opinions, as if all the Ruins of Antiquity lay fo
y on the Bones of us, that we cou'd not ftir Hand
iot : No, no, Sir, *ipfe dixit* is remov'd long ago,
l the Rubbifh of old Philofophy, that in a Man-
iry'd the Judgment of Mankind for many Cen-
is now carry'd off ; the vaft Tomes of *Ariftotle*
s Commentators are all taken to pieces, and their
bility is loft with all Perfons of a free and un-
lic'd Reafon.

:n above all Men living, why fhould the Poets be
/ink'd at this rate, and by what Authority fhould
'le's Rules of Poetry ftand fo fix'd and immutable ?
by the Authority of two thoufand Years ftanding,
fe thro' this long Revolution of Time the World
ill continu'd the fame ——— By the Authority
iir being receiv'd at *Athens*, a City the very fame
London in every Particular, their Habits the fame,
Humours alike, their public Tranfactions and pri-
Societies *Alamode de France* ; in fhort, fo very much
me in every Circumftance, that *Ariftotle's* Criticifms
give Rules to *Drury-Lane*, the *Areopagus* give Judg-
upon a Cafe in the *King's Bench*, and old *Solon* fhall
Laws to the *Houfe of Commons*.

t to examine this Matter a little further : All Arts
'rofeffions are compounded of thefe two Parts, a fpe-
ive Knowledge, and a practical Ufe ; and from an
llence in both thefe, any Perfon is rais'd to Emi-
s and Auth ity in his Calling. The Lawyer has

Years

his Years of Student in the Speculative Part of his Business ; and, when promoted to the Bar, he falls upon
the Practic, which is the Trial of his Ability.   Without all Dispute the great *Coke* had many a Tug at the
Bar, before he could raise himself to the Bench ; and had
made sufficiently evident his Knowledge of the Laws in
his Pleadings, before he was admitted to the Authority
of giving Judgment upon the Case.

The Physician, to gain Credit to his Prescriptions,
must labour for a Reputation in the Cure of such and such
Distempers ; and before he sets up for a *Galen* or *Hip-
pocrates,* must make many Experiments upon his Patients.
Philosophy itself, which is a Science the most abstract from
Practice, has its public Acts and Disputations ; it is
rais'd gradually, and its Professor commences Doctor by
Degrees ; he has the Labour of maintaining *Theses,* me-
thodizing his *Arguments,* and clearing *Objections* ; his Memory and Understanding is often puzzled by Oppositions
couch'd in Fallacies and Sophisms, in solving all which
he must make himself remarkable, before he pretends
to impose his own System upon the World.   Now if
the Case be thus in *Philosophy,* or in any Branch thereof, as in *Ethics, Physics,* which are call'd Sciences,
what must be done in *Poetry,* that is denominated an
Art, and consequently implies a Practice in its Perfection ?

Is it reasonable, that any Person that has never writ a
Distich of Verses in his Life, should set up for a *Dictator*
in Poetry ; and without the least Practice in his own Performance, must give Laws and Rules to that of others ?
Upon what Foundation is Poetry made so very cheap and
so easy a Task by these Gentlemen ? An excellent Poet is
the single Production of an Age, when we have Crowds
of Philosophers, Physicians, Lawyers, Divines, every
Day, and all of them competently famous in their Call-
ings.   In the two learned Commonwealths of *Rome* and
Athens, there was but one *Virgil* and one *Homer,* yet have
we above a hundred *Philosophers* in each, and most part
of 'em, forsooth, must have a touch at Poetry, drawing
it into *Divisions, Subdivisions* &c. when the Wit of 'em all
set together would not amount to one of *Martial's Epigrams.*

Of all these I shall mention only *Aristotle,* the first and
great *Lawgiver* in this respect, and upon whom all that
follow'd

follow'd him are only Commentators. Among all the vaſt Tracts of this voluminous Author, we don't find any Fragment of an Epic Poem, or the leaſt Scene of a Play, to authorize his Skill and Excellence in that Art. Let it not be alledg'd, that for aught we know he was an excellent Poet, but his more ſerious Studies would not let him enter upon Affairs of this Nature; for every body knows that *Ariſtotle* was no *Cynic*, but liv'd in the Splendor and Air of the Court; that he lov'd Riches as much as others of that Station, and being ſufficiently acquainted with his Pupil's Affection to Poetry, and his Complaint that he wanted an *Homer* to aggrandize his Actions, he would never have ſlipt ſuch an Opportunity of further ingratiating himſelf in the King's Favour, had he been conſcious of any Abilities in himſelf for ſuch an Undertaking; and having a more noble and copious Theme in the Exploits of *Alexander*, than what inſpir'd the blind Bard in his Hero *Achilles*. If his Epiſtles to *Alexander* were always anſwer'd with a conſiderable Preſent, what might we have expected from a Work like *Homer's* upon ſo great a Subject, dedicated to ſo mighty a Prince, whoſe greateſt Fault was his vain Glory, and that he took ſuch Pains to be deify'd among Men?

It may be objected, that all the Works of *Ariſtotle* are not recover'd; and among thoſe that are loſt, ſome Eſſays of this kind might have periſh'd. This Suppoſition is too weakly founded; for altho' the Works themſelves might have eſcap'd us, 'tis more than probable that ſome Hint or other, either in the Life of the Conqueror, or Philoſopher, might appear, to convince us of ſuch a Production: Beſides, as 'tis believ'd he writ *Philoſophy*, becauſe we have his Books; ſo I dare ſwear he writ no *Poetry*, becauſe none is extant, nor any Mention made thereof that ever I could hear of.

But ſtay—Without any further Enquiry into the Poetry of *Ariſtotle*, his Ability that Way is ſufficiently apparent by that excellent Piece he has left behind him upon that Subject——By your Favour, Sir, this is *Petitio Principii*, or in plain *Engliſh*, give me the Sword in my own Hand, and I'll fight with you——Have but a little Patience till I make a Flouriſh or two, and then if you are pleas'd to demand it, I'll grant you that and every Thing elſe.

D 3 How

How eafy were it for me to take one of Doctor *Tillot*
Sermons, and out of the *Oeconomy* of one of thofe
courfes, trump you up a Pamphlet, and call it, *The A*
Preaching? In the firft Place I muft take a *Text*, and
I muft be very learn'd upon the Etymology of this W
Text; then this Text muft be divided into fuch and
Partitions, which Partitions muft have their hard Na
and *Derivations*; then thefe muft be fpun into *Suba*
fions, and thefe back'd by Proofs of Scripture, *Ratioci*
Oratoris, Ornamenta Figurarum, Rhetoricarum, and *Aut*
tas Patrum Ecclefiæ, with fome Rules and Directions
thefe ought to be manag'd and apply'd: And clofing
this difficult Pedantry with the *Dimenfion of Time* for
an Occafion, you will pay me the Compliment of ar
cellent Preacher, and affirm that any Sermon whatfoe
either by a *Prefbyter* at *Geneva,* or *Jefuit* in *Spain,*
deviates from thefe Rules, deferves to be hifs'd, anc
Prieft kick'd out of his Pulpit. I muft doubt your C
plaifance in this Point, Sir; for you know the Forr
Eloquence are divers, and ought to be fuited to the
ferent Humour and Capacities of an Audience. You
fenfible, Sir, that the fiery choleric Humour of
Nation muft be entertain'd and mov'd by other Me
than the heavy flegmatic Complexion of another;
have obferv'd in my little Travels, that a Sermon of
Quarters of an Hour, that might pleafe the Congreg
at St. *James's*, would never fatisfy the Meeting-houfe i
City, where People expect more for their Money;
having more Temptations of Roguery, muft have a l
Portion of Inftruction.

Be pleas'd to hear another Inftance of a different K
tho' to the fame Purpofe: I go down to *Woolwich,*
there upon a Piece of Paper I take the Dimenfion o
Royal Sovereign, and from hence I frame a Model of a
of War: I divide the Ship into three principal Parts
Keel, the *Hull,* and the *Rigging*; I fubdivide thefe
their proper Denominations, and, by the help of a Sa
give you all the Terms belonging to every Rope,
every Office in the whole Ship; will you from hence i
that I am an excellent Shipwright, and that this Mo
proper for a *Trading Junk* upon the *Volga,* or a *Ven*
Galley in the *Adriatick Sea?*

But you'll object, perhaps, that this is no parallel Case, because that *Aristotle's Ars Poetica* was never drawn from such slight Observations, but was the pure Effect of his immense Reason through a nice Inspection into the very Bottom and Foundation of Nature.

To this I answer, That Verity is eternal, as that the Truth of two and two making four was as certain in the Days of *Adam* as it is now; and that, according to his own Position, Nature is the same *apud omnes Gentes.* Now if his Rules of Poetry were drawn from certain and immutable Principles, and fix'd on the Basis of Nature, why should not his *Ars Poetica* be as efficacious now as it was two thousand Years ago? And why should not a single Plot, with perfect Unity of Time and Place, do as well at *Lincoln's-Inn-Fields*, as at the Play-house in *Athens?* No, no, Sir, I am to believe that the Philosopher took no such Pains in Poetry as you imagine; the *Greek* was his Mother Tongue, and *Homer* was read with as much Veneration among the School-Boys, as we learn our *Catechism:* Then where was the great Business for a Person, so expert in Mood and Figure as *Aristotle* was, to range into some Order a Parcel of Terms of Art, drawn from his Observations upon the *Iliads*, and to call these the Model of an *Epic Poem?* Here, Sir, you may imagine that I am caught, and have all this while been spinning a Thread to strangle myself: One of my main Objections against *Aristotle's Criticisms*, is drawn from his Non-performance in Poetry; and now I affirm, that his Rules are extracted from the greatest Poet that ever liv'd which gives the utmost Validity to the Precept, and that is all we contend for.

Look'e, Sir, I lay it down only for a Supposition, that *Aristotle's* Rules for an *Epic Poem* were extracted from *Homer's Iliads*, and if a Supposition has weigh'd me down, I have two or three more of an equal Balance to turn the Scale.

The great Esteem of *Alexander the Great* for the Works of old *Homer*, is sufficiently testify'd by Antiquity, insomuch that he always slept with the *Iliads* under his Pillow: Of this the *Stagyric* to be sure was not ignorant; and what more proper Way of making his Court could a Man of Letters devise, than by saying something in Commenda-

tion

tion of the King's Favourite? A Copy of Commendatory
Verfes was too mean, and perhaps out of the Element;
then fomething he would do in his own Way, a Book muft
be made of the Art of Poetry, wherein *Homer* is prov'd a
Poet by Mood and Figure, and his Perfection tranfmitted
to Pofterity: And if Prince *Arthur* had been in the Place
of the *Iliads*, we fhould have had other Rules for *Epic
Poetry*, and Doctor B——*re* had carry'd the *Bays* from
Homer, in Spight of all the Critics in *Chriftendom*.. But
whether *Ariftotle* writ thofe Rules to compliment his Pupil,
whether he would made a Stoop at Poetry, to fhew that
there was no Knowledge beyond the Flight of his Genius,
there is no Reafon to allow that *Homer* compil'd his Heroic Poem by thofe very Rules which *Ariftotle* has laid
down: For, granting that *Ariftotle* might pick fuch and
fuch Obfervations from this Piece, they might be mere
Accidents refulting cafually from the Compofition of
the Work, and not any of the effential Principles of the
Poem. How ufual is it for Critics to find out Faults,
and create Beauties, which the Authors never intend for
fuch; and how frequently do we find Authors run down
in thofe very Parts, which they defign for the 'greateft
Ornament? How natural is it for afpiring, ambitious
School-men to attempt Matters of the higheft Reach; the
wonderful Creation of the World (which nothing but the
Almighty Power that ordered it can defcribe) is brought
into Mood and Figure by the Arrogance of *Philofophy*.
But till I can believe that the Vertigos of *Cartefius*, or the
Atoms of *Epicurus* can determine the Almighty *Fiat*, they
muft give me Leave to queftion the Infallibility of their
Rules in refpect of Poetry.

Had *Homer* himfelf by the fame Infpiration that he writ
his Poem, left us any Rules for fuch a Performance, all
the World muft have own'd it for authentic. But he
was too much a Poet to give Rules to that, whofe Excellence he knew confifted in a free and unlimited Flight of
Imagination; and to defcribe the Spirit of Poetry, which
alone, in the *True Art of Poetry*, he knew to be as impoffible, as for Human Reafon to teach the Gift of Pro-
phecy by a Definition.

Neither is *Ariftotle* to be allow'd any further Knowledge
in *Dramatic*, than in *Epic Poetry*: *Euripides*, whom he
seems

compliment by Rules adapted to the Modes of
, was either his Contemporary, or liv'd but a
ore him; he was not infenſible how much this
vas the Darling of the City, as appear'd by the
is Expence diſburs'd by the Public for the Or-
ſf his Plays; and 'tis probable, he might take
ortunity of improving his Intereſt with the Peo-
ulging their Inclination by refining upon the
f what they admir'd. And beſides all this, the
of *Dramatic* Rage was ſo freſh in his Memory,
rd Uſage that his Brother *Sophocles* not long before
upon the Stage, that it was convenient to hu-
: reigning Wit, leſt a ſecond *Ariſtophanes* ſhould
1 to taſk with as little Mercy, as poor *Socrates*
the Hands of the firſt.
: talk'd ſo long to lay a Foundation for theſe
g Concluſions: *Ariſtotle* was no Poet, and con-
ʃ not capable of giving Inſtructions in the Art of
his *Ars Poetica* are only ſome Obſervations
·om the Works of *Homer* and *Euripides*, which
mere Accidents reſulting caſually from the Com-
i of the Works, and not any of the eſſential
:s on which they are compil'd. That without
iimſelf the Trouble of ſearching into the Nature
y, he has only complimented the Heroes of Wit
ɔur of his Age, by joining with them in their
ition; with this Difference, that their Applauſe
n, and his more Scholaſtic.
ɔ leave theſe only as Suppoſitions to be reliſh'd
y Man at his Pleaſure, I ſhall without compli-
any Author, either ancient or modern, inquire
firſt Invention of Comedy; what were the true
and honeſt Intentions of that Art; and from a
lge of the *End*, ſeek out the *Means*, without
ɔtation of *Ariſtotle*, or Authority of *Euripides*.
Productions, either Divine or Human, the final
the firſt Mover, becauſe the End or Intention
rational Action muſt firſt be confider'd, before
eiial or efficient Cauſes are put in Execution.
determine the final Cauſe of Comedy, we muſt
k beyond the material and formal Agents, and
in it's very Infancy, or rather in the very firſt

Act of its Generation, when its primary Parent, by proposing such or such an End of his Labour, laid down the first Sketches or Shadows of the Piece. Now as all Arts and Sciences have their first Rise from a final Cause, so 'tis certain that they have grown from very small Beginnings, and that the Current of Time has swell'd them to such a Bulk, that no Body can find the Fountain, by any Proportion between the Head and the Body ; this with the Corruption of Time, which has debauch'd things from their primitive Innocence to selfish Designs and Purposes, render it difficult to find the Origin of any Offspring so very unlike its Parent.

This is not only the Case of Comedy, as it stands at present, but the Condition also of the ancient Theatres; when great Men made Shews of this Nature a rising Step to their Ambition, mixing many lewd and lascivious Representations to gain the Favour of the Populace, to whose Taste and Entertainment the Plays were chiefly adapted. We must therefore go higher than either *Aristophanes* or *Menander*, to discover Comedy in its primitive Institution, if we wou'd draw any moral Design of its Invention to warrant and authorize its Continuance.

I have already mention'd the Difficulty of discovering the Invention of any Art, in the different Figure it makes by Succession of Improvements; but there is something in the Nature of Comedy, even in its present Circumstances, that bears so great a Resemblance to the Philosophical *Mithology* of the Ancients, that old *Æsop* must wear the Bays as the first and original Author ; and whatever Alterations or Improvements farther Application may have subjoin'd, his *Fables* gave the first Rise and Occasion.

Comedy is no more at present than a *well-fram'd Tale handsomely told, as an agreeable Vehicle for Counsel or Reproof.* This is all we can say for the Credit of its Institution, and is the Stress of its Charter for Liberty and Toleration. Then where shou'd we seek for a Foundation, but in *Æsop's* symbolical Way of moralizing upon Tales and Fables, with this Difference, That his Stories were shorter than ours ? He had his Tyrant *Lyon*, his Statesman *Fox*, his Beau *Magpy*, his Coward *Hare*, his

Bravo

Bravo *Ass*, and his Buffoon *Ape*, with all the Characters that crowd our Stages every Day; with this Distinction nevertheless, That *Æsop* made his Beast speak good *Greek*, and our Heroes sometimes can't talk *English*.

But whatever Difference Time has produc'd in the Form, we must in our own Defence stick to the *End* and *Intention* of his *Fables*. *Utile Dulci* was his Motto, and must be our Business; we have no other Defence against the Presentment of the *Grand Jury*, and for aught I know it might prove a good Means to mollify the Rigour of that Persecution, to inform the Inquisitors, that the great *Æsop* was the first Inventor of these poor Comedies that they are prosecuting with so much Eagerness and Fury; that the first *Laureat* was as just, as prudent, as pious, as reforming, and as ugly as any of themselves; and that the Beasts which are lugg'd upon the Stage by the Horn are not caught in the City, as they suppose, but brought out of *Æsop's* own Forest. We shou'd inform them, besides, that these very Tales and Fables which they apprehend as Obstacles to Reformation, were the main Instruments and Machines us'd by the wise *Æsop* for its Propagation; and as he wou'd improve Men by the Policy of Beasts, so we endeavour to reform Brutes with the Examples of Men. *Fondlewife* and his young Spouse are no more than the *Eagle* and *Cockle*; he wanted Teeth to break the Shell himself, so somebody else run away with the Meat.——The Fox in the Play, is the same with the Fox in the Fable, who stuff'd his Guts so full, that he cou'd not get out at the same Hole he came in; so both *Reynards* being Delinquents alike, come to be truss'd up together. Here are Precepts, Admonitions, and Salutary *Inuendoes* for the ordering our Lives and Conversations, couch'd in these *Allegories* and *Allusions*. The wisdom of the Ancients was wrapt up in Veils and Figures; the *Egyptian Hieroglyphics*, and the History of the Heathen Gods are nothing else; but if these Pagan Authorities give Offence to their scrupulous Consciences, let them but consult the Tales and Parables of our *Saviour* in Holy Writ, and they may find this Way of Instruction to be much more Christian than they imagine: *Nathan's* Fable of the poor Man's Lamb had more Influence on the Conscience

of *David*, than any Force of downright Admonition
So that by ancient Practice and modern Example, by the
Authority of Pagans, Jews and Christians, the World is
furnish'd with this so sure, so pleasant, and expedient an
Art of schooling Mankind into better Manners. Now
here is the primary Design of Comedy illustrated from its
first Institution; and the same End is equally alledg'd
for its daily Practice and Continuance. Then without
all Dispute, whatever Means are most proper and expedient for compassing this End and Intention, they must
be the *just Rules of Comedy*, and the *true Art of the Stage*.

We must consider then, in the first Place, that our
Business lies not with a *French* or a *Spanish* Audience,
that our Design is not to hold forth to ancient *Greece*, nor
to moralize upon the Vices and Defaults of the *Roman*
Common-wealth: No, no; an *English* Play is intended
for the Use and Instruction of an *English* Audience,
People not only separated from the Rest of the World by
Situation, but different also from other Nations, as well
in the Complexion and Temperament of the Natural
Body, as in the Constitution of our Body Politic: As
we are a Mixture of many Nations, so we have the most
unaccountable Medley of Humours among us of any
People upon Earth; these Humours produce Variety of
Follies, some of 'em unknown to former Ages; their
new Distempers must have new Remedies, which are
nothing but new Counsels and Instructions.

Now, Sir, if our *Utile*, which is the End, be different
from the Ancients, pray let our *Dulce*, which is the
Means, be so too; for you know that to different Towns
there are different Ways; or if you wou'd have it more
Scholastically, *ad diversos fines non idem conducit medium*,
or Mathematically, One and the same Line cannot ter-
minate in two Centers. But waving this Manner of
concluding by Induction, I shall gain my Point a nearer
Way, and draw it immediately from the first Principle
set down: *That we have the most unaccountable Medley of
Humours among us of any Nation upon Earth*; and this is
demonstrable from common Experience: We shall find
Wildair in one Corner, and a *Morose* in another; nay
the Space of an Hour or two shall create such Vicissitude
of Temper in the same Person, that he can hardly be
take

to engage the Attention of so many different Hu-
and Inclinations? Will a single Plot satisfy every
Will the Turns and Surprizes, that may result
lly from the ancient Limits of Time, be sufficient
open the Spleen of some, and pacise the Melan-
of others, screw up the Attention of a Rover, and
to the Stage, in Spite of his volatile Temper,
Temptation of a Mask? To make the Moral in-
e, you must make the Story diverting: The
tic Wit, the Beau Courtier, the heavy Citizen,
Lady, and her fine Footman, come all to be in-
l, and therefore must all be diverted; and he that
this best, and with most Applause, writes the
medy, let him do it by what Rules he pleases, so
not offensive to Religion and good Manners.

ic labor, hoc opus; how must this Secret of pleasing
different Tastes be discover'd? Not by tumbling
olumes of the Ancients, but by studying the Hu-
of the Moderns: The Rules of *English* Comedy
in the Compass of *Aristotle*, or his Followers,
the Pit, Box, and Galleries. And to examine
Humour of an *English* Audience, let us see by
eans our own *English* Poets have succeeded in this
To determine a Suit at Law, we don't look into
hives of *Greece* or *Rome*, but inspect the Reports

malities; the Decorums of Time and Place, fo mu
cry'd up of late, had no Force of Decorum with ther
the Oeconomy of their Plays was *ad libitum*, and the E
tent of their Plots only limited by the Convenience
Action. I would willingly underftand the Regulariti
of *Hamlet, Macbeth, Harry the Fourth*, and of *Fletche*
Plays; and yet thefe have long been the Darlings of tl
Englifb Audience, and are like to continue with the fan
Applaufe, in Defiance of all the Criticifms that ev
were publifh'd in *Greek* and *Latin*.

But are there no Rules, no Decorums to be obferv
in Comedy? Muft we make the Condition of the *Engl*
Stage a State of Anarchy? No, Sir——For there a
Extremes in Irregularity, as dangerous to an Author,
too fcrupulous a Deference to Criticifm; and as I ha
given you an Inftance of One, fo I fhall prefent you
Example of the other.

There are a Sort of Gentlemen that have had t
jaunty Education of Dancing, French, and a Fiddl
who coming to Age before they arrive at Years of D
cretion, make a Shift to fpend a handfome Patrimony
Two or Three Thoufand Pounds, by foaking in tl
Tavern all Night, lolling a-bed all the Morning, a
fauntering away all the Evening between the Two Pla
houfes with their Hands in their Pockets; you fhall ha
a Gentleman of this Size, upon his Knowledge of *C
vent-Garden*, and a Knack of witticifing in his Cup
fet up immediately for a Play-wright. But befides tl
Gentleman's Wit and Experience, here is another M
tive: There are a Parcel of faucy impudent Fellov
about the Play-houfe, called Door-keepers, that can
let a Gentleman fee a Play in Peace, without joggir
and nudging him every Minute. *Sir, will you pleafe
pay?*——*Sir, the Act's done, will you pleafe to pay, Sir*
I have broke their Heads all round Two or Thr
Times, yet the Puppies will ftill be troublefome. Befo
gad, I'll be plagued with 'em no longer; I'll e'en wri
a Play myfelf; by which Means, my Character of W
fhall be eftablifh'd, I fhall enjoy the Freedom of tl
Houfe, and to pin up the Bafket, pretty Mifs ——
fhall have the Profits of my Third Night for her Maide
head. Thus we fee what a great Bleffing a Coming Gi

to a Play-house: Here is a Poet sprung from the Tail of an Actress, like *Minerva* from *Jupiter's* Head. But my Spark proceeds——my own Intrigues are sufficient to found the Plot, and the Devil's in't, if I can't make my Character talk as wittily as those in the *Trip to the Jubilee*——But stay——what shall I call it first? Let me see——*The Rival Theatres*——Very good, by gad, because I reckon the Two Houses will have a Contest about this very Play——Thus having found a Name for his Play, in the next Place he makes a Play to his Name, and thus he begins:

A C T I. *Scene* Covent-Garden. *Enter* Portico, Piazza, *and* Turnstile.

Here you must note, that *Portico* being a Compound of practical Rake and speculative Gentleman, is Ten to One the Author's own Character, and the leading Card in the Pack *Piazza* is his Mistress, who lives in the Square, and is Daughter to old *Pillariso*, an odd out o'the-way Gentleman, something between the Character of *Alexander the Great* and *Solon*, which must please, because 'tis new.

Turnstile is Maid and Confident to *Piazza*, who, for a Bribe of Ten Pieces, lets *Portico* in at the Back-door; so the First Act concludes.

In the Second, enter *Spigotoso*, who was Butler perhaps to the *Czar* of *Muscovy*, and *Fossetana* his Wife. After these Characters are run dry, he brings you in at the Third Act *Whinewell* and *Charmarillis* for a Scene of Love to please the Ladies, and so he goes on without Fear or Wit 'till he comes to a Marriage or two, and then he writes——*Finis*.

'Tis then whisper'd among his Friends at *Will's* and *Hippolito's*, that Mr. *Such-a-one* has writ a very pretty Comedy; and some of 'em, to encourage the young Author, equip him presently with *Prologue* and *Epilogue*. Then the Play is sent to Mr. *Rich* or Mr. *Betterton*, in a fair legible Hand, with the Recommendation of some Gentleman, that passes for a Man of Parts and a Critic. In short, the Gentleman's Interest has the Play acted, and the Gentleman's Interest makes a Present to

pretty

pretty Mifs ——— fhe's made his Whore, and the S
his Cully, that for the Lofs of a Month in Rehearf
and a Hundred Pounds in dreffing a confounded P
muft give the Liberty of the Houfe to him and
Friends for ever after.

  Now fuch a Play may be written with all the
aftnefs imaginable, in Refpeft of Unity in Time
Place; but if you enquire its Charaƈter of any Per
tho' of the meaneft Underftanding of the whole A
ence, he will tell you 'tis intolerable Stuff; and i
your demanding his Reafons, his Anfwer is, *I don't*
it. His Humour is the only Rule that he can judj
Comedy by, but you find that mere Nature is offer
with fome Irregularities; and though he be not fo lea
in the *Drama*, to give you an Inventory of the Fa
yet I can tell you, that one Part of the Plot had no
pendence upon another, which made this fimple
drop his Attention and Concern for the Event; ar
difengaging his Thoughts from the Bufinefs of the Aƈ
he fat there very uneafy, thought the Time very tedi
becaufe he had nothing to do. The Charaƈters wer
incoherent in themfelves, and compos'd of fuch Va
of Abfurdities, that in his Knowledge of Nature he c
find no Original for fuch a Copy; and being there
unacquainted with any Folly they reprov'd, or any
tue that they recommended, their Bufinefs was as
and tirefome to him, as if the Aƈtors had talk'd
bick.

  Now thefe are the material Irregularities of a Play,
thefe are the Faults which downright Mother-Senfe
cenfure and be offended at, as much as the moft lea
Critic in the Pit. And altho' the one cannot give
the Reafons of his Approbation or Diflike, yet I
take his Word for the Credit or Difrepute of a Com
fooner perhaps than the Opinion of fome *Virtuofoes*;
there are fome Gentlemen that have fortify'd their Sp
fo impregnably with Criticifm, and hold out fo f
againft all Attacks of Pleafantry, that the moft pow
Efforts of Wit and Humour cannot make the leaft Imp
fion. What a Misfortune is it to thefe Gentlemen t
Natives of fuch an ignorant felf-will'd, imperti
Ifland, where let a Critic and a Scholar find neve

many Irregularities in a Play, yet five hundred saucy People will give him the Lie to his Face, and come to see this wicked Play forty or fifty Times in a Year? But this *Vox Populi* is the Devil, tho' in a Place of more Authority than *Aristotle*, it is call'd *Vox Dei*. Here is a Play with a Vengeance (says a Critic) to bring the Transactions of a Year's Time into the Compass of three Hours, to carry the whole Audience with him from one Kingdom to another, by the changing of a Scene. Where's the Probability; nay, the Possibility of all this? The Devil's in the Poet sure, he don't think to put Contradictions upon us.

Look'e, Sir, don't be in a Passion, the Poet does not impose Contradictions upon you, because he has told you no Lie; for that only is a Lie, which is related with some fallacious Intention that you should believe it for a Truth: Now the Poet expects no more that you should believe the Plot of his Play, than old *Æsop* design'd the World should think his *Eagle* and *Lion* talk'd like you and I; which, I think, was every Jot as improbable as what you quarrel with; and yet the Fables took, and I'll be hang'd if you yourself don't like 'em. But besides, Sir, if you are so inveterate against Improbabilites, you must never come near the Play-house at all; for there are several Improbabilities, nay Impossibilities, that all the Criticisms in Nature cannot correct: As for Instance; in the Part of *Alexander the Great*, to be affected with the Transactions of the Play, we must suppose that we see that great Conqueror, after all his Triumphs, shunn'd by the Woman he loves, and importun'd by her he hates; cross'd in his Cups and Jollity by his own Subjects, and at last miserably ending his Life in a raging Madness: We must suppose, that we see the very *Alexander*, the Son of *Philip*, in all these unhappy Circumstances, else we are not touch'd by the Moral, which represents to us the Uneasiness of Human Life in the greatest State, and the Instability of Fortune in Respect of wordly Pomp; yet the whole Audience at the same Time knows, that this is Mr. *Betterton*, who is strutting upon the Stage, and tearing his Lungs for a Livelihood: And that the same Person should be Mr. *Betterton* and *Alexander the Great* at the same Time, is somewhat like an Impossibility in my Mind. Yet you

must

must grant this Impossibility, in Spite of your Teeth, if you ha'n't Power to raise the old Hero from the Grave to act his own Part.

Now for another Impossibility : The less rigid Criticks allow to a Comedy the Space of an artificial Day, or twenty-four Hours ; but those of the thorough Reformation will confine it to the natural or solar Day, which is but half the Time. Now admitting this for a Decorum absolutely requisite ; this Play begins when it is exactly Six by your Watch, and ends precisely at Nine, which is the usual Time of the Representation. Now is it feasible, *in rerum natura*, that the same Space or Extent of Time can be three Hours by your Watch, and twelve Hours upon the Stage, admitting the same Number of Minutes, or the same Measure of Sand to both ? I am afraid, Sir, you must allow this for an Impossibility too; and you may with as much Reason allow the Play the Extent of a whole Year ; and if you grant me a Year, you may give me seven, and so to a Thousand. For that a thousand Years should come within the Compass of three Hours, is no more an Impossibility, than that two Minutes should be contain'd in one; *Nullum minus continet in se majus*, is equally applicable to both.

So much for the Decorum of *Time*, now for the Regularity of *Place*. I might make the one a Consequence of t'other, and alledge, that by allowing me any Extent of Time, you must grant me any Change of Place, for the one depends upon t'other ; and having five or six Years for the Action of a Play, I may travel from *Constantinople* to *Denmark*, so to *France*, and home to *England*, and rest long enough in each Country besides. But you'll say, How can you carry us with you ? Very easily, Sir, if you will be willing to go : As for Example; Here is a new Play, the House is throng'd, the Prologue spoken, and the Curtain drawn represents you the Scene of *Grand Cairo*. Whereabouts are you now, Sir ? Were not you the very Minute before in the Pit in the *English* Play-house talking to a Wench, and now *præsto, pass*, you are spirited away to the Banks of the River *Nile*. Surely, Sir, this is a most intolerable Improbability ; yet this you must allow me, or else you destroy the very Constitution of Representation : Then in the second Act, with a Flourish of

the

s, I change the Scene to *Aſtrachan*. O *this is* ! Look'e, Sir, 'tis not a Jot more intolerable ther ; for you'll find that 'tis much about the ince between *Egypt* and *Aſtrachan*, as it is be-ry-*Lane* and *Grand Cairo* ; and if you pleaſe to ancy take Poſt, it will perform the Journey in Moment of Time, without any Diſturbance in to your Perſon.　You can follow *Quintus Cur-*r *Aſia* in the Train of *Alexander*, and trudge ibal, like a *Cadet*, through all *Italy*, *Spain* and the Space of four or five Hours ; yet the Devil ou will ſtir a Step over the Threſhold for the n *Chriſtendom*, tho' he make it his Buſineſs to roes more amiable, and to ſurprize you with derful Accidents and Events.

little a Friend to thoſe rambling Plays as any r have I ever eſpouſed their Party by my own yet I could not forbear ſaying ſomething in on of the great *Shakeſpear*, whom every little at can form an *Aoriſtus primus* will preſume to for Indecorums and Abſurdities ; Sparks that uce upon their *Greek* and *Latin*, that, like our 'ravels, they can reliſh nothing but what is fo-let the World know they have been abroad but it muſt be ſo, becauſe *Ariſtotle* ſaid it ; it muſt be otherwiſe, becauſe *Shakeſpear* ſaid it, ure that *Shakeſpear* was the greater Poet of the t you'll ſay, that *Ariſtotle* was the greater Cri-'hat's a Miſtake, Sir, for Criticiſm in Poetry is han Judgment in Poetry ; which you will find exicon.　Now if *Shakeſpear* was the better Poet, ave the moſt Judgment in his Art ; for every ows that Judgment is an eſſential Part of Poe-without it no Writer is worth a Farthing.　But o the Authority of either, without conſulting n of the Conſequence, is an Abuſe to a Man's iding ; and neither the Precept of the Philoſo-r Example of the Poet, ſhould go down with out examining the Weight of their Aſſertions. xpect no more Decorum or Regularity in any than the Nature of the Thing will bear : ie Stage cannot ſubſiſt without the Strength of

Suppo-

Suppofition, and Force of Fancy in the Audience, why fhould a Poet fetter the Bufinefs of his Plot, and ftarve his Action for the Nicety of an Hour, or the Change of a Scene, fince the Thought of Man can fly over a thou-fand Years with the fame Eafe, and in the fame Inftant of Time that your Eye glances from the Figure of fix or feven on the Dial-Plate; and can glide from the *Cape of Good Hope* to the *Bay of St. Nicolas*, which is quite crofs the World, with the fame Quicknefs and Activity, as between *Covent-Garden Church* and *Will's Coffee Houfe.* Then I muft beg of thefe Gentlemen to let our old *Eng-lifh* Authors alone——— If they have left Vice unpunifh'd, Virtue unrewarded, Folly unexpos'd, or Prudence un-fuccefsful, the contrary of which is the *Utile* of Comedy, let them be lafh'd to fome purpofe; if any Part of their Plots have been independent of the reft, or any of their Characters forc'd or unnatural, which deftroys the *Dulce* of Plays, let them be hifs'd off the Stage: But if, by a true Decorum in thefe material Points, they have writ fuccefsfully, and anfwer'd the End of Dramatic Poetry in every Refpect, let them reft in Peace, and their Me-mories enjoy the Encomiums due to their Merit, without any Reflection for waving thofe Niceties, which are nei-ther inftructive to the World, nor diverting to Mankind; but are like all the reft of the critical Learning, fit only to fet People together by the Ears in ridiculous Con-troverfies, that are not one Jot material to the Good of the Public, whether they be true or falfe.

And thus you fee, Sir, I have concluded a very un-neceffary Piece of Work; which is much too long, if you don't like it: But let it happen any Way, be affur'd, that I intended to pleafe you, which fhould partly excufe,

S I R,

Your moft humble Servant.

THE
STAGE-COACH,
A
FARCE,

As it is Acted at the

THEATRE-ROYAL
IN
DRURY-LANE.

Written by Mr. FARQUHAR.

LONDON:

Printed for T. LOWNDES in *Fleetstreet.*

MDCCLXXII.

Dramatis Perfonæ.

M E N.

Micher, the old Uncle and Guardian to *Ifabella*.
Nicodemus Somebody, a Country 'Squire.
Bafil, a Captain, in Love with *Ifabella*.
Fetch, Servant to *Bafil*.
Macahone, an *Irifhman*.
Tom Jolt, the Stage-Coachman.
Landlord of the Houfe.

W O M E N.

Ifabella, Niece to *Micher*, in Love with *Bafil*.
Dolly, Maid in the Houfe.
Oftler, and other Guefts in the Houfe.

S C E N E *an Inn on the Road between* Chefter
London.

THE

STAGE-COACH.

SCENE an Inn.

Enter Fetch, *with Cloak-Bag and Piſtols.*

HERE, Houſe! where are ye all? Now we'ave ſupt, I'll ſee if my Maſter's Bed be ready.——*Tom, John, Robin,* where a Plague are ye? All deaf? No Attendance in theſe Country Inns? This is worſe than the *Roſe Tavern* after Play, the *Sun Tavern* after 'Change, or the *Devil Tavern* after Church.

Enter Dolly.

Doll. D'ye call, Sir?

Fet. Call, Sir! What a Plague——Eigh! gad 'tis a pretty Girl. Hark you, Child, do you ſerve Travellers upon the Road here?

Dol. Yes, Sir.

Fet. Kiſs me, then.

Dol. That's the Chambermaid's Buſineſs.——D'ye want any thing elſe? I'm in haſte.

Fet. What Room does my Maſter lie in?

Dol. The Caſtle.

Fet. And what Room do I lie in?

Dol. The Garret.

Fet.

Fet. Very well ; and what Room do you lie in ?

Dol. Under you.

Fet. Say no more. I'll but take a Dram to digeſt Supper, lay theſe Things in my Maſter's Chamber, tl I'll talk with you in yours.

Dol. Are your Piſtols charg'd ?

Fet. Yes, yes, we always go charg'd, Child : A Brace Bullets, I aſſure you. [*Exit* Dol

Enter Captain Baſil.

Baſ. What a tedious, tireſome, dull, jolting Vehicle i Stage-Coach ? We that are in it, are more fatigued tl the Beaſts that draw it. This unlucky Hurt, *Fetch*, t I've got lately, has hinder'd my riding Poſt, and thrown into this confounded Company, a big-bellied Farm Daughter, an *Iriſh* Wit, a Canting Quaker, a City Whc and a Country Parſon.

Fet. And a diſbanded Captain, Sir ; for want of a ſtrolli Lawyer, or a Nurſe and a Child, to make up a clever Sta Coach Set.

Baſ. Ay, the ſwell'd Country Puſs plagu'd me with ſcreaming and wry Faces, the profound *Teague* with Nonſenſe, the Quaker with the Spirit, the Whore with Fleſh, and the fat Parſon with both.

Fet. Truly, Sir, I pity'd you ; for I don't think th was in the whole Company a Man of Parts, but and I.

Baſ. Muſt I be tormented two Days more with Coach, before I get to *London* ?

Fet. Too true, Sir.

Baſ. How can you tell ?

Fet. Nobody better, Sir ; my Father in *London* has Employment about the Coaches.

Baſ. What's his Employment ?

Fet. Sir, he's a very worthy Citizen, that attends *Bloſſom's* Inn, in the Quality of a Ticket Porter.

Baſ. I muſt get to *London* ſooner, or I ſhall ruin Affairs.——Let me talk with the Coach-man ; if it poſſible, I'll make him ſtretch for me : Call him hitl [*Exit* Fetc

Pſhaw ! here's that *Iriſh* Booby.

E

Enter Macahone.

Mac. By my Shoul, 'tis a brave Houfe! Sure the Shentle-
an of this Tavern muft be fome Perfon of very great
uality——Oh, my dear Mafter Captain, I am your moft
viog and much honour'd Friend.

Baf. Our Acquaintance, Sir, is a little too fhort for fo
uch Familiarity.

Mac. Our Acquaintance too fhort! Dear Joy, it is
ireefcore Miles long; and, by Shaint *Patrick*, I would be
ery joyful for being your efpecial Friend, becaufe I am
fraid we fhall never meet again.

Baf. May I crave your Name, Sir?

Mac. My Name is *Torlough Rauwer Macahone*, of the
?arifh of *Curoughabegley*, in the County of *Tiperary*, Efh-
quire, where is my Manfion-houfe, for me and my Prede-
:effors after me.

Baf. Very well; and pray, Sir, what Affairs carry you
to *London?*

Mac. No Affairs, my dear Joy; for I have tranfacted
my Bufinefs in *London* before I came there.

Baf. That's fomewhat an odd Way of doing Bufinefs.

Mac. By my Shoul, Sir, 'tis the quickeft Way tho'. I
was going to *London* to make my Fortune.

Baf. How, Sir?

Mac. Why, by the Law, Friend, or Phyfic, or a Merchant's Wife, or Back-gammon, or any of thefe honourable
Profeffions; 'tis all the fame to *Macahone*, faith. But I
have made my Fortune already, by my Gofhip's Hand.

Baf. How pray, Sir?

Mac. Becaufe, my dear Joy, you are my intimate Friend
and a Stranger, I will communicate that Secret into your
Breaft——The fine Lady in the Coach, Madam *Strowler*,
is a rich Merchant's Wife, in *Vinegar-yard*, by *Drury-lane* in
London, and fhe is fallen in downright Affections with me,
and treats me with mighty Civility, permitting me to pay
the Reckoning for her in every Place.

Baf. Jenny the Orange-Wench has fnapt this Booby;
and e'en let her make a Hand of him.——Are you fure
fhe's rich?

Mac. By my Shoul fhe fhew'd me a Diamond as big as a
Potatoe; and faith it look'd almoft as clear as Glafs: And
fhe keeps her flying Chariot too, fhe told me fo herfelf;

and, by my Shoul, I am fo cunning, that if another I
told me fo, I had not believ'd him.

Baf. You're plaguy cunning, indeed, Sir.

Mac. O chree, dear Joy, we are all fo, upon my Sho
Let an *Irifbman* alone for making his Fortune; he is as cu
ning as no Man alive——But, my dear Joy, I wifh I w
after going to Bed, to digeft my Supper: Here are t
Beds in your Chamber; and pray my dear Friend, tell n
do you intend to lie in 'em both?

Baf. 'Tis probable, Sir, I fhall ufe but one.

Mac. Then, Sir, with your Leave and Permiffion,
fhall ufe t'other: but pray let me not incommode yc
Perfon, if you intend to lie in both the Beds.

Baf. Not at all, Sir——Booby.　　　　[*Af*

Mac. Sir, I am your moft obliging Servant.

Baf. Coxcomb.　　　　[*Af.*

Mac. I render you many Thanks.　　　　[*Ex*

Enter Jolt, *and* Fetch.

Baf. Honeft Jolt! how is't? What fhall I give thee
drink?

Jolt. Thank you, Mafter, what you pleafe. Here's ra
Nantz in the Houfe; a Cogue, or fo, wou'd do no Har

Baf. Here, *Fetch*, bring us Half a Pint. [*Exit* Fetch
Well, *Jolt*, canft do a Man a Kindnefs upon Occafion?

Jolt. A Kindnefs! Ay, Mafter, an' that be all, we Coac
men are all mighty civil Fellows, you know.

Baf. Are your Horfes good?

Jolt. Good! Special Cattle, Mafter! A *London* Doft
would have fet up his Coach with 'em, if we had trufted
the Fall of the Leaf; and but t'other Day here, one
your Stockjobbers hir'd 'em for an Election; ecod, they h
almoft got him the Place.

Enter Fetch, *with Brandy.*

Baf. Here, *Jolt*, pull it off.

Jolt. Your Health, Mafter—— Rare Stuff, after m
twelve Eggs and Pound of Bacon.

Baf. Well, *Jolt*, can I be at *London*, by To-morro
Night?

Joit. To-morrow Night! Ay, Mafter, if you can fly.

[*Drink*

Baf. See here, *Jolt*——my Bufinefs is preffing; a goc
Share of this Purfe is thine, if thou wilt haften my Journe

Jo

Jolt. If that be all [*drinks*] 'tis done—we are to be in *London* the Day after To-morrow, by Ten o'Clock at Night— Now, Mafter, to oblige you, I'll be there by Nine.

Baf. Is the Fellow mad ? I tell thee I muft be there To-morrow.

Jolt. Ay, fo you may if you can; 'tis a long Way, Mafter, the Roads are deep, and I won't fpoil my Horfes— they are dearer to me, poor Beafts, than my Wife and Children.

Fet. Silly Fool, thou haft no more Senfe than thy Horfes ; why there's enough in that Purfe to bribe thy very Mafter, the Duke of *Mantua,* and two or three *German* Princes.

Jolt. Well, what there's in't, there's in't. [*Peeps in the empty Pot, and throws it down.*] What do you prate for ? Thefe Beau Footmen are as Cock-a-hoop of late, as if they had Places at Court. I'm an honeft Man.—Bribes won't pafs in the Country now.——Befides I muft not baulk my Stages, the Inn-keepers have brib'd me already. [*Exit.*

Baf. Well, tho' it kills me, I muft ride Poft.

Fet. But pray, Sir, what makes you in fuch Hafte ?

Baf. Why this Letter from my Miftrefs. [*Reads.*

Y O U've heard I've loft my dear Mother. My Uncle, to *whofe Care I am left, not confidering your Pretenfions, is refolved to marry me to another ; but what's worfe, the old Gentleman has got my Writings, and I muft feem to comply with his Defires. If you would prevent my being made a moft unfortunate Creature, fly to my Relief, my dear* Bafil, *with all the Speed which your Love and my Diftrefs require.*

                 I S A B E L L A.

I'm afraid I fhall come too late: Run to the Poft-Houfe, get us Horfes, and we'll mount this Moment. But whom have we here ?

Fet. Some of the Company that came in the *London* Coach, that fupp'd on t'other Side of the Houfe. :

Enter 'Squire Somebody, *with a Band-Box, a Mafk, and Fan, and other Luggage.*

'*Squi.* Come, Mrs. *Ifbel,* I've got your Things—Blefs us ! What a Parcel of Luggage thefe Women carry about 'em— And the poor Lover here muft be fubject to the Slavery of

Bundles and Band-boxes—Mrs. *Isbel*, why don't you co
away, I'm as tir'd as a *Scotch* Pedlar under his Pack.

Enter Isabella.

Isab. Ha !   [*Sees the Captain, and sta*

'*Squi.* Ha! What's the Matter, my dear Wife, that
to be ?

Isab. I miss my Watch; I fear I've left it in the Ro
where we supp'd; pray go and see.

'*Squi.* Ay, by all Means——Here, look to your Thin
there are Strangers about.   [*E*

Baf. Ha! What do I see! Look, *Fetch*, is not tl
Isabella ?

Isab. My dear *Bafil !*   [*Meet and embra*

Baf. My *Isabella !* What Miracle has brought y
hither ?

Isab. You received my Letter ?

Baf. Here it is, and it has brought me so far in t
Journey to you.

Isab. My Uncle, who knows you only by Name, dreadi
your Return to *London,* has thought fit to hurry me down
the Country House of that Blockhead that I sent just now
a Fool's Errand, under Pretence of losing my Watch. N
Uncle is at the Bar, haggling with the Landlady, and is
come up presently into the Room where we lie: Now
you can find a Way to rescue me from the old Knave, a
the young Fool——But here he comes: He's the Son
Sir *Aminadab Somebody* in *Lancashire.*

Enter '*Squire* Somebody.

'*Squi.* Gone, gone ! No Watch to be found ! Ecc
Gentlewoman, see what your Uncle will say to you ! You
make a rare Wife, faith, if you lose your Things so afor
hand——I won't lend you mine.

Isab. You need not, Sir, for the Watch is found agair
I had only put it in a wrong Pocket.

'*Squi.* Then that's Thirty Pounds in my Pocket.

Baf. Sure, I shou'd know that Voice, and Face to
Sir, are not you related to the Family of the *Somebody's ?*

'*Squi.* Yes, Sir, my Father is Sir *Aminadab Someboo*
Bart. and I am his eldest Son by the first Venter, *Nic
demus Somebody,* Esq;

B.

Baf. Sir, I am proud to embrace the Son of my old Friend Sir *Aminadab*—Pray, Sir, what Lady is that with you?

'Squi. 'Tis my Miſtreſs, at your Service ; we want but a Parſon, a Wedding-Dinner, a Pair of clean Sheets, and a Sack Poſſet, to ſend us the Way of all Fleſh.

Baf. Then, Sir, upon your Account, I'll preſume to pay my Reſpeſts to the Lady. [*Saluts her.*

'Squi. Sir, you're a verv reſpeſtful Perſon truly.—— Well, how d'ye like her? Wont ſhe make a rare 'Tit tor *Somebody?* She's a little in the Dumps at preſent, but we ſhall dump her out of that.

Baf. What! out of Humour, and ſo near her Marriage.

'Squi. Ay, there was a certain Captain that lov'd her, and ſhe lov'd that certain Captain : Now I can't tell how the Devil this Fellow windled himſelf into the Mother's Favour, and got her Conſent ; but as good Luck would have it, the old Woman was pleaſed to go where all old Wo-men ſhou'd go, and ſo Nuncle *Micher*, being a very honeſt Man, and mighty fit for a Guardian, but having a deadly Averſion to a Red Coat, ſtruck up a Bargain with Father for me, and we're going down to our Houſe, to take Poſ-ſeſſion of the Premiſes : So this ſame Scoundrel of an Officer is like to be diſbanded, and ſhe, forſooth, is vex'd becauſe ſhe can't ſerve under him. Ha, ha, ha, poor Dog, he's broke on all Sides,

Baf. Ha, ha, ſilly Fellow! he'll hang himſelf, that's certain. What ſhou'd Soldiers do elſe in Time of Peace?

'Squire. Ay, my dear Friend, I ſhou'd be glad if they were all hang'd; but for the Sake of the *French*——Perhaps you may know this ſame Captain ; 'tis one *Baſil*, a poor inſig-nificant Ringleader of fifty Rogues. Ha, ha.

Baf. Ha, ha, ha, ha, ha.

Jub. If you thought this Captain over-heard you, you durſt not talk at that Rate.

'Squi. Durſt not, ſay you? Odzookers, I fear neither Man, Woman, or Child. I wou'd tell him ſo to his Face— when my Friend ſtands by me here.

Baf. Softly, Madam, my Friend *Nicodemus* is a Perſon whom you ought to regard—in Time you'll have no Cauſe to complain.

E 3 *'Squi.*

'Squi. Ah, dear Sir, you do me more Honour than I deferve. But don't you think now that I am much more for her Turn than this fame Raggamuffin?

Baf. There's no Comparifon, Sir; and I think nobody can tell better than I; fo I can affure the Lady this is like to be the laft Trouble you fhall give her.

'Squi. Well faid, faith. Ecod, I've got a good Friend, and I did not think on't.

Ifab. Ay, but if *Bafil* were here, he wou'd be too hard for you and your Friend both.

Baf. Why, what wou'd you do, if *Bahl* were here?

Ifab. I would run away with him to the next Parfon, and leave *Nicodemus* here in the Lurch.

'Squi. Nicodemus thanks you with all his Heart———Did not I tell you now how fhe was bewitch'd by this Captain? The Devil's in the Captains, I believe. Ecod, I've a Mind to be a Captain too———Odzookers, now I think on't, my dear Friend, I'm a Captain already of the Militia; and do you think that we that pay them are no better Men than they?

Baf. Ay, to be fure.

Ifab. Well, but we cou'd do it, Sir, and you never the wifer; for while my Uncle and you were faft afleep, I could fteal out of my Chamber, fly into *Bafil's* Arms, and he fhould have a Coach ready to hurry me to *London*, before you were awake the next Morning.

'Squi. Odzooks, fhe's a cunning Jade; for all that I fhall have a rare Wife of her.

Baf. Well, well, Madam, I underftand you, we fhall take Care of that Matter.

'Squi. Ay, ay, fo we will; my dear Friend, here, and I, fhall watch your Waters, I'll warrant you———Oh here's Uncle *Micher.*

Enter Micher, *with a Bill.*

Micb. Hah! the Cut-throat Dogs: There's a Bill for you! That fat Jade at the Bar will fcore herfelf to the Devil, before any Solicitor, Taylor, Phyfic or Tipple Poifoner in *Europe.* [*Gives the 'Squire the Bill.*

'Squi. [*Reads*] For Bread and beer, Eight Shillings and Ten Pence. *Here's as much Bread and Drink as wou'd ferve all the* French *in* Spittal-fields *for a Week.* For a Calf's Head and Bacon, Ten Shillings. For a boil'd Pig and Colly-

ly-flowers, *that I befpoke,* Nine Shillings. For a Red
ring, *that was yours, Uncle,* One Shilling. For a Bottle
Jartſhorn, *that was your Supper, Miſtreſs,* Seven Pence.
  dey! what's here? Mull'd Sack, Dumplins, Cheeſe,
nges Toaſt and Butter, Fruit, Sallad, Wine, Cards,
ıdy, Tarts, and Tobacco, in all, Two Pounds Thirteen
lings and Three Pence Three Farthings, befides Fire—
: Devil fire the Houfe.   -

fich. Well, how fhall we club this Matter? There's the
Woman that has the King's Evil, and the t'other that
s the Coach ev'ry Minute to go behind a Bufh, they
't pay as much as we.

qui. Ecod, but they fhall; and for you, Miftrefs, you
pay but a Crown, becaufe you eat nothing; and that
mayn't think that you're hardly dealt by, I'll fing you
Song that makes it Stage-Coach Law.

The STAGE-COACH SONG.

> *Let's fing of Stage Coaches,*
> *And fear no Reproaches,*
> *For riding in one;*
> *But daily be jogging,*
> *While whiſtling and flogging,*
> *While whiſtling and flogging,*
> *The Coachman drives on.*
> *With a Hey, geeup, geeup hey, ho;*
> *With a Hey gee* Dobbin, *hey ho;*
> *Hey, geeup, geeup, geeup, hey ho,*
> *With a hey gee* Dobbin, *hey ho.*
>
> *In Coaches thus ſtrowling,*
> *Who would not be rowling,*
>   *With Nymphs on each Side;*
> *Still pratling and playing,*
> *Our Knees interlaying,*
>   *We merrily ride.*
> *With a Hey, &c.*
>
> *Here Chance kindly mixes*
> *All Sorts and all Sexes,*
>   *More Females than Men;*

We squeeze them, we ease them,
The jolting does please them;
Drive jolly then.
With a Hey, &c.

The harder you're driving,
The more 'tis reviving;
Nor fear we to fall;
For if the Coach tumble,
We have a rare Jumble;
We have a rare Jumble;
And then up Tails all.

With a Hey, geeup, geeup, hey ho;
With a Hey gee Dobbin, hey ho;
Hey, geeup, geeup, geeup, hey ho,
With a hey gee Dobbin, hey ho.

Mich. Well, now let's go to Bed, that we may be the sooner out of this confounded Inn next Morning.

'Squi. Well, dear Sir, the best Friends must part, tho' it be Man and Wife; but if you can step home with me, 'tis hard by, about Fourscore and Ten Miles off, and stay there a Week, I'll make you so drunk, you shan't find the Way back again in a Month.

Baf. Sir, you must excuse me, I am otherwise engag'd.

'Squi. Good Night, then.　　　　　　　　[*Exit.*

Ijab. Good Night, Sir.　　　[*Ex.* Micher, Isabella.

Baf. Your Servant, Madam. I hope you'll be in a better Humour To-morrow. Ha! *Fetch,* here's Fortune for you.——Now, my dear Lad, run, and at any Rate get us some Calash, Chariot, Coach, any thing, to hurry us to *London*; fly. In the mean time, I'll run to my Chamber, and get every thing ready.　　　　[*Exeunt severally.*

Enter Jolt.

Hush! Mum's the Word; there's a plaguy Candle stands in my Way; out, Informer, I'll spoil your peeping. The House is full, and Beds are scarce, therefore I can't lie in my own; so, good Wife at home, by your Leave, we Travellers are forc'd sometimes to lie two in a Bed. 'Tis main dark, rare driving now in a deep Road, and a rough Way————Odsnigs, now if *Dolly* shou'd be skittish, and won't let me; I'll knock at her Chamber Door, however, and if the Door will open, well said Door, I'll enter, and if *Dolly* will do like the rest of her Crew,
well

ll said *Dolly*. Pox on't, here's a Light, 'tis not yet right
itterwawling Time, fo I'll fheer off till anon.   [*Exit.*
    Enter Bafil *with Things,* Fetch *with a Candle.*

Baf. Well, *Fetch?*

Fet. I've done your Bufinefs, Sir—I've found in this very
n a Calafh, with four good Horfes, that fhould have gone
npty to *London* To-morrow Morning; I've agreed with
e Coachman to go with you immediately; he'll be ready
go with you at a Whiftle.

Baf. That was lucky, and I've got my Things; here
ey fhall lie till *Ifabella* comes out—I wifh fhe were here.

Fet. Sir, Sir, I think I hear a Noife.

Baf. Put out the Candle then, and let us ftep into that
orner, for here we muft wait for her.

Enter Jolt.

Jolt. Now the Coaft is clear—I have had a ftrange Han-
ering after this fame *Dull,* this great while, and for her
ake I fet up here at the *Angel*; now if fhe won't be civil,
'ye fee, I'll carry my Guefts to the *Saracen's-Head,* where
fhalt have the Oftler to take Care of my Horfes, and the
faid to take Care of me—Now for her Door.

Fet. Ods my Life, Sir; we've forgot one thing; the
Gate is lock'd up by this time, how fhall we get out?

Baf. What fhall we do?

Jolt. Hufh! I hear fomething; fhould this be fome
logue now creeping to *Dolly,* I'll put a Spoke in his
Wheel.

Fet. Stay, I've thought on't; the Maid's a good traftable
Wench, fhe'll do whatever we'll have her.

Jolt. Will fhe, faith, you Dog? Sirrah, I'll take Care
f that.

Fet. I'll knock at the Door; for a Piece of Money, I'll
arrant fhe'll do the Job.

Jolt. Perhaps I may do your Job firft, you
n of a Whore.

Fet. Tis well if I 'fcape a good Dab on the
—Confound that Poft, 'tis deadly hard——
w.] Her Door is on this Side, I'm fure.
m again.] Ha! what's that? Anotl
e third time.——Oh, fure here's
ftrikes Jolt *in the Teeth.*] *Dolly,* D
keep; fure I'm right; where's the
und it. [*Puts his Finger in* Jolt's

E 5

the Devil! the Devil! Help, Sir, help, I've got my Finger in a Rat-trap.

Baf. Where art thou?

Jolt. Gee, gee, ho, gee. [*Whips him.*

Fet. Murder! Murder! Help!

Baf. Hold, you Dog, or I'll kill you.

Jolt. Gee, gee, ho, gee ho.

Fet. Murder, Murder, Help! the Devil lays me on.

Enter Oſtler, with a Light.

Oſt. What's the Matter? What's the Matter?

Jolt. Come on, gee, gee, ho.

Oſt. What a Duce do you mean, Maſter *Jolt?*

Jolt. [*Yawns.*] What's the Matter? What's all this Buſtle for?

Oſt. What are you drunk or dreaming?

Jolt. What wou'd you have? Where am I? Oh! is it you, *Phil* the Oſtler? Odſnigs, I thought I had been in Bed; I dream'd that my Coach ſtuck in *Hockly the Hole*, and I was licking my Horſes till I made them ſmoke again —I beg your Pardon, Gentlemen, for taking you for my Beaſts.

Enter Dolly.

Dol. What's the Matter here; are not you aſham'd to diſturb People at this Time of Night?

Fet. You're come in good Time, Child, to ſave that Rogue a Beating, for now we've other Buſineſs; a Word with you.

Baf. Get you gone, Sirrah, or I'll cut your Ears out, you Dog; and you here with your Light, go off, and leave us to our Buſineſs. [*Exit Oſtler.*

Jolt. Odzookers, now they're driving the Bargain; Ecod I'll overturn the Coach To-morrow in a Slough, to cool that Dog of a Captain's Courage in a Puddle.

Fet. The Town's our own, Sir; I've given the Wench a Guinea, ſhe conſents, and I've got the Key.

Jolt. The Key! A Plague on her Lock; now has the Minx granted at once, what ſhe has deny'd me this Twelvemonth; but that Guinea is the Devil at a Key-hole: I warrant 'twou'd open a thouſand Spring Locks in *Covent-Garden*———I'll watch and ſee what all this will come to.

Enter Iſabella, *with a Trunk.*

Iſab. He ſhou'd be here!———Captain!

Baf.

af. My Dear!

olt. My Dear! Ah the damn'd Jade! She's come out im now.

Enter Micher *groping.*

fich. Does she walk in her Sleep? Where can she go at Time of Night? I'll watch her.

ab. Captain, where are you?

af. Here, here.

fich. Captain! Sure she can't have her Captain here.

olt. Odsnigs, they're going to't; but I'll spoil their 't.

ab. Come, I'm got out at last, and what's more, I've the Writings.

fich. Ah, you young Baggage, have I caught you; its here; Lights.

ab. Hist! I hear my Uncle's Voice, let's lose no Time.

af. Let's away, my Dear ———*Fetch,* take up the ogs. [*Exeunt.*

fich. Lights here, Lights.

[Fetch *takes up the Things, and drops the Key.* Exit.]

Enter Ofler *with a Light.*

ft. What's the Matter here, again?

ich. Ha! what a Devil, who are you?

olt. And who are you, an' that be all?

ich. Where's my Niece, ah, you Pimp? you're in the too; where's that damn'd Rogue the Captain?

olt. Your Niece! the Captain has other Work in hand; his is a rare Time to quit Scores with him. If you the Captain, you'll find him in that Room with his re.

ich. His Whore! the Dog make my Niece his Whore! a Constable, a Constable.

Enter 'Squire, *yawning.*

nui. Here, what the Devil's the Matter? Can't you let ly sleep among ye?

ich. Ah, *Nicodemus,* we're all undone; the Captain has way your Mistress into that Room; and what they are ;, Heaven knows.

nui. Ha! I hear some Noise; I hear some Noise with-hy dont you break the Door, Uncle?

ich. Why don't you?

nui. She's your Niece.

Mich,

Mich. She's your Wife that is to be.

'Squi. I can't tell that now.

Mich. Then let's have a Conſtable.

Jolt. I'll run and call up my Landlord ; he's a Conſtable.   [*Exit.*

[*Several People appear in Night-caps, in both Balconies.*

1. A Plague take you all, are you all aſleep, that ye make ſuch a Noiſe. What the De'il's the Matter with you?

'Squi. Nothing, nothing, no Harm, only a Gentleman who's making me a Cuckold before my Time.

Enter Landlord, Jolt *with a Leaver.*

Land. Here, where are theſe People?

'Squi. Here, Sir, in that Room.

Land. Come out here : I charge ye come out : I'm an Officer, won't you come out in the King's Name? why then ſtay where you are, in the Devil's Name : Break open the Door.   [Jolt *breaks open the Door.*

Land. Why don't you go in?

Jolt. Why don't you go in, you're an Officer?

Land. Then I command you to go in before me.

Jolt. Let the 'Squire go in, 'tis his Buſineſs.

'Squi. Let my Uncle go in, 'tis more his Buſineſs than mine.

Mich. Come, we'll all go in, tho' he be a Captain, he's but one.   [*Exeunt.*

Enter Dolly *at another Door.*

Dol. What can they be ſearching for in my Chamber?

Re-enter all.

'Squi. The Devil a Thing is there, but an old Pair of Boddice, a broken-back'd Chair, a Quire of Ballads, a Flock Bed, a Green Chamber-pot.

Dol. Why, Gentlemen, the People that you want are gone ; they took the Key from me, and went out.

'Squi. Gone! Oh ye Skies! *Sic tranſit Gloria Mundi.*

Mich. Here, here, let's follow 'em.

'Squi. Ay, ay, Horſes, Coaches, Spurs, Whips, Spatterdaſhes, Gambadoes, Boots, and Saſhoons, away.

Land. Hold, hold, Gentlemen, what's here? the Key of the great Gate ; they muſt be in the Houſe ſtill, if the Maid did not let 'em out.

Dol. Not I, upon my Word, Sir.

                                              Land.

Land. Then they muſt have dropp'd the Key, and are in
he Houſe ſtill.

'Squi. Huzza! have at 'em then; Halberts, Quarter-
ſtaffs, Muſkets, Pikes, and Pocket-piſtols.

Mich. Find 'em out, find 'em out, then.

[*Exit Landlord,* Jolt.
Why don't you go to help 'em, Nephew?

'Squi. Uncle, I ſtay to keep you Company.

Enter Baſil *in a Night-gown.*

Baſ. What's the Meaning of all this Noiſe? A Man
can't ſleep for ye.

'Squi. Ah, my dear Friend, ſtand by me now. Who
ſhou'd be here, but that damn'd Rogue of a Captain that
we talk'd of, and has run away with my Miſtreſs.

Baſ. The Devil he did; and how will you uſe him when
he's found?

'Squi. Uſe him! I'll pump him, I'll ſouſe him, flea him,
carbonade him, and eat him alive.

Baſ. But hark ye, Sir, don't make ſuch a Noiſe, you'll
diſturb my Wife.

'Squi. What, Sir, are you marry'd?

Baſ. Marry'd and bedded ſince I ſaw you.

'Squi. To whom?

Enter Iſabella, *Landlord,* Jolt, *and Servants.*

Baſ. To this Lady, Sir.

'Squi. Uncle!

Mich. Nephew!

'Squi. Speak you, 'tis more your Buſineſs than mine.

Mich. Marry'd! it can't be: How cou'd you be married
ſo ſuddenly?

Baſ. Very luckily, Sir; we intended to have it done
more decently, but my Blockhead dropp'd the Key, and
being ſtopp'd that Way, we ſaw a Light in the Miniſter's
Chamber that travell'd with me; we went up, found him
ſmoaking his Pipe; he firſt gave us his Bleſſing, then let us
his Bed.

'Squi. He was a very civil Gentleman.

Mich. Sir, this won't paſs upon me; what Evidence
have you for this?

Enter Macahone.

Mac. By my Shoul, he needs no Evidence, for I am
one. I was call'd to be a Witneſs; his Man did waken
me

me before I was afleep; and if you will believe nobody, you may go up, and afk the Miniſter.

Baſ. And in Return, my dear Countryman, I'll take Care to do you Service in relation to your pretended Merchant's Wife.

Mich. Then ſince it is ſo, much Good may't do you with your No-fortune; her Mother did not leave her a Groat.

'Squi. I'm glad on't with all my Heart.

Iſab. Sir, it will appear otherwiſe by my Writings.

Mich. Writings; what Writings? I've no Writings of yours.

Baſ. No more you han't, Sir; for here they are.

Mich. Confuſion! then I know what I've loſt.

'Squi. And ſo do I too. I've loſt my Lahour, I've loſt my Friend, I've loſt my Nuncle, and I've loſt my Wife.

> But ſince the Coach ſuch Novelties has bred,
> The 'Squire unmarry'd, and the Captain wed,
> I'll be reveng'd, and go———I'll go to Bed.
>
> [*Exeunt Omnes.*

Love and a Bottle,

A

COMEDY,

As it is Acted at the

THEATRE-ROYAL

IN

DRURY-LANE.

Vade, sed incultus, qualem decet exulis esse,
Ovid. Trist. El. 1.

LONDON,
Printed for the Executors of H. Lintot, and J. Clarke.
MDCCLXXII.

XXXXXXXXXXXXXX X XXXXXXXXXXXXX

PROLOGUE.

y *J. H.* ſpoken by Mr. *Powel*; a Servant
attending with a Bottle of Wine.

A S ſtubborn Atheiſts, who diſdain to pray,
 Repent, tho' late, upon their dying Day;
in their Pangs, moſt Authors rack'd with Fears,
plore your Mercy in our ſuppliant Pray'rs.
t our new Author has no Cauſe maintain'd,
t him not loſe what he has never gain'd.
ve and a Bottle are his Peaceful Arms;
dies and Gallants, have not theſe ſome Charms?
r Love, all Mankind to the Fair muſt ſue:
d, Sirs, the Bottle be preſents to you.
alth to the Play, (drinks) then let it fairly paſs,
re none ſit here that will refuſe their Glaſs!
there's a damning Soldier——let me think——
looks as he were ſworn——to what? To drink.   [drinks.
me on then; Foot to Foot be boldly ſet,
d our young Author's new Commiſſion wet.
and his Bottle here attend their Doom,
om you the Poet's Helicon *muſt come;*
be has any Foes, to make amends,
gives his Service (drinks) ſure you now are Friends.
Critic here will be provoke to fight,
e Day be theirs, he only begs his Night.
ay pledge him now, ſecur'd from all Abuſe,
en name the Health you love, let none refuſe,
t each Man's Miſtreſs be the Poet's Muſe.

          }

Drama-

Dramatis Personæ.

Roebuck.	An *Irish* Gentleman, of a wild roving Temper; newly come to *London*.	Mr. *Williams*.
Lovewell.	His Friend, sober and modest, in Love with *Lucinda*.	Mr. *Mills*.
Mockmode.	A young Squire, newly come from the University, and setting up for a Beau.	Mr. *Bullock*.
Lyrick.	A Poet.	Mr. *Johnson*.
Pamphlet.	A Bookseller.	
Rigadoon.	A Dancing-Master.	Mr. *Haynes*.
Nimblewrist,	A Fencing-Master.	Mr. *Afhton*.
Club.	Servant to *Mockmode*,	Mr. *Pinkethma*
Brush.	Servant to *Lovewell*.	Mr. *Fairbank*.

W O M E N.

Lucinda.	A Lady of considerable Fortune.	Mrs. *Rogers*.
Leanthe.	Sister to *Lovewell*, in Love with *Roebuck*, and disguis'd as *Lucinda*'s Page.	Mrs. *Maria Ah fon*.
Trudge.	Whore to *Roebuck*.	Mrs. *Mills*.
Bulfinch.	Landlady to *Mocmode*, *Lyrick*, and *Trudge*.	Mrs. *Powel*.
Pindress.	Attendant and Confident to *Lucinda*.	Mrs. *Moor*.

Bailiffs, Beggar, Porter, Masques, Attendants.

SCENE, *LONDON*.

L O V I

ove and a Bottle.

ACT I.

SCENE, Lincoln's-Inn-Fields.

ter Roebuck *in a Riding Habit* Solus, *repeating the following Line.*

THUS far our Arms have with Success been crown'd
———Heroically spoken, faith, of a Fellow that has not one Farthing in his Pocket. If I have one Penny buy a Halter withal in my present Necessity, may I be ng'd; tho' I am reduc'd to a fair way of obtaining one thodically very soon, if Robbery or Theft will purchase Gallows. But hold——can't I rob honourably by turn-Soldier?

Enter a Cripple begging.

Crip. One Farthing to the poor old Soldier, for the rd's sake.

Roeb. Ha!———a Glimpse of Damnation just as a Man ntering into Sin, is no great Policy of the Devil.——— how long did you bear Arms, Friend?

Crip. Five Years, an't please you, Sir.

Roeb. And how long has that honourable Crutch born t?

Crip. Fifteen, Sir.

Roeb. Very pretty! Five Years a Soldier, and fifteen a gar!———This is Hell right! An Age of Damnation,
for

for a momentary Offence. Thy Condition, Fellow, is preferable to mine; the merciful Bullet, more kind than thy ungrateful Country, has given thee a Debenture in thy broken Leg, from which thou canft draw a more plentiful Maintenance than I from all my Limbs in Perfection. Prithee, Friend, why would'ft thou beg of me? Doft think I am rich?

Crip. No, Sir, and therefore I believe you charitable. Your warm Fellows are fo much above the Senfe of our Mifery, that they can't pity us: and I have always found it, by fad Experience, as needlefs to beg of a rich Man, as a Clergyman. Our greateft Benefactors, the brave Officers, are all difbanded, and muft now turn Beggars like myfelf; and fo, Times are very hard, Sir.

Roeb. What! Are the Soldiers more charitable than the Clergy?

Crip. Ay, Sir, a Captain will fay Dam'me, and give me Sixpence; and a Parfon fhall whine out God blefs me, and give me not a Farthing: Now I think the Officer's Blefsing much the beft.

Roeb. Are the Beaus never compaffionate?

Crip. The great full Wigs they wear ftop their Ears fo clofe, that they can't hear us; and if they fhou'd, they never have any Farthings about 'em.

Roeb. Then I am a Beau, Friend; therefore pray leave me. Begging from a generous Soul that has not to beftow, is more tormenting than Robbery to a Mifer in his Abundance. Prithee, Friend, be thou charitable for once; I beg only the Favour which rich Friends beftow, a little Advice: I am as poor, as thou art, and am defigning to turn Soldier.

Crip. No, no, Sir; fee what an honourable Poft I am forc'd to ftand to, my Rags are Scare-crows fufficient to frighten any one from the Field; rather turn Bird of Prey at home. [*Shewing his Crutch.*

Roeb. Grammercy, old Devil; I find Hell has its Pimps of the poorer Sort, as well as of the wealthy. I fancy, Friend, thou haft got a Cloven Foot inftead of a broken Leg. 'Tis a hard Cafe that a Man muft never expect to go nearer Heav'n than fome Steps of a Ladder. But 'tis unavoidable; I have my Wants to lead, and the Devil to drive; and if I can't meet my Friend *Lovewell*, (which I
                                                                    think

think impoſſible, being ſo great a Stranger in Town) Fortune, thou haſt done thy worſt; I proclaim open War againſt thee.

I'll ſtab the next rich Darling that I ſee;
And killing him, be thus reveng'd on thee.

{*Goes to the back Part of the Stage, as into the Walks,*
making ſome Turns croſs the Stage in Diſorder, while
the next ſpeak. Exit Beggar.

Enter Lucinda *and* Pindreſs.

Luc. Oh! theſe Summer Mornings are ſo delicately fine, *Pindreſs,* it does me good to be abroad.

Pin. Ay, Madam, theſe Summer Mornings are as pleaſant to young Folks, as the Winter Nights to marry'd People, or as your Morning of Beauty to Mr. *Loveweil.*

Luc. I'm violently afraid the Evening of my Beauty will fall to his Share very ſoon; for I'm inclinable to marry him. I ſhall ſoon lie under an Eclipſe, *Pindreſs.*

Pin. Then it muſt be full Moon with your Ladyſhip. But why wou'd you chuſe to marry in Summer, Madam?

Luc. I know no Cauſe, but that People are apteſt to run mad in hot Weather, unleſs you take a Woman's Reaſon.

Pin. What's that, Madam?

Luc. Why, I am weary of lying alone.

Pin. Oh dear Madam! Lying alone is very dangerous; 'tis apt to breed ſtrange Dreams.

Luc. I had the oddeſt Dream laſt night of my Courtier that is to be, Squire *Mockmode.* He appeared crowded about with a Dancing-Maſter, Puſhing-Maſter, Muſic-Maſter, and all the Throng of Beau-makers; and methought he mimic'd Foppery ſo aukwardly, that his Imitation was downright burleſquing it. I burſt out a laughing ſo heartily, that I awaken'd myſelf.

Pin. But Dreams go by Contraries, Madam. Haven to you ſeen him yet?

Luc. No; but my Uncle's Letter gives Account that he's newly come to Town from the Univerſity, where his Education could reach no farther than to guzzle fat Ale, ſmoke Tobacco, and chop Logic——Faugh——it makes me ſick.

Pin. But he's very rich, Madam; his Concerns join to yours in the Country.

Luc.

Luc. Ay, but his Concerns shall never join to mine in the City : For since I have the Disposal of my own Fortune, *Lovewell*'s the Man for my Money.

Pin. Ay, and for my Money; for I've had above twenty Pieces from him since his Courtship began. He's the prettiest sober Gentleman; I have so strong an Opinion of his Modesty, that I'm afraid, Madam, your first Child will be a Fool.

Luc. Oh God forbid! I hope a Lawyer understands Business better than to beget any thing *non compos*——The Walks fill apace; the Enemy approaches, we must set out our false Colours,   [*Put on their Masks.*

Pin. We Masks are the purest Privateers! Madam, how would you like to cruise about a little ?

Luc. Well enough, had we no Enemies but our Fops and Cits : But I dread these blustring Men of War, the Officers, who after a Broad-side of Damme's and Sinkme's, are for boarding all Masks they meet as lawful Prize.

Pin. In Truth, Madam, and the most of them are lawful Prize, for they generally have *French* Ware under Hatches.

Luc. Oh hideous! O' my Conscience, Girl, thou'rt quite spoil'd. An Actress upon the Stage would blush at such Expressions.

Pin. Ay, Madam, and your Ladyship would seem to blush in the Box, when the Redness of your Face proceeded from nothing but the Constraint of holding your Laughter. Didn't you chide me for not putting a stronger Lace in your Stays, when you had broke one as strong as a hempen Cord with containing a violent Tehee at a smutty Jest in the last Play ?

Luc. Go, go, thou'rt a naughty Girl! that impertinent Chat has diverted us from our Bus'ness. I'm afraid *Lovewell* has miss'd us for Want of the Sign.——But whom have we here ? An odd Figure, some Gentleman in Disguise, I believe.

Pin. Had he a finer Suit on, I shou'd believe him in Disguise; for I fancy his Friends have only known him by that this Twelve-month.

Luc. His Mien and Air shew him a Gentleman, and his Cloaths demonstrate him a Wit. He may afford us some Sport. I have a Female Inclination to talk to him.

Pin.

Pin. Hold, Madam, he looks as like one of thofe dangerous Men of War you juft now mention'd as can be; you had beft fend out your Pinnace before, to difcover the Enemy.

Luc. No, I'll hale him myfelf: [*Moves towards him.* What, Sir, dreaming?
                    [*Slaps him o'th' Shoulder with her Fan.*
Roeb. Yes, Madam.   [*Sullenly.*
Luc. Of what?
Roeb. Of the Devil, and now my Dream's out.
Luc. What! Do you dream ftanding?
Roeb. Yes, faith, Lady, very often, when my Sleep's haunted by fuch pretty Goblins as you. You are a Sort of Dream I would fain be reading: I'm a very good Interpreter indeed, Madam.
Luc. Are you then one of the wife Men of the Eaft?
Roeb. No, Madam; but one of the Fools of the Weft.
Luc. Pray, what do you mean by that?
Roeb. An *Irifhman*, Madam, at your Service.
Luc. Oh horrible! an *Irifhman!* a mere Wolf-dog, I proteft.
Roeb. Ben't furpriz'd, Child; the Wolf-dog is as well-natur'd an Animal as any of your Country Bull-dogs, and a much more fawning Creature, let me tell ye.
                    [*Lays hold on her.*
Luc. Pray, good *Cæfar*, keep off your Paws; no fcraping Acquaintance, for Heaven's Sake. Tell us fome News of your Country; I have heard the ftrangeft Stories,——that the People wear Horns and Hoofs.
Roeb. Yes, faith, a great many wear Horns; but we had that, among other laudable Fafhions, from *London*. I think it came over with your Mode of wearing high Topknots; for ever fince, the Men and Wives bear their Heads exalted alike. They were both Fafhions that took wonderfully.
Luc. Then you have Ladies among you.
Roeb. Yes, yes, we have Ladies, and Whores; Colleges, and Play-houfes; Churches, and Taverns; fine Houfes, and Bawdy-houfes: In fhort, every Thing that you can boaft of, but Fops, Poets, Toads and Adders.
Luc. But have you no Beaus at all?
Roeb. Yes, they come over like Woodcocks, once a Year.

Luc.

Luc. And.have your Ladies no Springes to catch 'em in

Roeb. No, Madam; our own Country affords us muc
better Wild-fowl. But they are generally ftripped of thei
Feathers by the Play-houfe and Taverns; in both whicl
they pretend to be Critics; and our ignorant Nation ima
gines a full Wig as infallible a Token of a Wit as th
Laurel.

Luc. Oh Lard! and here 'tis, the certain Sign of i
Blockhead. But why no Poets in *Ireland,* Sir?

Roeb. Faith, Madam, I know not, unlefs St. *Patric*
fent them a packing with other venomous Creatures out o:
Ireland. Nothing that carries a Sting in its Tongue ca
live there. But fince I have defcribed my Country, let me
know a little of *England,* by a Sight of your Face.

Luc. Come you to Particulars firft. Pray, Sir, unmafk,
by telling who you are; and then I'll unmafk, and fhew
who I am.

Roeb. You muft difmifs your Attendant then, Madam;
for the diftinguifhing Particular of me is a Secret.

Pin. Sir, I can keep a Secret as well as my Miftrefs; and
the greater the Secrets are, I love 'em the better.

Luc. Can't they be whifper'd, Sir?

Roeb. Oh yes, Madam, I can give you a Hint, by which
you may underftand 'em———

                       [Pretends to whifper, and kiffes her.

Luc. Sir, you're impudent.

Roeb. Nay, Madam, fince you're fo good at minding
Folks, have with you.   *[Catches her faft, carrying her off.*

Luc. }
Pin. } Help! help! help!

               Enter Lovewell.

Love. Villain, unhand the Lady, and defend thyfelf.
                                      [Draws.

Roeb. What! Knight Errants in this Country! Now has
the Devil very opportunely fent me a Throat to cut; pray
Heaven his Pockets be well lin'd.——*[Quits 'em, they go off.*
——Have at thee——St. *George* for *England.*

          [They fight, after fome Paffes Roebuck *ftarts*
——My Friend *Lovewell!*   *back and paufes.*

Love. My dear *Roebuck!*

             [Fling down their Swords and embrace.
Shall I believe my Eyes?

                                     Roeb.

ou may believe your Ears ; 'tis I, egad.
Vhy, thy being in *London* is fuch a Myftery, that
e the Evidence of more Senfes than one to con-
: its Truth.————But pray unfold the Riddle.
Vhy faith 'tis a Riddle. You wonder at it before
nation, then wonder more at yourfelf for not
.——What is the univerfal Caufe of the continued
Iankind ?
The univerfal Caufe of our continued Evils is
fure.
Io, 'tis the Flefh, *Ned*————That very Woman
: us all out of *Paradife* has fent me a packing out

Iow fo ?
nly tafting the forbidden Fruit; that was all.
s fimple Fornication become fo great a Crime
to be punifhable by no lefs than Banifhment?
gad, mine was double Fornication, *Ned*————
was fo pregnant to bear Twins, the Fruit grew in
and my unconfcionable Father, becaufe I was a
debauching her, wou'd make me a Fool by wed-
But I would not marry a Whore, and he wou'd
difobedient Son, and fo————
But was fhe a Gentlewoman ?
'fhaw ! No, fhe had no Fortune. She wore in-
k Mantua and High-head ; but thefe are grown
gns of Gentlity now-a-days, as that is of Chaf-

But what Neceflity forc'd you to leave the King-

'll tell you——To fhun th' infulting Authority of
'd Father, the dull and often repeated Advice of
nt Relations, the continual Clamours of a furious
and the fhrill Bawling of an ill natur'd Baftard—
which, good Lord deliver me.
And fo you left them to Grand Dadda !————Ha,

Heav'n was pleas'd to leffen my Affliction, by
'ay the She-brat ; but the other is, I hope, well,
brave Boy, whom I chriften'd *Edward*, after thee,
; I made bold to make my Man ftand for you,
Sifter fent her Maid to give her Name to my

L   F   Love.

Love. Now you talk of my Sifter, pray how does fhe?

Roeb. Dear *Lovewell,* a very Miracle of Beauty an Goodnefs.————But I don't like her.

Love. Why?

Roeb. She's virtuous;————and I think Beauty and Virtu are as ill joined as Lewdnefs and Uglinefs.

Love. But I hope your Arguments could not make her Profelyte to this Profeffion?

Roeb. Faith I endeavour'd it; but that plaguy Honou ————Damn it for a Whim————Were it as honourable fo Women to be Whores, as Men to be Whore-mafters, we fhou'd have Lewdnefs as great a Mark of Quality among the Ladies, as 'tis now among the Lords.

Love. What! do you hold no innate Principle of Virtu in Woman?

Roeb. I hold an innate Principle of Love in them: Their Paffions are as great as ours, their Reafon weaker. We admire them, and confequently they muft us. And I tell thee once more, That had Woman no Safe-guard but your innate Principle of Virtue, honeft *George Roebuck* wou'd have lain with your Sifter, *Ned,* and fhou'd enjoy a Countefs before Night.

Love. But methinks, *George,* 'twas not fair to tempt my Sifter.

Roeb. Methinks 'twas not fair of thy Sifter, *Ned,* to tempt me. As fhe was thy Sifter, I had no Defign upon her; but as fhe's a pretty Woman, I could fcarcely forbear her, were fhe my own.

Love. But, upon ferious Reflection, cou'd not you have liv'd better at home by turning thy Whore into thy Wife than here by turning other Men's Wives into Whores. There are Merchants Ladies in *London,* and you muft trad with them, for aught I fee.

Roeb. Ay, but is the Trade open? Is the Manufactur encourag'd, old Boy?

Love. Oh, wonderfully!————a great many poor Peopl live by't. Tho' the Hufbands are for engroffing the Trade the Wives are altogether for encouraging Interlopers. Bu I hope you have brought fome fmall Stock to fet up with.

Roeb. The Greatnefs of my Wants, which wou'd forc me to difcover 'em, makes me blufh to own 'em. [*Afid* Why faith, *Ned,* I had a great Journey from *Ireland* hither

I wou'd burthen myſelf ·with no more than juſt neceſſary arges.

Love. Oh, then you have brought Bills.

Roeb. No, faith. Exchange of Money from *Dublin* hir, is ſo unreaſonable high, that———

Love. What!

Roeb. That———Zoons, I have not one Farthing———w you underſtand me.

Love. No, faith, I never underſtand one that comes *in wa pauperis*; I ha'nt ſtudy'd the Law ſo long for nothing. —But what Proſpect can you propoſe of a Supply?

Roeb. I'll tell you. When you appear'd, I was juſt thanking my Stars for ſending me a Throat to cut, and conſequently a Purſe. But my Knowledge of you prevented me that Way, and therefore I think you're oblig'd in Return iſſiſt me by ſome better Means. You were once an hoſt Fellow; but ſo long Study in the Inns may alter a Man ngely, as you ſay.

Love. No, dear *Roebuck*, I am ſtill a Friend to thy Virs, and eſteem thy Follies as Foils only to ſet them off. id but rally you; and to convince you, here are ſome ces, Share of what I have about me: Take them as rneſt of my farther Supply; you know my Eſtate is ſufent to maintain us both, if you will either reſtrain your travagancies, or I retrench my Neceſſaries.

Roeb. Thy Profeſſion of Kindneſs is ſo great, that I cou'd aoſt ſuſpect it of Deſign. But come, Friend, I am hearr tir'd with the Fatigue of my Journey, beſides a violent of Sickneſs which detain'd me a Month at *Coventry*, to ? exhauſting of my Health and Money. Let me only ruit by a Reliſh of the Town in Love and a Bottle, and n——Oh Heavens! and Earth!

[*As they are going off,* Roebuck *ſtarts back ſurpriz'd.*

Love. What's the matter, Man?

Roeb. Why, Death and the Devil! or, what's worſe, a oman and a Child —— Oons! don't you ſee Mrs. *Trudge* th my Baſtard in her Arms croſſing the Field towards us? —Oh the indefatigable Whore, to follow me all the Way *London!*

Love. Mrs. *Trudge!* my old Acquaintaince.

Roeb. Ay, ay, the very ſame; your old Acquaintance;

and

and for aught I know, you might have clubb'd about getting the Brats.

Love. 'Tis but reafonable then I fhou'd pay Share of the Reckoning. I'll help to provide for her; in the mean Time you had beft retire.——*Brufh*, conduct this Gentleman to my Lodgings, and run from thence to Widow *Bullfinch's*, and provide a Lodging with her for a Friend of mine. —— Fly, and come back prefently.——[*Exeunt* Roeb. *and* Brufh.]——So; my Friend comes to Town like the Great *Turk* to the Field, attended by his Concubines and Children; and I'm afraid thefe are but Part of his Retinue——but hold——I fhan't be able to fuftain the Shock of this Woman's Fury. I'll withdraw till fhe has difcharg'd her firft Volley, then furprize her.

Enter Trudge, *with a Child crying.*

Hufh, hufh, hufh—— And indeed it was a young Traveller.——And what wou'd it fay? It fays that Daddy is a falfe Man, a cruel Man, an ungrateful Man.——In troth fo he is, my dear Child.——What fhall I do with it, poor Creature!——Hufh, hufh, hufh —— Was ever poor Woman in fuch a lamentable Condition? Immediately after the Pains of one Travail, to undergo the Fatigues of another!——But I'm fure he can never do well; for tho' I can't find him, my Curfes, and the Mifery of this Babe, will certainly reach him.

Love. M.thinks I fhou'd know that Voice——[*Moving forward.*] What! Mrs. *Trudge!* and in *London!* whofe brave Boy haft thou got there?

Trud. Oh Lord! Mr. *Lovewell!* I am very glad to fee you——and yet I am afham'd to fee you. But indeed he promis'd to marry me. [*Crying*] and you know, Mr *Lovewell*, that he's fuch a handfome Man, and fo many Ways of infinuating! that the Frailty of Woman's Nature cou'd not refift him.

Love. What's all this?——A handfome Man! Ways of infinuating! Frailty of Nature!——I don't underftand thefe ambiguous Terms.

Trud. Ah, Mr. *Lovewell!* I am fure you have feen Mr. *Roebuck*, and I am fure 'twou'd be the firft Thing he wou'd tell you. I refer to you, Mr. *Lovewell*, if he is not an ungrateful Man, to deal fo barbaroufly with any Woman that

had

had us'd him fo civilly. I was kinder to him than I wou'd have been to my own born Brother.

Love. O then I find Kiffing goes by Favour, Mrs. *Trudge.*

Trud. Faith you're al! alike ; you Men are alike——Poor Child ! he's as like his own Dadda, as if he were fpit out of his Mouth. See, Mr. *Lovewell,* if he has not Mr. *Roebuck's* Nofe to a Hair ; and you know he has a very good Nofe ; and the little Pigfny his Mamma's Mouth.——Oh the little Lips ! and 'tis the beft natur'd little Dear——[*Smuggles and kiffes it.*]——And wou'd it afk it's Godfather's Bleffing !——Indeed, Mr. *Lovewell,* I believe the Child knows you.

Love. Ha, ha, ha! Well, I will give it my Bleffing.
[*Gives it Gold.*

[*As he gives her the Gold, enter* Lucinda *and*
Pindrefs, *who feeing them ftand, abfcond.*
Come, Madam, I'll firft fettle you in a Lodging, and then find the falfe Man, as you call him——
[*Exit* Lovewell.

Lucinda *and* Pindrefs *come forward.*

Luc. The falfe Man is found already——Was here ever fuch a lucky Difcovery ?——My Care for his Prefervation brought me back, and now behold how my Kindnefs is return'd !——Their Fighting was a downright Trick to frighten me from the Place, thereby to afford him an Opportunity of entertaining his Whore and Brat.

Pin. Your Conjecture, Madam, bears a Colour ; for looking back, I could perceive 'em talk very familiarly ; fo that they cou'd not be Strangers, as their pretended Quarrel would intimate.

Luc. 'Tis all true, as he is falfe.——What ! flighted ! defpis'd ! my honourable Love truck'd for a Whore ! Oh Villain ! Epitome of the Sex !——But I'll be re-veng'd. I'll marry the firft that afks me the Queftion ; nay, though he be a difbanded Soldier, or a poor Poet, or a fenfelefs Fop !—— Nay, tho' impotent, I'll marry him.

Pin. Oh, Madam ! that's to be reveng'd on yourfelf.

Luc. I care not, Fool ! I deferve Punifhment for my Credulity, as much as he for his Falfhood.——And you
deferve

deserve it too, Minx; your Persuasions drew me to
Assignation : I never lov'd the false-Man.

Pin. That's false, I am sure.   [*A*

Luc. But you thought to get another Piece of G
We shall have him giving you Money on the same Sc
he was so liberal to his Whore just now.

[*Walks about in a Pa*

Enter Lovewell.

Love. So much for Friendship——now for my L
——I ha'nt trangressed much——Oh, there she is—
Oh my Angel !   [*Runs to*

Luc. Oh thou Devil !   [*Starts b*

Love. Not unless you damn me, Madam.

Luc. You're damn'd already ; you're a Man.

[*Exit, pushing* Pind

Love. You're a Woman, I'll be sworn.——Hey d
what giddy Female Planet rules now ! By the Lord, t
Women are like their Maidenheads, no sooner so
than lost.——Here, *Brush,* run after *Pindress,* and k
the Occasion of this.——[Brush *runs.*]——Stay, c
back.——Zoons, I'm a Fool.

Brush. That's the first wise Word you have spo
these two Months.

Love. Trouble me with your untimely Jests, Sir.
and I'll——

Brush. Your Pardon, Sir; I'm in downright Ear
'Tis a less Slavery to be Apprentice to a famous C
surgeon, than to a Lover. He falls out with me,
cause he can't fall in with his Mistress. I can bear i
longer.

Love. Sirrah, what are you a mumbling ?

Brush. A short Prayer before I depart, Sir.—I I
been these three Years your Servant, but now, Sir,
your humble Servant.   [*Bows as g*

Love. Hold, you shan't leave me.

Brush. Sir, you can't be my Master.

Love. Why so?

Brush. Because you are not your own Master ; yet
would think you might, for you have lost your Mist
Oons ! Sir, let her go, and a fair Riddance. Who th
away a Tester and a Mistress, loses Six-pence.
little pimping *Cupid* is a blind Gunner. Had he sho

n

)arts as I have carry'd *Billet Deux*, he wou'd have
· kicking with her Heels up ere now. In short,
r Patience is worn to the Stumps with attending ;
)es and Stockings are upon their last Legs with
g between you. I have sweat out all my Moisture
Hand with palming your clammy Letters upon
[have———

. Hold, Sir ; your Trouble is now at an End, for
1 to marry her.

). And have you courted her these three Years, for
; but a Wife ?

. Do you think, Rascal, I wou'd have taken so
'ains to make her a Miss ?

). No, Sir ; the tenth Part on't wou'd ha'done.
: if you are resolv'd to marry, God b'w'ye.

. What's the Matter now, Sirrah ?

). Why, the Matter will be, that I must then
or her.——Hark ye, Sir, what have you been doing
s while, but teaching her the Way to cuckold
·Take care, Sir; look before you leap. You
ticklish Point to manage.————Can you tell,
1at's her Quarrel to you now ?

. I can't imagine. I don't remember that ever I
:d her.

). That's it, Sir. She resolves to put your Easi-
the Test now, that she may with more Security
on't hereafter.——Always suspect those Women of
s that are for searching into the Humours of their
:rs ; for they certainly intend to try them when
marry'd.

. How cam'st thou such an Engineer in Love ?

). I have sprung some Mines in my Time, Sir;
1ce I have trudg'd so long about your amorous
es, I have more Intrigue in the Sole of my Feet,
)me Blockheads in their whole Body.

. Sirrah, have you ever discover'd any Behaviour
Lady, to occasion this suspicious Discourse ?

). Sir, has this Lady ever discover'd any Beha-
)f yours to occasion this suspicious Quarrel ? I be-
he Lady has as much of the innate Principle of
(as the Gentleman said) as any Woman. But
aggage, her Attendant, is about ravishing her

F 4 *Lady's*

Lady's Page every Hour. 'Tis an old Saying, *Li | Master, like Man*; why not as well, *Like Miſtreſs, k | Maid?*

Love. Since thou art for trying Humours, have wi | you, Madam *Lucinda.* Beſides, ſo fair an Opportuni | offers, that Fate ſeem'd to deſign it.——Have you· le | the Gentleman at my Lodgings?

Bruſh. Yes, Sir, and ſent a Porter to his Inn to brin | his Things thither.

Love. That's· right.———Love, like other Diſeaſe | muſt ſometimes have a deſperate Cure. The School· | *Venus* impoſes the ſtrict Diſcipline; and awful *Cupid* is | chaſtning God : He whips ſeverely.———

Bruſh. Not if we kiſs the Rod. [*Exeun*

The End of the Firſt Act.

A C T II.

S C E N E, *Lovewell's Lodgings.*

Enter Lovewell, Roebuck *dreſs'd, and* Bruſh.

Love. O'My Conſcience, the fawning Creature lov | you.

Roeb. Ay, the conſtant Effects of debauching a Wc | man are, that ſhe infallibly loves the Man for doing th | Buſineſs, and he certainly hates her.——But what Con | pany is ſhe like to have at this ſame Widow's, *Bruſh?*

Bruſh. Oh the beſt Company, Sir; a Poet lives then | Sir.

Roeb. They're the worſt Company, for they're il | natur'd.

Bruſh. Ah, Sir, but it does no Body any Harm; fc | theſe Fellows that get Bread by their Wits are alwa; | forc'd to eat their Words. They muſt be good-ni | tur'd, 'ſpight of their Teeth, Sir. 'Tis ſaid he pays h | Lodging by cracking ſome ſmutty Jeſts with his Lanc | lady over-night; for ſhe's very well pleas'd with h | Natural Parts. [*While* Roeb. *and* Bruſh *talk,* Lovewe | *ſeems to project ſomething by himſe* | *Roe*

Roeb. What other Lodgers are there ?

Bruſh. One newly enter'd, a young Squire, juſt come from the Univerſity.

Roeb. A mere Peripatetic, I warrant him. —— A very pretty Family; a Heathen Philoſopher, an *Engliſh* Poet, and an *Iriſh W'hore.* Had the Landlady but an *Highland* Piper to join with 'em, ſhe might ſet up for a Collection of Monſters.—Any Body within ? [*Slaps Lovewell on the Sboulder.*

Love. Yes, you are my Friend. All my Thoughts were employ'd about you. In ſhort, I have one Requeſt to make, That you would renounce your looſe wild Courſes, and lead a ſober Life, as I do.

Roeb. That I will, if you'll grant me a Boon.

Love. You ſhall have it, be't what it will.

Roeb. That you wou'd relinquiſh your preciſe ſober Behaviour, and live like a Gentleman as I do.

Love. That I can't grant.

Roeb. Then we're off: Tho' ſhou'd your Women prove no better than your Wine, my Debaucheries will fall of themſelves, for Want of Temptation.

Love. Our Women are worſe than our Wine; our Claret has but little of the *French* in't, but our Wenches have the Devil and all: They are both adulterated; to prevent the Inconveniencies of which, I'll provide you an honourable Miſtreſs.

Roeb. An honourable Miſtreſs ; what's that ?

Love. A virtuous Lady, whom you muſt love and court; the ſureſt Method of reclaiming you.——As thus :——Thoſe ſuperfluous Pieces you throw away in Wine, may be laid out——

Roeb. To the Poor ?

Love. No, no : In Sweet Powder, Cravats, Garters, Snuff-boxes, Ribbons, Coach-hire, and Chair-hire. Thoſe idle Hours which you miſpend with lewd ſophiſticated Wenches muſt be dedicated——

Roeb. To the Church ?

Love. No ; to the innocent and charming Converſation of your virtuous Miſtreſs; by which Means, the two moſt exorbitant Debaucheries, Drinking and Whoring, will be retrench'd.

Roeb.

Roeb. A very fine Retrenchment truly! I muft firft defpife the honeft jolly Converfation at the Tavern, for the foppifh, affected, dull, infipid Entertainment at the Chocolate-houfe; muft quit my Freedom with ingenious Company, to harnefs myfelf to Foppery among the fluttering Crowd of *Cupid*'s Livery-boys.————The fecond Articles is, That I muft refign the Company of lewd Women for that of my innocent Miftrefs; that is, I muft change my eafy natural Sin of Wenching, to that conftrain'd Debauchery of Lying and Swearing.———— The many Lies and Oaths that I made to thy Sifter, will go nearer to damn me, than if I had enjoy'd her a hundred times over.

Love. Oh *Roebuck!* your Reafon will maintain the contrary when you're in Love.

Roeb. That is, when I have loft my Reafon: Come, come, a Wench, a Wench, a foft, white, eafy, confenting Creature!————Prithee, *Ned*, leave Muftinefs, and fhew me the Varieties of the Town.

Love. A Wench is the leaft Variety——Look out—— See what a numerous Train trip along the Street there.—
[*Pointing outwards.*

Roeb. Oh *Venus!* all thefe fine ftately Creatures! Fare you well, *Ned.*——
[*Runs out*; Lovewell *catches him, and pulls him back.*] Prithee let me go; 'tis a Deed of Charity; I'm quite ftarv'd. I'll juft take a fnap, and be with you in the Twinkling——As you're my Friend——I muft go.

Love. Then we muft break for all together———— [*Quits him.*]————He that will leave his Friend for a Whore, I reckon a Commoner in Friendfhip as in Love.

Roeb. If you faw how ill that ferious Face becomes a Fellow of your Years, you wou'd never wear it again. Youth is taking in any Mafquerade but Gravity.

Love. Tho' Lewdnefs fuits much worfe with your Circumftances, Sir.

Roeb. Ay, thefe Circumftances! Damn thefe Circumftances.—There he has hamftring'd me. This Poverty! how it makes a Man fneak!————Well, prithee let's know this devilifh virtuous Lady. By the Circumftances of my Body, I fhall foon be off or on with her.
Love.

Love. Know then, for thy utter Condemnation, that she's a Lady of Eighteen, Beautiful, Witty, and nicely Virtuous.

Roeb. A Lady of Eighteen! Good———Beautiful! Better———Witty! Best of all.———Now with these three Qualifications, if she be nicely virtuous, then I'll henceforth adore every thing that wears a Petticoat ———Witty and Virtuous! Ha, ha, ha! Why, 'tis as inconsistent in Ladies as Gentlemen; and were I to debauch one for a Wager, her Wit shou'd be my Bawd. ———Come, come, the forbidden Fruit was pluck'd from the Tree of Knowledge, Boy.

Love. Right———But there was a cunninger Devil than you to tempt.———I'll assure you, *George,* your Rhetoric wou'd fail you here; she wou'd worst you at your own Weapons.

Roeb. Ay, or any Man in *England,* if she be Eighteen, as you say.

Love. Have a Care, Friend; this Satire will get you torn in Pieces by the Females; you'll fall into *Orpheus's* Fate.

Roeb. *Orpheus* was a Blockhead, and deserv'd his Fate.

Love. Why?

Roeb. Because he went to Hell for a Wife.

Love. This happens right———[*Aside*]———But you shall go to Heav'n for a Mistress; you shall court this Divine Creature———I don't desire you to fall in Love with her; I don't intend you shou'd marry her neither: But you must be convinc'd of the Chastity of the Sex; tho' if you shou'd conquer her, the Spoil, you Rogue, will be glorious, and infinitely worth the Pains in attaining.

Roeb. Ay, but *Ned,* my Circumstances, my Circumstances.———

Love. Come, you shan't want Money.

Roeb. Then I dare attempt it. Money is the Sinews of Love, as of War. Gad, Friend, thou art the bravest Pimp I ever heard of———Well, give me Directions to sail by, the Name of my Port, lade my Pockets, and then for the Cape of Good Hope.

Love. You need no Directions as to the Manner of Courtship.

Roeb.

Ro.b. No; I have feen fome few Principles, on which my Courtfhip's founded, which feldom fail. To let a Lady rely upon my Modefty, but to depend myfelf altogether upon my Impudence; to ufe a Miftrefs like a Deity in public, but like a Woman in private: To be as cautious then of afking an impertinent Queftion, as afterwards of telling a Story; remembring, that the Tongue is the only Member that can't hurt a Lady's Honour, though touched to the tendereft Part.

Love. Oh! but to a Friend, *George*; you'll tell a Friend your Succefs.

Ro.b. No, not to her very felf; it muft be as private as Devotion——No babbling, unlefs a fqualling Brat peeps out to tell Tales——But where lies my Courfe?

Love. *Brufh* fhall fhew you the Houfe; the Lady's Name is *Lucinda*; her Father and Mother dead; fhe's Heirefs to Twelve Hundred a Year: But above all, obferve this; She has a Page, which you muft get on your fide: 'Tis a very pretty Boy; I prefented him to the Lady about a Fortnight ago; he's your Countryman too; he brought me a Letter from my Sifter, which I have about me.————Here, you may read it.

Roeb. Ay, 'tis her Hand; I know it well; and I almoft blufh to fee it. [*Afide.*

[*Reads*] Dear Brother,

A Lady of my Acquaintance lately dying, begg'd me as her laft Requeft, to provide for this Boy, who was her Page: I hope I have obey'd my Friend's laft Command, and oblig'd a Brother, by fending him to you. Pray difpofe of him as much as you can for his Advantage. All Friends are well, and I am Your affectionate Sifter, *Leanthe.*

[*While he reads,* Lovewell *talks to* Brufh, *and gives him fome Directions feemingly.*

All Friends are well: Is that all? Not a Word of poor *Reebuck*———I wonder fhe mention'd nothing of my Misfortunes to her Brother. But fhe has forgot me already. True Woman ftill———Well, I may excufe her, for I am making all the Hafte I can to forget her.

Love.

e. Be fure you have an Eye upon him, · and come to
efently at Widow *Bullfinch's* ————[*To* Brufh.]————
George, you won't communicate your Succefs ? [*Afide.*
. You may guefs what you pleafe ———— I'm as
after a Miftrefs as after· a Bottle ————All Air ;
ull of Joy, like a Bumper of Claret, fmiling and
ng. ·
e. Then you'll certainly run over.·
5. No, no, nor fhall I drink to any Body.——
·· [*Exeunt feverally.*

N E *changes to a Dining-room in Widow* Bullfinch's
*fe; a Flute, Mufic-book upon the Table; Cafe of Toys
ring up.*————

Rigadoon *the Dancing-Mafter, leading in* Mockmode
*oth Hands, as teaching him the Minuet; he fings, and
:kmode dances aukwardly;* Club *follows.*

. Tal—dal—deral—One—Two——Tal——dal
—deral—Coupé—Tal—dal—deral——Very well —
deral—Wrong—Tal—dal—deral—Toes out —Tal
-—deral——Obferve Time: ——Very well in-
Sir; you fhall dance as well as any Man in *England*;
ve an excellent Difpofition in your Limbs, Sir——
e me, Sir.
· *the Mafter dances a new Minuet; and at every Cut
· Club makes an aukward Imitation by leaping up.*]
) forth, Sir.
t. I'm afraid we fhall difturb my Landlady.
Landlady! You muft have a care of that; fhe'll
pardon you.———Landlady! Every Woman, from a
:fs to a Kitchen-wench, is *Madam*; and every Man,
Lord to a Lacquey, *Sir.*
t. Muft I then lofe my Title of 'Squire, 'Squire
ode ?
By all means, Sir; 'Squire and Fool are the fame
here.
t. That's very comical, faith——But is there an
Parliament for that, Mr. *Rigadoon ?*——Well,
can't be a 'Squire, I'll do as well; I have a great
and want only to be a great Beau to qualify me
for a Knight or a Lord. By the Univerfe, I have a
great

great Mind to bind myfelf 'Prentice to a Beau——Cou'd I but dance well, pufh well, play upon the Flute, and fwear the moft modifh Oaths, I wou'd fet up for Quality with e'er a young Nobleman of 'em all——Pray what are the moft fafhionable Oaths in Town ? *Zoons,* I take it, is a very becoming one.

Rig. Zoons is only us'd by the difbanded Officers and Bullies : But Zauns is the Beaux Pronunciation.

Mock. Zauns.

Club. Zauns.

Rig. Yes, Sir, we fwear as we dance; fmooth, and with a Cadence.——Zauns! 'Tis harmonious, and pleafes the Ladies, becaufe 'tis foft——Zauns, Madam——is the only Compliment our great Beaux pafs on a Lady.

Mock. But fuppofe a Lady fpeaks to me, what muft I fay ?

Rig. Nothing, Sir——you muft take Snufh, grin, and make her an humble Cringe——Thus——
   [*He bows Foppifhly, and takes Snufh*; Mockmode *imitates him aukwardly; and taking Snufh, fneezes.*

Rig. O Lard, Sir, you muft never fneeze; 'tis as unbecoming after *Orangeree,* as Grace after Meat.

Mock. I thought People took it to clear the Brain.

Rig. The Beaux have no Brains at all, Sir; their Skull is a perfect Snufh-box; and I heard a Phyfician fwear, who open'd one of 'em, that the three Divifions of his Head were fill'd with *Orangeree, Bourgamot,* and *Plain Spanifh.*

Mock. Zauns, I muft fneeze——[*Sneezes*]——Blefs me.

Rig. O fie, Mr. *Mockmode!* What a ruftical Expreffion that is !——Blefs me !——You fhou'd upon all fuch Occafions cry, Dem me. You would be as naufeous to the Ladies, as one of the old Patriarchs, if you us'd that obfolete Expreffion.

Club. I find that going to the Devil is very modifh in this Town——Pray, Mafter Dancing-mafter, what Religion may thefe Beaux be of ?

Rig. A Sort of *Indians* in their Religion ; they worfhip the firft thing they fee in the Morning.

Mock. What's that, Sir ?

Rig. Their own Shadows in the Glafs ; and fome of 'em fuch Hellifh Faces, that may frighten 'em into Devotion.

Mock.

Mock. Then they are *Indians* right, for they worship the Devil.

Rig. Then you shall be as great a Beau as any of 'em. But you must be sure to mind your Dancing.

Mock. Is not Music very convenient too?————I can play the *Rolls* and *Maiden Fair* already. *Alamire, Befabemi, Cefolfa, Delafol, Ela, Effaut. Gefolreut.* I have 'em all by heart already. But I have been plaguily puzzled about the Etymology of these Notes; and certainly a Man cannot arrive at any Perfection, unless he understands the Derivation of the Terms.

Rig. O Lard, Sir! That's easy. *Effaut* and *Gefolreut* were two famous *German* Musicians, and the rest were *Italians*.

Mock. But why are they only seven?

Rig. From a prodigious great Bass-Viol with seven Strings that played a Jig, call'd the *Music of the Spheres :* The seven Planets were nothing but Fiddle-strings.

Mock. Then your Stars have made you a Dancing-Master?

Rig. O Lard, Sir! *Pythagoras* was a Dancing-Master; he shews the Creation to be a Country Dance, where, after some antic Changes, all the Parts fell into their Places, and there they stand ready, till the next Squeak of a Philosopher's Fiddle sets them a dancing again.

Club. Sir, here comes the Pushing-Master.

Rig. Then I'll be gone. But you must have a care of pushing, 'twill spoil the Niceness of your Steps. Learn a Flourish or two; and that's all a Beau can have Occasion for.

Enter Nimblewrist.

Mock. Oh, Mr. *Nimblewrist!* I crave you ten thousand Pardons, by the Universe.

Nimb. That was a home Thrust. Good Sir, I hope you're for a Breathing this Morning. [*Takes down a Foil.*] ————I'll assure you, Mr. *Mockmode*, you will make an excellent Swordsman; you're as well shap'd for Fencing as any Man in *Europe.* The Duke of *Burgundy* is just of your Make; he pushes the finest of any Man in *France*————Sa, sa————like Lightning.

Mock. I'm much in love with Fencing : But, I think, Backsword is the best Play.

Nimb.

Nimb. Oh Lard, Sir!———Have you ever been in *France*, Sir?

Mock. No, Sir; but I understand the Geography of it————*France* is bounded on the North with the *Rhine.*———

Nimb. No, Sir; a *Frenchman* is bounded on the North with Quart, on the South with Tierce, and so forth. 'Tis a noble Art, Sir; and every one that wears a Sword is obliged by his Tenure to learn. The Rules of Honour are engraved on my Hilt, and my Blade must maintain 'em. My Sword's my Herald, and the bloody Hand my Coat of Arms.

Mock. And how long have you profefs'd this noble Art, Sir?

Nimb. Truly, Sir, I serv'd an Apprenticefhip to this Trade, Sir.

Mock. What, are ye a Corporation then?

Nimb. Yes, Sir; the Surgeons have taken us into theirs, becaufe we make fo much Work for 'em.———But, as I was telling you, Sir, I profefs'd this Science till the Wars broke out; but then, when every body got Commiffions, I put in for one, serv'd the Campaigns in *Flanders*; and when the Peace broke out, was difbanded; fo, among a great many other poor Rogues, am forc'd to betake to my old Trade. Now the public Quarrel's ended, I live by private ones. I live ftill by dying, as the Song goes, Sir. While we have *Englifh* Courage, *French* Honour, and *Spanifh* Blades among us, I fhall live, Sir.

Mock. Surely your Sword and Skill did the King great Service abroad.

Nimb. Yes, Sir; I kill'd above fifteen of our own Officers by private Duels in the Camp, Sir; kill'd 'em fairly; kill'd 'em thus, Sir—Sa, fa, fa, fa, Parry, parry, parry.—

[*He pufhes* Mockmode *on the Ribs; he ftrikes* Nimblewrift *over the Head, and breaks the Foil.*

Club. What's the Name of that Thruft, pray, Sir?

Nimb. Oh Lard, Sir! he did not touch me, not in the leaft, Sir; the Foil was crack'd, a palpable Crack.

[*Blood runs down his Face.*

Club. A very palpable Crack, truly. Your Skull is only crack'd, palpably crack'd, that's all.

Moc. Well, Sir, if you pleafe to teach me my Honour.—

My

My Dancing-matter has forbid me any more, left I fhould
difcompofe my Steps.

Nimb. Your Dancing-mafter is a Blockhead, Sir.

Enter Rigadoon.

Rig. I forgot my Gloves, and fo——————

Mock. Oh Sir! he calls you Blockhead, by the Univerfe.

Rig. Zauns, Sir—————— [*Foppifhly.*

Nimb. Zoons, Sir—————— [*Bluffifhly.*

Rig. I have more Wit in the Sole of my Foot, than you
have in your whole Body.

Nimb. Ay, Sir, you Caperers dance all your Brains into
your Heels, which makes you carry fuch empty Noddles.
Your Rational's revers'd, carrying your Underftandings in
your Legs. Your Wit is the perfeft *Antipodes* to other
Men's.

Rig. And what are you, good Monfieur, fa, fa? Stand
upon your Guard, Mr. *Mockmode*, he's the greateft falffier
in his Art; he'll fill your Head fo full of *French* Principles
of Honcur, that you won't have one of Honefty left. His
Breaft-plate there he calls the Butt of Honour; at which
all the Fools in the Kingdom fhoot, and not one can hit the
Mark.

Nimb. You talk of *Robin Hood*, who never fhot in his
Bow, Sir.—————You Dancers are the Battledores of the
Nation, that tofs the light foppifh Shttleccks to and again,
to get yourfelves in heat.——Have a care, Mr. *Mockmode*;
this Fellow will make a mere Grafhopper of you.—————
Sir, you're the grand Pimp to Foppery and Lewdnefs; and
the Devil and a Dancing-mafter dance a Corante over the
whole Kingdom.

Rig. A Pimp, Sir! What then, Sir? I engage Couples
into the Bed of Love, but you match 'em into the Bed of
Honour. We only juggle People out of their Chaftity,
but you cheat 'em out of their Lives. We fhall have you,
Mr. *Mockmode*, grinning in the Bed of Honour, as if you
laugh'd at the Fool who muft be hang'd for you—Which is
beft, Mr. *Nimblewrift*, an eafy Minuet, or a *Tyburn* Jigg?

Nimb. Don't provoke my Sword, Sir, left that Art you
fo revile fhou'd revenge itfelf; for every one of you that
live by Dancing, fhou'd die by Pufhing, Sir.

Rig. And every Man that lives by Pufhing, fhou'd die
Dancing, I take it.

Nimb.

Nimb. Zoons, Sir! What d'ye mean?

Rig. Nothing, Sir;——Tal——dal——deral—— [*Dances.*]——This takes the Ladies, Mr. *Mockmode*; this runs away with all the great Fortunes in Town. Tho' you be a Fool, a Fop, a Coward, dance well, and you captivate the Ladies. The moving a Man's Limbs pliantly, does the Bufinefs, If you want a Fortune, come to me—— Tal——dal——deral—— [*Dances.*

Nimb. No, no, to me, Sir,——fa, fa,——does your Bufinefs fooneft with a Woman: A clean and manly Extenfion of all your Parts—Ha—Carrying a true Point is the Matter.——Sa, fa, fa, fa,——Defend yourfelf. [*Pufhing at* Rigadoon, *who dances and fings, retiring off the Stage.* *Enter* Bullfinch.

Bull. O Goodnefs! What a Room's here! Could not Fellows wipe their Feet before they came up? And here's fuch a tripping and fuch a ftamping, that they have broke down all the Cieling. You Dancing and Fencing-mafters have been the Downfal of many Houfes. Get out of my Doors; my Houfe was never in fuch a Pickle.——You Country Gentlemen, newly come to *London*, like your own Spaniels out of a Pond, muft be fhaking the Water off, and befpatter every Body about you.——
  [*Mockmode having taken Snufh, offering to fneeze, fneezes in her Face.*

Mock. Zauns, Madam, [*Sneezes*]——Blefs me!——Dem me, I mean.

Bull. He's tainted. Thefe curfed Flies have blown upon him already.

Mock. Sa, fa,——Defend Flankonade, Madam.

Bull. Ah, Mr. *Mockmode*, my Pufhing and Dancing Days are done: But I had a Son, Mr. *Mockmode*, that wou'd match you——Ah, my poor *Robin!* He dy'd of an Apoplexy: He was as pretty a young Man as ever ftep'd into a black Leather Shoe: He was as like you, Mr. *Mockmode*, as one Egg is like another; he dy'd like an Angel——But I am fure he might have recover'd but for the Phyficians ——Oh thefe Doctors, thefe Doctors!

Mock. Blefs the Doctors, I fay; for I believe they kill'd my honeft old Father.

Bull. Ay, that's true: If my *Robin* had left me an Eftate, I fhou'd have faid fo too.—— [*Cries.*
                                                              Mock.

Mock. Zauns, Madam ; you muſt not be melancholy, Madam.

Bull. Well, Sir, I hope you'll give us the Beverage of our fine Cloaths. I'll aſſure you, Sir, they fit you very well, and I like your Fancy mightily.

Mock. Ay, ay, Madam. But what's moſt modiſh for Beverage ? For, I ſuppoſe, the Faſhion of that alters always with the Cloaths.

Bull. The Taylors are the beſt Judges of that——— Champaigne, I ſuppoſe.

Mock. Is Champaigne a Taylor ? Now, methinks, that were a fitter Name for a Wig-maker——I think they call my Wig a Champaigne.

Bull. You're clear out, Sir, clear out. Champaigne is a fine Liquor, which all your great Beaux drink to make 'em witty.

Mock. Witty ! Oh, by the Univerſe, I muſt be witty. I'll drink nothing elſe ; I never was witty in all my Life. I love Jokes dearly.———Here, *Club,* bring us a Bottle of what d'ye call it ; the witty Liquor.

Bull. But I thought all you that were bred at the Univerſity ſhou'd be Wits naturally.

Mock. The quite contrary, Madam; there's no ſuch thing there. We dare not have Wit there, for fear of being counted Rakes. Your ſolid Philoſophy is all read there, which is clear another thing. But now I will be a Wit, by the Univerſe. I muſt get acquainted with the great Poets ; Landlady, you muſt introduce me.

Bull. Oh dear me, Sir; wou'd you ruin me ? I introduce you ! No Widow dare be ſeen with a Poet, for fear ſhe ſhou'd be thought to keep him.

Mock. Keep him ! What's that ? They keep nothing but Sheep in the Country : I hope they don't fleece the Wits ?

Bull. Alas, Sir, they have no Fleeces ; there's a great Cry, but little Wool. However, if you wou'd be acquainted with the Poets, I can prevail with a Gentleman of my Acquaintance to introduce you ; 'tis one *Lovewell,* a fine Gentleman that comes here ſometimes.

Mock. Lovewell ! By the Univerſe, my Rival : I heard of him in the Country : This puts me in mind of my Miſtreſs ——Zauns, I'm certainly become a Beau already ; or I was ſo in Love with myſelf, I quite forgot her.——I

have

have a Note in my Pocket-book to find her out by.——-

[Pulls out a large Pocket-book; turning over t

Leaves, reads to himfel

Six-pence for wafhing —— Two-pence to the Maid. —
Six-pence for Snufh——One Shilling for Butter'd Ale.——B
the Univerfe, I have loft the Directions.——-Hark y
Madam, does this fame *Lovewell* come often here, fay you

Bull. Yes, Sir, very of:en——There's a Lady of his A
quaintance, a Lodger in the Houfe juft now.

Mock. A Lady of his Acquaintance, a Lodger in th
Houfe juft now; of his Acquaintance, do you fay ?

Bull. Yes, and a pretty Lady too.

Mock. And he comes often here, you fay. By the Un
verfe! fhou'd I happen to lodge in the fame Houfe wit
my Miftrefs: I gad it muft be the fame. Can you tell t
Woman's Name ?—— Stay——Is her Name *Lucinda* ?

Bull. Perhaps it may, Sir; but I believe fhe's a Widov
for fhe has a young Son, and I'm fure 'tis legitimately be
gotten; for it is the braveft Child you fhall fee in a Sun
mer's Day; 'tis not like one of our puling Brats o'th' Tow
here, born with the Difeafes of half a Dozen Fathe
about it.

Mock. By the Univerfe, I don't remember whether m
Miftrefs is a Maid or Widow: But if a Widow, fo mue
the better; for all your *London* Widows are devilifh rick
they fay. She came in a Coach, did fhe not, Madam ?

Bull. Yes, Sir, yes.

Mock. Then 'tis infallibly fhe———Does fhe not alway
go out in her Coach ?

Bull. She has not ftirr'd abroad fince fhe came, Sir.

Mock. Oh, I was told that fhe was very referv'd, the
'tis very much of a Widow. I have often heard my Moth
fay, that fitting at home and Silence were very becoming i
a Maid; and fhe has often chid my Sifter *Dorothy* for ga
ding out to the Meadows, and tumbling among the Cock
wit the Hay-makers. I gad I'm the moft lucky Son of
Whore; I was wrapt in the Tail of my Mother's Smock
Landlady.

Enter Servant.

Bull. Oh, but this Lady, Sir———

Ser. Madam, here's a Gentleman below wants to fpea
with you inftantly.

Bu

Bull With me, Child! Sir, I'll wait on you in a Mi-
ate. [*Exit with Servant.*

Enter Club *with Wine and Glasses.*

Mock. Is that the witty Liquor? Come, fill the Glasses.
low that I have found my Miftrefs, I must next find my
Vits.

Club. So you had need, Mafter; for they that find a
Miftrefs, are generally out of their Wits.——
[*Gives him a Glafs.*

Mock. Come, fill yourfelf. [*They jingle and drink.*
Jut where's the Wit now, *Club?* Have you found it?

Club. I gad, Mafter, I think 'tis a very good Jeft.

Mock. What?

Club. What! why drinking. You'll find, Mafter, that
his fame Gentleman in the Straw Doublet, this fame *Will
'th' Whifp,* is a Wit at the Bottom. [*Fills.*]——Here,
iere, Mafter; how it puns and quibbles in the Glafs!

Mock. By the Univerfe, now I have it; the Wit lies
n the Jingling: All Wit confifts moft in Jingling. Hear
iow the Glaffes rhime to one another.

Club. What, Mafter, are thefe Wits fo apt to clafh?
[*Jingles the Glaffes.*

Mock. Oh by the Univerfe, by the Univerfe, this is
Wit. [*Breaks e'm.*] My Landlady is in the right.——
have often heard there was Wit in breaking Glaffes. It
vould be a very good Joke to break the Flafk now.

Club. I find then that this fame Wit is very brittle
Ware.—But I think, Sir, 'twere no Joke to fpill the Wine.

Mock. Why, there's the Jeft, Sirrah; all Wit confifts in
ofing; there was never any thing got by't. I fancy
his fame Wine is all fold at *Will's* Coffee-houfe. Do you
now the Way thither, Sirrah? I long to fee Mr. *Comick*
nd Mr. *Tagrhime,* with the reft of 'em. I wonder how
hey look! Certainly thefe Poets muft have fomething
xtraordinary in their Faces. Of all the Rarities in the
own, I long to fee nothing more than the *Poets,* and
Iedlam.——Come in, *Club;* I muft go practife my Honours
-Tal—dal—deral— [*Exit dancing, and* Club *toping.*

Enter Lovewell *and* Bullfinch.

Bull. Oh Mr. *Lovewell!* you come juft in the Nick;
was ready to fpoil all, by telling him fhe was a Stranger,
nd juft now come.

Love.

Love. Well, dear Madam, be cautious for the future 'tis the moſt fortunate Chance that ever befel me. 'Twere convenient we had the other Lodgers of our Side.

Bull. There's nobody but Mr. *Lyrick*; and you had a ſafely tell a Secret over a Groaning-Cheeſe, as to him.

Love. How ſo?

Bull. Why, you muſt know, that he has been lying-in theſe four Months of a Play; and he has got all the Muſes about him; a Parcel of the moſt tattling Goſſips.

Love. Come, come; no more Words; but to our Buſineſs. I will certainly reward you. But have you any good Hopes of its ſucceeding?

Bull. Very well of the 'Squire's Side. But I'm afraid your Widow will never play her Part, ſhe's ſo aukward and ſo ſullen.

Love. Go you and inſtruct her, while I manage Affairs abroad.

Bull. She's always raving of one *Roebuck*. Prithee, who is this ſame *Roebuck?*——Ah Mr. *Lovewell*, I'm afraid this Widow of yours is ſomething elſe at the Bottom; I'm afraid there has been a Dog in the Well. [*Exit.*

Enter Bruſh.

Love. So, Sirrah! where have you left the Gentleman?

Bruſh. In a Friend's Houſe, Sir.

Love. What Friend?

Bruſh. Why, a Tavern.

Love. What took him there?

Bruſh. A Coach, Sir.

Love. How d'ye mean?

Bruſh. A Coach and Six, Sir; no leſs, I'll aſſure you, Sir.

Love. A Coach and Six!

Bruſh. Yes, Sir, ſix Whores and a carted Bawd: He pick'd 'em all up in the Street, and is gone with this ſplendid Retinue into the Sun by *Covent-Garden.* I aſk'd him what he meant? He told me, that he only wanted to whet, when the very Sight of 'em turn'd my Stomach.

Love. The Fellow will have his Swing, tho' he hang for't. However, run to him, and bid him take the Name of *Mockmode*; call himſelf *Mockmode* upon all Occaſions; and tell him that he ſhall find me here about Four in the Afternoon—Aſk no Queſtions, but fly——
.So ;——

So:——His ufurping that Name gives him a Title to
court *Lucinda*, by which I fhall difcover her Inclination
to [*Exit.* Brufh.] this *Mockmode*, whofe coming to Town
has certainly occafion'd her Quarrel with me; while I
fet the Hound himfelf upon a wrong Scent, and ten to
one provide for Miftrefs *Trudge* by the Bargain. 'Tis faid
one can't be a Friend and a Lover.

- *But oppofite to that, this Plot fhall prove,*
  I'll ferve my Friend by what affifts my Love.   [Exit.

The End of the Second Act.

ACT III.

SCENE, Lucinda's *Houfe.*

Enter Leanthe fola, *drefs'd like a* Page.

METHINKS this Livery fuits ill my Birth; but Slave
to Love, I muft not difobey; his Service is the
hardeft Vaffalage, forcing the Powers divine to lay their
Godfhips down to be more Gods, more happy here below.——Thus I, poor Wanderer, have left my Country,
difguis'd myfelf fo much, I hardly know whether this
Habit, or my Love, be blindeft; to follow one, perhaps,
who loves me not, tho' every Breath of his foft Words
was Paffion, and every Accent Love. Oh *Roebuck!*
                                                    [*Weeps.*

Enter Roebuck.

Roeb. This is the Page, Love's Link-Boy, that muft
light me the Way.——How now, pretty Boy; has your
Lady beaten you? ha!——This Lady muft be a *Venus*,
for fhe has got a *Cupid* in her Family. 'Tis a wondrous
pretty Boy——[Leanthe *ftarts, and ftares at him.*] but a
very comical Boy——What the Devil does he ftare at?

Lean. Oh Heav'ns! is the Object real, or are my Eyes
falfe? Is that *Roebuck*, or am I *Leanthe?* I'm afraid he's
not the fame; and too fure I'm not myfelf——   [*Weeps.*

Roeb. What Offence could fuch pretty Innocence commit, to deferve a Punifhment to make you cry?

Lean. Oh, Sir! a wondrous Offence.

                                                    Roeb.

Roeb. What was it, my Child?

Lean. I prick'd my Finger with a Pin, till I made it bleed.

Roeb. Such little Boys as you should have a care of sharp Things.

Lean. Indeed, Sir, we ought; for it prick'd me so deep, that the Sore went to my very Heart.

Roeb. Poor Boy! here's a Plaister for your sore Finger——— [*Gives him Gold.*

Lean. Sir, you had best keep it for a sore Finger. [*Returns it.*

Roch. O' my Conscience the Boy's witty, but not very wise in returning Gold——Come, come, you shall take it. [*Forces it upon him and kisses him.*

Lean. That's the fitter Cure for my sore Finger —The same dear Lips still. Oh, that the Tongue within them were as true! [*Aside.*

Roeb. By Heav'ns, this Boy has the softest Pair of Lips I ever tasted. I ne'er found before, that Ladies kiss'd their Pages; but now if this Rogue were not too young, I shou'd suspect he were before-hand with me. I gad, I must kiss him again—Come, you shall take the Money. [*Kisses*

Lean. Oh how he bribes me into Bribery!——— But what must I do with this Money, Sir?

Roeb. You must get a little Mistress, and treat her with it.

Lean. Sir, I have one Mistress already; and they say, no Man can serve two Masters, much less two Mistresses. How many Mistresses have you, pray?

Roeb. Umh! I gad the Boy has pos'd me——How many, Child? Why, let me see.——There was Mrs. *Mary*, Mrs. *Margaret*, Mrs. *Lucy*, Mrs. *Susan*, Mrs. *Judy*, and so forth; to the Number of five and twenty, or thereabouts.

Lean. Oh ye Powers! and did you love 'em all?

Roeb. Yes, desperately.——— I wou'd have drank and fought for any one of them: I have sworn and ly'd to every one of 'em, and have lain with 'em all: That's for your Encouragement, Boy; learn betimes, Youth; young Plants shou'd be water'd. Your Smock-Face was made for a Chamber-Utensil.

Lean. And did not one escape ye?

Roeb. Yes.

. Yes, one did ;——the Devil take her.

. What, don't you love her then ?

. No, faith ; but I bear her an amorous Grudge ſomething between Love and Spight.——I cou'd kill th Kindneſs.

t. I don't believe it, Sir ; you cou'd not be ſo hard-l ſure : Her honourable Paſſion, I think, ſhou'd you beſt.

. O Child ! Boys of your Age are continually g Romances, filling your Heads with that old Bum-'Love and Honour : But when you come to my you'll underſtand better Things.

z. And muſt I be a falſe, treacherous Villain, when e to your **Years,** Sir ? Is Falſhood and Perjury eſ-to the perfect State of Manhood ?

b. Pſhaw, Children and old Men always talk thus ily——You underſtand nothing, Boy.

n. Yes, Sir, I have been in Love, and much more ou, I perceive.

b. It appears then, that there's no Service in the I ſo educating to a Boy as a Lady's——By *Jove,* park may be older than I imagine. Hark ye, Sir ; u never pull off your Lady's Shoes and Stockings ? ou never reach her the——Pincuſhion ? Do you ſit on her Bed-ſide, and ſing to her ? Ha !——, tell me, that's my good Boy.——

[Makes much of him.

n. Yes, I do ſing her aſleep ſometimes.

b. But do you never waken her again ?

n. No, but I conſtantly wake myſelf ; my Reſt's s diſturbed by Viſions of the Devil.

b. Who wou'd imagine now, that this young Sha-ou'd dream of a Woman ſo ſoon ?—But what Songs our Lady delight in moſt ?

n. Paſſionate ones, Sir : I'll ſing you one of 'em, if ſtay.

b. With all my Heart, my little Cherubim. The e is fond of ſhewing his Parts.—Come, begin.

A SONG: Set by Mr. *Richardson.*

I.

How bless'd are Lovers in Disguise!
 Like Gods they see,
 As I do thee,
Unseen by human Eyes.
 Expos'd to View,
 I'm hid from you,
I'm alter'd, yet the same :
 The Dark conceals me ;
 Love reveals me ;
Love, which lights me by its Flame.

II.

Were you not false, you me wou'd know ;
 For tho' your Eyes
 Cou'd not devise,
Your Heart had told you so.
 Your Heart wou'd beat
 With eager Heat,
And me by Sympathy wou'd find :
 True Love might see
 One chang'd like me,
False Love is only blind.

Roeb. Oh my little Angel in Voice and Shape!——
[*Kisses her.*] I cou'd wish myself a Female for thy Sake.
Lean. You're much better as you are for my Sake.
             [*Aside.*

Roeb. Or if thou wert a Woman, I wou'd——
Lean. What would you ? marry me ? wou'd you marry
me ?

Roeb. Marry you, Child! no, no; I love you too
well for that ; you shou'd not have my Hand, but all my
Body at once.——But to our Business: Is your Lady
at home ?
Lean. My Lady! What Business have you with my
Lady, pray, Sir ?
Roeb. Don't ask Questions. You know Mr. *Lovewell.*
Lean. Yes, very well. He's my great Friend, and one
I wou'd serve above all the World,—— but his Sister.
Reeb. His Sister!——Ha, that gives me a Twinge for
my Sin.——Pray, Mr. *Page,* was *Leanthe* well when you
left her ?

              Lean.

Lean. Yes, Sir ; but wondrous melancholy, by the Departure of a dear Friend of her's to another World.

Roeb. O, that was the Person mention'd in her Letter, whose Departure occasion'd your Departure for *England*.

Lean. That was the Occasion of my coming, too sure, Sir :————Oh, 'twas a dear Friend to me ! the Loss makes me weep.

Roeb. Poor tender-hearted Creature!————But I still find there was not a Word of me.————Pray, good Boy, let your Mistress know, here's one to wait on her.

Lean. Your Business is from Mr. *Lovewell*, I suppose, Sir.

Roeb. Ye, yes.

Lean. Then I'll go. [*Exit.*

Roeb. I've thrown my Cast, and am fairly in for't : But a'n't I an impudent Dog ? Had I as much Gold in my Breeches, as Brass in my Face, I durst attempt a whole Nunnery. This Lady is a reputed Virtue of good Fortune and Quality; I am a rakehelly Rascal, not worth a Groat ; and without any farther Ceremony, am going to debauch her.————But hold ;—She does not know that I'm this rakehelly Rascal ; and I know that she's a Woman, one of Eighteen too ; beautiful, witty.————O' my Conscience, upon second Thoughts, I am not so very impudent neither.————Now as to my Management, I'll first try the whining Addresses, and see if she'll bleed in the soft Vein.

Enter Lucinda.

Luc. Have you any Bus'ness with me, Sir ?

Roeb. Thus look'd the forbidden Fruit, luscious and tempting. 'Tis ripe, and will soon fall, if one will shake the Tree. [*Aside.*

Luc. Have you any Bus'ness with me, Sir ?
[*Comes nearer.*

Roeb. Yes, Madam, the Bus'ness of Mankind ; to adore you—My Love, like my Blood, circulates thro' my Veins, and at every Pulse of my Heart, animates me with a fresh Passion————Wonder not, Madam, at the Power of your Eyes, whose pointed Darts have struck on a young and tender Heart, which they easily pierced, and which, unaccustomed to such Wounds, finds the Smart more painful.

[*Lean.*

[*Lean. peeps.*] Oh Traytor! Juſt ſuch Words he ſpake to me.

Luc. Hey-day; I was never ſo attack'd in all my Life. In Love with me, Sir! Did you ever ſee me before?

Roeb. Never, by *Jove*——[*Aſide.*] Oh, ten thouſand Times, Madam. Your lovely Idea is always in my View, either aſleep or awake, eating or drinking, walking, ſitting or ſtanding; alone, or in Company, my Fancy wholly feeds upon your dear Image, and every Thought is you——Now have I told about fifteen Lyes in a Breath. [*Aſide.*

Luc. I ſuppoſe, Sir, you are ſome conceited young Scribbler, who has got the Benefits of a firſt Play in your Pocket, and are now going a Fortune-hunting.

Roeb. But why a Scribbler, Madam? Are my Cloaths ſo coarſe, as if they were ſpun by thoſe lazy Spinſters the Muſes? Does the Parting of my Fore-top ſhew ſo thin, as if it reſembled the two wither'd Tops of *Parnaſſus?* Do you ſee any thing peculiarly whimſical or ill-natur'd in my Face? Is my Countenance ſtrain'd, as if my Head were diſtorted by a Strangury of Thought? Is there any thing proudly, ſlovenly, or affectedly careleſs in my Dreſs? Do my Hands look like Paper-moths? I think, Madam, I have nothing poetical about me.

Luc. Yes, Sir, you have Wit enough to talk like a Fool; and are Fool enough to talk like a Wit.

Roeb. You call'd me Poet, Madam; and I know no better Way of Revenge, than to convince you that I am one by my Impudence—— [*Offers to kiſs her Hand.*

Luc. Then make me a Copy of Verſes upon that, Sir. [*Hits him on the Ear, and Exit.*

Leanthe *entering.*

How d'ye like the Subject, Sir?

Roeb. 'Tis a very copious one——[*Spitting.*]——It has made my Jolls rhime in my Head. This it is to be thought a Poet; every Minx muſt be caſting his Profeſſion in his Teeth.———What! Gone!

Lean. Ay, ſhe knows that making Verſes requires Solitude and Retirement.

Roeb. She certainly was afraid I intended to beg Leave to dedicate ſomething——If ever I make Love like a

Poetical

Fool again, may I never receive any Favour but
it for a Copy of Verses.

Re-enter Lucinda.

I won't difmifs him thus, for Fear he lampeen
-Well, Sir, have you done them?

Yes, Madam; will you pleafe to read?

[Catches her and kiffes her three or four Times.

Oh, Heaven! I can never bear it. I muft devife
leans to part 'em. *Exit.*

Sir, your Verfes are too rough and conftrain'd.
:r, becaufe I gave the Occafion, I'll pardon what's

;. By the Lord, fhe was angry only becaufe I did
ce the firft Offer to her Lips. *[Afide.]*——Then,
, the Peace is concluded?

Yes, and therefore both Parties fhould draw out
?ield. *[Going.*

Not till we make Reprizals. I make Peace with
in Hand, Madam; and till you return my Heart,
you have taken, or your own in Exchange, I will
t up. And fo, Madam, I proclaim open War
——————— . *[Catches her.*

Enter Leanthe.

. Oh, Madam! Yonder's poor little *Crab*, your
g, has got his Head between two of the Window-
ad is like to be ftrangled.

[The Dog howls behind the Scenes.

Oh Lard, my poor *Crabby!* I muft run to the
of my poor Dog; I'll wait on you inftantly.——
come, Page——Poor *Crabby!* *[Exit with* Leanthe.

. Oh the Devil choak *Crabby!*——Well, I find
much more Rhetoric in the Lips than the Tongue
Had Bufs been the firft Word of my Courtfhip. I
have gain'd the Out-works by this. Impudence in
s like Courage in War; tho' both blind Chances,
: Women and Fortune rule them.

Re-enter Leanthe.

. Sir, my Lady begs your Pardon; there's fome-
xtraordinary happen'd, which prevents her waiting
, as fhe promis'd.

. What, has Monfieur *Crabby* rubb'd fome of the
off his Neck? has he diforder'd his pretty Ears?
n't come again then?

Lean. No, Sir; you muſt excuſe her.

Roeb. Then I'll go and be drunk——Hark'e, Sirrah; I have half a Dozen delicious Creatures waiting for me at the *Sun*; you ſhall along with me and have your Choice. I'll enter you into the School of *Venus*, Child. 'Tis Time you had loſt your Maidenhead; you're too old for Play-things.

Lean. Oh Heavens! I had rather he ſhou'd ſtay than go there. [*Aſide.*] But why will you keep ſuch Company, Sir?

Roeb. Nay, if you're for Advice, farewel:

Men of ripe Underſtanding ſhou'd always deſpiſe
What Babes only practiſe, and Dotards adviſe.

[*Exit ſinging.*

Lean. Wild as Winds, and unconfin'd as Air.——Yet I may reclaim him. His Follies are weakly founded upon the Principles of Honour, where the very Foundation helps to undermine the Structure. How charming wou'd Virtue look in him, whoſe Behaviour can add a Grace to the Unſeemlineſs of Vice!

Enter Lucinda.

Luc. What, is the Gentleman gone?

Lean. Yes, Madam. He was inſtantly taken ill with a violent Pain in his Stomach, and was forc'd to hurry away in a Chair to his Lodging.

Luc. Oh poor Gentleman! He's one of thoſe conceited Fools that think no Female can reſiſt their Temptations. Blockheads, that imagine all Wit to conſiſt in blaſpheming Heav'n and Women.——I'll feed his Vanity, but ſtarve his Love.

And may all Coxcombs meet no better Fate,
Who doubt our Sex's Virtue, or dare prompt our Hate.

[*Exit.*

SCENE Lyrick's *Chamber in Widow* Bullfinch's *Houſe; Papers ſcatter'd about the Table, himſelf ſitting writing in a Night-Gown and Cap.*

Lyr. Two as good Lines as ever were written—[*riſing.*] I gad I ſhall maul theſe topping Fellows.——Says Mr. *Lee*,

Let there be not one Glimpſe, one ſtarry Spark,
But Gods meet Gods, and joſtle in the Dark.

Says

: *Lyrick,*

he Lights be burnt cut to a Snuff,
ds meet Gods, and play at Blindman's buff.
l!

s meet Gods, and so—fall out and cuff.

much mended. They're as noble Lines as ever
1'd. Oh! Here comes my damn'd Muse; I am
the Humour of writing Elegy after a little of
·ation.

Enter Bullfinch.

Ar. *Lyrick,* what do you mean by all this? Here
lodg'd two Years in my House, promis'd me
·pence a Week for your Lodging, and I have
iv'd eighteen Farthings; not the Value of that
k. [*Snaps with her Fingers.*] You alway· put me
elling me of your Play, your Play————Sir, you
no more with me, I'm in earnest.

his living on Love is the dearest Lodging—a
:rnally dunn'd, tho' perhaps he has less of one
in than t'other.————There's more Trouble
than you imagine, Madam.

:here's more Trouble with a Lodger than you
r. *Lyrick.*

irst, there's the Decorum of Time.

Thich you never observe; for you keep the worst
any Lodger in Town.

hen there's the Exactness of Characters.————

nd you have the most scandalous one I ever heard.

hen there's laying the Drama.

:hen you foul my Napkins and Towels.

hen there are Preparations of Incidents, working
ns, Beauty of Expression, Closeness of Plot, Just-
Place, Turn of Language, opening the Cata-

———

Then you wear out my Sheets, burn my Fire and
l:rty my House, eat my Meat, destroy my Drink,
my Furniture————I have lent you Money out
cket.

'as ever poor Rogue so ridden? If ever the
d a Horse, I am he.-————Faith, Madam, poor
jaded.

Bull.

Bull. Come, come, Sir, he fhan't flip his Neck out of the Collar for all that. Money I will have, and Money I muft have ; let your Play and you both be damn'd.

Lyr. Well. Madam, my Bookfeller is to bring me fome twenty Guineas for a few Sheets of mine prefently, which I hope will free me from your Sheets.

Bull. My Sheets, Mr. *Lyrick !* Pray what d'ye mean ? I'll affure you, Sir, my Sheets are finer than any of your Mufes fpinning —————— Marry come up.

Lyr. Faith you have fpun me fo fine, that you have almoft crack'd my Thread of Life, as may appear by my Spindle-fhanks.

Bull. Why fure——Where was your *Thalia,* and your *Melpomene,* when the Taylor wou'd have ftripped you of your Silk Waiftcoat, and have clapp'd you on a Stone Doublet ? Wou'd all your Golden Verfes have paid the Serjeant's Fees ?

Lyr. Truly, you freed me from Gaol, to confine me in a Dungeon ; you did not ranfom me, but bought me as a Slave ; fo, Madam, I'll purchafe my Freedom as foon as poffible. Flefh and Blood can't bear it.

Bull. Take your Courfe, Sir——There were a couple of Gentlemen juft now to enquire for you; and if they come again, they fha'n't be put off with the old Story of your being abroad, I'll promife you that, Sir.   [*Exit.*

Lyr. Zoons! If this Bookfeller does not bring me Money.——

Enter Pamphlet.

Oh! Mr. *Pamphlet,* your Servant. Have you perus'd my Poems ?

Pam. Yes, Sir; and there are fome things very well, extraordinary well, Mr. *Lyrick:* But I don't think 'em for my Purpofe————Poetry is a mere Drug, Sir.

Lyr. Is that becaufe I take Phyfic when I write ? —— Damn this coftive Fellow, now he does not apprehend the Joke.   [*Afide.*

Pam. No, Sir; but your Name does not recommend 'em. One muft write himfelf into a Confumption before he gain Reputation.

Lyr. That's the Way to lie abed when his Name's up. Now I lie abed before I can gain Reputation.

Pam. Why fo, Sir ?

Lyr.

Becaufe I have fcarcely any Cloaths to put on——
Man did Penance in a white Sheet——

You ftand only fometimes in a white Sheet for
ences with your Landlady. Faith, I have often
d how your Mufe cou'd take fuch Flights, yoak'd
a Cart-load as fhe is.

Oh! they are like the *Irifh* Horfes, they draw beft
Tail—Have you ever feen any of my Burlefque,
mphlet? I have a Project of turning three or
our moft topping Fellows in Doggrel. As for
:;—— [*Reads.*

ft with Laurels has our Arms adorn'd,
ome in Tears of Blood our Anger mourn'd.
utchers with Rofemary have our Beef adorn'd,
has in Gravy Tears our Hunger mourn'd.

re like it, Mr. *Pamphlet*, ha?——Well——

'ods, we pafs'd the rugged Alpine *Hills;*
l our way, and drove our hiffing Wheels;
cloudy Deluges, eternal Rills.

ferve, Mr. *Pamphlet*; pray obferve.

'azors keen, our Knives cut Paffage clean
gh Rills of Fat, and Deluges of Lean.

Very well, upon my Soul.

Hurl'd dreadful Fire, and Vinegar infus'd.

Ay, Sir, Vinegar! how patly that comes in for
; Mr. *Lyrick!* 'Tis all wondrous fine indeed.
This is the moft ingenious Fellow of his Trade
ve feen; he underftands a good thing.——[*Afide.*]
: as to our Bus'nefs——What are you willing to
thefe Poems? Prithee fay fomething. There are
ree thoufand Lines.——Here, take 'em for a
f Guineas.

No, Sir; Paper is fo exceffive dear, that I dare
ure upon 'em.

Well, becaufe you're a Friend, I'll beftow 'em
u.——Here, take 'em all——There's the Hopes
lication ftill. [*Afide.*

I give you a thoufand Thanks, Sir; but I dare
ure the Hazard; they'll never quit Coft, indeed,

Lyr. This Fellow is one of the greateſt Blockheads that ever was a Member of a Corporation———How ſhall I be reveng'd?

Enter Boy.

Boy. Sir, there are two Men below deſire to have the Honour of kiſſing your Hand.

Lyr. They muſt be Knaves or Fools by their fulſome Compliment. Hark ye———[*Wiſpers the Boy.*]———Bid 'em walk up.

Pam. Since you have got Company, Sir, I'll take my Leave.

Lyr. No, no, Mr. *Pamphlet*, by no means! We muſt drink before we part. Boy, a Pint of Sack and a Toaſt. Theſe are two Gentlemen out of the Country, who will be for all the new things lately publiſhed; they'll be good Cuſtomers———Come, ſit down———You have not ſeen my Play yet———Here, take the Pen, and if you ſee any thing amiſs, correct it: I'll go bring 'em up.———Stay, lend me your Hat and Wig, or I ſhall take cold going down Stairs. [*He takes* Pamphlet's *Hat and Wig, and puts his Cap on* Pamphlet's *Head.*

Pam. [*Solus.*] This is a right Poetical Cap; 'tis Baize the Outſide, and the Lining Fuſtain———[*Reading.*]——— This is all Stuff, worſe than his Poems.

Enter two Bailiffs behind him, and clap him on the Shoulder.

1ſt Bail. You're the King's Priſoner.

Pam. That's a good Fancy enough, Mr. *Lyrick.* But pray don't interrupt me, I m in the beſt Scene.——— I gad the Drama is very well laid.

2d Bail. Come, Sir.

Pam. Well, well, Sir, I'll pledge ye. Prithee now, good Mr. *Lyrick*, don't diſturb me.———

And furious Lightnings brandiſh'd in her Eyes.

That's true Spirit of Poetry.

1ſt Bail. Zoons, Sir, d'ye banter us?

[*Takes him under each Arm, and hauls him up.*

Pam. Gentlemen———I beg your Pardon. How d'ye like the City, Gentlemen? If you have any occaſion for Books to carry into the Country, I can furniſh you as well as any Man about *Paul's.* Where's Mr. *Lyrick?*

1ſt Bail.

1st Bail. Thefe Wits are damnable cunning. I always have double Fees for arrefting one of you Wits. All your Evafions won't do; we underftand Trap, Sir; you muft not think to catch old Birds with Chaff, Sir.

Pam. Zoons, Gentlemen, I'm not the Perfon! I'm a Freeman of the City; I have good Effects, Gentlemen; good Effects. D'ye think to make a Fool of me! I'm a Bookfeller, no Poet.

2d Bail. Ah, Sir, we know what you are by your Fool's Cap there.

1st Bail. Yes, one of you Wits wou'd have paf'd upon us for a Corn-cutter yefterday; and was fo like one, we had almoft believ'd him.   [*Hauls him.*

Pam. Why Gentlemen, Gentlemen, Officers, have a little Patience, and Mr. *Lyrick* will come up Stairs.

1st Bail. No, no; Mr. *Lyrick* fhall go down Stairs. He wou'd have us wait till fome Friends come in to refcue him. Ah! Thefe Wits are devilifh cunning.
                              [*Exeunt, hauling Pamphlet.*

Enter Lyrick, Mockmode, *and* Club; Lyrick *dreſs'd.*

Lyr. Ha, ha, ha! Very poetical, faith; a good Plot for a Play, Mr. *Mockmode*; a Bookfeller bound in Calves Leather———Ha, ha, ha!——How they walk'd along like the three Volumes of the *Englifh Rogue* fqueez'd together on a Shelf.

Mock. What was it? What was it, Mr. *Lyrick?*

Lyr. Why, I am a Statefman, Sir.——I can't but laugh, to think how they'll fpunge the Sheet before the Errata be blotted out; and then how he'll hamper the Dogs for falfe Imprifonment.

Mock. But pray, what's the Matter, Mr. *Lyrick?*

Lyr. Nothing, Sir, but a fharking Bookfeller that ow'd me about forty Guineas for a few Lines. He wou'd have put me off, fo I fent for a couple of Bull-dogs, and arrefted him.

Mock. Oh Lard! Mr. *Lyrick*, Honefty's quite out of Doors; 'tis a rare thing to find a Man that's a true Friend; a true Friend is a rare thing indeed!——Mr. *Lyrick*, will you be my Friend? I only want that Accomplifhment. I have got a Miftrefs, a Dancing and Fencing Mafter; and now I want only a Friend to be a Fine Gentleman.

Lyr. Have you never had a Friend, Sir?

Mock.

You ... a very ... Fellow: our Friendſhip com-
... ... and we lov'd one another
... ... we ... fell out afterwards at
... ...

... ... of ye int by the Set.—
... ... can't recommend me
... ...

... ... —You ... be a Man of
... ... a ... Sir.

... ... me ... was ... of a Friend, Sir?
... That ... tell ... serves m. and be my Second.—
Now, Sir, ... We ... ... tell in eng a Secret, becauſe
... ... a ... ... Prejudice will ... thought Malice.
... ... of Courage by your
... ... —

... ... I ... am King of Me.
... ... be a plaguy
... ... Enſſn when I read

... Sir ... ... of what we write as little as Divines
... ... —Beſides, Sir, there are other
... ... of a Friend; he muſt lend you Mo-
... Now, ... me taſte Friend, for I want forty
Guineas.

... Sir, I am here ... fifty upon good Security.—
Those ... ... Words my Father ſpoke on his Death-bed,
... I ... a never lend Money without Security.

... Fie, Sir. Security from a Friend, and a Man of
Honour as an Protection too!

Mrs. By the Univerſe, that's true, you are my Friend.
Then I'll tell you a Secret—   [They whiſper.

Cla. Now will this plaguy Wit turn my Noſe out of
Joint.—I was my Mother's Friend before, tho' I never
found the Shock of borrowing Money; tho' I have receiv'd ſome Marks of his Friendſhip, ſome ſound Drubs
about the Head and Shoulders, or ſo. I have been bound
for him too in the Stocks, for his breaking Windows
very often.

... Mr. Mockmode, you may be impos'd upon. I
... this Lady you court. I know Mr. Lovewell
... nam'd Lucinda; but that ſhe lodges in this
much doubt.

                                                    Mock.

Mock. Impos'd upon! that's very comical.—Ha, ha, ha! You shall see, Sir; come—Pray, Sir, you're my Friend.

Lyr. Nay, pray, indeed, Sir, I beg your [*They compliment for the Door.*] Pardon; you're a 'Squire, Sir.

Mock. Zauns, Sir, you lie; I'm not a Fool; I'll take an Affront from no Man.—Draw, Sir. [*Draws.*

Club. Draw, Sir.———I gad I'll put his Nose out of Joint now.

Lyr. Unequal Numbers, Gentlemen.

Club. I'm only my Master's Friend, his Second, or so, Sir.

Lyr. What's the Matter, noble 'Squire?

Mock You lie again, Sir: Zauns, draw. [*Strikes him with his Sword.*

Lyr. Ha! a Blow!———*Essex*, a Blow——yet I will be calm.

Club. Zoons, draw Sir. [*Strikes him.*

Lyr. Oh Patience, Heaven!—Thou art my Friend still.

Mock. You lie, Sir.

Lyr. Then thou art a Traitor, Tyrant, Monster.

Mock. Zauns, Sir, you're a Son of a Whore, and a Rascal.

Club. A Scribbler.

Lyr. Ah, ah———That stings home.——Scribbler?

Mock. Ay, Scribbler, Ballad-maker.

Lyr. Nay then———I and the Gods will fight it with ye all. [*Draws.*

Enter Roebuck *drunk and singing.*

France *ne'er will comply*
Till her Claret runs dry ;
Then let's pull away to defeat her :
He hinders the Peace,
Who refuses his Glass,
And deserves to be hang'd for a Traitor.

Now, my Mirmidons, fall on; I have taken off the Odds.

Dub a dub, dub a dub, to the Battle. [*Sings.*

Zoons, Gentlemen, why don't you fight? Blood, fight. Oblige me so far to fight a little; I long to see a little Sport.

Lyr. Sir, I scorn to shew Sport to any Man. [*Puts up.*
Mock.

Mock. And so do I, by the Universe.

Club. And I, by the Universe.

Lyr. I shall take another Time.   [*Exit.*

Roeb. Here, Rascal, take your Chopping-knife———
[*Gives* Club *his Sword.*] and bring me a Joint of that
Coward's Flesh for your Master's Supper——Fly, Dog.
[*Takes him by the Nose.*

Club. Ah———This Fellow's likeliest to put my
Nose out of Joint.

Roeb. Now, Sir, tell me, how you durst be a Coward.

Mock. Coward, Sir? I'm a Man of a great Estate.
Sir; I have five Thousand Acres of good fighting Ground
as any in *England*, good *Terra firma*, Sir: Coward, Sir!
Have a Care what you say, Sir———My Father was
a Parliament Man, Sir; and I was bred at the College,
Sir.

Roeb. O then I know your Genealogy; your Father
was a Senior-Fellow, and your Mother was an Air-pump.
You were suckled by *Platonic* Ideas, and you have some
of your Mother's Milk in your Nose yet.

Mock. From the Proposition by Mode and Figure, Sir.

Roeb. I told you so———Blow your Nose, Child;
and have a Care of dirtying your Philosophical Slabber-
ing-Bib.

Mock. What d'ye mean, Sir?

Roeb. Your starch'd Band, set by Mode and Figure,
Sir.

Mock. Band, Sir!——This Fellow's blind drunk. I
wear a Cravat, Sir.

Roeb. Then set a good Face upon the Matter. Throw
off Childishness and Folly, with your Hanging-sleeves.
Now you have left the University, learn, learn.

Mock. This Fellow's an Atheist, by the Universe!
I'll take Notice of him, and inform against him for
being drunk.——Pray, Sir, what's your Name?

Roeb. My Name! by the Lord, I have forgot———
Stay, I shall think on't by and by.

Mock. Zauns, forget your own Name! your Memory
must be very short, Sir.

Roeb. Ay, so it seems, for I was but christen'd this
Morning, and I have forgot it already.

Mock.

Mock. Was your Worſhip then *Turk* or *Jew* before?—
I knew he was ſome damn'd bloody Dog.　　*[Aſide.*

Roeb. Sir, I have been *Turk,* or *Jew* rather, ſince ;
for I have got a plaguy Heatheniſh Name—Pox on't :
—Oh! now I have it——*Mo*—*Mock-mo*——*Mockmode.*

Mock. Mockmode! Mockmode ! Sir, pray how do you
ſpell it ?

Roeb. Go you to your A, B, C, you came laſt from the
Univerſity.

Mock. I'm call'd *Mockmode.*——What Family are
you of, Sir ?

Roob. What Family are you of, Sir ?

Mock. Of *Mockmode-Hall* in *Shropſhire.*

Roeb. Then I'm of the ſame, I believe.——I fancy,
Sir, that you and I are near Relations.

Mock. Relations! Sir, there are but two Families :
my Father's, who is now dead ; and his Brother Colonel
Peaceable Mockmode.

Roeb. Ay, ay, the very ſame Colonel *Peaceable*——
Is not he Colonel of *Militia ?*

Mock. Yes, Sir.

Roeb. And was not he High-Sheriff of the County
laſt Year ?

Mock. The very ſame, Sir.

Roeb. The very ſame : I'm of that Family.——And
your Father dy'd about ——let me ſee——

Mock. About half a Year ago.

Roeb. Exactly ; by the ſame Token you got drunk at
a Hunting Match that very Day ſeven-night he was
bury'd.

Mock. This Fellow's a Witch——But it looks very
ſtrange that you ſhou'd be chriſten'd this Morning.
I'm ſure your Godfathers had a plaguy deal to anſwer for.

Roeb. Oh, Sir, I'm of Age to anſwer for myſelf.

Mock. One would not think ſo, you're ſo forgetful.
'Tis two and twenty Years ſince I was chriſten'd, and I
can remember my Name ſtill.

Roeb. Come, we'll take a Glaſs of Wine, and that
will clear our Underſtanding. We'll remember our
Friends.

Mock. You muſt excuſe me, Sir——This is ſome
Sharper.　　　　　　　　　　　　　　　　*[Aſide*
　　　　　　　　　　　　　　　　　　　Roeb.

Roeb. Nay, prithee, Coufin, good Coufin *Mockmode*, one Glafs. I know you are an honeft Fellow. We muft remember our Relations in the Country indeed, Sir.

Mock. Oh Sir, you're fo fhort of Memory, you can never call 'em to mind. You have forgot yourfelf, Sir; *Mockmode* is a heathenifh Name, Sir; and all that, Sir. And fo I beg your Pardon, Sir. ——— [*Exit.*

Roeb. Now were I Lawyer enough, by that little Enquiry into that Fellow's Concerns, I could bring in a falfe Deed to cheat him of his Eftate.

Enter Brufh.

Where the Devil is thy Mafter! You faid I fhou'd find him here,

Brufh. 'Tis impoffible for you or me, or any body to find him.

Roeb. Why?

Brufh. Becufe he has loft himfelf. The Devil has made a Juggler's Ball of him, I believe. He's here now; then, *Præfto*, pafs in an Inftant. He has got fome damn'd Bufinefs to-Day in hand.

Roeb. Ah, fo it feems——I muft be 'Squire *Mockmode*, and court an honourable Miftrefs, in the Devil's Name! Well, let my fober thinking Friend plot on, and lay Traps to catch Futurity; I'm for holding faft to the prefent.———I have got about twenty Guineas in my Pocket; and whilft they laft, the Devil take *George* if he thinks of Futurity; I'll go hand in hand with Fortune.

She is an honeft, giddy, reeling Punk;
My Head, her Wheel, turn round, and fo we both are drunk.
[*Exit reeling.*

The End of the Third Act.

ACT IV.

SCENE, Lucinda's *Houfe.*

Enter Leanthe, *and* Pindrefs *following with a Paper of Sweetmeats in her Hand.*

Pind. HERE, here, Page, your Lady has fent you fome Sweetmeats; but indeed you fha'nt have 'em till you hire me.

Lean.

She sent sour Sauce, when she made you the

[*Aside.*

Prithee now, what makes you constantly so
oly? Come. you must be merry, and shall be
I'll get you some Play-things.

I believe you want Play-things more than I. ——
ou'd be private, *Pindress.*

Well, my Child, I'll be private with you!
d Girls shou'd still be private together; and we
as retir'd as we please; for my Mistress is reader Closet, and all the Servants are below.———

at Concerns have you? I'm sure, such a little
have no great Business in private.

I will try thee for once—[*Aside.*]—Yes, Mrs.
I have great Inclinations——

To what? To do what, Sir?—Don't name
'Tis all in vain;——you shan't do it; you need
it.

Only to kiss you.   [*Kisses her.*

Oh fie, Sir! Indeed I'll have none of your Kisses.
back again. [*Kisses him.*] Is not the Taste of the
eats very pretty about my Lips?

Oh hang your liquorish Chaps: you'd fain be
your Lips, I find that.

Indeed, Mr. *Page,* I won't pay you the Kisses
from me last Night at Cross-purposes; and you
hink to keep my Pawn neither.——Pray give me
gary Bottle—As I hope to be sav'd, I will have
gary Bottle—[*Rummaging him*]——I'm stronger
a——I'll carry you in, and throw you upon the
d take it from you.——[*Takes him up in her Arms.*

Help! help! I shall be ravish'd! Help! help!

Enter Lucinda.

What's the Matter? Oh bless me!

Oh dear, Madam, this unlucky Boy had almost
me. Did not your Ladyship hear me cry, I
e ravish'd? I was so weak, I cou'd not resist the
ong Rogue; he whipt me up in his Arms, like
and had not your Ladyship come in——

What, Sirrah! wou'd you debauch my Maid,
e Cock-Sparrow? must you be Billing too? I
reat mind to make her whip you, Sirrah.

Pind.

Pind. O, dear Madam, let me do't. I will take him into the Room, and I will fo chaſtiſe him———

Luc. But do you think you'll be able, *Pindreſs ?* I'll fend one of my Men to help you.

Pind. No, no, Madam : I cou'd manage him with one Hand. ——— See here, Madam.

　　　　　[*Takes him in her Arms, and is running away.*

Luc. Hold, hold ! Is this you that the little ſtrong Rogue had almoſt raviſh'd ? He ſnatch'd you up in his Arms like a Baby ! Ah *Pindreſs ! Pindreſs !* I ſee y'are very weak indeed.———Are not you aſham'd, Girl, to debauch my little Boy ?

Pind. Your Ladyſhip gave me Orders to make him merry, and divert his Melancholy : and I know no better Way than to teaze him a little. I'm afraid the Boy is troubled with the Rickets, and a little ſhaking wou'd do him ſome good.

Lean. I'm tir'd with Impertinence, and have other Buſineſs to mind.　　　　　　　　　[*Aſide,* Exit.

Pind. I hope your Ladyſhip entertains no ill Opinion of my Virtue.

Luc. Truly I don't know what to think on't : But I've ſo good an Opinion of your Senſe, as to believe you wou'd not play the Fool with a Child.

Pind. We're all ſubjeƈt to playing the Fool, if you continue your Reſolution in marrying the firſt Man that aſks you the Queſtion.

Luc. No, my Mind's chang'd ; I'll never marry any Man.

Pind. I dare ſwear that Reſolution breaks ſooner than the former. [*Aſide.*] Ah, Madam, Madam ! if you never believe Man again, you muſt never be Woman again ; for tho' we are as cunning as Serpents, we are naturally as flexible too. Speak ingenuouſly, Madam ; if Mr. *Lovewell* ſhou'd, with an amorous Whine, and ſuppliant Cringe, tell you a formal Story, contrary to what we ſuſpeƈt, would you not believe him ?

Luc. What, believe his vain Aſſertions, before the Demonſtration of my Senſes ! No, no ; my Love's not ſo blind. Did I not ſee his Miſs and his Child ? Did I not behold him giving her Money ? Did I not hear him declare, he would ſettle her in a Lodging ?

　　　　　　　　　　　　　　　　　　Pind.

d. But, Madam, upon ſerious Reflection, where's
reat Harm in all this? Moſt Ladies wou'd be over-
at ſuch a Diſcovery of their Lover's Ability. The,
ſeem'd a luſty chopping Boy; and let me tell you,
m, it muſt be a luſty chopping Boy that got it.

. Urge no farther in his Defence; he's a Villain,
f all Villains I hate moſt an hypocritical one. The
s gives him the Epithet of modeſt, and the Gen-
n that of ſober *Lovewell.* Now methinks, ſuch a
of Debauchery fits ſo aukwardly on a Perſon of
haracter, that it adds an Unſeemlineſs to the natu-
ileneſs of the Vice; and he that dares to be a Hy-
:e in Religion, will certainly be one in Love.——
is not that he? *[Pointing outwards.*
d. Yes, Madam; I believe he is going to the

. Call a couple of Chairs quickly: we'll thither
ied. This Day's Adventures argue ſome intended
ipon me, which I may countermine by only ſetting
: upon the Matter. *[Puts her Maſque on.*

qs *Hypocriſy in Men can move,*
's *the beſt Hypocrite in female Love.*
even *Scores deſigning Heaven took care,*
:e *Men falſe Hearts, that we falſe Faces wear.*

[Exeunt

SCENE, *the Park.*

ter Lovewell *and* Lyrick *meeting;* Lyrick *reading.*

rack *thy Reputation, blaſt thy Fame,*
l *in ſtrong grinding Satire, gibbet up thy Name.*

e. What! in a Rapture, Mr. *Lyrick?*
. A little poetical Fury, that's all.————I'll
e him; I'll draw his Character for the Buffoon of.
ce; he ſhall be as famous in Ballad as *Robin*
or *Little John:* My Muſes ſhall haunt him like
s; they ſhall make him more ridiculous than *Don*

e. Becauſe he encounter'd your Windmill-Pate.——
——Ha, ha, ha!——Come, come, Mr. *Lyrick,* you
)e pacify'd.

Lyr.

Lyr. Pacify'd, Sir! Zoons, Sir, he's a Fool, and has not a grain of Senſe. Were he an ingenious Fellow, or a Man of Parts, I cou'd bear a Kicking from him: But an Abuſe from a Blockhead! I can never ſuffer it.

> *Pert Blockhead, who has purchas'd by the School,*
> *Juſt Senſe enough to make a noted Fool.*

That ſtings, Mr. *Lovewell.*

Love. Pray, Sir, let me ſee it.

Lyr. This is imperfect, Sir; But if you pleaſe to give your Judgment on this Piece.—[*Gives him a Paper.*] 'Tis a Burleſque on ſome of our late Writings.

Love. Ay, you Poets mount firſt on the Shoulders of your Predeceſſors, to ſee farther in making Diſcoveries; and having once got the upper-hand, you ſpurn them under-foot. I think you ſhou'd bear a Veneration to their very Aſhes.

Lyr. Ay, if moſt of their Writings had been burnt! I delare, Mr. *Lovewell,* their Fame has only made them the more remarkably faulty: Their great Beauties only illuſtrate their greater Errors.

Love. Well, you ſaw the new Tragedy laſt Night; how did it pleaſe ye?

Lyr. Very well; it made me laugh heartily.

Love. What, laugh at a Tragedy!

Lyr. I laugh to ſee the Ladies cry; to ſee ſo many weep at the Death of the fabulous Hero: Who wou'd but laugh, if the Poet that made 'em were hang'd! On my Conſcience, theſe Tragedies make the Ladies vent all their Love and Honour at their Eyes, when the ſame white Handkerchief that blows their Noſes, muſt be a Winding-Sheet to the deceaſed Hero.

Love. Then there's ſomething in the Handkerchief to embalm him. Mr. *Lyrick;* Ha, ha, ha!——But what Reliſh have you of Comedy?

Lyr. No ſatisfactory one.——My Curioſity is fore-ſtall'd by a Fore-knowledge of what ſhall happen: For as the Hero in Tragedy is either a whining, cringing Fool, that's always a ſtabbing himſelf; or a ranting, hectoring Bully, that's for killing every body elſe: ſo the Hero in Comedy is always the Poet's Character.

Love. What's that?

Lyr.

. A Compound of practical Rake, and speculative
eman, who always bears off the great Fortune in
ay, and shams the Beau and 'Squire with a Whore or
bermaid; and as the Catastrophe of all Tragedies
ath, so the End of Comedies is Marriage.

ε. And some think that the most Tragical Con-
a of the two.

. And therefore my Eyes are diverted by a better
dy in the Audience, than that upon the Stage.—I
ften wonder'd, why Men should be fond of seeing
ill represented, when, at the same Time and Place,
may behold the mighty Originals acting their
to the Life in their Boxes.————

ε. Oh, be favourable to the Ladies, Mr. *Lyrick*;
your Interest. Beauty is the Deity of Poetry; and
i rebel, you'll certainly run the Fate of your first
: the Devil.

. You're out, Sir. Beauty is a merciful Deity,
llows us sometimes to be a little Atheistical: and
ɔ indulgent to Wit, that it is pleas'd with it, tho'
: worst Habit, that of Satire. Besides, there can
r no greater Argument of our Esteem, than Rail-
becaufe it is still founded upon Jealousy; occasion'd
eir preferring senseless Fops, and wealthy Fools,
n of Wit and Merit, the great Upholders of the
·e.

ε. Now I think these Favourites of the Ladies are
witty than you.

. How so, pray, Sir?

ε. Becaufe they play the Fool, conscious that it
leafe; and you're a Wit, when sensible that Cox-
ι only are encourag'd. I wonder, Mr. *Lyrick*, that
n of your Sense shou'd turn Poet; you'll hardly
ind a Man that is capable of the Employment will
take it.

. The Reason of that is, every one that knows not
ɟe of the Matter, pretends to be a Judge of it.————
e Lard, Mr. *Loveavell*, I put the Critics next
: Plague, Pestilence, and Famine, in my Litany.—
ɣoo feen 'em last Night in the Pit, with such demure
cilious Faces————their contemplative Wigs thrust
iously backwards; their Hands rubbing their Temples,

ples, to chafe Ill-nature; and with a hiffing venomous
Tongue, pronouncing Pifh! Stuff! Intolerable! Damn
him!———Lord have Mercy upon us!

Love. Ay, and you fhall have others as foolifh as they
are ill-natur'd; fond of being thought Wits, who fhall
laugh outrageoufly at every fmutty Jeft; cry very well,
by Gad; that's fine by Heavens; and if a Diftich of Rhime
happens, they clap fo loud, that they drown the Jeft.

Lyr. That's the Jeft. The Wit lies in their Hands;
and if you would tell a Poet his Fortune, you muft ga-
ther it from the Palmiftry of the Audience; for as nothing's ill faid, but what's ill taken; fo nothing's well
faid, but what's well taken. And between you and I,
Mr. *Lovewell*, Poetry, without thefe laughing Fools,
were a Bell without a Clapper; an empty founding Bufinefs, good for nothing; and all we Profeffors might go
hang ourfelves in the Bell ropes.

Love. Ha, ha, ha!———But I thought Poetry was inftructive.

Lyr. Oh, Gad forgive me, that's true: To Ladies
it is morally beneficial; for you muft know, they are
too nice to read Sermons; fuch Inftructions are too grofs
for their refin'd Apprehenfions; but any Precepts that
may be inftill'd by eafy Numbers, fuch as of *Rochefter*,
and others, make great Converts. Then they hate to
hear a Fellow in a Church preach methodical Nonfenfe,
with a *Firftly, Secondly,* and *Thirdly:* But they take up
with fome of our modern Plays in their Clofet, where the
Morality muft be devilifh inftructive———But I muft be
gone; here comes the 'Squire. What, in the Name of
Wonder, has he got with him!

Love. That which fhall afford you a more plentiful Revenge than your Lampoon, if you join with me in the
Plot. To the better effecting of which, you muft be
feemingly reconciled to him.———Let's ftep afide, and obferve 'em, while I give you a Hint of the Matter.

[*Exeunt between the Scenes, and feem to confer and
hearken.*

Enter Mockmode, *leading* Trudge *drefs'd like a Widow.*

Mock. This is very fine Weather, bleffed Weather indeed, Madam; 'twill do Abundance of Good to the Grafs
and Corn.

Trud.

Trud. Ay, Sir, the Days are grown a great length; nd I think the Weather much better here than in *Ireland*.

Mock. Why, Madam, were you ever there?

Trud. Oh, no! Not I indeed, Sir; but I have heard ny firſt Huſband (reſt his Soul) ſay ſo; he was an *Iriſh* Gentleman.

Mock. I find, Madam, you have lov'd your firſt Huſband mightily, for you affect his Tone in Diſcourſe.—— 'ray, Madam, what did that Mourning coſt a Yard?

Trua. O, Lard! What ſhall I ſay now? 'Tis none of nine. [*Aſide*] It coſt, Sir; let me ſee————it coſt about ————but it was my Steward bought it for me; I never ſay ſuch ſmall Things.

Mock. By the Univerſe, ſhe muſt be plaguy rich! I will ſe briſk. [*Aſide.*] Pray, Madam——I——I pray, Madam, vill you give us a Song?

Trud. A Song! Indeed then I had a good Voice, before Mr. *Roebuck* ſpoil'd it.

Mock. Mr. *Roebuck!* Was that your firſt Huſband's Name, Madam?

Love. behind. She'll ſpoil all.

Trud. No, Sir; *Roebuck* was a Doctor that let me Blood under the Tongue for the Quinſey, and made me hoarſe ever ſince.

Mock. By the Univerſe ſhe's a Widow, and I'll be a little briſk. Madam, will you grant me a ſmall Favour, and I will bend upon my Knees to receive it.——[*Kneels.*

Trud. What is it, pray?

Mock. Only to take off your Garter.

Lovewell *enters.*

Love. Zoons, her thick Leg will diſcover all—By your Leave, Sir, have you any Pretenſions to this Lady?

[*Puſhes* Mockmode *down.*

Mock. I don't know whether this be an Affront or not. —[*Aſide.*]——Pretenſions, Sir! I have ſo great a Veneration for the Lady, that I honour any Man that has Pretenſions to her.—Dem me, Sir, may I crave the Honour of your Acquaintance?

Love. No, Sir.

Mock. No, Sir! I gad that muſt be Wit, for it can't be good Manners.——Sir, I reſpect all Men of Senſe, and wou'd therefore beg to know your Name.

Love.

Love. No Matter, Sir ; I know your Name's *Mockmede*

Mock. By the Univerfe, that's very comical ! that a Fellow fhould pretend to tell me my own Name !——Another Queftion if you pleafe, Sir.

Love. What is it, Sir ?

Mock. Pray Sir, what's my Chriften'd Name ?

Love. Sir, you don't know.

Mock. Zauns, Sir, would you perfuade me out of my Chriften'd Name ? I'll lay you a Guinea that I do know, by the Univerfe——[*Pulls a handful of Money out*] Here's Silver, Sir ; here's Silver, Sir : I can command as much Money as another, Sir ; I am at Age, Sir ; and I won't be banter'd, Sir.

Love. Sir, you muft know, that I baptize you Rival; for your Love to this Lady is the only Sign of Chriftianity you can boaft of.—And now, Sir, my Name's *Lovewell.*

Mock. Then I fay, Sir, that your Love to that Lady is the only Sign of a *Turk* you can brag of.——I wifh *Club* were come.   [*Afide.*

Love. Sir, I fhall certainly circumcife you, if you make any fahther Pretenfions to Madam *Lucinda* here.

Mock. Circumcife me ! Circumcife a Pudding's End, Sir.——Zauns, Sir, I'll be judged by the Lady, who merits Circumcifion moft, you or I, Sir. Thefe *London* Blades are all ftark mad. [*Lucinda enters; and obferves Lovewell courting Trudge in dumb Signs.*] I met one about two Hours ago, that had forgot his Name, and this Fellow wou'd perfuade me now, that I had forgot mine. Mr. *Lyrick* is the only Man that fpeaks plain to me. I muft be Friends with him, becaufe I find I may have Occafion for fuch a Friend ; I'll find him out ftrait.   [*Exit.*

Love. Madam, will you walk—[*Exit with* Trudge.

      Lucinda *and* Pindrefs *come forward.*

Luc. Now my Doubts are remov'd.

Pind. Mine are more puzzling. There muft be fomething in this more than we imagine. You had beft to talk with him.

Luc. Yes, if my Tongue bore Poifon in it, and that I could fpit Death in his Face.

Pind. If he is loft, your hard Ufage this Morning has occafion'd it.

Luc. I am glad on't; I've gain'd by the Lofs; I de-
ife him more now than ever I lov'd him. That Paffion
iich can ftoop fo low as that Blowze, is an Object too
ean for any Thing but my Scorn to level at.

Pind. This were a critical Minute for your new Lover
e 'Squire, I fancy; Mr. *Lovewell*'s Difgrace wou'd
ing him into Favour prefently.

Luc. It certainly fhall, if he be not as great a Fool as
)ther's falfe.

Pind. You may be miftaken in your Opinion of him,
much as you have been in Mr. *Lovewell.*

Luc. No, *Pindrefs*; I fhall find what I read in the laft
ifcellanies very true:

But two Diftinctions their whole Sex does part;
All Fools by Nature, or all Rogues by Art.

SCENE *continues.*

ter feveral Mafques croffing the Stage, and Roebuck *fol-*
lowing.

Roeb. 'Sdeath; What a Coney-borough's here! The
rade goes fwimmingly on. This is the great Empory
Lewdnefs, as the Change is of Knavery.——The Mer-
ints cheat the World there, and their Wives gull them
re.——I begin to think Whoring fcandalous, it is
own fo mechanical.——My Modefty will do me no
)od; I fear——Madam, are you a Whore?
                                    [*Catches a Mafque.*
1ft *Maf.* Yes, Sir.

Roeb. Short and Pithy.——If ever Woman fpake
ruth, I believe thou haft.   [*Second Mafque pulls him by*
e *Elbow.*] Have you any Bufinefs with me, Madam?
:ad *Maf.* Pray, Sir, be civil; you're miftaken, Sir-
have had an Eye upon this Fellow all this Afternoon.
(*fide*)—You're miftaken, Sir

Roeb. Very likely, Madam; for I imagin'd you modeft.
2d *Maf.* So I am, for I'm marry'd.

Roeb. And marry'd to your Sorrow; I warrant you!
2d *Maf.* Yes, upon my Honour, Sir.

Roeb. I knew it. I have met above a Dozen this Even-
g all marry'd to their Sorrow——Then I fuppofe.
VOL. I.   H   you're

you're a Citizen's Wife; and by the Broadness of your Bottom, I shou'd guess you sat very much behind a Counter.

2d Maf. My Husband's no Mercer, he's a Judge.

Roeb. Zoons, a Judge; I shall be arraign'd at the Bar for keeping on my Hat so long——'Tis very hard, Madam, he should not do you Justice: Has not he an Estate in Tail, Madam?

2d Maf. I seldom examine his Papers: They are a Parcel of old dry shrivell'd Parchments; and this Court-hand is so devilish crabbed, I can't endure it.

Roeb. Umph!——Then I suppose, Madam, you want a young Lawyer to put your Case to: But sure, Madam, I am a Judge too.

Enter Lovewell.

2d Maf. O, Heavens forbid! such a young Man!

Roeb. That is, I'll do nothing without a Bribe.—— Pray, Madam, how does the Watch strike?

2d Maf. It never strikes, it only points to the Business, as you must do, without telling Tales. Dare ye meet me two Hours hence?

Roeb. Ah, Madam, but I shall never hit the Time exactly without a Watch.

2d Maf. Well, take it.——At Ten exactly, at the Fountain in the *Middle-Temple*. *Cook upon Littleton* be the Word.

Roeb. So——If the Law be all such Volumes as these, Mercy on the poor Students! From *Cook upon Littleton* in Sheets deliver me.

Love. What, engag'd? *Myrmidon!* I find you'll never quit the Battle, till you have crack'd a Pike in the Service.

Roeb. Oh, dear Friend! Thou'rt critically come to my Relief; for faith I'm almost tir'd.

Love. What a miserable Creature is a Whore! whom every Fool dares pretend to love, and every wise Man hates.

Roeb. What? Moralizing again! Oh, I'll make thee a Man: I'm enter'd in the Inns, by the Lord!

Love. Pshaw!

Roeb. Nay, if you won't believe me, see my Bond of Admission, in Oil——[*Shews the Watch.*

Love. A Gold Watch! Boy!

Roeb.

Roeb. Ay, a Gold Watch, Boy.

Love. Whence had you Money to buy it?

Roeb. I took it upon Tick, and I defign to pay honeftly.

Love. I don't like this running o'th' Score.——But what ews from *Lucinda,* Boy? is fhe kind? Ha?

Enter a Mafque croffing the Stage.

Roeb. Ha! there's a ftately Cruifer; I muft give her ne Chace——I'll tell you when I return. [*Exit running.*

Love. I find he has been at a Lofs there, which occa- ous his Eagernefs for the Game here. I begin to repent e of my Sufpicion; I believe her Virtue fo facred, that is a Piece of Atheifm to diftruft its Exiftence. But Jea- ufy in Love, like the Devil in Religion, is ftill raifing oubts, which, without a firm Faith in what we adore, ill certainly damn us.

Enter a Porter.

Por. Is your Name Mr. *Roebuck,* Sir?

Love. What wou'd you have with Mr. *Roebuck,* Sir?

Por. I have a fmall Note for him, Sir.

Love. Let me fee't.

Por. Ay, Sir, if your Name be Mr. *Roebuck,* Sir.

Love. My Name is *Roebuck,* Blockhead.

Por. God blefs you, Mafter.

[*Gives him a Letter, and Exit.*

Love. This is fome tawdry Billet, with a fcrawling Adieu t the End on't. Thefe ftrolling Jades know a young holefome Fellow newly come to Town, as well as a Par- in's Wife does a fat Goofe. 'Tis certainly fome Secret, nd therefore fhall be known. [*Opens the Letter.*

S I R, *Tuefday,* Three o'Clock.

MY Behaviour towards you this Morning was fomewhat ftrange; but I fhall tell you the Caufe of it, if you meet us at Ten this Night in our Garden. The Back-door fhall be per. Yours, *Lucinda.*

My Heart! Certainly it can't be L, U, C, Y, M, D, A; hat fpells Woman. 'Twas never written fo plain before. *Roebuck,* thou'rt as true an Oracle, as fhe's a falfe one. Oh, thou damn'd *Sybil!* I have courted thee thefe three Years, and cou'd never obtain above a Kifs of the Hand, nd this Fellow in an Hour or two has obtain'd *the Back-*

H 2 *door*

door open. Mr. *Roebuck,* fince I have difcover'd fo
your Secrets, I'll make bold to open fome more c
———But how fhall I fhake him off?——Oh, I ha
I'll feek him inftantly.

Enter Roebuck *meeting the Porter.*

Roeb. Here, you, Sir, have you a Note for one Ro
Por. I had, Sir; but I gave it to him juft now.
Roeb. You lie, Sirrah; I am the Man.
Por. I an't pofitive I gave it to the right Perfon
I'm very fure I did, for he anfwer'd the Defcriptio
Page gave to a T, Sir.
Roeb. 'Twas well I met that Page, Dog, or now
I cut thy Throat, Rafcal.
Por. Blefs your Worfhip, noble Sir.
Roeb. At Ten, in the Garden! The Back-door
Oh, the delicious Place and Hour! Soft panting B
trembling Joints! melting Sighs! and eager Emb
Oh, Extafy!—But how to fhake off *Lovewell!*—
his nicely Virtuous! Ha, ha, ha!—This is his
Principle of Virtue! Ha, ha, ha!

Enter Lovewell.

Love. How now! Why fo merry?
Roeb. Merry! Why, 'twould make a Dog fplit,
Ha, ha, ha!———The Watch, Sir, the Watch
ha, ha!
Love. What of the Watch? You laugh by the
you'll be run down by and by, fure!
Roeb. Ah, but I fhall be wound up again. This
I had for a Fee, Lawyer——Shou'd I ever be try'd,
this Judge, how I fhou'd laugh to fee how grave
Goofe Cap fits upon a Pair of Horns; Ha, ha, he
Love. Thou'rt Horn-mad. Prithee leave Imperti
———I receiv'd a Note juft now.
Roeb. A Note! 'Sdeath, what Note! What Sir,
Who brought it?
Love. A Gentleman; 'tis a Challenge.
Roeb. Oh, Thanks to the Stars! I'm glad on't. (
Love. And you may be fignally ferviceable to
this Affair. I can give you no greater Teftimony
Affection, than by making fo free with you.——
Roeb. What needs all this Formality! I'll be th
cond, without all this Impertinence.

Love. There's more than that, Friend.——In the firſt Place, I don't underſtand a Sword; and again, I'm to be call'd to the Bar this Term, and ſuch a Buſineſs might prejudice me extremely. So, Sir, you muſt meet and fight for me.

Roeb. Faith, Leviroull, I ſha'n't ſtick to cut a Throat for my Friend at any Time; ſo I may do it fairly, or ſo ——The Hour and Place?

Love. This very Evening in *Moorfields.*

Roeb. Umph! How will you employ yourſelf the while?

Love. I'll follow you at a Diſtance, leſt you have any foul Play.

Roeb. Which if you do——No, faith *Ned,* ſince I'm to anſwer an Appointment for you, you muſt make good an Aſſignation for me. I'm to meet one of your Ladies at the Fountain in the *Temple* To-night. You may be call'd to the Bar there, if you will. This Watch will tell you the Hour, and ſhall be your Paſſport. Let me have yours.—— *[Change Watches.*

Love. Oh! Was that the Jeſt? Ha, ha, ha!—— Well, I will anſwer an Aſſignation for you ſure enough. Ha, ha, ha!——How readily does the Fool run to have his Throat cut? *[Aſide.*

Roeb. How eagerly now does my Moral Friend run to the Devil, having Hopes of Profit in the Wind! I have nabb'd him off purely.——But prithee, *Ned,* where had you this fine Jewel! *[Viewing one ty'd to the Watch.*

Love. Pſhaw! A Trifle; a Trifle; from a Miſtreſs— Take care on't tho'. But hark ye, *George;* don't puſh too home; have a Care of whipping thro' the Guts.

Roeb. 'Gad, I'm afraid one or both of us may fall. But d'ye hear, *Ned,* remember you ſent me on this Er-rand, and are therefore anſwerable for all Miſchief; if I do whip my Adverſary thro' the Lungs or ſo, remember you ſet me upon't.

Love. Well, honeſt *George,* you won't believe how much you oblige me in this Courteſy.

Roeb. You know always I oblige myſelf by ſerving my Friend——I never thought this Spark was a Coward be-fore. *[Aſide.*

Love.

Love. I never imagin'd this Fellow was so easy before.
[*Aside.*] Well, good Success to us both; and when we meet,
we'll relate all Transactions that pass.

Roeb. That you're a Fool.

Love. That you're an Ass. [*Exeunt severally, laughing.*
Re-enter Lovewell *crossing the Stage hastily,* Mockmode *and*
Lyrick *following him.*

Lyr. Mr. *Lovewell,* a Word w'ye

Love. Let it be short, pray Sir, for my Bus'ness is urgent,
and 'tis almost dark.

Lyr. I'm reconcil'd to the 'Squire, and want only the
Pretensment of a Copy of Verses to ingratiate myself
wholly, thoroughly. Let me have that Piece I lent you
just now.

Love. Ay, ay, with all my Heart.—Here.—Farewel.
[*Pulls the Poem hastily, and jostles out a Letter with it,
which* Mockmode *takes up.*

Lyr. Now, Sir, here's a Poem, which (according to the
Way of us Poets) I say, was written at fifteen, but between
you and I, it was made at five and twenty.

Mock. Five and twenty!——When is a Poet at Age, pray,
Sir.

Lyr. At the third Night of his first Play; for he's never a
Man till then.

Mock. But when at Years of Discretion?

Lyr. When they leave Writing; and that's seldom or
never.

Mock. But who are your Guardians?

Lyr. The Criticks, who, with their good Will, won't
never let us come to Age. But what have you got there?

Mock. By the Universe, I don't know; 'tis a Woman's
Hand; some Billet-Deux, I suppose; it jostled out of *Love-*
well's Pocket. We'll to the next Light and read it.
[*Exeunt.*

SCENE *a dark Arbour in* Lucinda's *Garden.*
Enter Roebuck *Solus.*

Roeb. Oh, how I reverence a Back-door half open, half
shut? 'Tis the narrow Gate to the Lover's Paradise; *Cupid*
stood Centry at the Entrance, *Love* was the Word, and he
let me pass.——Now is my Friend pleading for Life; he
has a puzzling Case to manage, ten to one he's non-suited;
I have gull'd him fairly.

Enter

Enter Lovewell.

Love. I've got in. Thanks to my Stars, or rather the Clouds, whose Influence is my best Friend at present. Now is *Roebuck* gazing, or rather groping about for a Fellow with a long Sword; and I know his Fighting Humour will be as mad to be baulk'd by any Enemy, as by a Mistress.

Roeb. Hark, Hark! I hear a Voice; it must be she—— *Lucinda?*

Love. True to the Touch, I find. Is it you, my Dear?

Roeb. Yes, my Dear.

Love. Let me embrace thee, my Heart.

Roeb. Come to my arms.

[*Run into each other's Arms. Finding the Mistake, start back.*

Love. 'Slife! a Man!

Roeb. 'Sdeath! a Devil!—— And wert thou a Legion, here's a Wand thou'd conjure thee down— [*Draws.*

Love. We shall find whose Charm is strongest. [*Draws.*

They pass by one another; Roebuck passes out at the opposite Door; and as Lovewell is passing out on the other Side of the Stage,

Enter Leanthe, *with a Night-Gown over his Cloaths.*

Lean. Mr. *Roebuck!* Sir! Mr. *Roebuck!*

Love. That's a Woman's Voice, I'll swear——Madam.

Lean. Sir.

Love. Come, my dear *Lucinda;* I've staid a little too long; but making an Apology now were only lengthening the Offence. Let's into the Arbour, and make up for the Moments mispent.

Lean. Hold, Sir: Do you love this *Lucinda* you're so fond of hauling into the Arbour?

Love. Yes, by all that's powerful.

Lean. False, false *Roebuck!*——[*Aside.*]—— I am lost.

Love. Madam, do you love this *Roebuck,* that you open'd the Garden-door to so late?

Lean. I'm afraid I do too well.

Love. And did you never own an Affection to another?

Lean. No; witness all those Powers you just now mention'd,

Love. Revenge yourselves, ye Heavens. Behold in me your Accuser, and your Judge. Behold *Lovewell,* injur'd

Lovewell.

Lovewell.——This Darkness, which opportunely hides
Blushes, makes your Shame more monstrous.

Lean. Ha! *Lovewell!* I'm vex'd it is he, but glad
mistaken ———Now, Female Policy, assist me.

Love. Yes, Madam, your Silence proclaims you g
——Farewel, Woman.

Lean. Ha, ha, ha!

Love. What am I made your Scorn?

Lean. Ha! ha, ha!———This happens better th
expected.———Ha, ha, ha!———Mr. *Lovewell!*

Love. No Counter-plotting, Madam: the Mine's sp
already, and and all your Deceit discovered.

Lean. Indeed you're a fine Fellow at discovering Dec
I must confess, that cou'd not find whether I was a Ma
a Woman all this Time.

Love. What, the Page!

Lean. No Counter-plotting, good Sir; the Mine's sp
already.———Ah, Sir, I fancy Mr. *Roebuck* is better at
covering a Man from a Woman in the dark, than you.

Love. This Discovery is the greatest Riddle!——Pri
Child, what makes thee disguis'd? But, above all,
meant that Letter to *Roebuck?*

Lean. Then I find you intercepted it.——Why, Sir
Lady had a Mind to put a Trick upon the impudent Fel
made him an Assignation, and sent me in her Stead, to
ter him. But when I tell her how you fell into the Su
and how jealous you were——Ha, ha, ha!

Love. Oh my little dear Rogue! was that the Matte
[*Hugs her.*] On my Conscience, thou'rt so soft, I be
thou'rt a Woman still.———But who was that Man I
counter'd just now?

Lean. A Man! 'Twas certainly *Roebuck.*———[s
Some of the Footmen, I suppose.———Come, Sir, I
conduct you out immediately, lest some more of 'em i
you.   [*Conducts him to the Door and re*
He certainly was here, and I have miss'd him.
Fortune delights with Innocence to play,
And loves to hoodwink those already blind.
Wary Deceit can many By-ways tread,
To shun the Blocks in Virtue's open Road,
Whilst heedless Innocence still falls on Ruin;

Yet, whilft by Love infpir'd, I will purfue,
What Men by Courage, we by Love can do.
Not even his Falfhood fhall my Claim remove;
From mutual Fires none can true Paffion prove;
For like to like, is Gratitude, not Love.

The End of the Fourth ACT.

ACT V.

SCENE, *An Anti-chamber in* Lucinda's *Houfe;
the Flat Scene half open, difcovers a Bed-chamber:*
Lucinda *in her Night-gown, and reading by a
Table.*

Enter Roebuck, *groping his Way.*

Roeb. ON what new happy Climate am I thrown?
This Houfe is Love's Labyrinth; I have
ftumbled into it by Chance.——Ha! an Illufion! let me
look again.——Eyes, if you play me falfe, [*Looking
about.*] I'll pluck ye out——'Tis fhe! 'tis *Lucinda!* alone,
undrefs'd, in a Bed-chamber, between Eleven and Twelve
o'Clock ——A bleffed Opportunity!——Now if her
innate Principle of Virtue defend her, then is my innate
Principle of Manhood not worth Two-pence.——Hold, fhe
comes forward.—— [Lucinda *approaches reading.*
Luc. Unjuft Prerogative of faithlefs Man,
Abufing Pow'r which partial Heav'n has granted!
In former Ages, Love and Honour flood
As Props and Beauties to the Female Caufe:
But now lie proftitute to Scorn and Sport.
Man, made our Monarch, is a Tyrant grown,
And Woman-kind muft bear a fecond Fall.
Roeb. [*Afide.*] Ah, and a third too, or I'm miftaken.——
I muft divert this plaguy Romantic Humour.
Luc. While Virtue guided Peace, and Honour War,
Their Fruits and Spoils were Off'rings made to Love.
Roeb. And 'tis foftill: for [*raifing his Voice.*]
Beau with earlieft Cherries Mifs does grace,
And Soldier offers Spoils of *Flanders* Lace.
Luc. Ha!——Protect me, Heav'ns! what art thou?
H 5 *Roeb.*

whole Modesty and

Roeb. A Man, Madam.

Luc. What accursed Spirit has driven you hither?

Roeb. The Spirit of Flesh and Blood, Madam.

Luc. Sir, what Encouragement have you ever receiv'd to prompt you to this Impudence?

Roeb. Umph! I must not own the Reception of a Note from her. [*Aside.*] Faith, Madam, I know not whether to attribute it to Chance, Fortune, my good Stars, my Fate, or my Destiny: But here I am, Madam, and here I will be.   [*Taking her by the Hand.*

Luc. [*Pulling her Hand away.*] If a Gentleman, my Commands may cause you to withdraw; if a Ruffian, my Footman shall dispose of you.

Roeb. Madam, I'm a Gentleman; I know how to oblige a Lady, and how to save her Reputation. My Love and Honour go link'd together; they are my Principles; and if you'll be my Second, we'll engage immediately.

Luc. Stand off, Sir; the Name of Love and Honour are burlesqu'd by thy professing 'em. Thy Love is Impudence, and thy Honour a Cheat. Thy Mien and Habit shew thee a Gentleman; but thy Behaviour is brutal. Thou art a *Centaur*; only one part Man, and the other Beast.

Roeb. Philosophy in Petticoats! No wonder Women wear the Breeches; [*Aside.*] and, Madam, you are a Demi-Goddess; only one part Woman, t'other Angel; and thus divided, claim my Love and Adoration.

Luc. Honourable Love is the Parent of Mankind; but thine is the Corrupter and Debaser of it.——The Passion of you Libertines is like your Drunkenness; heat of Lust, as t'other is of Wine, and off with the next Sleep.

Roeb. No, Madam; an Hair of the same—is my Receipt.—Come, come, Madam, all things are laid to rest that will disturb our Pleasure; whole Nature favours us; the kind indulgent Stars that directed me hither, wink at what we are about. —— 'Twere jilting of Fortune to be now idle; and she, like a true Woman, once baulk'd, never affords a second Opportunity.—I'll put out the Candle, the Torch of Love shall light us to Bed.

Luc. To Bed, Sir!——Thou hast Impudence enough to draw thy Rationality in Question. Whence proceeds it? From a vain Thought of thy own Graces, or an Opinion of my Virtue:—If from the latter, know that I am a Woman,

whose

whofe Modefty dare not doubt my Virtue; yet have fo much Pride to fupport it, that the dying Groans of thy whole Sex at my Feet, fhould not extort an immodeft Thought from me.

Roeb. Your Thoughts may be as modeft as you pleafe, Madam.——You fhall be as virtuous to-morrow Morning as e'er a Nun in *Europe*; the Opinion of the World fhall pro-claim you fuch, and that's the fureft Charter the moft rigid Virtue in *England* is held by. The Night has no Eyes to fe, nor have I a Tongue to tell: One Kifs fhall feal up my Lips for ever.

Luc. That uncharitable Cenfure of Women, argues the Meannefs of thy Converfation.

Roeb. Her fuperior Virtue awes me into Coldnefs.—'Slife! it can't be Twelve fure.——Night's a Lyar.

[Draws out his Watch.

Luc. Sir, if you won't be gone, I muft fetch thofe fhall conduct you hence.——My Eyes are dazzled fure.

[Paffing by him towards the Door, fhe perceives the Jewel ty'd to the Watch.

Pray, Sir, let me fee that Jewel.

Roeb. By Heavens, fhe has a mind to't!——Oh, 'tis at your Service with all my Soul.

Luc. Wrong not my Virtue by fo poor a Thought.—— But anfwer directly, as you are a Gentleman, to what I now fhall afk: whence had you that Jewel?

Roeb. I exchanged Watches with a Gentleman, and had this Jewel into the Bargain. He valu'd it not; 'twas a Trifle from a Miftrefs.

Luc. A Trifle! faid he——Oh Indignation, am I flight-ed thus!——I'll put a Jewel out of his Power, that he wou'd pawn his Soul to retrieve.——If you be a Gentleman, Sir, whom Gratitude can work up to Love, or a virtuous Wife reclaim, I'll make you a large Return for that Trifle.

Roeb. Hey-day! a Wife, faid fhe.

Luc. What's your Name, Sir, and of what Country?

Roeb. My Name's *Roebuck*, Madam.

Luc. Roebuck.

Roeb. 'Sdeath! I forgot my Inftructions.——*Mockmode*, Madam.——*Roebuck Mockmode*, my Name, and Surname.

Luc. Mockmode, my 'Squire! it can't be! But if it fhou'd, I've made the better Exchange.——Of what Family are you, Sir?

H 6 *Roeb.*

Roeb. Of, *Mockmode-Hall* in *Shropshire*, Madam; My Father's lately dead; I came lately from the University; I've fifteen hundred Acres of as good fighting Ground as any in *England*. ——'Twas lucky I met that Blockhead to-day. [*Aside.*

Luc. The very same.——And had you any Directions to court a Lady in *London?*

Roeb. Umph!——How shou'd I have found the way hither else, Madam? What the Devil will this come to? [*Aside.*

Luc. My Fool that I dreamt of, I find a pretty Gentleman.——Dreams go by Contraries.——Well, Sir, I am the Lady; and if your Designs are honourable, I'm yours; take a turn in the Garden, 'till I send for my Chaplain: You must take me immediately, for if I cool, I'm lost for ever. [*Exit.*

Roeb. I think I am become a very sober *Shropshire* Gentleman in good earnest; I don't start at the Name of the Parson.——Oh Fortune! Fortune! what art thou doing? If thou and my Friend will throw me into the Arms of a fine Lady, and a great Fortune, how the Devil can I help it! Oh but, Zoons, there's Marriage! Ay, but there's Money.——Oh but there are Children, squawking Children! Ay, but then there are *Rickets* and *Small-Pox*, which perhaps may carry them all away.——Oh but there's Horns! Horns! Ay, but then I shall go to Heaven; for 'tis but reasonable, since all Marriages are made in Heaven, that all Cuckolds should go thither.——But then, there's *Leanthe!* that sticks. I love her, witness, Heaven; I love her to that Degree.——Pshaw, I shall whine presently. I love her as well as any Woman, and what can she expect more? I can't drag a Lover's Chain a hundred Miles by Land, and a hundred Leagues by Water.——Fortune has decreed it otherwise.——So lead on, blind Gude, I'll follow thee; and when the Blind leads the Blind, no wonder they both fall into——Matrimony. [*Going out, meets* Leanthe.] Oh my dear auspicious little *Mercury!* let me kiss thee.——Go tell thy charming Mistress, I obey her Commands. [*Exit.*

Enter Leanthe.

Lean. Her Commands! Oh Heavens! I must follow him. [*Going.*

Luc. Page, Page.

Lean.

Lean. Oh, my curs'd Fortune! baulk'd again!—Madam.

Luc. Call my Chaplain; I'm to be marry'd presently.

Lean. Marry'd so suddenly! To whom, pray, Madam?

Luc. To the Gentleman you met going hence just now.

Lean. Oh Heavens! your Ladyship is not in earnest, Madam?

Luc. What, is Matrimony to be made a Jest of? Don't be impertinent, Boy; call him instantly.

Lean. What shall I do?—Oh, Madam, suspend it till the Morning, for Heav'ns sake. Mr. *Lovewell's* in the House; I met him not half an Hour ago; and he will certainly kill the Gentleman, and perhaps harm your Ladyship.

Luc. Lovewell in my House! how came he hither?

Lean. I know not, Madam. I saw him, and talk'd to him; he had his Sword drawn, and he threaten'd every body. Pray delay it to-night, Madam.

Luc. No, I'm resolv'd; and I'll prevent his discovering me: I'll put on a Suit of your Cloaths, and order *Pindress* to carry her Night-Gown to the Gentleman in the Garden, and bid him meet me in the lower Arbour, in the West Corner, and send the Chaplain thither instantly.

Lean. Hold, Fortune, hold; thou hast entirly won!
For I am lost. Thus long I have been rack'd
On thy tormenting Wheel, and now my Heart-strings break.
Discovering who I am, exposes me to Shame;
Then what on Earth can help me?

Enter Pindress.

Pin. Oh Lord, Page, what's the matter? Here's old doings, or rather new doings. Prithee, let you and I throw in our Two-pence a-piece into this Marriage-Lottery.

Lean. You'll draw nothing but Blanks, I'll assure you, from me.—But stay, let me consider o'th' Business.

Pin. No Consideration; the ————— must be done hand-over-head. ——————————

Lean. Well, I ————————— and wish you, *Pindress.* ——— her Hand.

Pin. You exper

Lean. No, no, ————
————, 'tis a Ma———
West Corner———
diately with———

muſt paſs upon the Chaplain for my Lady and the Gentleman——Haſte.

Pin. Sha'n't I put on my new Gown firſt?

Lean. No, no; you ſhall have a Green Gown for your
Wedding in the Arbour.

Pin. A Green-Gown!—Well, all Fleſh is Graſs.

Lean. Make haſte, my Spouſe, fly.

Pin. And will you come? will you be ſure to come?—
O my little Green Gooſeberry, my Teeth waters at ye.—

Lean. Now Chance, No thou'rt blind.

Then Love, be thou my Guide, and ſet me right;
Tho' blind, like Chance, you have beſt Eyes by Night. [Ex.

SCENE Bollfinch's House.

Enter Lovewell, Bruſh, *and* Servant.

Love. Mr. *Lyrick* abroad, ſay'ſt thou! and *Mockmode* with
him!

Serv. All abroad, my Miſtreſs and all.

Love. I don't underſtand this.——*Bruſh,* run to *Lucinda*'s
Lodgings, and obſerve what's doing there: I ſpy'd ſome
haſty Lights glancing thro' the Rooms: I'll follow you preſently. [*Exit* Bruſh.]——Can't you inform me which Way
they went?

Serv. Perhaps Mr. *Mockmode*'s Man can inform ye.

Love. Pray call him.

Serv. Mr. *Club,* Mr. *Club.*

Love. What! is the Fellow deaf?

Serv. No, Sir; but he's aſleep, and in Bed.—Mr. *Club,*
Mr. *Club.*

Club. Augh.—[*Yawning.*] I'm aſleep, I'm aſleep; don't
wake me.—Augh.

Serv. Here's a Gentleman wants ye.

Enter Club, *with his Coat unbutton'd, his Garters unty'd,*
ſcratching and yawning, as newly waken'd from Bed.

Club. Pox o' your *London* Breeding; what makes you
waken a Man out of his Sleep that way?

Love. Where's your Maſter, pray, Sir?

Club. Augh——'Tis a ſad thing to be broken of one's
Reſt this way.

Love. Can you inform me where your Maſter's gone?

Club. My Maſter!—Augh—— [*Stretching and yawning.*
                                                           Love.

Love. Feb, Sir, your Master——

Club. My Master!—Augh—What o'Clock is it, Sir. I believe 'tis past Midnight, for I have got my first Sleep—Augh——

Love. Thou'rt asleep still, Blockhead. Answer me, or—Where's your Master?

Club. Augh—I had the pleasantest Dream, when you call'd me——Augh——I thought my Master's great black Stone-horse had broke loose among the Mares—Augh—; And so, Sir, you call'd me——Augh—And so I awaken'd.

Love. Sirra, [*Strikes him.*]—— Now your Dream's out, I hope.

Club. Zauns, Sir! what d'ye mean, Sir? My Master's as good a Man as you, Sir; Dem me, Sir.

Love. Tell me presently where your Master is, Sirrah, or I'll dust the Setter out of your Jacket.

Club. Oh, Sir, your Name's *Lovewell*, Sir!

Love. What then, Sir?

Club. Why then my Master is—where you are not, Sir.—My Master's in a fine Lady's Arms, and you are——here, I take it.   [*Shrugging.*

Love. Has he got a Whore a-bed with him?

Club. He may be Father to the Son of a Whore by this time, if your Mistress *Lucinda* be one. Mr. *Lyrick* did his Bus'ness, and my Master will do her Business I warrant him, if o'th' right *Shropshire* Breed. which I'm sure he is, for my Mother nurs'd him on my Milk.

Love. Two Calves suckled on the same Cow——Ha, ha, ha! Gramercy, Poet; has he brought the Play to a Catastrophe so soon? A rare Executioner, to clap him in the Female Pillory already! Ha, ha, ha!

Club. Ay, Sir; and a Pillory, that you wou'd give your Ears for; I warrant you think my Master's over Head and Ears in the *Irish* Quagmire; you wou'd have drown'd him in. But, Sir, we have found the Bottom on't.

Love. He may pass over the Quagmire, Sirrah, for there were stepping Stones laid in his Way.

Club. He has got over dry-shod, I'll assure you —Pray, Sir, did not you receive a Note from *Lucinda*, the true *Lucinda*, to meet her at Ten in her Garden, to-night?—Why don't you laugh now? Ha, ha, ha!

Love. 'Sdeath, Rascal, what Intelligence cou'd you have of that?

Club

Club. Hold, Sir, I have more Intelligence. You threw Mr. *Lyrick* his Poem, in a hurry, in the *Park*, and jufled that fweet Letter out of your Pocket, Sir. This Letter fell into my Mafter's Hands, Sir, and difcover'd your Sham, Sir, your Trick, Sir. Now, Sir, I think you are as deep in the Mud as he is in the Mire.

Love. Curs'd Misfortune!——And where are they gone, Sir? Quickly, the Truth, the whole Truth, Dog, or I'll fpit you like a Sparrow.

Club. I defign to tell you, Sir. Mr. *Lyrick*, Sir, being my Mafter's intimate Friend, or fo, upon a Bribe of a Hundred Pounds, or fo, has fided with him, taken him to *Lucinda's* Garden in your ftead, and there's a Parfon, and all, and fo forth.—Now, Sir, I hope the Poet has brought the Play to a very good Cata—Cata—what d'ye call him, Sir?

Love. 'Twas he I encounter'd in the Garden.—— 'Sdeath! Trick'd by the Poet; I'll cut off one of his Limbs; I'll make a Synalœpha of him; I'll——

Club. He, he, he!——Two Calves fuckled on the fame Cow!——He, he, he!

Love. Nay, then I begin with you.   [*Drubs him.*

Club. Zauns! Murder! Demme! Zauns! Murder! Zauns!   [*Runs off; Lovewell after him.*

SCENE *changes to the Anti-chamber in* Lucinda's *Houfe; a Hat and a Sword on the Table.*

Enter Brufh.

Brufh. I have been peeping and crouching about like a Cat a moufing. Ha! I fmell a Rat—a Sword and a Hat! —There are certainly a Pair of Breeches appertaining to thefe, and may be lap'd up in my Lady's Lavender, who knows?   [*Liftens.*

Enter Lovewell *in a hurry.*

Love. What, Sir? What are you doing? I'm ruin'd, trick'd.——

Brufh. I believe fo too, Sir—See here!——
          [*Shews the Hat and Sword.*

Love. By all my Hopes, *Roebuck's* Hat and Sword. This is Mifchief upon Mifchief. Run you to the Garden, Sirrah, and if you find any Body, fecure 'em, I'll fearch the Houfe— I'm ruin'd!—Fly! *Roebuck?*—What hoa—*Roebuck?*—hoa!
                                                  Enter

Enter Roebuck *unbutten'd, runs to* Lovewell *and embraces him.*

Roeb. Dear, dear *Lovewell*, wish me Joy; with me Joy, my Friend.

Love. Of what, Sir?

Roeb. Of the dearest, tenderest, whitest, softest Bride, that ever blest Man's Arms. I'm all Air, all a *Cupid*, all Wings, and must fly again to her Embraces. Detain me not, my Friend.

Love. Hold Sir, I hope you mock me! tho' that itself's unkind.

Roeb. Mock you!——By Heaven's, no. She's more than Sense can bear, or Tongue express ——O *Lucinda?* Shoo'd Heaven——

Love. Hold, Sir; no more.

Roeb. I'm on the Rack of Pleasure, and must confess all. When her soft melting, white, and yielding Waist, Within my pressing Arms was folded fast, Our Lips were melted down by Heat of Love, And lay incorporate in liquid Kisses, Whilst in soft broken Sighs, we catch'd each other's Souls.

Love. Come, come, *Roebuck*, no more of this Extravagance——By Heav'n I swear you sha'n't marry her.

Roeb. By Heav'n I swear so too; for I'm marry'd already.

Love. Then thou'rt a Villain.

Roeb. A Villain, Man!——Pshaw, that's Nonsense. A poor Fellow can no sooner get marry'd, than you imagine he may be called a Villain presently——You may call me a Fool, a Blockhead, or an Ass, by the Authority of Custom: But why a Villain, for God's sake?

Love. Did not you engage to meet and fight a Gentleman for me in *Moorfields?*

Roeb. Did not you promise to engage a Lady for me at the *Fountain*, Sir?

Love. This *Lucinda* is my Mistress, Sir.

Roeb. This *Lucinda*, Sir, is my Wife.

Love. Then this decides the Matter.——Draw:

[*Throws* Roebuck *his Sword, and draws his own.*

Roeb. Prithee be quiet, Man; I've other Business to mind on my Wedding-night. I must in to my Bride. [*Going.*

Love. Hold, Sir; move a Step, and by Heavens I'll stab thee.

Roeb.

Roeb. Put up, put up; Pshaw, I a'n't prepar'd to day; I a'n't, Devil take me.

Love. Do you dally with me, Sir?

Roeb. Why you won't be fo unconfcionable as to kill a Man fo fuddenly; I han't made my Will yet. Perhaps I may leave you a Legacy.

Love. Pardon me, Heavens, if prefs'd by ftinging Taunts, my Paffion urge my Arm to act what's foul.
[Offers to pufh at him.

Roeb. Hold. [*Taking up his Sword.*] 'Tis fafeft making Peace, they fay, with Sword in Hand. ——— I'll tell thee what, *Ned,* I would not lofe this Night's Pleafure for the Honour of fighting and vanquifhing the Seven Champions of *Chriftendom:* Permit me then but this Night to return to the Arms of my dear Bride, and Faith and Troth I'll take a fair Thruft with you To-morrow Morning.

Love. What! beg a poor Reprieve for Life! ——— Then thou art a Coward.

Roeb. You imagined the contrary, when you employed me to fight for you in *Moorfields.*

Love. Will nothing move thy Gall? ——— Thou'rt bafe, ungrateful.

Roeb. Ungrateful! I love thee, *Ned*; by Heavens, my Friend, I love thee; therefore name not that Word again, for fuch a Repetition would overpay all thy Favours.

Love. A cheap, a very cheap way of making Acknow-ledgment, and therefore thou haft catched it, which makes thee more ungrateful.

Roeb. My Friendfhip even yet does balance Paffion; but throw in the leaft Grain more of an Affront, and by Heaven you turn the Scale.

Love. [*Paufing.*] No, I've thought better; my Reafon clears: She's not worth my Sword; a Bully only fhou'd draw in her Defence, for fhe's falfe, a Proftitute.
[Puts in his Sword.

Roeb. A Proftitute! by Heavens thou ly'ft. [*Draws.*]— Thou haft blafphemed. Her Virtue anfwers the uncor-rupted State of Woman; fo much above Modefty, that it mocks Temptation. She has convinc'd me of the bright Honour of our Sex, and I ftand Champion now for the fair Female Caufe.

Love. Then I have loft what nought on Earth can pay. Curfe on all Doubts, all Jealoufies, that deftroy our prefent

but Happiness, by mistrusting the future. Thus Misbe-
lievers making their Heaven uncertain, find a certain
Hell —— And is she virtuous? found the bold Charge
aloud, which does proclaim me guilty.

Roeb. By Heavens, as virtuous as thy Sister.

Love. My Sister!——Ha!——I fear, Sir, your Marriage with *Lucinda* has wrong'd my Sister; for her you
courted, and I heard she lov'd you.

Roeb. I courted her, it is true, and lov'd her also; nay,
my Love to her rival'd my Friendship tow'rds——and
had my Fate allow'd me Time for Thought, her dear Remembrance might have stop'd the Marriage. But since
'tis past, I must own to you, to her, and all the World,
that I cast off all former Passion, and shall henceforth
confine my Love to the dear Circle of her charming Arms
from whom I just now parted.

—Enter Leanthe *in Woman's loose Apparel.*

Lean. I take you at your Word. These are the Arms
that held you.

Roeb. Oh Gods and Happiness! *Leanthe!*

Love. My Sister! Heavens! It cannot be.

Roeb. By Heavens it can, it shall, it must be so——
or none on Earth cou'd give such Joys but she.——Who
would have thought my Joys cou'd bear Increase? *Lovewell,* my Friend! This is thy Sister! 'Tis *Leanthe!* My
Mistress, my Bride, my Wife!

Lean. I am your Sister, Sir; as such I beg you to pardon the Effect of violent Passion, which has driven me
to imprudent Actions: But none such as may blot the
Honour of my Virtue, or Family. To hold you no
longer in Suspence, 'twas I brought the Letter from
Leanthe; 'twas I manag'd the Intrigue with *Lucinda;* I
sent the Note to Mr. *Roebuck* this Afternoon; and I——

Roeb. That was the Bride of happy me.

Love. Thou art my Sister and Guardian-Angel; for
you hast bless'd thyself, and bless'd thy Brother. *Lucinda*
still is safe, and may be mine.

Roeb. May!——She shall be thine, my Friend.

Love. Where is *Lucinda?*

Enter Mockmode.

Mock. Not far off; tho' far enough from you, by the
universe.

Lean.

Lean. You muſt give me leave not to believe you, Sir.

Mock. Oh, Madam! I crave you ten thouſand Pardons, by the Univerſe, Madam; Zauns, Madam; Dem me, Madam.   [*Offers to ſalute her awkwardly.*

Love. By your Leave, Sir. ———   [*Thruſts him back.*

Roeb. Ah, Couſin *Mockmode!*—How do all our Friends in *Shropſhire* ?———

Mock. Now, Gentlemen, I thank you all for your Trick, your Sham. You imagine I have got your Whore, Couſin, your Crack. But, Gentlemen, by the Aſſiſtance of a Poet, your *Sheely* is metamorphos'd into the real *Lucinda;* which your Eyes ſhall teſtify. Bring in the Jury there. —Guilty or not Guilty ?

Enter Lyrick *and* Trudge.

Trud. Oh, my dear *Roebuck!* [Trudge *ſeeing* Roebuck, *throws off her Maſque, flies to him, takes him about the Neck and kiſſes him.*] And Faith is it you, dear Joy ? And where have you been theſe ſeven long Years ?

Mock. Zauns !

Roeb. Hold off, ſtale Iniquity.—Madam, you'll pardon this ?   [*To* Leanthe.

Trud. Indeed I won't live with that Stranger. You promis'd to marry me, ſo you did.—Ah, Sir, *Neddy's* a brave Boy, God bleſs him; he's a whole Armful ; Lord knows, I had a heavy Load of him.

Love. Guilty or not Guilty, Mr. *Mockmode ?*

Mock. 'Tis paſt that; I am condemn'd; I'm hang'd in the Marriage Nooſe.—Hark ye, Madam, was this the Doctor that let you Blood under the Tongue for the Quinſey ?

Trud. Yes, that it was, Sir.

Mock. Then he may do ſo again ; for the Devil take me if ever I breathe a Vein for ye.—Mr. *Lyrick,* is this your Poetical Friendſhip ?

Lyr. I had only a mind to convince you of your 'Squire-ſhip.

Love. Now, Siſter, my Fears are over.—But where's *Lucinda ?* How is ſhe diſpos'd of ?

Lean. The Fear ſhe lay under of being diſcover'd by you, gave me an Opportunity of impoſing *Pindreſs* upon her inſtead of this Gentlewoman, whom ſhe expected to wear one of *Pindreſs's* Night-Gowns as a Diſguiſe. To

make

e the Cheat more current, she difguis'd herfelf in my
aths, which has made her pafs on her Maid for me;
I by that Opportunity putting on a Suit of her's, pafs'd
n this Gentleman for *Lucinda*: My next Bufinefs is
nd her out, and beg her Pardon, endeavour her Re-
cilement to you, which the Difcovery of the Miftakes
ween both will eafily effect.

eb. Well, Sir, [*To* Lyrick,] how was your Plot car-
on ?

yr. Why this 'Squire (will you give me Leave to call
fo now ?) this 'Squire had a mind to perfonate *Love-*
, to catch *Lucinda*.—So I made *Truage* to perfonate
nda, and fnap him in this very Garden.—Now, Sir,
'll give me Leave to write our *Epithalamium*.

ock. My *Epithalamium* ! my *Epitaph* ! Screech-Owl,
I'm buried alive. But I hope you'll return my hun-
Pounds I gave you for marrying me.

yr. No ; but for five hundred more I'll unmarry you.
fe are hard Times, and Men of Induftry muft make

Here's the Money, by the Univerfe, Sir ; a Bill
e hundred Pounds Sterl— upon My

Bring me a pit

Lay it in the Geth n's Hand.

Execationer fhall cut the Rope.

ve. What, Pope *Joan* re you the

ll. Of the Poet's Ordination.

r. Ay, ay, before the Time of Chriftianity the Poets
Priefts.

ck. No Wonder then that all the World were Hea-

r. How d'ye like the P t? Wou'd it not do well
Play !—My Money, Si — [*To* Roebuck,

eb. No, Sir ; it belongs to this Gentlewoman.—
it to Trudge.] You have divorc'd her, and muft
give

give her separate Maintenance.—There's another Turn
of Plot you were not aware of, Mr. *Lyrick.*

Enter Lucinda, Leanthe, *and* Pindress.

Luc. You have told me Wonders.

Lean. Here are these can testify the Truth. This Gentleman is the real Mr. *Mockmode,* and much such another
Person as your Dream represented.

Roeb. I hope, Madam, you'll pardon my dissembling,
since only the Hopes of so great a Purchase cou'd cause it.

Luc. Let my wishing you much Joy and Happiness in
your Bride, testify my Reconciliation; and at the Request of your Sister, Mr. *Lovewell,* I pardon your past
Jealousies. You threatened me, Mr. *Lovewell,* with an
Irish Entertainment at my Wedding. I wish it present
now, to assist at your Sister's Nuptials.

Lean. At my last going hence, I sent for 'em, and they're
ready.

Love. Call 'em in then.

[*An Irish Entertainment of three Men and three Women, dress'd after the* Fingalian *Fashion.*

Luc. I must reward your Sister, Mr. *Lovewell,* for the
many Services done me as my Page. I therefore settle
my Fortune and myself, on you, on this Condition, That
you make over your Estate in *Ireland* to your Sister and
that Gentleman.

Love. 'Tis done, only with this Proviso, Brother, That
you forsake your Extravagancies.

Roeb. Brother, you know I always slighted Gold,
But most when offer'd as a sordid Bribe,
I scorn to be brib'd even to Virtue,
But for bright Virtue's sake, I here embrace it.

[*Embracing* Leanthe.

I have espous'd all Goodness with *Leanthe,*
And am divorc'd from all my former Follies.

Woman's our Fate. Wild and unlawful Flames
Debauch us first, and softer Love reclaims;
Thus *Paradise* was lost by *Woman's* Fall,
But virtuous *Woman* thus restores it all. [*Exeunt omnes.*

EPILOGUE

XXXXXXXXXXXXXXXX X XXXXXXXXXXXXXX

EPILOGUE.

Written and spoke by *Jo. Haynes* in Mourning.

Come not here, your Poet's Fate to fee,
He and his Play both be damn'd for me:
Royal Theatre, I come to Mourn for thee,
&c.

[Looking up at it.

[Mocking the late Singers.

When their Male Thruſh up Singer drew your Money;
got you an Eunuch's Pipe, Signior Rampony.
Beardleſs Songſter que coh'd ne'er make much on;
Females found a damn'd Blotch in his Scutcheon.
Italian never ſure ſo got of mighty Fame,
Fideli—There's Muſic in his Name;
is like the Muſic of the Spheres,
be Heavenly for the Price it bears. [20 l. a time.

He's

EPILOGUE

He's a handsome Fellow too, looks brisk and trim:
If he don't take ye, then the De'el take him.
Besides, lest our white Faces always mayn't delight ye,
We've pickt up Gipsies now to please or fright ye.

Lastly, to make our House more courtly shine,
As Travel does the Men of Mode refine,
So our Stage-Heroes did their Tour design.
To mend their Manners, and coarse English Feeding,
They went to Ireland, to improve their Breeding;
Yet, for all this, we still are at a loss,
Oh Collier! Collier! thou'st frighted away Miss C——s:
She, to return our Foreigner's Complaisance,
At Cupid's call, has made a Trip to France.
Love's Fire Arms here, are since not worth a Sous:
We've lost the only Touch-hole of our House.

Losing that Jewel, gave us a fatal Blow:
Well, if this Audience must Jo. Haynes undo;
Well, if 'tis decreed, nor can thy Fate, O Stage!
Resist the Vows of this obdurate Age;
I'll then grow wiser, leave off playing the Fool,
And hire this Play-house for a Boarding-School.
D'ye think the Maids won't be in a sweet Condition,
When they are under Jo. Haynes's grave Tuition?
They'll have no Occasion then, I'm sure, to Play,
They'll have such Comings in another way.

THE

Conſtant Couple;

OR, A

Trip to the Jubilee.

A

C O M E D Y,

As it is Acted at the

T H E A T R E - R O Y A L

IN

D R U R Y - L A N E.

Sive favore tuli, ſive hanc ego Carmine famam;
Jure tibi grates, candide lector, ago.
Ovid. Trift. lib. iv. Eleg. 10.

LONDON:

Printed for T. LOWNDES, T. CASLON, S. BLADON,
C. CORBETT, and W. NICOLL.

M. DCC. LXXII.

PREFACE

To the Reader.

*A*N affected Modesty is very often the greatest Vanity, and
Authors are sometimes prouder of their Blushes, than of the
Praises that occasion'd them. I sha'n't therefore, like a
foolish Virgin, fly to be pursu'd, and deny what I chiefly wish
for. I am very willing to acknowledge the Beauties of this
Play, especially those of the third Night, which not to be proud
of, were the Height of Impudence: Who is asham'd to value
himself upon such Favours, undervalues those who conferr'd them.

As I freely submit to the Criticisms of the Judicious, so I can-
not allow this an ill Play, since the Town has allow'd it such
Success. When they have pardon'd my Faults, 'twere very ill
Manners to condemn their Indulgence. Some may think (my
Acquaintance in Town being too slender to make a Party for the
Play) that the Success must be deriv'd from the pure Merits
of the Cause. I am of another Opinion ; I have not been long
enough in Town to raise Enemies against me ; and the English
are still kind to Strangers. I am below the Envy of great
Wits, and above the Malice of little ones. I have not displeased
the Ladies, nor offended the Clergy ; both which are now pleas'd
to say, that a Comedy may be diverting without Smut and
Profaneness.

Next to those Advantages, the Beauties of Action gave the
greatest Life to the Play, of which the Town is so sensible,
that all will join with me in Commendation of the Actors, and
allow (without detracting from the Merit of others) that the
Theatre-Royal affords an excellent and compleat Set of Come-
dians. Mr. Wilks's Performance has set him so far above
Competition in the Part of Wildair, that none can pretend to
envy the Praise due to his Merit. That he made the Part, will
appear from hence, that whenever the Stage has the Misfortune
to lose him, Sir Harry Wildair may go to the Jubilee.

A great many quarrel at the Trip to the Jubilee for a
Misnomer : I must tell them, that perhaps there are greater
Trips in the Play ; and when I find that more exact Plays have
had better Success, I'll talk with the Critics about Decorums,
&c. However, if I ever commit another Fault of this Nature, I'll endeavour to make it more excusable.

I 2 PRO-

PROLOGU

By a FRIEND.

POETS will think nothing so checks their Fury
    As Wits, Cits, Beaux, and Women for their Jury.
Our Spark's half dead to think what Medley's come,
With blended Judgments to pronounce his Doom.
'Tis all false Fear; for in a mingled Pit,
Why, what your grave Don thinks but dully writ,
His Neighbour i'th' great Wig may take for Wit.
Some Authors court the Few, the Wise if any;
Our Youth's content, if he can reach the many,
Who go with much like Ends to Church and Play,
Not to observe what Priests or Poets say,
No! no! your Thoughts, like theirs, lie quite another way
The Ladies safe may smile, for here's no Slander,
No Smut, no lewd-tongu'd Beau, no double Entendre.
'Tis true, he has a Spark just come from France,
But then so far from Beau—why, he talks Sense!
Like Coin oft carry'd out, but—seldom brought from thence
There's yet a Gang to whom our Spark submits,
Your Elbow-shaking Fool, that lives by's Wits,
That's only witty tho', just as he lives, by fits.
Who, Lion-like, through Bailiffs, scours away,
Hunts, in the Face, a Dinner all the Day,
At Night with empty Bowels grumbles o'er the Pla
And now the modish 'Prentice he implores,
Who, with his Master's Cash, stol'n out of Doors,
Employs it on a Brace of——Honourable Whores:
While their good bulky Mother pleas'd, sits by,
Bawd Regent of the Bubble Gallery.
Next to our mounted Friends, we humbly move,
Who all your Side-box Tricks are much above,
And never fail to pay us with your Love.
Ah Friends! poor Dorset Garden-house *is gone;*
Our merry Meetings there are all undone:

PROLOGUE.

Quite loft to us, fure for fome ftrange Mifdeeds,
That ftrong Dog Sampfon's pull'd it o'er our Heads,
Snaps Rope like Thread; but when his Fortune's told him,
He'll hear perhaps of Rope will one Day hold him :.
At leaft, I hope, that our good-natur'd Town
Will find a way to pull his Prices down.
   Well, That's all! Now, Gentlemen, for the Play,
On fecond Thoughts, I've but two Words to fay ;
Such as it is for your Delight defign'd,
Hear it, read, try, judge, and fpeak as you find.

       Drama-

Dramatis Personæ,

At Drury-Lane, 1771.

MEN.

Sir Harry Wildair	- - -	Mrs. *Barry.*
Beau Clincher	- - -	Mr. *Jefferson.*
Colonel Standard	- - -	Mr. *Aickin.*
Alderman Smuggler	- - -	Mr. *Parsons.*
Clincher junior	- - -	Mr. *W. Palmer.*
Vizard	- - - -	Mr. *Packer.*
Dicky	- - -	Mr. *Waldron.*
Tom Errand	- - -	Mr. *Ackman.*

WOMEN.

Angelica	- - - -	Miss *Rogers.*
Lady Darling	- - -	Mrs. *Cross.*
Parly	- - -	Mrs. *Love.*
Lady Lurewell	- - -	Mrs. *Baddeley.*

Constable, Mob, Porter's Wife, Servants, &c.

SCENE, *LONDON.*

TH

THE
Conſtant Couple.

❀✤❀✤❀✤❀✤❀✤❀✤❀✤❀✤❀✤❀✤❀✤❀✤

ACT I.

SCENE, *The Park.*

Enter Vizard *with a Letter, a Servant following.*

VIZARD.

*A*NGELICA ſend it back unopen'd ! ſay you ?
    Serv. As you ſee, Sir.

Viz. The Pride of theſe virtuous Women is more
inſufferable than the Immodeſty of Proſtitutes—After all
my Encouragement to ſlight me thus !

Serv. She ſaid, Sir, that imagining your Morals ſincere, ſhe gave you Acceſs to her Converſation ; but that
your late Behaviour in her Company has convinc'd her,
that your Love and Religion are both Hypocriſy, and
that ſhe believes your Letter like yourſelf, fair on the
Outſide, foul within ; ſo ſent it back unopen'd.

Viz. May Obſtinacy guard her Beauty till Wrinkles
bury it ; then may Deſire prevail to make her curſe that
untimely Pride her diſappointed Age repents—I'll be
reveng'd the very firſt Opportunity——Saw you the old
Lady *Darling,* her Mother ?

Serv.

Serv. Yes, Sir, and she was pleas'd to say much in your Commendation.

Viz. That's my Cue——An Esteem grafted in Old Age is hardly rooted out; Years stiffen their Opinions with their Bodies, and old Zeal is only to be cozen'd by young Hypocrisy.—— [*Aside.*

Run to the Lady *Lurewell's*, and know of her Maid, whether her Ladyship will be at home this Evening. Her Beauty is sufficient Cure for *Angelica's* Scorn.

[*Exit Servant.* Vizard *pulls out a Book, reads, and walks about.*

Enter Smuggler.

Smug. Ay, there's a Pattern for the young Men o'th' Times, at his Meditation so early, some Book of pious Ejaculations, I'm sure.

Viz. This *Hobs* is an excellent Fellow! [*Aside.*] O Uncle *Smuggler!* To find you at this End o'th' Town is a Miracle.

Smug. I have seen a Miracle this Morning indeed, Cousin *Vizard.*

Viz. What is it, pray, Sir?

Smug. A Man at his Devotion so near the Court—I'm very glad, Boy, that you keep your Sanctity untainted in this infectious Place; the very Air of this Park is Heathenish, and every Man's Breath I meet scents of Atheism.

Viz. Surely, Sir, some great Concern must bring you to this unsanctify'd End of the Town.

Smug. A very unsanctify'd Concern truly, Cousin.

Viz. What is it?

Smug. A Law-Suit, Boy——Shall I tell you?——My Ship the *Swan* is newly arriv'd from *St. Sebastian*, laden with *Portugal* Wines: Now the impudent Rogue of a Tide-waiter has the Face to affirm it is *French* Wines in *Spanish* Casks, and has indicted me upon the Statute—— O Conscience! Conscience! These Tide-waiters and Surveyors plague us more with their *French* Wines, than the War did with *French* Privateers————Ay, there's another Plague of the Nation——

Enter Colonel Standard.

A red Coat and Feather.

Viz. Col. *Standard,* I'm your humble Servant.

Stand.

d. May be not, Sir.

. Why fo ?

d. Becaufe——I'm difbanded.

. How ! Broke ?

. This very Morning, in *Hde-Park,* my brave
ient, a thoufand Men that look'd like Lions Yef-
, were fcatter'd, and look'd as poor and fimple as
erd of Deer that graz'd befide 'em.

g. Tal, al,. deral [*Singing.*] I'll have a Bonfire
ight as high as the Monument.

d. A Bonfire ! Thou dry, wither'd, Ill nature ;
t thofe brave Fellows Swords defended you, your
had been a Bonfire e'er this about your Ears.——
e not venture our Lives, Sir ?

g. And did we not pay for your Lives, Sir ?——
re your Lives! I'm fure we ventur'd our Money,
at's Life and Soul to me.——Sir, we'll maintain
longer.

d. Then your Wives fhall, old *Acteon.* There are
d thirty ftrapping Officers gone this Morning to
on free Quarter in the City.

g. O Lord! O Lord! I fhall have a Son within
ine Months born with a leading Staff in his Hand.
r, you are——

d. What, Sir.

. Sir, I fay that you are. ——

d. What, Sir ?

. Difbanded, Sir, that's all——I fee my Law-
der. [*Exit.*

Sir, I'm very forry for your Misfortune.

. Why fo? I don't come to borrow Money of
f you're my Friend, meet me this Evening at the
; I'll pay my Foy, drink a Health to my King,
ity to my Country, and away for *Hungary* to-
Morning.

What! you won't leave us ?

. What ! A Soldier ftay here, to look like an
ir of Colours in *Weftminfter Hall,* ragged, and
No, no——I met Yefterday a broken Lieu-
he was afham'd to own that he wanted a Dinner,
g'd Eighteen-pence of me to buy a new Scabbard,
Sword...

I 5 *Wizes.*

Viz. O, but you have good Friends, Colonel!

Stand. O, very good Friends! My Father's a Lord, and my elder Brother a Beau; mighty-good Friends indeed!

Viz. But your Country may perhaps want your Sword again.

Stand. Nay, for that Matter, let but a single Drum beat up for Volunteers between *Ludgate* and *Charing-Cross*, and I shall undoubtedly hear it at the Walls of *Buda.*

Viz. Come, come, Colonel, there are Ways of making your Fortune at Home—Make your Addresses to the Fair, you're a Man of Honour and Courage.

Stand. Ay, my Courage is like to do me wondrous Service with the Fair: This pretty cross Cut over my Eye will attract a Dutchess—I warrant 'twill be a mighty Grace to my Ogling——Had I us'd the Stratagem of a certain Brother Colonel of mine, I might succeed.

Viz. What was it, pray?

Stand. Why, to save' his pretty Face for the Women, he always turn'd his Back upon the Enemy.———He was a Man of Honour for the Ladies.

Viz. Come, come, the Loves of *Mars* and *Venus* will never fail; you must get a Mistress.

Stand. Prithee, no more on't——You have awaken'd a Thought, from which, and the Kingdom, I wou'd have stol'n away at once.———To be plain, I have a Mistress.

Viz. And she's cruel?

Stand. No.

Viz. Her Parents prevent your Happiness?

Stand. Nor that.

Viz. Then she has no Fortune?

Stand. A large one: Beauty to tempt all Mankind, and Virtue to beat off their Assaults. O *Vizard!* such a Creature!

Enter Sir Harry Wildair, *crosses the Stage singing, with Footmen after him.*

Hey-day! Who the Devil have we here?

Viz. The Joy of the Play-house, and Life of the Park; Sir *Harry Wildair*, newly come from *Paris.*

Stand.

Stand. Sir *Harry Wildair!* Did not he make a Campaign in *Flanders* some three or four Years ago?

Viz. The same.

Stand. Why, he behaved himself very bravely.

Viz. Why not? Do'ft think Bravery and Gaiety are inconsistent? He's a Gentleman of most happy Circumstances, born to a plentiful Estate; has had a genteel and easy Education, free from the Rigidness of Teachers, and Pedantry of Schools. His florid Constitution being never ruffled by Misfortune, nor stinted in its Pleasures, has render'd him entertaining to others, and easy to himself.—Turning all Passion into Gaiety of Humour, by which he chuses rather to rejoice with his Friends, than be hated by any; as you shall see.

Re-enter Wildair.

Wild. Ha, *Vizard!*

Viz. Sir *Harry!*

Wild. Who thought to find you out of the *Rubrick* so long? I thought thy Hypocrisy had been wedded to a Pulpit-Cushion long ago.——Sir, if I mistake not your Face, your Name is *Standard.*

Stand. Sir *Harry,* I'm your humble Servant.

Wild. Come, Gentlemen, the News, the News o'th' Town, for I'm just arriv'd.

Viz. Why, in the City-end o'th' Town we're playing the Knave, to get Estates.

Stand. And in the Court-end playing the Fool, in spending 'em.

Wild. Just so in *Paris.* I'm glad we're grown so modish.

Viz. We are so reform'd, that Gallantry is taken for Vice.

Stand. And Hypocrify for Religion.

Wild. Alamode de Paris again.

Viz. Not one Whore between *Ludgate* and *Aldgate.*

Stand. But ten Times more Cuckolds than ever.

Viz. Nothing like an Oath in the City.

Stand. That's a Mistake; for my Major swore a hundred and fifty last Night to a Merchant's Wife in her Bedchamber.

Wild. Pshaw, this is trifling; tell me News, Gentlemen. What Lord has lately broke his Fortune at the Groom-Porter's? or his Heart at *New-Market,* for the

Loſs of a Race? What Wife has been lately ſuing
Doctors-Commons for Alimony; or, what Daughter ran
away with her Father's *Valet*? What Beau gave the
nobleſt Ball at the *Bath*, or had the fineſt Coach in the
Ring? I want News, Gentlemen.

Stand. Faith, Sir, theſe are no News at all.

Viz. But pray, Sir *Harry*, tell us ſome News of your
Travels.

Wild. With all my Heart.—You muſt know then, I
went over to *Amſterdam* in a *Dutch* Ship: I there had a
Dutch Whore for five Stivers. I went from thence to
Landen, where I was heartily drub'd in the Battle with
the But-end of a *Swiſs* Muſket. I thence went to *Paris*,
where I had half a Dozen Intrigues, bought half a
Dozen new Suits, fought a Couple of Duels, and here I
am again *in ſtatu quo.*

Viz. But we heard that you deſign'd to make the Tour
of *Italy*; what brought you back ſo ſoon?

Wild. That which brought you into the World, and
may perhaps carry you out of it; a Woman.

Stand. What! quit the Pleaſures of Travel for a
Woman!

Wild. Ay, Colonel, for ſuch a Woman! I had rather
ſee her *Ruelle* than the Palace of *Lewis le Grand*: There's
more Glory in her Smile, than in the *Jubilee* at *Rome*;
and I wou'd rather kiſs her Hand, than the Pope's Toe.

Viz. You, Colonel, have been very laviſh in the Beauty
and Virtue of your Miſtreſs; and Sir *Harry* here has been
no leſs eloquent in the Praiſe of his. Now will I lay you
both ten Guineas a-piece, that neither of them is ſo
pretty, ſo witty, or ſo virtuous, as mine.

Stand. 'Tis done.

Wild. I'll double the Stakes—But, Gentlemen, now I
think on't, how ſhall we be reſolv'd? For I know not
where my Miſtreſs may be found; ſhe left *Paris* about a
Month before me, and I had an Account——

Stand. How, Sir! left *Paris* about a Month before you?

Wild. Yes, Sir, and I had an Account that ſhe lodg'd
ſomewhere in St. *James's.*

Viz. How! ſomewhere in St. *James's*, ſay you?

Wild. Ay, Sir, but I know not where, and perhaps
mayn't find her this Fortnight.

Stand. Her Name, pray, Sir *Harry.*

Viz. Ay, ay, her Name; perhaps we know her.

Wild. Her Name! Ay,——fhe has the fofteft, whiteft Hand that e'er was made of Flefh and Blood; her Lips fo balmy fweet——

Stand. But her Name, Sir.

Wild. Then her Neck and Breaft;——her Breafts do fo heave, fo heave.   [*Singing.*

Viz. But her Name, Sir; her Quality.

Wild. Then her Shape, Colonel!

Stand. But her Name I want, Sir.

Wild. Then her Eyes, *Vizard!*

Stand. Pfhaw, Sir *Harry,* her Name, or nothing.

Wild. Then if you muft have it, fhe's call'd the Lady —————But then her Foot, Gentlemen; fhe dances to a Miracle. *Vizard,* you have certainly loft your Wager.

Viz. Why, you have certainly loft your Senfes; we fhall never difcover the Picture, unlefs you fubfcribe the Name.

Wild. Then her Name is *Lurewell.*

Stand. 'Sdeath, my Miftrefs.   [*Afide.*

Viz. My Miftrefs, by *Jupiter.*   [*Afide.*

Wild. Do you know her, Gentlemen?

Stand. I have feen her, Sir.

Wild. Can'ft tell where fhe lodges? Tell me, dear Colonel.

Stand. Your humble Servant, Sir.   [*Exit* Stand.

Wild. Nay, hold, Colonel; I'll follow you, and will know.   [*Runs out.*

Viz. The Lady *Lurewell,* his Miftrefs! He loves her: But fhe loves me.——But he's a Baronet, and I plain *Vizard;* he has a Coach and Six, and I walk on Foot; I was bred in *London,* and he in *Paris.*——That very Circumftance has murder'd me——Then fome Stratagem muft be laid to divert his Pretenfions.

Re-enter Wildair.

Wild. Prithee, *Dick,* what makes the Colonel fo out of Humour?

Viz. Becaufe he's out of Pay, I fuppofe.

Wild. 'Slife, that's true; I was beginning to miftruft fome Rivalfhip in the Cafe.

Viz. And fuppofe there were, you know the Colonel can fight, Sir *Harry.*

Wild.

Wild. Fight! Pshaw! but he can't dance, ha! We contend for a Woman, *Vizard!* 'Slife, Man, if Ladies were to be gain'd by Sword and Pistol only, what the Devil should all we Beaux do?

Viz. I'll try him farther. [*Aside.*] But wou'd not you, Sir Harry, fight for this Woman you so much admire?

Wild. Fight! Let me consider. I love her——that's true;—but then I love honest Sir *Harry Wildair* better. The Lady *Lurewell* is divinely charming——right—— but then a Thrust i'th' Guts, or a *Middlesex* Jury, is as ugly as the Devil.

Viz. Ay, Sir *Harry,* 'twere a dangerous Cast for a Beau Baronet to be tried by a Parcel of greasy, grumbling, bartering Boobies, who wou'd hang you, purely because you're a Gentleman.

Wild. Ay, but, on t'other Hand, I have Money enough to bribe the Rogues with: So upon mature Deliberation, I would fight for her.——But no more of her. Prithee, *Vizard,* can't you recommend a Friend to a pretty Mistress by the by, till I can find my own? You have Store I'm sure; you cunning poaching Dogs make surer Game, than we that hunt open and fair. Prithee now, good *Vizard.*

Viz. Let me consider a little.——Now Love and Revenge inspire my Politics. [*Aside.*

[*Pauses whilst Sir* Harry *walks singing.*

Wild. Pshaw! thou'rt as long studying for a new Mistress, as a Drawer is piercing a new Pipe.

Viz. I design a new Pipe for you, and wholesome Wine; you'll therefore bear a little Expectation.

Wild. Ha! say'st thou, dear *Vizard?*

Viz. A Girl of Sixteen, Sir *Harry.*

Wild. Now sixteen thousand Blessings light on thee.

Viz. Pretty and witty.

Wild. Ay, ay, but her Name, *Vizard.*

Viz. Her Name! yes,—— she has the softest whitest Hand that e'er was made of Flesh and Blood; her Lips so balmy sweet——

Wild. Well, well, but where shall I find her, Man?

Viz. Find her!——but then her Foot, Sir *Harry;* she dances to a Miracle.

Wild. Prithee don't distract me.

Viz.

I think, Madam, I'm like to be very virtuous
Service, if you teach me all thoſe Tricks that you
our Lovers.

You're a Fool, Child! obſerve this, that tho'
ıan ſwear, forſwear, lie, diſſemble, back-bite,
d, vain, malicious, any Thing, if ſhe ſecures the
hance, ſhe's ſtill virtuous; that's a Maxim.

I can't be perſuaded tho', Madam, but that you
ɔv'd Sir *Harry Wildair* in *Paris.*

Of all the Lovers I ever had, he was my greateſt
for I cou'd never make him uneaſy: I left him
l in a Duel upon my Account: I long to know
· the Fop be kill'd or not.

Enter Standard.

rd! no ſooner talk of killing, but the Soldier is
l up. You're upon hard Duty, Colonel, to ſerve
ng, your Country, and a Miſtreſs too.

'. The latter, I muſt confeſs, is the hardeſt; for
, Madam, we can be reliev'd in our Duty; but
ɛ, who wou'd take our Poſt, is our Enemy;
ion in Glory is tranſporting, but Rivals here in-
e.

Thoſe that bear away the Prize in the Field,
boaſt the ſame Succeſs in the Bed-chamber;
hink, conſidering the Weakneſs of our Sex, we
make thoſe our Companions who can be our
ons.

'. I once, Madam, hop'd the Honour of defend-
from all Injuries, thro' a Title to your lovely
but now my Love muſt attend my Fortune. My
ſſion, Madam, was my Paſs-port to the Fair;
a Nobleneſs to my Paſſion, it ſtampt a Value in
e; 'twas once the Life of Honour, but now its
g-Sheet, and with it muſt my Love be buried.

What! diſbanded, Colonel?

'. Yes, Mrs. *Parly.*

Faugh, the nauſeous Fellow! he ſtinks of Poverty
[*Aſide.*

His Misfortune troubles me, 'cauſe it may pre-
ɾ Deſigns. [*Aſide.*

'. I'll chuſe, Madam, rather to deſtroy my Paſ-
Abſence abroad, than have it ſtarv'd at home.

L

Lure. I'm forry, Sir, you have fo mean an Opinion of my Affection, as to imagine it founded upon your Fortune. And to convince you of your Miftake, here I vow by all that's facred, I own the fame Affection now as before. Let it fuffice, my fortune is confiderable.

Stand. No, Madam, no; I'll never be a Charge to her I love! The Man that fells himfelf for Gold, is the worft of Proftitutes.

Lure. Now were he any other Creature but a Man, I coo'd love him.　　　　　　　　　[*Afide.*

Stand. This only laft Requeft I make, that no Title recommend a Fool, no Office introduce a Knave, nor Coat a Coward, to my Place in your Affections; fo farewel my Country, and adieu my Love.　　[*Exit.*

Lure. Now the Devil take thee for being fo honourable: Here, *Parly*, call him back, I fhall lofe half my Diverfion elfe. Now for a trial of Skill. [*Re-enter* Colonel. Sir, I hope you'll pardon my Curiofity: When do you take your Journey?

Stand. To-morrow morning, early, Madam.

Lure. So fuddenly! which way are you defign'd to travel?

Stand. That I can't yet refolve on.

Lure. Pray, Sir, tell me; pray, Sir; I intreat you, why are you fo obftinate?

Stand. Why are you fo curious, Madam?

Lure. Becaufe————

Stand. What!

Lure. Becaufe, I, I, ————

Stand. Becaufe! What, Madam?—Pray tell me.

Lure. Becaufe I defign to follow you.　　[*Crying.*

Stand. Follow me! By all that's great, I ne'er was proud before.
But fuch Love from fuch a Creature
Might fwell the Vanity of the proudeft Prince.
Follow me! By Heavens thou fhalt not.
What! expofe thee to the Hazards of a Camp———
Rather I'll ftay, and here
Bear the Contempt of Fools, and worft of Fortune.

Lure. You need not, fhall not; my Eftate for both is fufficient.

Stand. Thy Eftate! No, I'll turn a Knave, and purchafe one myfelf; I'll cringe to the proud Man I under-
　　　　　　　　　　　　　　　　　　　　mine

mine, and fawn on him that I wou'd bite to Death; I'll
tip my Tongue with Flattery, and smooth my Face with
Smiles; I'll turn Pimp, Informer, Office-broker, nay
Coward, to be great; and sacrifice it all to thee, my
generous Fair.

Lure. And I'll dissemble, lie, swear, jilt, any thing,
but I'll reward thy Love, and recompense thy noble
Passion.

Stand. Sir *Harry*, ha, ha, ha! poor Sir *Harry*, ha,
ha, ha! Rather kiss her Hand, than the Pope's Toe,
ha, ha, ha!

Lure. What Sir *Harry*, Colonel! What Sir *Harry!*

Stand. Sir *Harry Wildair*, Madam.

Lure. What! Is he come over?

Stand. Ay, and he told me—but I don't believe a
Syllable on't.

Lure. What did I tell you?

Stand. Only called you his Mistress, and pretending to
be extravagant in your Commendation, would vainly
insinuate the Praise of his own Judgment and good Fortune in a Choice.———

Lure. How easily is the Vanity of Fops tickled by our
Sex!

Stand. Why, your Sex is the Vanity of Fops.

Lure. On my Conscience, I believe so. This Gentleman, because he danc'd well, I pitch'd on for a Partner at
a Ball in *Paris*, and ever since he has so persecuted me
with Letters, Songs, Dances, Serenading, Flattery,
Foppery, and Noise, that I was forc'd to fly the Kingdom——And I warrant you he made you jealous.

Stand. Faith, Madam, I was a little uneasy.

Lure. You shall have a plentiful Revenge; I'll send
him back all his foolish Letters, Songs and Verses, and
you yourself shall carry 'em; 'twill afford you Opportunity of triumphing, and free me from his farther Impertinence; for of all men he's my Aversion. I'll run and
fetch them instantly.

Stand. Dear Madam, a rare Project! How shall I
bait him like *Actæon* with his own Dogs.——Well, Mrs.
Parly, it is order'd by *Act of Parliament*, that you receive
no more Pieces, Mrs. *Parly*.———

Par. 'Tis provided by the same Act, that you send no
more Messages by me, good Colonel; you must not pre-

tend

tend to ſend any more Letters, unleſs you can pay the Poſtage.

Stand. Come, come, don't.be mercenary ; take Example by your Lady, be honourable.

Par. A-lack-a-day, Sir, it ſhews as ridiculous and haughty for us to imitate our Betters in their Honour, as in their Finery ; leave Honour to Nobility that can ſupport it : We poor Folks, Colonel, have no Pretence to't ; and truly, I think, Sir, that your Honour ſhou'd be caſhier'd with your Leading-ſtaff.

Stand. 'Tis one of the greateſt Curſes of Poverty, to be the Jeſt of Chambermaids !

Enter Lurewell.

Lure. Here's the Packet, Colonel ; the whole Magazine of Love's Artillery,   [*Gives him the Packet.*

Stand. Which ſince I have gain'd, I will turn upon the Enemy. Madam, I'll bring you the News of my Victory this Evening. Poor Sir *Harry*, ha, ha, ha ! [*Exit.*

Lure. To the right about as you were ; march, Colonel ! ha, ha, ha !

Vain Man, who boaſts of ſtudy'd Parts and Wiles !
Nature in us, your deepeſt Art beguiles,
Stamping deep Cunning in our Frowns and Smiles.
You toil for Art, your Intellects you trace ;
Woman, without a Thought, bears Policy in her Face.

The End of the firſt ACT.

❖❖❖❖❖❖❖❖❖❖❖❖❖§❖§❖❖❖❖❖❖❖❖❖❖❖

ACT II.

SCENE, Clincher *Junior's Lodgings.*

Enter Clincher *opening a Letter, Servant following.*

Dear Brother.

Clin.—reads. I *Will ſee you preſently ; I have ſent this Lad to wait on you, he can inſtruct you in the Faſhions of the Town ; I am your affectionate Brother,*
Clincher.

Very well, and what's your Name, Sir ?

Dick.

Dick. My Name is *Dicky*, Sir?

Clin. *Dicky!*

Dick, Ay, *Dicky,* Sir.

Clin. Very well, a pretty Name! And what can you do, Mr. *Dicky?*

Dicky. Why, Sir, I can powder a Wig, and pick up a Whore.

Clin. O Lord! O Lord! A Whore! Why are there many Whores in this Town?

Dick. Ha, ha, ha! many Whores? There's a Queftion indeed; why, Sir, there are above five hundred Surgeons in Town.—Haik'e, Sir, do you fee that Woman there in the Velvet Scarf, and red Knots?

Clin. Ay, Sir, what then?

Dick. Why fhe fhall be at your Service in three Minutes, as I'm a Pimp.

Clin. O *Jupiter Ammon!* Why fhe's a Gentlewoman.

Dick. a Gentlewoman! Why fo are all the Whores in Town, Sir.

Enter Clincher *Senior.*

Clin. fen. Brother, you're welcome to *London!*

Clin. jun. I thought, Brother, you ow'd fo much to the Memory of my Father, as to wear Mourning for his Death.

Clin. fen. Why fo I do, Fool; I wear this becaufe I have the Eftate, and you wear that, becaufe you have not the Eftate. You have caufe to mourn indeed, Brother. Well, Brother, I'm glad to fee you, fare you well. *[Going.*

Clin. jun. Stay, ftay, Brother; where are you going?

Clin. fen. How natural 'tis for a Country Booby to afk impertinent Queftions. Hark'e, Sir, is not my Father Dead?

Clin. jun. Ay, ay, to my Sorrow.

Clin. fen. No matter for that, he's dead; and am not I a young powder'd extravagant *Englifh* Heir?

Clin. jun. Very right, Sir.

Clin. fen. Why then, Sir, you may be fure that I am going to the *Jubilee,* Sir.

Clin. jun. *Jubilee!* What's that?

Clin. fen. *Jubilee!* Why the *Jubilee* is——faith, I don't know what it is.

Dick.

Dick. Why, the *Jubilee* is the fame thing with our *Lord Mayor's* Day in the City; there will be *Pageants*, and *Squibs*, and *Raree Shows*, and all that, Sir.

Clin. jun. And muft you go fo foon, Brother?

Clin. fen. Yes, Sir, for I muft ftay a Month in *Amfter-dam*, to ftudy Poetry.

Clin. jun. Then I fuppofe, Brother, you travel through *Mufcovy* to learn Fafhions, don't you, Brother?

Clin. fen. Brother! Prithee, *Robin*, don't call me Brother; Sir will do every jot as well.

Clin. jun. O *Jupiter Ammon!* Why fo?

Clin. fen. Becaufe People will imagine that you have a Spite at me.————But have you feen your Coufin *Ange-lica* yet, and her Mother the Lady *Darling?*

Clin. jun. No, my Dancing-mafter has not been with me yet. How fhall I falute them, Brother?

Clin. fen. Pfhaw, that's eafy; 'tis only two Scrapes, a Kifs, and your humble Servant. I'll tell you more when I come from the *Jubilee.* Come along. [*Exeunt.*

SCENE, *Lady* Darling's *Houfe.*

Enter Wildair *with a Letter.*

Wild. *L* Ike *Light and Heat incorporate we lay,*
We blefs'd the Night, and curs'd the coming Day.

Well, if this Paper-kite flies fure, I'm fecure of my Game—Humph! The prettieft *Bordel* I have feen, a very ftately genteel one. [*Footmen crofs the Stage.*
Hey day! Equipage too! Now for a Bawd by the *Cur-tefy*, and a Whore with a *Coat of Arms.*—'Sdeath, I'm afraid I've miftaken the Houfe.

Enter Lady Darling.

No, this muft be the Bawd by her Bulk.

Darl. Your Bufinefs, pray, Sir?

Wild. Pleafure, Madam.

Darl. Then, Sir, you have no Bufinefs here.

Wild. This Letter, Madam, will inform you farther; Mr. *Vizard* fent it, with his humble Service to your Ladyfhip.

Darl. How does my Coufin, Sir?

Wild. Ay, her Coufin too; that's right Procurefs again.
Madam,

Madam,

Darl. reads. EArneſt Inclination to ſerve——Sir Harry—— ——Madam——Court my Couſin—— Gentleman————Fortune————

Your Ladyſhip's moſt humble Servant.

VIZARD.

Sir, Your Fortune and Quality are ſufficient to recommend you any where; but what goes farther with me, is the Recommendation of ſo ſober and pious a young Gentleman as my Couſin *Vizard.*

Wild. A right ſanctify'd Bawd o'my Word.

Darl. Sir *Harry*, your Converſation with Mr. *Vizard* argues you a Gentleman, free from the looſe and vicious Carriage of the Town; I'll therefore call my Daughter.
[*Exit.*

Wild. Now go thy way for an illuſtrious Bawd of *Babylon*——She dreſſes up a Sin ſo religiouſly, that the Devil wou'd hardly know it of his making.

Re enter Darling *with* Angelica.

Darl. Pray, Daughter, uſe him civilly; ſuch Matches don't offer every Day.

Wild. O all ye Powers of Love! An Angel! 'Sdeath, what Money have I got in my Pocket! I can't offer her leſs than twenty Guineas——and by *Jupiter* ſhe's worth a hundred.

Angel. 'Tis he! The very ſame! And his Perſon as agreeable as his Character of good Humour——Pray Heav'n his Silence proceed from Reſpect.

Wild. How innocent ſhe looks! How would that Modeſty adorn Virtue, when it makes even Vice look ſo charming!——By Heaven there's ſuch a commanding Innocence in her Looks, that I dare not aſk the Queſtion.

Angel. Now all the Charms of real Love and feign'd Indifference aſſiſt me to engage his Heart, for mine is loſt already.

Wild. Madam—I, I——Zoons, I cannot ſpeak to her——But ſhe's a Whore, and I will——Madam, in ſhort, I, I——O Hypocriſy, Hypocriſy, what a charming Sin art thou?

Angel. He is caught; now to ſecure my Conqueſt—— I thought, Sir, you had Buſineſs to communicate.

Wild. Business to communicate! How nicely she words it! Yes, Madam, I have a little Business to communicate. Don't you love singing Birds, Madam?

Angel. That's an odd Question for a Lover———Yes, Sir.

Wild. Why then, Madam, here is a Nest of the prettiest Goldfinches that ever chirp'd in a Cage; twenty young ones, I assure you, Madam.

Angel. Twenty young ones! What then, Sir?

Wild. Why then, Madam, there are—twenty young ones ——'Slife, I think twenty is pretty fair.

Angel. He's mad, sure— Sir *Harry*, when you have learn'd more Wit and Manners, you shall be welcome here again.

Wild. Wit and Manners! Egad, now I conceive there is a great deal of Wit and Manners in twenty Guineas—I'm sure 'tis all the Wit and Manners I have about me at present. What shall I do?

Enter Clincher *junior and* Dicky.

What the Devil's here? Another Cousin, I warrant ye! Hark'e, Sir, can you lend me ten or a dozen Guineas instantly? I'll pay you fifteen for them in three Hours, upon my Honour.

Clin. jun. These *London* Sparks are plaguy impudent! This Fellow, by his Wig and Assurance, can be no less than a Courtier.

Dick. He's rather a Courtier by his borrowing.

Clinch. jun Faith, Sir, I ha'n't above five Guineas about me.

Wild. What Business have you here then, Sir? For to my Knowledge twenty won't be sufficient.

Clinch. jun. Sufficient! For what, Sir?

Wild What, Sir! Why, for that, Sir; what the Devil should it be, Sir? I know your Business, notwithstanding all your Gravity, Sir.

Clinch. jun. My Business! Why my Cousin lives here.

Wild. I know your Cousin does live here, and *Vizard's* Cousin, and every Body's Cousin.———Hark'e, Sir, I shall return immediately; and if you offer to touch her till I come back, I shall cut your Throat, Rascal.   [*Exit.*

Clinch jun. Why the Man's mad, sure?

Dick. Mad, Sir, ay; why he's a Beau.

Clinch.

Clinch. jun. A Beau! What's that? Are all Madmen
lux?

Dick. No, Sir; but moſt Beaux are Madmen. But now
your Couſin: Remember your three Scrapes, a Kiſs,
I your humble Servant. [*Exeunt, as into the Houſe.*

SCENE, *the Street.*

Enter Wildair, *Colonel following.*

Stand. Sir *Harry*, Sir *Harry!*

Wild. I'm in haſte, Colonel; beſides, if you're in no
tter Humour than when I parted with you in the Park
is Morning, your Company won't be very agreeable.

Stand. You're a happy Man, Sir *Harry*, who are never
t of Humour: Can nothing move your Gall, Sir *Harry?*

Wild. Nothing but Impoſſibilities, which are the ſame as
thing.

Stand. What Impoſſibilities?

Wild. The Reſurrection of my Father to diſinherit me,
an Act of Parliament againſt Wenching. A Man of
ght thouſand Pounds *per Annum* to be vext! No, no;
ager and Spleen are Companions for younger Brothers.

Stand. Suppoſe one call'd you Son of a Whore behind
ur Back.

Wild. Why, then wou'd I call him Raſcal behind his
ick; ſo we're even.

Stand. But ſuppoſe you had loſt a Miſtreſs.

Wild. Why, then I wou'd get another.

Stand. But ſuppoſe you were diſcarded by the Woman
u love, that wou'd ſurely trouble you.

Wild. You're miſtaken, Colonel; my Love is neither ro-
antically honourable, nor meanly mercenary; 'tis only a
ach of Gratitude; while ſhe loves me, I love her; when
e deſiſts, the Obligation's void.

Stand. But to be miſtaken in your Opinion, Sir; if the
ady *Lurewell* (only ſuppoſe it) had diſcarded you—I ſay,
ly ſuppoſe it——and had ſent your Diſcharge by me.

Wild. Pſhaw! that's another Impoſſibility.

Stand. Are you ſure of that?

Wild. Why, 'twere a Soleciſm in Nature. Why ſhe's a
lib of me, Sir. She dances with me, ſings with me, plays
ith me, ſwea-- with me, lies with me.

VOL. I.   K   *Stand.*

Stand. How, Sir?

Wild. I mean in an honourable Way; that is, ſhe for me. In ſhort, we are as like one another as a couple of Guineas.

Stand. Now that I have rais'd you to the higheſt Pinnacle of Vanity, will I give you ſo mortifying a Fall, ſhall daſh your Hopes to Pieces.——I pray your Honour peruſe theſe Papers.   [*Gives him the Packet*

Wild. What is't, the Muſter-Roll of your Regiment, Colonel?

Stand. No, no, 'tis a Liſt of your Forces in your Love Campaign; and, for your Comfort, all diſbanded.

Wild. Prithee, good Metaphorical Colonel, what d' mean?

Stand. Read, Sir, read; theſe are the *Sibyls* Leaves that will unfold your Deſtiny.

Wild. So it be not a falſe Deed to cheat me of Eſtate, what care I——[*Opening the Packet*] Humph! Hand! To the Lady *Lurewell*—To the Lady *Lurewell* To the Lady *Lurewell*——What the Devil haſt thou been tampering with, to conjure up theſe Spirits?

Stand. A certain familiar of your Acquaintance, Sir Read, read.

Wild [*Reading*]—Madam, my Paſſion—ſo natural—ye Beauty contending—Force of Charms——Mankind—Eternal Admirer *Wildair!* I ne'er was aſham'd of my Name before.

Stand. What, Sir *Harry Wildair* out of Humour! ha, ha! Poor Sir *Harry*; more Glory in her Smile than in the *Jubilee* at *Rome*, ha, ha, ha! But then her Foot, Sir *Harry* ſhe dances to a Miracle! ha, ha, ha! Fie, Sir *Harry*, Man of your Parts write Letters not worth keeping! What ſay'ſt thou, my dear Knight Errant? ha, ha, ha! you muſt ſeek Adventures now indeed.

Wild. [*ſings*] No, no, let her wander, &c.

Stand. You are jilted to ſome Tune, Sir; blown up with falſe Muſic, that's all.

Wild. Now, why ſhould I be angry that a Woman is Woman? Since Inconſtancy and Falſhood are grounded their Natures, how can they help it?

Stand. Then they muſt be grounded in your Nature; ſhe's a Rib of you, Sir *Harry*.

Wi.

Here's a Copy of Verſes too; I muſt turn Poet in
l's Name——Stay—'Sdeath, what's here? This is
l—Oh the charming Characters! *My dear* Wildair.
] That's I egad! *this buff bluff Colonel*——that's
re rareſt fool in Nature—the Devil he is!—*and as
t I us'd bim*—with all my Heart, faith——*I had no
ay of letting bim know that I lodge in St.* James's *near*
Lamb. *Lurewell.* Colonel, I am your moſt humble

Hold, Sir, you ſha'n't go yet; I ha'n't deliver'd
Meſſage.
Upon my Faith but you have, Colonel.
Well, well, own your Spleen; out with it, I know
ke to burſt.
I am ſo, egad! ha, ha, ha!
　　　　　　　[*Laugh and point at one another.*
, Ay, with all my Heart, ha, ha!
ell, that's forc'd, Sir *Harry.*
I was never better pleas'd in all my Life, by

. Well, Sir *Harry,* 'tis Prudence to hide your Con-
ten there's no Help for't—: But to be ſerious now.
ly has ſent you back all your Papers there—I was
s not to look upon 'em.
I'm glad on't, Sir; for there were ſome Things that
not have you ſee.
. All this ſhe has done for my Sake, and I deſire
uld decline any farther Pretenſions for your own
c, honeſt, good-natur'd Sir *Harry,* I'm your humble
　　　　　　　[*Exit.*
Ha, ha, ha, poor Colonel! O the Delight of an
as Miſtreſs! what a Life and Briſkneſs it adds
mour, like the Loves of mighty *Jove,* ſtill ſuing in
: Shapes. A *Legerdemain Miſtreſs,* who, *Præſto!*
nd ſhe's vaniſh'd; then *Hey!* in an Inſtant in your
gain. 　　　　　　　[*Going.*

　　　　Enter Vizard.

Well met, Sir *Harry;* what News from the Iſland
:?
. Faith, we made but a broken Voyage by your
but now I am bound for another Port: I told you
onel was my Rival.
　　　K 2　　　　　　　　*Viz.*

Viz. The Colonel! curs'd Misfortune! another!

[*Aſide.*

Wild. But the civileſt in the World; he brought me Word where my Miſtreſs lodges: The Story's too long to tell you now, for I muſt fly.

Viz. What! have you given over all Thoughts of *Angelica?*

Wild. No, no, I'll think of her ſome other Time. But now for the Lady *Lurewell:* Wit and Beauty calls.

That Miſtreſs ne'er can pall her Lover's Joys,
Whoſe Wit can whet, when'er her Beauty cloys.
Her little amorous Frauds all Truths excel,
And make us happy, being deceiv'd ſo well.   *Exit.*

Viz. ſolus.——The Colonel my Rival too! how ſhall I manage? There is but one Way—him and the Knight will I ſet a tilting, where one cuts t'other's Throat, and the Survivor's hang'd: So there will be two Rivals pretty decently diſpos'd of. Since Honour may oblige them to play the Fool, why ſhould not Neceſſity engage me to play the Knave.

[*Exit*

S C E N E, Lurewell's *Lodgings.*

Lurewell *and* Parly.

Lure. Has my Servant brought me the Money from my Merchant?

Par. No, Madam; he met Alderman *Smuggler* at *Charing Croſs,* who has promis'd to wait on you himſelf immediately.

Lure. 'Tis odd that this old Rogue ſhou'd pretend to love me, and at the ſame Time cheat me of my Money.

Par. 'Tis well, Madam, if he don't cheat you of your Eſtate; for you ſay the Writings are in his Hands.

Lure. But what Satisfaction can I get of him? Oh! here he comes.

Enter Smuggler.

Mr. Alderman, your Servant; have you brought me any Money, Sir?

Smug. Faith, Madam, Trading is very dead; what with paying the Taxes, raiſing the Cuſtoms, Loſſes at Sea abroad,

and

and maintaining our Wives at home, the Bank is reduc'd very low.

Lure. Come, come, Sir, thefe Evafions won't ferve your Turn; I mull have Money, Sir——I hope you don't defign to cheat me.

Smug. Cheat you, Madam! have a care what you fay: I'm an Alderman, Madam! Cheat you, Madam! I have been an honeft Citizen thefe five and thirty Years!

Lure. An honeft Citizen! bear witnefs, *Parly!* I fhall trap him in more Lies prefently.——Come, Sir, tho' I am a Woman, I can take a Courfe.

Smug. What Courfe, Madam? You'll go to Law, will ye? I can maintain a Suit of Law, be it right or wrong, thefe forty Years, I am fure of that, thanks to the honeft Practice of the Courts.

Lure. Sir, I'll blaft your Reputation, and fo ruin your Credit.

Smug. Blaft my Reputation! he, he, he! Why, I'm a religious Man, Madam! I have been very inftrumental in the Reformation of Manners. Ruin my Credit! ah, poor Woman. There is but one Way, Madam,—you have a fweet leering Eye.

Lure. You inftrumental in the Reformation! How?

Smug. I whipt all the *Whores, Cut and Long-Tail,* out of the *Parifh:*——Ah! that leering Eye!——Then I voted for pulling down the Playhoufe:——Ah! that Ogle, that Ogle:—— Then my own pious Example:——Ah! that Lip, that Lip!

Lure. Here's a religious Rogue for you now!——As I hope to be fav'd, I have a good mind to beat the Old Monfter.

Smug. Madam, I have brought you about a hundred and fifty Guineas, (a great deal of Money as Times go) and——

Lure. Come, give 'em me.

Smug. Ah! that Hand, that Hand, that pretty foft, white—I have brought it, you fee; but the Condition of the Obligation is fuch, that whereas that leering Eye, that pouting Lip, that pretty foft Hand, that——you underftand me; you underftand, I'm fure you do, you little Rogue——

Lure. Here's a Villain now, fo covetous, that he won't Wench upon his own Coft, but would bribe me with my own Money. I'll be reveng'd——Upon my Word, Mr. Alderman, you make me blufh; what d'ye mean, pray?

Smug.

Smug. See here, Madam.

                    [*Puts a Piece of Money in his Mouth.*
Buſs and Guinea, Buſs and Guinea, Buſs and Guinea.

  Lure. Well, Mr. Alderman, you have ſuch pretty win-
ning Ways, that I will, ha, ha, ha, ha!

  Smug. Will you indeed, he, he, he! my little Cocket;
and when? and where? and how?

  Lure. 'Twill be a difficult Point, Sir, to ſecure both our
Honours; you muſt therefore be diſguis'd, Mr. Alderman.

  Smug. Pſhaw! no matter, I am an old Fornicator, I'm
not half ſo religious as I ſeem to be. You little Rogue;
why, I'm diſguis'd as I am; our Sanctity is all Outſide, all
Hypocriſy.

  Lure. No Man is ſeen to come into this Houſe after
Night-fall; you muſt therefore ſneak in, when 'tis dark, in
Woman's Cloaths.

  Smug. With all my Heart.—I have a Suit on purpoſe, my
little Cocket: I love to be diſguis'd, I cod, I make a very
handſome Woman, I cod I do.

Enter Servant, whiſpers Lurewell.

  Lure. Oh! Mr. Alderman, ſhall I beg you to walk into
the next Room? here are ſome Strangers coming up.

  Smug. Buſs and Guinea firſt; ah, my little Cocket
                                   [*Exit*

Enter Wildair.

  Wild. My Life, my Soul, my all that Heaven can give.

  Lure. Death's Life with thee, without thee Death to live.

Welcome, my dear Sir *Harry*; I ſee you got my Directions

  Wild. Directions! in the moſt charming Manner, thou
dear *Machiavel* of Intrigue.

  Lure. Still briſk and airy, I find, Sir *Harry.*

  Wild. The Sight of you, Madam, exalts my Air, and
makes Joy lighten in my Face.

  Lure. I have a thouſand Queſtions to aſk you, Sir *Harry*
How d'ye like *France?*

  Wild. Ah! *eſt le plus beau Pais du Monde.*

  Lure. Then what made you leave it ſo ſoon?

  Wild. Madam, *vous voyez que je vous ſuy par-tout.*

  Lure. O Monſieur, *je vouz ſuis fort obligée*—But, where'
the Court now?

                                        Wil

At *Marli*, Madam.

And where my Count *La Valier?*

His Body's in the Church of *Nôtre Dame*; I don't
here his Soul is.

What Difeafe did he die of?

A *Duel*, Madam; I was his *Doctor.*

How d'ye mean?

As moft Doctors do, I kill'd him.

En Cavalier, my dear Knight Errant; well, and
nd how; what Intrigues, what Gallantries are car-
n in the *Beau Monde?*

I fhou'd afk you that Queftion, Madam, fince your
p makes the *Beau Monde* wherever you come.

Ah! Sir *Harry*, I've been almoft ruin'd, pefter'd to
here, by the inceffant Attacks of a mighty Colonel;
xfieg'd me as clofe as our Army did *Namur.*

I hope your Ladyfhip did not furrender tho'.

No, no, but was forced to capitulate; but fince
come to raife the Siege, we'll dance, and fing, and

And love and kifs—*Montrez moy votre Chambre.*

Attande, attande, un peu—I remember, Sir *Harry*,
omis'd me in *Paris*, never to afk that impertinent
n again.

Pfhaw, Madam, that was above two Months ago;
Madam, Treaties made in *France* are never kept.

Wou'd you marry me, Sir *Harry?*

Oh! *Le marriage eft une grand male.*——But I will
you.

Your Word, Sir, is not to be rely'd on; if a Gentle-
ill forfeit his Honour in Dealings of Bufinefs, we may
bly fufpect his Fidelity in an Amour.

My Honour in Dealings of Bufinefs! why, Ma-
never had any Bufinefs all my life.

Yes, Sir *Harry*, I have heard a very odd Story,
forry that a Gentleman of your Figure fhou'd un-
he Scandal.

Out with it, Madam.

Why, the Merchant, Sir, that tranfmitted your
Exchange to you in *France*, complains of fome in-
ınd difhonourable Dealings.

K 4 *Wild.*

Wild. Who, old *Smuggler!*

Lure. Ay, ay, you know him I find.

Wild. I have ſome Reaſon, I think; why, the Rogue has cheated me of above five hundred Pounds within theſe three Years.

Lure. 'Tis your Buſineſs then to acquit yourſelf publicly; for he ſpreads the Scandal every where.

Wild. Acquit myſelf publicly! —— Here, Sirrah, my Coach; I'll drive inſtantly into the City, and cane the old Villain round the *Royal Exchange*; he ſhall run the Gauntlet through a thouſand bruſht Beavers and formal Cravats.

Lure. Why, he is in the Houſe now, Sir.

Wild. What, in this Houſe?

Lure. Ay, in the next Room.

Wild. Then, Sirrah, lend me your Cudgel.

Lure. Sir *Harry,* you won't raiſe a Diſturbance in my Houſe?

Wild. Diſturbance, Madam, no, no; I'll beat him with the Temper of a Philoſopher. Here, Mrs. *Parly,* ſhew me the Gentleman.　　　　　　　　[Exit. *with Parly*

Lure. Now ſhall I get the old Monſter well beaten, and Sir *Harry* peſter'd next Term with Bloodſheds, Batteries Coſts and Damages, Solicitors and Attorneys; and if they don't teize him out of his good Humour, I'll never play again.　　　　　　　　　　　　　　　　[*Exit*

SCENE *changes to another Room in the ſame Houſe.*
Enter Smuggler.

Smug. O, this damn'd Tide-waiter! A Ship and Cargo worth five thouſand Pounds! why, 'tis richly worth five hundred Perjuries.

Enter Wildair.

Wild. Dear Mr. Alderman, I'm your moſt devoted and humble Servant.

Smug. My beſt Friend, Sir *Harry,* you're welcome to *England.*

Wild. I'll aſſure you, Sir, there's not a Man in the King's Dominions I am gladder to meet, dear, dear Mr. Alderman
　　　　　　　　　　　　　　　　[*Bowing very low*
　　　　　　　　　　　　　　　　　　　　Smug.

Smug. O Lord, Sir, you Travellers have the moft obliging ways with you.

Wild. There is a Bufinefs, Mr. Alderman, fall'n out,
which you may oblige me infinitely by——I am very forry
that I am forc'd to be troublefome; but Neceffity, Mr.
Alderman.

Smug. Ay, Sir, as you fay, Neceffity——But upon my
Word, Sir, I am very fhort of Money at prefent, but——

Wild. That's not the Matter, Sir; I'm above an Obligation
that way; but the Bufinefs is, I'm reduc'd to an indifpenfible
Neceffity of being oblig'd to you for a Beating——Here take
this Cudgel.

Smug. A Beating, Sir *Harry!* ha, ha, ha! I beat a Knight
Baronet! an Alderman turn Cudgel-Player! ha, ha, ha!

Wild. Upon my Word, Sir, you muft beat me, or I
cudgel you; take your Choice.

Smug. Pfhaw, pfhaw, you jeft.

Wild. Nay, 'tis fure as Fate: fo, Alderman, I hope you'll
pardon my Curiofity. [*Strikes him.*

Smug. Curiofity! Duce take your Curiofity, Sir; what
'ye mean?

Wild. Nothing at all; I'm but in jeft, Sir.

Smug. O, I can take any thing in jeft; but a Man might
imagine by the Smartnefs of the Stroke, that you were in
downright earneft.

Wild. Not in the leaft, Sir; [*Strikes him.*], not in the
leaft indeed, Sir.

Smug. Pray, good Sir, no more of your Jefts, for they are
the blunteft Jefts that ever I knew.

Wild. [*Strikes.*] I heartily beg your Pardon, with all my
Heart, Sir.

Smug. Pardon, Sir! well, Sir, that is Satisfaction enough
from a Gentleman: But ferioufly now, if you pafs any
more of your Jefts upon me, I fhall grow angry.

Wild. I humbly beg your Permiffion to break one or two
more. [*Strikes him.*

Smug. O Lord, Sir, you'll break my Bones: Are you
mad, Sir? Murder, Felony, Manflaughter!
[Wild. *knocks him down.*

Wild. Sir, I beg you ten thoufand Pardons; but I am
abfolutely compell'd to't, upon my Honour, Sir: nothing
K 5. can

can be more averſe to my Inclinations, than to
with my honeſt, dear, loving, obliging Friend, the A
man.

[*Striking him all this while,* Smuggler *tumbles
and over. and ſhakes out his Pocket-Book on the F*
Lurewell *enters, takes it up*]

Lure. The old Rogue's Pocket-book; this may h
uſe. [*Aſide.*] O Lord, Sir *Harry's* murdering the poo
Man.——

Smug. O dear Madam. I was beaten in jeſt, 'till
murder'd in good earneſt.

Lure. Well, well, I'll bring you off, *Senior—Fra*
Frapez!

Smug. O! for Charity's Sake, Madam, reſcue a
Citizen.

Lure. O you barbarous Man! Hold! hold! *Frapez*
rudiment!

Frapez! I wonder you are not aſham'd, [*Holding* Wild
poor reverend honeſt Elder—[*Helps* Smug. *up.*] It m
me weep to ſee him in this Condition, poor Man!
Now the Devil take you, Sir *Harry*—For not beating
harder. Well, my Dear, you ſhall come at Night, and
make you amends.   [*Here Sir* Harry *takes S*

Smug. Madam, I will have Amends before I leave
Place.

Sir how durſt you uſe me thus?

Wild. Sir?

Smug. Sir, I ſay that I will have Satisfaction.

Wild. With all my Heart.   [*Throws Snuff into his.*

Smug. O! Murder, Blindneſs, Fire! O Madam, Mac
get me ſome Water! Water, Fire, Fire, Water!

                               [*Exit with* Lure

Wild. How pleaſant is reſenting an Injury without Paſ
'Tis the Beauty of Revenge.

Let Stateſmen plot, and under Buſineſs groan,
And ſtilling public Quiet, loſe their own;
Let Soldiers drudge and fight for Pay, or Fame,
For when they're ſhot, I think 'tis much the ſame;
Let Scholars vex their Brains with Mood and Tenſe,
And mad with Strength of Reaſon, Fools commence,
Loſing their Wits in ſearching after Senſe;

                                                    ſ

Their Summum Bonum *they muſt toil to gain,*
And ſeeking Pleaſure, ſpend their Life in Pain :
I make the moſt of Life, no Hour miſſpend,
Pleaſure's the Mean, and Pleaſure is my End.
No Spleen, no Trouble ſhall my Time deſtroy,
Life's but a Span, I'll every Inch enjoy.   [Exit.

The End of the Second Act.

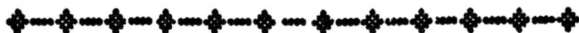

✦━✦━✦━✦━✦ ━ ✦━✦━✦━✦━✦

ACT III.

SCENE, *The Street.*

Enter Standard *and* Vizard.

Stand. I Bring him Word where ſhe lodg'd ! I the civileſt
Rival in the World ! 'Tis impoſſible.

Viz. I ſhall urge it no farther, Sir.
I only thought, Sir, that my Character in the World might
add Authority to my Words without ſo many Repetitions.

Stand. Pardon me, dear *Vizard.*
Our Belief ſtruggles hard before it can be brought to yield
to the Diſadvantage of what we love ;
'Tis ſo great an Abuſe to our Judgment, that it makes the
Faults of our Choice our own Failing.,
But what ſaid Sir *Harry ?*

Viz. He pitied the poor credulous Colonel, laugh'd
heartily.
Flew away with all the Raptures of a Bridegroom, repeating
theſe Lines,

A Miſtreſs ne'er can pall her Lover's Joys,
Whoſe Wit can whet, whene'er her Beauty cloys.

Stand. A Miſtreſs ne'er can pall ! By all my Wrongs he
whores her ! And I'm made their Property. Vengeance !
Vizard, you muſt carry a Note for me to Sir *Harry.*

Viz. What ! a Challenge ! I hope you don't deſign to
fight ?

K 6   *Stand.*

Stand. What! Wear the Livery of my King, and pock
an Affront! 'Twere an Abuse to his Sacred Majesty;
Soldier's Sword, *Vizard*, should start of itself to redress it
Master's Wrong.

Viz. However, Sir, I think it not proper for me to carr
any such Message between Friends.

Stand. I have ne'er a Servant here, what shall I do?

Viz. There's *Tom Errand*, the Porter, that plies at th
Blue Posts, one who knows Sir *Harry* and his Haunts ver
well; you may send a Note by him.

Stand. Here you, Friend.

Viz. I have now some Business, and must take my Leave
I would advise you nevertheless against this Affair.

Stand. No wispering now, nor telling of Friends to pre
vent us. He that disappoints a Man of an honourable Re
venge, may love him foolishly like a Wife, but never value
him as a Friend.

Viz. Nay, the Devil take him that parts you, say I.

Enter Porter running.

Err. Did your Honour call Porter?

Stand. Is your Name *Tom Errand?*

Err. People call me so, an't like your Worship——

Stand. D'ye know Sir *Harry Wildair?*

Err. Ay, very well, Sir; he's one of my best Masters
many a round Half-crown have I had of his Worship; he'
newly come home from *France*, Sir.

Stand. Go to the next Coffee-house, and wait for me
O Woman, Woman, how blest is Man, when favour'd b
your Smiles, and how accurs'd when all those Smiles ar
found but wanton Baits to sooth us to Destruction?

1   *chief Joys with base Allays are curst,*
     our best Things, when once corrupted, worst. [Exit

Enter Wildair *and* Clincher *senior following.*

, *sen.* Sir, Sir, Sir, having some Business of Im
s to communicate to you, I wou'd beg your Atten
ro a trifling Affair that I wou'd impart to your Under
ing.

. What is your trifling Business of Importance, pray

Clinch

b. *fen.* Pray, Sir, are the Roads deep between this
·is.

. Why that Queftion, Sir?

b. *fen.* Becaufe I defign to go to the *Jubilee*, Sir;
ftand that you are a Traveller, Sir; there is an
Travel in the Tie of your Cravat, Sir; there is in-
ir——I fuppofe, Sir, you bought this Lace in *Flan-*

. No, Sir, this Lace was made in *Norway.*

b. *fen. Norway,* Sir!

. Yes, Sir, of the Shavings of Deal-boards.

b. *fen.* That's very ftrange now, faith——Lace made
Shavings of Deal-boards! Egad, Sir, you Travel-
very ftrange Things abroad, very incredible Things
indeed. Well, I'll have a Cravat of the very fame
:fore I come home.

. But, Sir, what Preparations have you made for
urney?

b. *fen.* A Cafe of Pocket-piftols for the Bravo's——
wimming Girdle.

. Why thefe, Sir?

b. *fen.* O Lord! Sir, I'll tell you——fuppofe us in
ow; away goes I to fome Ball—for I'll be a mighty
Then, as I faid, I go to fome Ball, or fome Bear-
, 'tis all one you know——then comes a fine *Italian*
!oba, and plucks me by the Sleeve, *Signior Angle,*
Angle—fhe's a very fine Lady, obferve that—*Signior*
fays fhe.—*Signora,* fays I, and trips after her to the
of a Street, fuppofe it *Ruffel-Street* here, or any
ftreet; then you know, I muft invite her to the
, I can do no lefs.—There up comes her Bravo; the
grows faucy, and I give him an *Englifh* Doufe of the
I can Box, Sir, box tightly; I was a 'Prentice, Sir,
hen, Sir, he whips out his *Stilletto,* and I whips out
l-Dog——flaps him through, trips down Stairs, turns
rner of *Ruffel-Street* again, and whips me into the
ador's Train, and there I'm fafe as a Beau behind
nes.

. Is your Piftol charg'd, Sir?

b. *fen.* Only a Brace of Bullets, that's all, Sir.

. 'Tis a very fine Piftol, truly; pray let me fee it.

b. *fen.* With all my Heart, Sir.

Wild;

Wild. Hark'e, Mr. *Jubilee*, can you digeſt a Brace of
Bullets ?

Clincb. ſen. O by no Means in the World, Sir !

Wild. I'll try the Srength of your Stomach, however.
Sir, you're a dead Man. [*Preſenting the Piſtol to bis Breaſt.*

Clincb. ſen. Conſider, dear Sir ! I am going to the *Jubilee*, when I come home again, I am a dead Man at your
Service.

Wild. O very well, Sir ! but take heed you are not ſo
choleric for the future.

Clincb. ſen. Choleric, Sir ! Oons ! I deſign to ſhoot
ſeven *Italians* a Week, Sir.

Wild. Sir, you won't have Provocation.

Clincb. ſen. Provocation, Sir ! Zauns, Sir, I'll kill any
Man for treading upon my Corns, and there will be a de-
viliſh Throng of People there ; they ſay that all the Princes
in *Italy* will be there.

Wild. And all the Fops and Fiddlers in *Europe*—But the
Uſe of your ſwimming Girdle, pray, Sir ?

Clincb. ſen. O Lord, Sir ! That's eaſy. Suppoſe the Ship
caſt away ; now, whilſt other fooliſh People are buſy at their
Prayers, I whip on my ſwimming Girdle, clap a Month's
Proviſion into my Pocket, and ſails me away like an Egg
in a Duck's Belly.—And hark'e, Sir, I have a new Project
in my Head. Where d'ye think my ſwimming Girdle ſhall
carry me upon this Occaſion ? 'Tis a new Project.

Wild. Where, Sir ?

Clincb. ſen. To *Civita Vecchia*, faith and troth, and ſo
ſave the Charges of my Paſſage. Well, Sir, you muſt pardon me now, I'm going to ſee my Miſtreſs.   [*Exit.*

Wild. This Fellow's an accompliſh'd Aſs before he goes
abroad. Well ! This *Angelica* has got into my Heart, and I
can't get her out of my Head. I muſt pay her t'other Viſit.

SCENE, *Lady* Darling's *Houſe.*

Angelica *ſola.*

Angel. Unhappy State of Woman ! whoſe chief Virtue is
but Ceremony, and our much boaſted Modeſty but a ſlaviſh
Reſtraint. The ſtrict Confinement on our Words, makes
our Thoughts ramble more ; and what preſerves our outward Fame, deſtroys our inward Quiet.——'Tis hard that
Love ſhou'd be deny'd the Privilege of Hatred ; that Scandal

dal and Detraction ſhou'd be ſo much indulg'd, yet ſacred Love and Truth debar'd our Converſation.

Enter Darling, Clincher jun. *and* Dicky.

Darl. This is my Daughter, Couſin.

Dick. Now, Sir, remember your three Scrapes.

Clinch. ſaluting Angelica.]——One, two, three, Your humble Servant. Was not that right, *Dicky?*

Dick. Ay, faith, Sir; but why don't you ſpeak to her?

Clinch. jun. I beg your Pardon, *Dicky*, I know my Diſtance. Wou'd you have me ſpeak to a Lady at the firſt Sight?

Dick. Ay, Sir, by all means; the firſt Aim is the ſureſt.

Clinch. jun. Now for a good Jeſt, to make her laugh heartily.——By *Jupiter Ammon* I'll go give her a Kiſs.

[*Goes towards her.*

Enter Wildair, *interpoſing.*

Wild. 'Tis all to no Purpoſe, I told you ſo before; your pitiful five Guineas will never do—you may go, I'll out-bid you.

Clinch. jun. What the Devil! The Madman's here again.

Darl. Bleſs me, Couſin! What d'ye mean? Affront a Gentleman of his Quality in my Houſe!

Clinch. jun. Quality——Why, Madam, I don't know what you mean by your Madmen, and your Beaux, and your Quality—They're all alike, I believe.

Darl. Pray, Sir, walk with me into the next Room.

[*Exit* Darl. *leading* Clin. Dicky *follows.*

Angel. Sir, if your Converſation be no more agreeable than 'twas the laſt Time, I wou'd adviſe you to make your Viſit as ſhort as you can.

Wild. The Offences of my laſt Viſit, Madam, bore their Puniſhment in the Commiſſion; and have made me as un-eaſy till I receive Pardon, as your Ladyſhip can be till I ſue for it.

Angel. Sir *Harry*, I did not well underſtand the Offence, and muſt therefore proportion it to the Greatneſs of your Apology; if you wou'd therefore have me think it light, take no great Pains in an Excuſe.

Wild. How ſweet muſt the Lips be that guard that Tongue! Then, Madam, no more of paſt Offences, let us prepare for Joys to come; let this ſeal my Pardon.[*Kiſſes her Hand*] And this [*Again*] initiate me to farther Happineſs.

Angel. Hold, Sir,——one Queſtion, Sir *Harry*, and pray anſwer plainly—D'ye love me?

Wild.

Wild. Love you! Does Fire aſcend? Do Hypocrites diſ-ſemble? Uſurers love Gold, or great Men Flattery? Doubt theſe, then queſtion that I love.

Angel. This ſhews your Gallantry, Sir, but not your Love.

Wild. View your own Charms, Madam, then judge my Paſſion; your Beauty raviſhes my Eye, your Voice my Ear, and your Touch has thrill'd my melting Soul.

Angel. If your Words be real, 'tis in your Pow'r to raiſe an equal Flame in me.——

Wild. Nay, then——I ſeize——

Angel. Hold, Sir, 'tis alſo poſſible to make me deteſt and ſcorn you worſe than the moſt profligate of your deceiving Sex.

Wild. Ha! A very odd Turn this. I hope, Madam, you only affect Anger, becauſe you know your Frowns are becoming.

Angel. Sir *Harry*, you being the beſt Judge of your own Deſigns, can beſt underſtand whether my Anger ſhou'd be real or diſſembled; think what ſtrict Modeſty ſhou'd bear, then judge of my Reſentments.

Wild. Strict Modeſty ſhou'd bear! Why faith, Madam, I believe, the ſtricteſt Modeſty may bear fifty Guineas, and I don't believe 'twill bear one Farthing more.

Angel. What d'ye mean, Sir?

Wild. Nay, Madam, what do you mean? if you go to that. I think now fifty Guineas is a fine Offer for your ſtrict Modeſty, as you call it.

Angel. 'Tis more charitable, Sir *Harry*, to charge the Impertinence of a Man of your Figure on his Defect in Underſtanding, than on his Want of Manners.—I'm afraid you're mad, Sir.

Wild. Why, Madam, you're enough to make any Man mad. 'Sdeath, are you not a——

Angel. What, Sir?

Wild. Why, a Lady of—ſtrict Modeſty, if you will have it ſo.

Angel. I ſhall never hereafter truſt common Report, which repreſented you, Sir, a Man of Honour, Wit, and Breeding; for I find you very deficient in them all three.   [*Exit.*

Wild. ſolus. Now I find that the ſtrict Pretences which the Ladies of Pleaſure make to ſtrict Modeſty, is the Reaſon why thoſe of Quality are aſham'd to wear it.

Enter

Enter Vizard.

c. Ah! Sir *Harry*, have I caught you? Well, and Succeſs?

ld. Succeſs! 'Tis a Shame for you young Fellows in a here, to let the Wenches grow ſo ſaucy: I offer'd her Guineas, and ſhe was in her Airs preſently, and flew in a Huff. I cou'd have had a Brace of Counteſſes *ris* for half the Money, and *Je vous remercie* into the iin.

c. Gone in her Airs, ſay you! And did not you foler?

ld. Whither ſhou'd I follow her?

c. Into her Bed-chamber, Man; ſhe went on Purpoſe, a Man of Gallantry, and not underſtand that a Lady's)leas'd when ſhe put on her Airs, as you call it?

ld. She talk'd to me of ſtrict Modeſty, and Stuff.

c. Certainly. Moſt Women magnify their Modeſty, e ſame Reaſon that Cowards boaſt their Courage, bethey have leaſt on't. Come, come, Sir *Harry*, when make your next Aſſault, encourage your Spirits with *Burgundy*; if you ſucceed, 'tis well; if not, you have Excuſe for your Rudeneſs. I'll go in, and make your : for what's paſt. Oh! I had almoſt forgot——Col. 'ard wants to ſpeak with you about ſome Buſineſs.

ld. I'll wait upon him preſently; d'ye know where he)e found?

c. In the Piazza of *Covent-Garden*, about an Hour ', I promis'd to ſee him; and there you may meet to have your Throat cut. [*Aſide.*] I'll go in and inle for you.

ld. But no foul Play with the Lady, *Vizard*.   [*Exit.*

c. No fair Play, I can aſſure you.   [*Exit.*

NE, *The Street before* Lurewell*'s Lodgings*; Clincher ſen. *and* Lurewell *coquetting in the Balcony.*

Enter Standard.

ad. How weak is Reaſon in Diſputes of Love? That g Reaſon which ſo oft pretends to queſtion Works of Omnipotence, yet poorly truckles to our weakeſt Paſand yields implicit Faith to fooliſh Love, paying blind to faithleſs Women's Eyes. I've heard her Falſhood uch preſſing Proofs, that I no longer ſhould diſtruſt it.

Yet

Yet ſtill my Love wou'd baffle Demonſtration, and make
Impoſſibilities ſeem probable. [*Looks up*] Ha! That Fool
too! What, ſtoop ſo low as that Animal!—'Tis true, Women once fall'n, like Cowards in Deſpair, will ſtick at nothing; there's no Medium in their Actions. They muſt be
bright as Angels, or black as Fiends. But now for my Revenge, I'll kick her Cully before her Face, call her Whore,
curſe the whole Sex, and leave her.　　　　[*Goes in.*

Lurewell *comes down with* Clincher. *The Scene changes to a*
Dining-Room.

Lure. O Lord, Sir, it is my Huſband! What will become of you?

Clinch. Ah! Your Huſband! Oh, I ſhall be murdered:
What ſhall I do! Where ſhall I run! I'll creep into an
Oven; I'll climb up the Chimney; I'll fly; I'll ſwim; —
I wiſh to the Lord I were at the *Jubilee* now.——

Lure. Can't you think of any thing, Sir?

Clinch. Think! not I; I never cou'd think to any Purpoſe in my Life.

Enter Tom Errand.

Lure. What do you want, Sir?

Err. Madam, I am looking for Sir *Harry Wildair*; I
ſaw him come in here this Morning; and did imagine he
might be here ſtill, if he is not gone.

Lure. A lucky Hit! Here, Friend, change Cloaths with
this Gentleman, quickly, ſtrip.

Clinch. Ay, ay, quickly, ſtrip: I'll give you half a Crown
to boot. Come here; So.　　　　[*They change Cloaths.*

Lure. Now ſlip you [*To* Clinch.] down Stairs, and wait
at the Door till my Huſband be gone; and get you in there
[*To the Porter.*] till I call you. [*Puts* Errand *in the next Room.*

Enter Standard.

Oh, Sir! Are you come? I wonder, Sir, how you have
the Confidence to approach me after ſo baſe a Trick?

Stand. O Madam, all your Artifices won't avail.

Lure. Nay, Sir, your Artifices won't avail. I thought,
Sir, that I gave you Caution enough againſt troubling me
with Sir *Harry Wildair*'s Company when I ſent his Letters
back by you; yet you, forſooth, muſt tell him where I
lodg'd, and expoſe me again to his impertinent Courtſhip!

Stand. I expoſe you to his Courtſhip!

　　　　　　　　　　　　　　　　　　　　　Lure.

Lure. I'll lay my Life you'll deny it now. Come, come, Sir; a pitiful Lie is as scandalous to a Red Coat as an Oath to a Black. Did not Sir *Harry* himself tell me, that he found out by you where I lodg'd?

Stand. You're all Lies: First, your Heart is false; your Eyes are double; one Look belies another; and then your Tongue does contradict them all—Madam, I see a little Devil just now hammering out a Lie in your *Pericranium.*

Lure. As I hope for Mercy, he's in the right on't. [*Aside.*] Hold, Sir, you have got the Play-house Cant upon your Tongue; and think, that Wit may privilege your railing: But I must tell you, Sir, that what is Satire upon the Stage, is ill Manners here.

Stand. What is feign'd upon the Stage, is here in Reality real Falshood. Yes, yes, Madam,——I expos'd you to the Courtship of your Fool *Clincher*, too; I hope your Female Wiles will impose that upon me——also——

Lure. *Clincher!* Nay, now you're stark mad. I know no such Person.

Stand. O Woman in Perfection! not know him? 'Slife, Madam, can my Eyes, my piercing jealous Eyes, be so deluded? Nay, Madam, my Nose could not mistake him; for I smelt the Fop by his *Pulvilio* from the Balcony down to the Street.

Lure. The Balcony! Ha, ha, ha! the Balcony; I'll be hang'd but he has mistaken Sir *Harry Wildair's* Footman with a new *French* Livery, for a Beau.

Stand. 'Sdeath, Madam, what is there in me that looks like a Cully! Did not I see him?

Lure. No, no, you cou'd not see him; you're dreaming, Colonel. Will you believe your Eyes, now that I have rubb'd them open?—Here, you Friend.

Enter Errand *in* Clincher's *Cloaths.*

Stand. This is Illusion all; my Eyes conspire against themselves. 'Tis Legerdemain.

Lure. Legerdemain! Is that all your Acknowledgment for your rude Behaviour?——Oh, what a Curse is it to love as I do!—But don't presume too far, Sir, on my Affection: For such ungenerous Usage will soon return my tir'd Heart. —Be gone, Sir, [*To the Porter.*] to your impertinent Master, and tell him I shall never be at Leisure to receive any of his troublesome

troubleſome Viſits.—Send to me to know when I ſhou'd be at home!——Be gone, Sir :—I am ſure he has made me an unfortunate Woman.				[*Weep.*

Stand. Nay, then there is no Certainty in Nature ; and Truth is only Falſhood well diſguis'd.

Lure. Sir, had not I own'd my fond fooliſh Paſſion, I ſhou'd not have been ſubject to ſuch unjuſt Suſpicions : But it is an ungrateful Return.				[*Weeping.*

Stand. Now, where are all my firm Reſolves ? I will be-lieve her juſt. My Paſſion rais'd my Jealouſy ; then why mayn't Love be as blind in finding Faults, as in excuſing them ?—I hope, Madam, you'll pardon me, ſince Jealouſy, that magnify'd my Suſpicion, is as much the Effect of Love, as my Eaſineſs in being ſatisfy'd.

Lure. Eaſineſs in being ſatisfy'd ! You Men have got an inſolent Way of extorting Pardon, by perſiſting in your Faults. No, no, Sir ; cheriſh your Suſpicions, and feed up-on your Jealouſy : 'Tis fit Meat for your ſqueamiſh Stomach.

With me all Women ſhou'd this Rule purſue :
Who think us falſe, ſhou'd never find us true.

				[*Exit in a Rage.*

Enter Clincher *in the Porter's Cloaths.*

Clinch. Well, Intriguing is the prettieſt, pleaſanteſt Thing for a Man of my Parts :—How ſhall we laugh at the Huſ-band, when he is gone ?—How ſillily he looks! He's in labour of Horns already.—To make a Colonel a Cuckold! 'Twill be rare News for the Alderman.

Stand. All this Sir *Harry* has occaſion'd ; but he's brave, and will afford me a juſt Revenge :—O! this is the Porter I ſent the Challenge by -——Well, Sir, have you found him?

Clinch. What the Devil does he mean now ?

Stand. Have you given Sir *Harry* the Note, Fellow ?

Clinch. The Note! What Note ?

Stand. The Letter, Blockhead, which I ſent by you to Sir *Harry Wildair*; have you ſeen him ?

Clinch. O Lord, what ſhall I ſay now ? Seen him ? Yes, Sir—No, Sir.—I have, Sir—I have not, Sir.

Stand. The Fellow's mad. Anſwer me directly, Sirrah, or I'll break your Head.

Clinch. I know Sir *Harry* very well, Sir ; but as to the Note, Sir, I can't remember a Word on't : Truth is, I have a very bad Memory.

				Stand.

'. O Sir, I'll quicken your Memory.   [*Strikes him.*

h. Zauns, Sir, hold!—I did give him the Note.

'. And what Anfwer?

h. I mean, I did not give him the Note.

'. What d'ye banter, Rafcal?   [*Strikes him again.*

h. Hold, Sir, hold! He did fend an Anfwer.

'. What was't, Villain?

h. Why, truly Sir, I have forgot it: I told you

iad a very treacherous Memory.

'. I'll engage you fhall remember me this Month,

[*Beats him off, and* Exit.

Enter Lurewell *and* Parly.

Fortboon, fortboon, fortboon! This is better than

led; but Fortune ftill helps the Induftrious.

Enter Clincher.

h. Ah! The Devil take all Intriguing, fay I, and

io firft invented Canes.—That curs'd Colonel has

h a Knack of beating his Men, that he has left

rk of a Collar of Bandileers about my Shoulders.

. O, my poor Gentleman! And was it beaten?

h. Yes, I have been beaten. But where's my

s? my Cloaths?

, What, you won't leave me fo foon, my Dear,

?

h. Will ye! If ever I peep into a Colonel's Tent

may I be forc'd to run the Gauntlet.—But my

s, Madam.

. I fent the Porter down Stairs with them: Did not

et him?

h. Meet him! No, not I.

No! He went out of the Back-door, and is run

way, I'm afraid.

h. Gone, fay you! and with my Cloaths! my fine

Cloaths!—O, the Rogue, the Thief!—I'll have

ng'd for Murder.—But how fhall I get home in this

?

I'm afraid, Sir, the Colonel will be back pre-

for he dines at home.

h. O, then I muft fneak off!

ver fuch an Unfortunate Beau,

re his Coat well thrafh'd, and lofe his Coat alfo?

Lure.

Lure. Thus the noble Poet fpoke Truth:

Nothing fuits worfe with Vice than want of Senfe:
Fools are ftill wicked at their own Expence.

Par. Methinks, Madam, the Injuries you have fuffer'd by Men muft be very great, to raife fuch heavy Refentments againft the whole Sex.

Lure. The greateft Injury that Woman cou'd fuftain; they robb'd me of that Jewel, which preferv'd, exalts our Sex almoft to Angels; but deftroy'd, bebafes us below the worft of Brutes, Mankind.

Par. But I think, Madam, your Anger fhou'd be only confin'd to the Author of your Wrongs.

Lure. The Author! Alas, I know him not, which makes my Wrongs the greater.

Par. Not know him! 'Tis odd, Madam, that a Man fhould rob you of that fame Jewel you mentioned, and you not know him.

Lure. Leave trifling;—'tis a Subject that always fours my Temper: But fince, by thy faithful Service, I have fome Reafon to confide in your Secrecy, hear the ftrange Relation.——Some twelve Years ago, I liv'd at my Father's Houfe in *Oxfordfhire*, bleft with Innocence, the ornamental, but weak Guard of blooming Beauty: I was then juft Fifteen, an Age fatal to the Female Sex: Our Youth is tempting, our Innocence credulous, Romances moving, Love powerful, and Men are—Villains. Then it happened, that three young Gentlemen from the Univerfity coming into the Country, and being benighted, and Strangers, call'd at my Father's: He was very glad of their Company, and offer'd them the Entertainment of his Houfe.

Par. Which they accepted, no doubt: Oh! thefe ftrolling Collegians are never abroad, but upon fome Mifchief.

Lure. They had fome private Frolic or Defign in their Heads, as appear'd by their not naming one another, which my Father perceiving, out of Civility, made no Enquiry into their Affairs; two of them had a heavy, pedantic, Univerfity Air, a Sort of a difagreeable Scholaftic Boorifhnefs in their Behaviour; but the third!

Par. Ah! the third, Madam;—the third of all things, they fay, is very critical.

Lure. He was—but in fhort, Nature cut him out for my undoing ; he feem'd to be about Eighteen.

Par. A fit Match for your Fifteen as cou'd be.

Lure. He had a genteel Sweetnefs in his Face, a grace-ful Comelinefs in his Perfon, and his Tongue was fit to footh foft Innocence to ruin. His very Looks were witty, and his expreffive Eyes fpoke fofter, prettier things, than Words cou'd frame.

Par. There will be Mifchief by and by ; I never heard a Woman talk fo much of Eyes, but there were Tears prefently after.

Lure. His Difcourfe was directed to my Father, but his Looks to me. After Supper I went to my Chamber, and read *Caffandra*, then went to Bed, and dreamt of him all Night, rofe in the Morning, and made Verfes, fo fell defperately in Love.—My Father was fo well pleas'd with his Converfation, that he begg'd their Company next Day ; they confented, and next Night, *Parly*————

Par. Ah, next Night, Madam,—next Night (I'm afraid) was a Night indeed.

Lure. He brib'd my Maid, with his Gold, out of her Honefty ; and me, with his Rhetoric, out of my Honour. —She admitted him to my Chamber, and there he vow'd, and fwore, and wept, and figh'd——and conquer'd.

[Weeps.

Par. A-lack-a-day, poor Fifteen ! *[Weeps.*

Lure. He fwore that he wou'd come down from *Oxford* in a Fortnight, and marry me.

Par. The old Bait ! the old Bait!—I was cheated juft fo myfelf. [*Afide.*] But had not you the Wit to know his Name all this while ?

Lure. Alas! what Wit had Innocence like mine ? He told me, that he was under an Obligation to his Compa-nions of concealing himfelf then, but that he wou'd write to me in two Days, and let me know his Name and Qua-lity. After all the binding Oaths of Conftancy, joining Hands, exchanging Hearts, I gave him a Ring with this Motto, *Love and Honour* ; then we parted, but I never faw the dear Deceiver more.

Par. No, nor never will, I warrant you.

Lure. I need not tell my Griefs, which my Father's Death made a fair Pretence for ; he left me fole Heirefs

and

and Executrix to Three Thousand Pounds a Y(
laſt, my Love for this ſingle Diſſembler turn'd t
tred of the whole Sex; and reſolving to divert
ſancholy, and make my large Fortune ſubſervie
Pleaſure and Revenge, I went to travel, where,
Courts of *Europe,* I have done ſome Execution.
will play my laſt Scene; then retire to my Countr
live ſolitary, and die a Penitent.

Par. But don't you ſtill love this dear Diſſeml

Lure. Moſt certainly: 'Tis Love of him that l
Anger warm, repreſenting the Baſeneſs of Manl
in view; and makes my Reſentments work——
have that old impotent Lecher, *Smuggler,* here to
I have a Plot to ſwinge him, and his preciſe l
Vizard.

Par. I think, Madam, you manage every be
comes in your way.

Lure. No, *Parly;* thoſe Men, whoſe Pretenſions
juſt and honourable, I fairly diſmiſs'd, by lettir
know my firm Reſolutions never to marry. B
Villains that wou'd attempt my Honour, I'v(
fail'd to manage.

Par. What d'ye think of the Colonel, Madam
poſe his Deſigns are honourable.

Lure. That Man's a Riddle; there's ſomething
nour in his Temper that pleaſes; I'm ſure he k
too, becauſe he's ſoon jealous, and ſoon ſatisfy'
he's a Man ſtill.——When I once tried his Pulſ
Marriage, his Blood ran as low as a Coward's.
indeed, that he lov'd me, but cou'd not marry
ſooth, becauſe he was engag'd elſewhere. So po
tence made me diſdain his Paſſion, which otherwi
have been uneaſy to me.——But hang him, I have te
enough.——Beſides, *Parly,* I begin to be tir'd of
venge:——But this Buſs and Guinea I muſt maul on
I'll hanſel his Woman's Cloaths for him. G(
Pen and Ink; I muſt write to *Vizard* too.

Fortune, this once aſſiſt me as before;
Two ſuch Machines can never work in vain,
As thy propitious Wheel, and my projecting Brain.

　　The End of the Third Act.

ACT IV.

SCENE, *Covent-Garden.*

Wildair *and* Standard *meeting.*

I Thought, Sir *Harry,* to have met you ere this
in a more convenient Place; but since my
;s were without Ceremony, my Revenge shall be
Draw, Sir!

1. Draw, Sir! What shall I draw?

ıd. Come, come, Sir, I like your facetious Humour
nough; it shews Courage and Unconcern. I know
ave; and therefore use you thus. Draw your Sword.

d. Nay, to oblige you, I will draw; but the Devil
ne if I fight.—Perhaps, Colonel, this is the prettiest
you have seen.

ıd. I doubt not but the Arm is good; and therefore
both worth my Resentment. Come, Sir.

'd. But, prithee Colonel, dost think that I am such
lman, as to send my Soul to the Devil, and Body to
'orms upon every Fool's Errand? [*Aside.*

nd. I hope you're no Coward, Sir.

ld. Coward, Sir! I have Eight Thousand Pounds a
Sir.

:nd. You fought in *Flanders,* to my Knowledge.

ld. Ay, for the same Reason that I wore a red Coat;
ıse 'twas fashionable.

ınd. Sir, you fought a *French* Count in *Paris.*

'ld. True, Sir; but there was no Danger of Lands,
Tenements: Besides, he was a Beau, like myself.
you're a Soldier, Colonel, and Fighting's your Trade,
I think it downright Madness to contend with any
in his Profession.

ınd. Come, Sir, no more dallying: I shall take very
:mly Methods, if you don't shew yourself a Gentle-

ild. A Gentleman! Why there again now. A Gen-
an! I tell you once more, Colonel, that I am a Ba-
t, and have Eight Thousand Pounds a Year. I can
e, sing, ride; fence, understand the Languages.
:, I can't conceive how running you through the Body

ɒL. I.   L   shou'd ſhou'd contribute one Jot more to my Gentility. But pray, Colonel, I had forgot to aſk you, What's the Quarrel?

Stand. A Woman, Sir.

Wild. Then I put up my Sword. Take her.

Stand. Sir, my Honour's concerned.

Wild. Nay, if your Honour be concern'd with a Woman, get it out of her Hands as ſoon as you can. An honourable Lover is the greateſt Slave in Nature; ſome will ſay, the greateſt Fool. Come, come, Colonel, this is ſomething about the Lady *Lurewell*, I warrant; I can give you Satisfaction in that Affair.

Stand. Do ſo then immediately.

Wild. Put up your Sword firſt; you know I dare fight: But I had much rather make you a Friend than an Enemy. I can aſſure you, this Lady will prove too hard for one of your Temper. You have too much Honour, too much in Conſcience, to be a Favourite with the Ladies.

Stand. I'm aſſur'd, Sir, ſhe never gave you any Encouragement.——

Wild. A Man can never hear Reaſon with a Sword in his Hand. Sheath your Weapon; and then if I don't ſatisfy you, ſheath it in my Body.

Stand. Give me but Demonſtration of her granting you any Favour, and it is enough.

Wild. Will you take my Word?

Stand. Pardon me, Sir, I cannot.

Wild. Will you believe your own Eyes?

Stand. 'Tis ten to one whether I ſhall or no, they have deceiv'd me already.

Wild. That's hard—But ſome means I ſhall deviſe for your Satisfaction—We muſt fly this Place, elſe that cluſter of Mob will overwhelm us. [*Exeunt.*

Enter Mob, Tom Errand's *Wife hurrying in* Clincher ſenior *in* Errand's *Cloaths.*

Wife. O, the Villain, the Rogue, he has murder'd my Huſband:—Ah! my poor *Timothy!* [*Crying.*

Clin. Dem your *Timothy!*—your Huſband has murder'd me, Woman; for he has carry'd away my fine *Jubilee* Cloaths.

Wife. Ay, you Cut-throat, have you not got his Cloaths upon your Back there?—Neighbours, don't you know poor *Timothy's* Coat and Apron?

Mob.

Ay, ay, it is the ſame.

Mob. What ſhall we do with him, Neighbours?

Mob. We'll pull him in pieces.

Mob. No, no; then we may be hang'd for Mur-
it we'll drown him.

Ah, good People, pray don't drown me; for I
arnt to ſwim in all my Life. Ah, this plaguy in-
·!

Away with him, away with him to the *Thames.*

Oh, if I had but my *Swimming Girdle* now.

Enter Conſtable.

Hold, Neighbours, I command the Peace.

O, Mr. Conſtable, here's a Rogue that has
d my Huſband, and robb'd him of his Cloaths.

. Murder and Robbery! then he muſt be a Gen-
Hands off there; he muſt not be abus'd.—
Account of yourſelf. Are you a Gentleman?

No, Sir, I am a Beau.

. A Beau! Then you have kill'd nobody, I'm
ed. How came you by theſe Cloaths, Sir?

You muſt know, Sir, that walking along, Sir, I
now how, Sir; I can't tell where, Sir; and ſo
ter and I chang'd Cloaths, Sir.

. Very well! the Man ſpeaks Reaſon, and like
leman.

. But pray, Mr. Conſtable, aſk him how he chang'd
¡ with him.

. Silence, Woman! and don't diſturb the Court.
, Sir, how did you change Cloaths?

Why, Sir, he pull'd off my Coat, and I drew off
ɔ I put on his Coat, and he put on mine.

. Why, Neighbour, I don't find that he's guilty:
him; and if he carries no Arms about him, we'll
¡ go. [*They ſearch his Pockets, and pull out his Piſtols.*
. O *Gemini!* My *Jubilee* Piſtols!

! What, a Caſe of Piſtols! Then the Caſe is plain.
what are you, Sir? Whence came you, and whi-
¡ you?

. Sir, I came from *Ruſſel-Street*, and am going to
bilee.

. You ſhall go to the Gallows, you Rogue.

Conſt.

Conſt. Away with him, away with him to *Newgate,* ſtraight.

Clin. I ſhall go to the *Jubilee* now, indeed. [*Exeunt.*

Re-enter Wildair *and* Standard.

Wild. In ſhort, Colonel, 'tis all Nonſenſe: Fight for a Woman! Hard by is the Lady's Houſe, if you pleaſe we'll wait on her together: You ſhall draw your Sword; I'll draw my Snuff-Box: You ſhall produce your Wounds receiv'd in War; I'll relate mine by *Cupid's* Dart: You ſhall look big; I'll ogle:—You ſhall ſwear; I'll ſigh:— You ſhall *ſa, ſa,* and I'll *Coupee;* and if ſhe flies not to my Arms like a Hawk to its Perch, my Dancing-Maſter deſerves to be damn'd.

Stand. With the generality of Women, I grant you theſe Arts may prevail.

Wild. Generality of Women! Why there again, you're out. They're all alike, Sir; I never heard of any one that was particular, but one.

Stand. Who was ſhe, pray?

Wild. Penelope, I think ſhe's call'd, and that's a Poetical Story too. When will you find a Poet in our Age make a Woman ſo chaſte?

Stand. Well, Sir *Harry,* your facetious Humour can diſguiſe Falſhood, and make Calumny paſs for Satire; but you have promis'd me ocular Demonſtration that ſhe favours you: Make that good, and I ſhall then maintain Faith and Female to be as inconſiſtent as Truth and Falſhood.

Wild. Nay, by what you told me, I am ſatisfied that ſhe impoſes on us all: And *Vizard* too ſeems what I ſtill ſuſpected him: But his honeſty once miſtruſted, ſpoils his Knavery:——But will you be convinc'd, if our Plot ſucceeds?

Stand. I rely on your Word and Honour, Sir *Harry;* which if I doubted, my Diſtruſt wou'd cancel the Obligation of their Security.

Wild. Then meet me half an Hour hence at the *Rummer:* You muſt oblige me by taking a hearty Glaſs with me toward the fitting me out for a certain Project, which this Night I undertake.

Stand. I gueſs by the Preparation, that Woman's the Deſign.

Wild.

Wild. Yes, faith.—I am taken dangerous ill with two fooliſh Maladies, Modeſty and Love; the firſt I'll cure with *Burgundy,* and my Love by a Night's Lodging with the Damſel. A ſure Remedy. *Probatum eſt.*

Stand. I'll certainly meet you, Sir. [*Exeunt ſeverally.*

Enter Clincher junior *and* Dicky.

Clin. Ah! *Dicky,* this *London* is a ſad Place, a ſad vicious Place: I wiſh that I were in the Country again: And this Brother of mine! I'm ſorry he's ſo great a Rake: I had rather ſee him dead than ſee him thus.

Dick. Ay, Sir, he'll ſpend his whole Eſtate at this ſame Jubilee. Who d'ye think lives at this ſame Jubilee?

Clin. Who, pray?

Dick. The Pope.

Clin. The Devil he does! My Brother go to the Place where the Pope dwells! He's bewitch'd ſure!

Enter Tom Errand *in* Clincher ſenior's *Cloaths.*

Dick. Indeed, I believe he is, for he's ſtrangely alter'd.

Clin. Alter'd! Why he looks like a Jeſuit already.

Err. This Lace will ſell. What a Blockhead was the Fellow to truſt me with his Coat! If I can get croſs the Garden, down to the Water-ſide, I am pretty ſecure.
[*Aſide.*

Clin. Brother!—Alaw! O *Gemini!* Are you my Brother?

Dick. I ſeize you in the King's Name, Sir.

Err. O Lord! Shou'd this prove ſome Parliament Man now!

Clin. Speak, you Rogue, what are you?

Err. A poor Porter, Sir, and going of an Errand.

Dick. What Errand? Speak, you Rogue.

Err. A Fool's Errand, I'm afraid.

Clin. Who ſent you?

Err. A Beau, Sir.

Dick. No, no; the Rogue has murder'd your Brother, and ſtript him of his Cloaths.

Clin. Murder'd my Brother! O *Crimini!* O my poor Jubilee Brother!—Stay, by *Jupiter Ammon,* I'm Heir tho: Speak. Sirrah, have you kill'd him? Confeſs that you have kill'd him, and I'll give you Half a Crown.

Err. Who, I, Sir? Alack-a-day, Sir, I never kill'd any Man, but a Carrier's Horſe once.

L 3   *Clin.*

Clin. Then you fhall certainly be hang'd ; but co
that you kill'd him, and we'll let you go.

Err. Telling the Truth hangs a Man, but conf
a Lie can do no Harm ; befides, if the worft come t
worft, I can but deny it again—Well, Sir, fince I
tell you, I did kill him.

Clin. Here's your Money, Sir.—But are you fure
kill'd him dead ?

Err. Sir, I'll fwear it before any Judge in *Englan*

Dick. But are you fure that he's *Dead in Law ?*

Err. Dead in Law ? I can't tell whether he be *D*
Law. But he's as dead as a Door-Nail ; for I gave
feven Knocks on the Head with a Hammer.

Dick. Then you have the Eftate by Statute. Any
that's knock'd o'th' Head is *Dead in Law.*

Clin. But are you fure he was *Compos Mentis* whe
was kill'd ?

Err. I fuppofe he was, Sir ; for he told me nothi
the contrary afterwards.

Clin. Hey ! Then I go to the *Jubilee*—Strip, Sir,
By *Jupiter Ammon*, ftrip.

Dick. Ah I don't fwear, Sir.

[*Puts on his Brother's Cl*

Clin. Swear, Sir! Zoons, han't I got the Eftate,
Come, Sir, now I'm in Mourning for my Brother.

Err. I hope you'll let me go now, Sir.

Clin. Yes, yes, Sir ; but you muft do me the Favo
fwear pofitively before a Magiftrate, that you kill'd
dead, that I may enter upon the Eftate without any T
ble. By *Jupiter Ammon*, all my Religion's gone, fi
put on thefe fine Cloaths—Hey, call me a Coach f
body.

Err. Ay, Mafter, let me go, and I'll call one ir
diately.

Clin. No, no ; *Dicky*, carry this Spark before a Ju
and when he has made Oath, you may difcharge
And I'll go fee *Angelica*. [*Exeunt* Dick *and* Err
Now that I'm an elder Brother, I'll court, and fwear,
rant, and rake, and go to the *Jubilee* with the be
them. [

SCENE, Lurewell's *House.*

Enter Lurewell *and* Parly.

re. Are you fure that *Vizard* had my Letter?

ar. Yes, yes, Madam; one of your Ladyfhip's Foot-
gave it to him in the Park, and he told the Bearer,
all Tranfports of Joy, that he wou'd be punctual to
inute.

re. Thus moft Villains fome time or other are punc-
to their Ruin; and Hypocrify, by impofing on the
ld, at laft deceives itfelf. Are all Things prepar'd
iis Reception?

ar. Exactly to your Ladyfhip's Order; the Alderman
is juft come, drefs'd and cook'd up for Iniquity.

re. Then he has got Woman's Cloaths on?

ar. Yes, Madam, and has pafs'd upon the Family for
: Nurfe.

re. Convey him into that Clofet, and put out the
dles, and tell him, I'll wait on him prefently.

[*As* Parly *goes to put out the Candles, fomebody knocks.*
re. This muft be fome Clown without Manners, or
entleman above Ceremony. Who's there?

Wildair fings.

Thus Damon *knock'd at* Celia's Door,
He figh'd, and begg'd, and wept, and fwore,
   The Sign was fo,
      [Knocks.]
   She anfwer'd, No.
      [Knocks thrice.]
   No, no, no.
Again he figh'd, again he pray'd,
No, Damon, *no, I am afraid:*
Confider, Damon, *I'm a Maid.*
      Confider,
         No,
      I'm a Maid.
         No, &c.
At laft his Sighs and Tears made Way,
She rofe, and foftly turn'd the Key:
Come in, faid fhe, but do not ftay.
      I may conclude
      You will be rude,
      But if you are, you may.
         Enters.   [*Exit* Parly.

L 4   Lure.

Lure. 'Tis too early for Serenading, Sir *Harry.*

Wild. Wheresoever Love is, there Music is proper; there's an harmonious Consent in their Natures, and when rightly join'd, they make up the Chorus of Earthly Happiness.

Lure. But, Sir *Harry,* what Tempest drives you here at this Hour?

Wild. No Tempest, Madam, but as fair Weather as ever entic'd a Citizen's Wife to cuckold her Husband in fresh Air. Love, Madam. [*Wild. taking her by the Hand.*

Lure. *As pure and white as Angels soft Desires.*

Wild. *Fierce, as when ripe consenting Beauty fires.* Is't not so?

Lure. O Villain! What Privilege has Men to our Destruction, that thus they hunt our Ruin? [*Aside.*] If this be a Love Token, [*Wild. drops a Ring, she takes it up.*] your Mistresses Favours hang very loose about you, Sir.

Wild. I can't, justly, Madam, pay your Trouble of taking it up by any Thing, but desiring you to wear it.

Lure. You Gentlemen have the cunningest Ways of playing the Fool, and are so industrious in your Profuseness. Speak seriously, am I beholden to Chance or Design for this Ring?

Wild. To Design, upon my Honour. And I hope my Design will succeed.   [*Aside.*

Lure. *And what shall I give you for such a fine Thing?*

Wild. *You'll give me another, you'll give me another fine Thing.*   [*Both sing.*

Lure. Shall I be free with you, Sir *Harry?*

Wild. With all my Heart, Madam, so I may be free with you.

Lure. Then plainly, Sir, I shall beg the Favour to see you some other Time; for at this very Minute I have two Lovers in the House.

Wild. Then to be as plain, I must be gone this Minute, for I must see another Mistress within these two Hours.

Lure. Frank and free.

Wild. As you with me——Madam, your most humble Servant.   [*Exit.*

Lure. Nothing can disturb his Humour. Now for my Merchant and *Vizard.* [*Exit and takes the Candles with her.*

Enter Parly, *leading in* Smuggler, *dress'd in Woman's Cloaths.*

Par. This Way, Mr. Alderman.

                                                    Smug.

Smug. Well, Mrs. *Parly,*—I'm oblig'd to you for this Trouble, here are a Couple of Shillings for you. Times are hard, very hard, indeed; but next Time I'll fteal a Pair of Silk Stockings from my Wife, and bring them to you——What are you fumbling about my Pockets for?—

Par. Only fetting the Pleats of your Gown; here, Sir, get into this Clofet, and my Lady will wait on you pré-fently.　　　[*Puts him into the Clofet, runs out, and returns with* Vizard.

Viz. Where would'ft thou lead me, my dear aufpicious little Pilot?

Par. You're almoft in Port, Sir; my Lady's in the Clofet, and will come out to you immediately.

Viz. Let me thank thee as I ought.　　[*Kiffes her.*

Par. Pfhaw, who has hir'd me beft; a Couple of Shil-lings, or a Couple of Kiffes?

Viz. Propitious Darknefs guides the Lovers Steps, and Night that fhadows outward Senfe, lights up our inward Joy. Night! The great awful Ruler of Mankind, which, like the *Perfian* Monarch, hides its Royalty to raife the Veneration of the World. Under thy eafy Reign Dif-femblers may fpeak Truth; all flavifh Forms and Cere-monies laid afide, and generous Villany may act without Conftraint.

Smug. [*Peeping out of the Clofet.*] Blefs me! What Voice is this?

Viz. Our hungry Appetites, like the wild Beafts of Prey, now fcour about, to gorge their craving Maws; the Pleafure of Hypocrify, like a chain'd Lion, once broke loofe, wildly indulges its new Freedom, ranging through all unbounded Joys.

Smug. My Nephew's Voice, and certainly poffefs'd with an Evil Spirit; he talks as prophanely as an Actor pof-fefs'd with a Poet.

Viz. Ha! I hear a Voice: Madam,——my Life, my Happinefs, where are you, Madam?

Smug. Madam! He takes me for a Woman too: I'll try him. Where have you left your Sanctity, Mr. *Vizard.*

Viz. Talk no more of that ungraceful Subject—I left it where it has only Bufinefs, with Day-light; 'tis need-lefs to wear a Mafk in the dark.

Smug. O the Rogue, the Rogue!——The World ta[...] you for a very ſober, virtuous Gentleman.

Viz. Ay, Madam, that adds Security to all my Pleaſu[...] —With me a Cully-'Squire may ſquander his Eſtate, [...] ne'er be thought a Spendthrift——With me a holy El[...] may zealouſly be drunk, and toaſt his tuneful Noiſ[...] Sack, to make it hold forth clearer——But what is [...] my Praiſe, the formal Rigid ſhe, that rails at Vice [...] Men, with me ſecures her looſeſt Pleaſures, and her ſtri[...] Honour———ſhe who with ſcornful Mien, and virtu[...] Pride, diſdains the Name of Whore, with me can wan[...] and laugh at the deluded World.

Smug. How have I been deceived! Then you are [...] great among the Ladies.

Viz. Yes, Madam, they know that like a Mole in [...] Earth, I dig deep, but inviſible; not like thoſe ſlutter[...] noiſy Sinners, whoſe Pleaſure is the Proclamation of t[...] Faults; thoſe empty Flaſhes, who no ſooner kindle, [...] they muſt blaze to alarm the World. But come, Mad[...] you delay our Pleaſures.

Smug. He ſurely takes me for the Lady *Lurewell*— has made him an Appointment too—but I'll be reven[...] of both——Well, Sir, what are thoſe you are ſo intim[...] with?

Viz. Come, come, Madam, you know very well— thoſe who ſtand ſo high, that the Vulgar envy even t[...] Crimes, whoſe Figure adds Privilege to their Sin, makes it paſs unqueſtion'd: fair, high, pamper'd Fem[...] whoſe ſpeaking Eyes, and piercing Voice, would arm [...] Statue of a *Stoick*, and animate his cold Marble with [...] Soul of an *Epicure*, all raviſhing, lovely, and ſoft, [...] kind, like you———

Smug. I'm very lovely and ſoft indeed! you ſhall fin[...] much harder than you imagine, Friend——Well, Sir, [...] I ſuppoſe your Diſſimulation has ſome other Motive [...] ſides Pleaſure?

Viz. Yes, Madam, the honeſteſt Motive in the Wo[...] Intereſt—You muſt know, Madam, that I have an [...] Uncle, Alderman *Smuggler*, you have ſeen him, I ſupp[...]

Smug. Yes, yes, I have ſome ſmall Acquaintance [...] him.

Vix. 'Tis the moſt knaviſh, preciſe, covetous old Rogue, that ever died of the Gout.

Smug. Ah! The young Son of a Whore! Well, Sir, and what of him?

Vix. Hell hungers not more for wretched Souls, than he for ill-got Pelf——and yet (what's wonderful) he that would ſtick at no profitable Villany himſelf, loves Holineſs in another—he prays all *Sundays* for the Sins of the Week paſt——he ſpends all Dinner-time in two tedious Graces; and what he deſigns a Bleſſing to the Meat, proves a Curſe to his Family——he's the moſt——

Smug. Well, well, Sir, I know him very well.

Vix. Then, Madam, he has a ſwinging Eſtate, which I deſign to purchaſe as a Saint, and ſpend like a Gentleman. He got it by Cheating, and ſhould loſe it by Deceit. By the Pretence of my Zeal and Sobriety, I'll cozen the old Miſer one of theſe Days out of a Settlement and Deed of Conveyance——

Smug. It ſhall be a Deed to convey you to the Gallows, then, ye young Dog. [*Aſide.*

Vix. And no ſooner he's dead, but I'll rattle over his Grave with a Coach and Six, to inform his covetous Ghoſt how genteelly I ſpend his Money.

Smug. I'll prevent you, Boy, for I'll have my Money bury'd with me. [*Aſide.*

Vix. Bleſs me, Madam! Here's a Light coming this Way. I muſt fly immediately; when ſhall I ſee you, Madam?

Smug. Sooner than you expect, my Dear.

Vix. Pardon me, dear Madam, I would not be ſeen for the World. I wou'd ſooner forfeit my Life, nay my Pleaſure, than my Reputation. [*Exit.*

Smug. Reputation! Reputation! That poor Word ſuffers a great deal——Well! thou art the moſt accompliſh'd Hypocrite that ever made a grave plodding Face over a Diſh of Coffee and a Pipe of Tobacco! he owes me for ſeven Years Maintenance, and ſhall pay me by ſeven Years Impriſonment; and when I die, I'll leave him the Fee-ſimple of a Rope and a Shilling. Who are theſe? I begin to be afraid of ſome Miſchief——I wiſh that I were ſaſe within the City Liberties——I'll hide myſelf.

[*Stands cloſe.*

L 6   *Enter*

Enter Butler, *with other Servants and Lights.*

But. I say there are two Spoons wanting, and I'll search the whole House—Two Spoons will be no small Gap in my Quarter's Wages.————

Serv. When did you miss 'em, *James?*

But. Miss them! Why I miss them now! in short they must be among you, and if you don't return them, I'll go to the Cunning-man To-morrow Morning; my Spoons I want, and my Spoons I will have.

Serv. Come, come, search about.

[*Search and discover* Smuggler.

But. Hark'e, good Woman, what makes you hide yourself? What are you asham'd of?

Smug. Asham'd of! O Lord, Sir, I'm an honest old Woman that never was asham'd of any Thing.

But. What are you, a Midwife then? Speak, did not you see a Couple of stray Spoons in your Travels?

Smug. Stray Spoons!

But. Ay, ay, stray Spoons; in short you stole them, and I'll shake your old Limbs to Pieces, if you don't deliver them presently.

Smug. Bless me; a reverend Elder of seventy Years old accus'd for *Petty Larceny!*—Why search me, good People, search me; and if you find any Spoons about me, you shall burn me for a Witch.

But. Ay, we will search you, Mistress.

[*They search and pull the Spoons out of his Pocket.*

Smug. Oh! the Devil, the Devil!

But. Where, where is he? Lord bless us! she is a Witch in good Earnest, may be.

Smug. O, it was some Devil, some *Covent-Garden* or St. *James's* Devil, that put them in my Pocket.

But. Ay, ay, you shall be hang'd for a Thief, burnt for a Witch, and then carted for a Bawd. Speak, what are you?

Enter Lurewell.

Smug. I'm the Lady *Lurewell's* Nurse.

Lure. What Noise is this?

But. Here is an old *Succubus*, Madam, that has stole two Silver Spoons, and says she's your Nurse.

Lure. My Nurse! O the impudent old Jade, I never saw the wither'd Creature before.

Smug.

Smug. Then I'm finely caught. O Madam, Madam, don't you know me? don't you remember Bufs and Guinea?

Lure. Was ever fuch Impudence? I know thee! why thou'rt as brazen as a Bawd in the Side-box.—Take her before a Juftice, and then to *Newgate*, away.

Smug. O! confider, Madam, that I'm an Alderman.

Lure. Confider, Sir, that you're a compound of Covetoufnefs, Hypocrify, and Knavery, and muft be punifh'd accordingly—You muft be in Petticoats, gouty Monfter, muft ye! You muft Bufs and Guinea too; you muft tempt a Lady's Honour, old Satyr; away with him.

[*Hurry him off.*

Still may our Sex thus Frauds of Men oppofe,
Still may our Arts delude thefe tempting Fees.
May Honour rule, and never fall betray'd,
But Vice be caught in Nets for Virtue laid.

The End of the Fourth Act.

ACT V.

SCENE, *Lady* Darling's *Houfe.*

Darling *and* Angelica.

Darl. DAughter, fince you have to deal with a Man of fo peculiar a Temper, you muft not think the general Arts of Love can fecure him; you may therefore allow fuch a Courtie. fome Encouragement extraordinary, without Reproach to your Modefty.

Angel. I am fenfible, Madam, that a formal Nicety makes our Modefty fit aukward, and appears rather a Chain to enflave, than Bracelet to adorn us;—it fhould fhew, when unmolefted, eafy and innocent as a Dove, but ftrong and vigorous as a Faulcon, when affaulted.

Darl. I'm afraid, Daughter, you miftake Sir *Harry's* Gaiety for Difhonour.

Ang. Tho' Modefty, Madam, may wink, it muft not fleep, when powerful Enemies are abroad—I muft confefs, that of all Men's, I wou'd not fee Sir *Harry Wildair's* Faults;

Pret . . . riv. . . . . Words . . . . like Honour——But Madam, in spite of Love, I must name him, and curb those Practices which taint our Nobility, and rob all virtuous Women of the truest Men.——

Cler. You must certainly be mistaken, *Angelica*; for his Artistry . . . Sir *Harry*'s Designs are only to court, and marry you.

Ang. His Presence, perhaps, was such; but Women now, like *Enemies*, are attack'd; whether by Treachery, or fairly conquer'd, the Glory of the Triumph is the Same——Pray, Madam, by what Means were you made acquainted with his Designs?

Cler. Means. I'll . . . say, my Cousin *Vizard*, who, I'm sure, is your sincere Friend, sent him. He brought me this Letter from my Cousin.——

[Gives her the Letter, which she opens.

Ang. His Tears then I'm assur'd in Earnest.—— Trust Sir *Harry*, by his Instigation, fix a base Affront upon me? No, I can't suspect him of so ungenteel a Crime——This Letter shall make me Truth——[*Aside.*] My Suspicions, Madam, are much clear'd; and I hope in satisfy your Ladyship in my Management, when next I see Sir *Harry*.

Your Servant.

Serv. Madam, here's a Gentleman below calls himself *Wildair*.

Darl. Conduct him up. Daughter, I won't doubt your Discretion.　　　　　　　　　[*Exit* Darling.

Enter Wildair.

Wild. O, the Delights of Love and *Burgundy!*—— Madam, I have toasted your Ladyship fifteen Bumpers successively, and swallow'd *Cupids* like *Loches* to every Glass.

Ang. And what then, Sir?

Wild. Why then, Madam, the Wine has got into my Head, and the *Cupids* into my Heart; and unless by quenching quick my Flame, you kindly ease the Smart I'm a lost Man, Madam.

Ang. Drunkenness, Sir *Harry*, is the worst Pretence a Gentleman can make for Rudeness; for the Excuse is as scandalous as the Fault.——Therefore, pray confide

wh

o you are fo free with, Sir; a Woman of Condition,
it can call half a Dozen Footmen upon Occafion.

Wild. Nay, Madam, if you have a Mind to tofs me
a Blanket, half a Dozen Chamber-maids would do
tter Service.—Come, come, Madam, tho' the Wine
kes me lifp, yet it has taught me to fpeak plainer.
all the Duft of my ancient Progenitors, I muft this
ight reft in your Arms.

Aug. Nay then, who waits there? [*Enter Footmen.*
ke hold of that Madman, and bind him.

Wild. Nay, then *Burgundy's* the Word, Slaughter will
fue. Hold,—do you know, Scoundrels, that I have
en drinking victorious *Burgundy?* [*Draws.*

Servants. We know you're drunk, Sir.

Wild. Then how have you the Impudence, Rafcals,
affault a Gentleman with a Couple of Flafks of
ourage in his Head?

Servants. We muft do as our young Miftrefs com-
ands us.

Wild. Nay, then have among ye, Dogs.

[*Throws Money among them; they fcramble and take it
up. He pelting them out, fbuts the Door, and returns.*

afcals, Poltroons,—I have charm'd the Dragon, and
w the Fruit's my own.

Aug. O, the mercenary Wretches! This was a Plot to
tray me.

Wild. I have put the whole Army to Flight: And now
il take the General Prifoner. [*Laying hold on her.*

Aug. I conjure you, Sir, by the facred Name of
onour, by your dead Father's Name, and the fair
eputation of your Mother's Chaftity, that you offer
t the leaft Offence—Already you have wrong'd me
aft Redrefs.

Wild. Thou art the moft unaccountable Creature.

Aug. What Madnefs, Sir *Harry!* what wild Dream
f loofe Defire cou'd prompt you to attempt this Bafe-
efs? View me well.——The Brightnefs of my Mind,
ethinks, fhould lighten outwards, and let you fee your
liftake in my Behaviour. I think it fhines with fo
uch Innocence in my Face, that it fhould dazzle all
our vicious Thoughts: Think not I am defencelefs
aufe alone. Your very felf is Guard againft yourfelf:

I'm.

I'm fure, there's fomething generous in your Soul; my Words fhall fnatch it out, and Eyes fhall fire it for my own Defence.

Wild. [*Mimicking.*] Tal tidum, ti dum, tal ti didi, didum. A Million to one now, but this Girl is juft come flefh from reading the *Rival Queens*——'I gad, I'll at her in her own Cant.

O my Satyra, O my angry Dear, turn thy Eyes on me, behold thy Beau in Bufkins.

Ang. Behold me, Sir; view me with a fober Thought, free from thofe Fumes of Wine that throw a Mift before your Sight, and you fhall find that every Glance from my reproaching Eyes is arm'd with fharp Refentment, and with a virtuous Pride that looks Difhonour dead.

Wild. This is the firft Whore in *Heroics* that I have met with. [*Afide.*] Look ye, Madam, as to that flender Particular of your Virtue, we fhan't quarrel about it; you may be as virtuous as any Woman in *England*, if you pleafe; you may fay your Prayers all the Time :— But pray, Madam, be pleas'd to confider what is this fame Virtue that you make fuch a mighty Noife about: Can your Virtue befpeak you a Front Row in the Boxes ? No, for the Players can't live upon Virtue. Can your Virtue keep you a Coach and Six ? No, no; your Virtuous Women walk on Foot——Can your Virtue hire you a Pew in the Church ? Why, the very Sexton will tell you, No. Can your Virtue ftake for you at Picquet ? No. Then, what Bufinefs has a Woman with Virtue ?— Come, come, Madam, I offer'd you fifty Guineas,— there's a Hundred.—The Devil! Virtuous ftill! Why, it is a Hundred, five Score, a Hundred Guineas.

Ang. O Indignation! Were I a Man, you durft not ufe me thus; but the mean, poor Abufe you throw on me, reflects upon yourfelf; our Sex ftill ftrikes an Awe upon the Brave, and only Cowards dare affront a Woman.

Wild. Affront! S'death, Madam, a hundred Guineas will fet you up a Bank at Baffet; a Hundred Guineas will furnifh out your Lodgings with China; a Hundred Guineas will give you an Air of Quality; a Hundred Guineas will buy you a rich Efcritoir for your *Billet-deux*, or a fine *Common-Prayer Book* for your Virtue. A
Hundred

ıdred Guineas will buy a Hundred fine Things, and
Things are for fine Ladies ; and fine Ladies are for
Gentlemen ; and fine Gentlemen are—'I Egad, this
gundy makes a Man ſpeak like an Angel——Come,
ıe, Madam, take it, and put it to what Uſe you pleaſe.
ſng. I'll uſe it as I would uſe the baſe unworthy
·er ! thus ! [*Throws down the Purſe and ſtamps upon it.*
Vild. I have no Mind to meddle in State Affairs ; but
·è Women will make me a Parliament Man ſpite of
Teeth, on purpoſe to bring in a Bill againſt their
ortion. She tramples under Foot that Deity which
:he World adores.——O the blooming Pride of beau-
l Eighteen ! Pſhaw, I'll talk to her no longer ;
make my Markets with the old Gentlewoman,
knows Buſineſs better.——[*Goes to the Door.*] Here,
, Friend, pray deſire the old Lady to walk in.——
.rk'e, Egad, Madam, I'll tell your Mother.

Enter Lady Darling.

)arl. Well, Sir *Harry*, and how d'ye like my Daughter,
ı ?
'ild. Like her, Madam !——Heark'e, will you take
Why faith, Madam !——take the Money, I ſay, or
l, all's out.
'ng. All ſhall out ; Sir, you're a Scandal to the
ne of Gentleman.
'ild. With all my Heart, Madam :—In ſhort, Ma-
, your Daughter has us'd me ſomewhat too fami-
y, tho' I have treated her like a Woman of Quality.
arl. How, Sir ?
'ild. Why, Madam, I have offer'd her a Hundred
neas.
arl. A Hundred Guineas ! upon what Score ?
'ild. Upon what Score ! Lord, Lord, how theſe old
nen love to hear Bawdy. Why, faith, Madam, I
: never a double *Entendre* ready at preſent, but I'll
you a Song.

> *Behold the Goldfinches, tall al de rall,*
> *And a Man of my Inches, tall al de rall,*
> *You ſhall take um, believe me, tall al de rall,*
> *If you will give me your—tall al de rall.*

odiſh Minuet, Madam, that's all.

Darl.

Darl. Sir, I don't underſtand you.

Wild. Ay, ſhe will have it in plain Terms; Madam, in downright *Engliſh*, I offer'd your Da a hundred Guineas to———

Ang. Hold, Sir; ſtop your abuſive Tongue, too for modeſt Ears to hear.—Madam, I did before ſ that his Deſigns were baſe, now they're too plain Knight, this mighty Man of Wit and Humour, is a Tool to a Knave: *Vizard* has ſent him on a E Errand to affront a Woman; but I ſcorn the Abuſe him that offer'd it.

Darl. How, Sir, come to affront us! D'ye knov we are, Sir?

Wild. Know who you are! Why, your Da there, is Mr. *Vizard's*—Couſin, I ſuppoſe:—Aı you, Madam—now to call her Procureſs Alamo *France,* [*Aſide.*] *J'eſtime votre Occupation.*———

Darl. Pray, Sir, ſpeak *Engliſh*.

Wild. Then to define her Office, Alamode de *Lo* [*Aſide.*] I ſuppoſe your Ladyſhip to be one of thoſe obliging, diſcreet, old Gentlewomen, who keep viſiting Days for the Entertainment of their pret Friends, whom they treat with Imperial Tea, a ſ Room, and a Pack of Cards. Now I ſuppoſe y underſtand me.

Darl. This is beyond Sufferance! But ſay, thou a Man, what Injury have you ever receiv'd from ɪ mine, thus to engage you in this ſcandalous Aſper

Ang. Yes, Sir, what Cauſe, what Motives coɪ duce you thus to debaſe yourſelf below your Rank i

Wild. Hey day! Now dear *Roxana*, and you n *Statyra*, be not ſo very Heroic in your Stiles; *V* Letter may reſolve you, and anſwer all the impeɪ Queſtions you have made me.

Both Women. We appeal to that.

Wild. And I'll ſtand to't; he read it to me, a Contents were pretty plain, I thought.

Ang. Here, Sir, peruſe it, and ſee how much ɪ injur'd, and you deceiv'd.

Wild. [*Opening the Letter.*] But hold, Madam *Darling.*] before I read I'll make ſome Condition: *Vizard* ſays here, that I won't ſcruple 30 or 40 ʃ

Now, Madam, if you have clapt in another Cypher to
the Account, and made it 3 or 4 Hundred, egad I will
not stand to't

Ang. Now I can't tell whether Disdain or Anger be
the most just Resentment for this Injury.

Darl. The Letter, Sir, shall answer you.

Wild. Well then [*Reads.*]

> *Out of my earnest Inclination to serve your Ladyship, and*
> *my Cousin* Angelica, Ay, ay, the very Words, I
> can say it by Heart——*I have sent Sir* Harry
> Wildair—*to*—What the Devil's this? *Sent Sir*
> Harry Wildair *to court my Cousin*——He read to
> me quite a different thing.—*He's a Gentleman of*
> *great Parts and Fortune*——He's a Son of a Whore
> and a Rascal——*And won'd make your Daughter*
> *very happy (Whistles) in a Husband. (Looks foolish,*
> *and hums a Song.)* Oh, poor Sir *Harry,* what
> have the angry Stars defign'd?

Ang. Now, Sir, I hope you need no Instigation to
redress our Wrongs, since even the Injury points the
Way.

Darl. Think, Sir, that our Blood for many Gene-
rations, has run in the purest Channel of unsully'd
Honour.

Wild. Ay, Madam.   [*Bows to her.*

Ang. Consider what a tender Flower is Woman's Reputation, which the least Air of foul Detraction blasts.

Wild. Yes, Madam.   [*Bows to t'other.*

Darl. Call then to mind your rude and scandalous
Behaviour.

Wild. Right, Madam,   [*Bows again.*

Ang. Remember the base Price you offer'd me. [*Exit.*

Wild. Very true, Madam; was ever Man so catechiz'd?

Darl. Then think that *Vizard,* Villain *Vizard,* caus'd
all this, yet lives: That's all; farewel.

Wild. Stay, Madam, (*To Darling*) one Word; is
there no other Way to redress your Wrongs, but by
fighting?

Darl. Only one, Sir, which if you can think of, you
may do; you know the Business I entertain'd you for.

                             Wild.

Wild. I underſtand you, Madam. [*Exit* Darl
Here am I brought to a very pretty Dilemma, I
commit Murder, or commit Matrimony; which is
now ? A Licenſe from *Doctors Commons*, or a Sen
from the *Old Bailey ?* If I kill my Man, the Law h
me : If I marry my Woman, I ſhall hang myſe
But, Damn it,—Cowards dare fight; I'll marry, t
the moſt daring Action of the two : So my dear C
Angelica, have at you.

SCENE *Newgate.* Clincher ſenior *ſolus.*

Clin. How ſevere and melancholy are *Newgate*
flections! Laſt Week my Father died ; yeſterday I t
Beau; To-day I am laid by the Heels, and To-mo
ſhall be hung by the Neck—I was agreeing wi
Bookſeller about printing an Account of my Jou
through *France* and *Italy*; but now the Hiſtory o
Travels muſt be thro' *Holbourn* to *Tyburn.—The laſ
dying Speech of* Beau Clincher, *that was going to th
bilee—Come a Half-penny a-piece.* A ſad ſound, :
ſound, faith ! 'Tis one way to have a Man's I
make a great Noiſe in the World.

Enter Smuggler *and* Gaoler.

Smug. Well, Friend, I have told you who I am
ſend theſe Letters into *Thames Street,* as directed ;
are to Gentlemen that will bail me. [Exit *Gaoler.*]
this *Newgate* is a very populous Place : Here's
bery and Repentance in every Corner.——Well, Fr
what are you ? a Cut-throat or a Bum-Bailiff ?

Clinch. What are you, Miſtreſs ? a Bawd or a W
Heark'e, if you are a Witch, d'ye ſee, I'll give :
hundred Pounds to mount me on a Broom-ſtaff, and
me away to the *Jubilee.*

Smug. The *Jubilee !* O, you young Rake-hell,
brought you here ?

Clin. Ah, you old Rogue, what brought you he:
you go to that ?

Smug. I knew, Sir, what your powdering, your p
ing, your dancing, and your friſking, would come :

Clin. And I knew what your Cozening, your Exto:
and your Smuggling wou'd come to.

Smug. Ay, Sir, you muſt break your Indentures, and nn to the Devil in a full bottom Wig, muſt you?

Clin. Ay, Sir, and you muſt put off your Gravity, nd run to the Devil in Petticoats :—You deſign to ſwing n Maſquerade, Maſter, d'ye?

Smug. Ay, you muſt go to the Plays too, Sirrah : Lord, ᴸord! What Buſineſs has a 'Prentice at a Play-houſe, ᴉnleſs it be to hear his Maſter made a Cuckold, and his Miſtreſs a Whore? It is ten to one now, but ſome maᴉcious Poet has my Character upon the Stage within this Month: 'Tis a hard matter now, that an honeſt ſober Man can't ſin in private for this plaguy Stage. I gave an ᴉoneſt Gentleman five Guineas myſelf towards writing a Book againſt it : And it has done no good, we ſee.

Clin. Well, well, Maſter, take Courage! our Comᷓort is, we have liv'd together, and ſhall die together, ᴼᵃly with this difference, that I have liv'd like a Fool, ᴉnd ſhall die like a Knave; and you have liv'd like a Knave, and ſhall die like a Fool.

Smug. No, Sirrah! I have ſent a Meſſenger for my Cloaths, and ſhall get out immediately, and ſhall be ᴉpon your Jury by and by.—Go to Prayers, you Rogue, to Prayers. [*Exit.* Smug.

Clin. Prayers! it is a hard taking when a Man muſt ſay Grace to the Gallows.—Ah, this curſed Intriguing! Had I ſwung handſomely in a ſilken Garter now, I had died in my Duty; but to hang in Hemp, like the Vulgar, it is very ungenteel.

Enter Tom Errand.

A Reprieve! a Reprieve! thou dear, dear—damn'd Rogue. Where have you been? Thou art the moſt welcome—Son of a Whore; where's my Cloaths?

Err. Sir, I ſee where mine are: Come, Sir, ſtrip, Sir, ſtrip.

Clin. What, Sir, will you abuſe a Gentleman?

Err. A Gentleman! Ha, ha, ha! d'ye know where you are, Sir? We're all Gentlemen here.—I ſtand up for Liberty and Property.—*Newgate*'s a Commonwealth. No Courtier has Buſineſs among us ; come, Sir.

Clin. Well, but ſtay, ſtay, till I ſend for my own Cloaths : I ſhall get out preſently.

Err. No, no, Sir! I'll ha' you into the Dungeon, and ᴉncaſe you.

Clin.

Clin. Sir, you can't maſter me; for I'm twenty th
ſand ſtrong.　　　　　　　　　　[Exeunt ſtruggl

SCENE, *Changes* to *Lady* Darling's *Houſe.*

Enter Wildair *with Letters, Servants following.*

Wild. Here, fly all around, and bear theſe ꞇs
rected; you to *Weſtminſter,*—you to St. *James's,* and
into the City.—Tell all my Friends, a Bridegroo
Joy invites their Preſence. Look all of ye like Bri
grooms alſo: All appear with hoſpitable Looks,
bear a Welcome in your Faces.——Tell 'em I'm marr
If any aſk to whom, make no Reply; but tell 'em ꞇ
I'm marry'd, that Joy ſhall crown the Day, and L
the Night. Be gone, fly.

Enter Standard.

A thouſand Welcomes, Friend; my Pleaſure's ꞇ
complete, ſince I can ſhare it with my Friend: B
Joy ſhall bound from me to you; then back agꞃ
and, like the Sun, grow warmer by Reflection.

Stand. You're always pleaſant, Sir *Harry;* but
tranſcends yourſelf: Whence proceeds it?

Wild. Canſt thou not gueſs, my Friend? Whence fl
all Earthly Joy? What is the Life of Man, and Sou
Pleaſure?—*Woman*——What fires the Heart with Tꞃ
ſport, and the Soul with Raptures? *Lovely Woma*
What is the Maſter-ſtroke and Smile of the Creati
but *charming virtuous Woman?*—When Nature in the
neral Compoſition, firſt brought Woman forth, lik
fluſh'd Poet, raviſh'd with his Fancy, with Ecſtaſꞁ
bleſt the fair Production!—Methinks, my Friend,
reliſh not my Joy. What is the Cauſe?

Stand. Canſt thou not gueſs.—What is the Bane of M
and Scourge of Life, but *Woman?*—What is the heathe
Idol Man ſets up, and is damn'd for worſhippiꞇ
Treacherous Woman.—What are thoſe, whoſe Eyes,
Baſiliſks, ſhine beautiful for ſure Deſtruction, wl
Smiles are dangerous as the Grin of Fiends, but *falſe,*
luding Woman?—Woman! whoſe Compoſition inverts ꞇ
manity; their Bodies heavenly; but their Souls are C

Wild. Come, come, Colonel, this is too much
know your Wrongs receiv'd from *Lurewell* may ex

ꞇ

entments againſt her.   But it is unpardonable to
the Failings of a ſingle Woman upon the whole
I have found one, whoſe Virtues.——

So have I, Sir *Harry*; I have found one whoſe
above yielding to a Prince.   And if Lying, Diſ-
3, Perjury and Falſhood, be no Breaches in a
' s Honour, ſhe's as innocent as Infancy.

Well, Colonel, I find your Opinion grows
by Oppoſition; I ſhall now therefore wave the
nt, and only beg you for this Day to make a
' Complaiſance at leaſt.—Here comes my charm-
le.

Enter Darling *and* Angelica.

. [Saluting *Angelica*.] I wiſh you, Madam, all
of Love and Fortune.

Enter Clincher junior.

Gentlemen and Ladies, I'm juſt upon the Spur,
e only a Minute to take my Leave.

Whither are you bound, Sir?

Bound, Sir! I'm going to the *Jubilee*, Sir.

Bleſs me, Couſin! how came you by theſe
?

Cloaths! ha, ha, ha! the rareſt Jeſt! Ha, ba, ha!
urſt, by *Jupiter Ammon*, I ſhall burſt!

What's the matter, Couſin?

The Matter! Ha, ha, ha! Why, an honeſt Por-
ha, ha! has knock'd out my Brother's Brains, ha,

. A very good Jeſt, i'faith, ha, ha, ha!

Ay, Sir, but the Jeſt of all is, he knock'd out
ins with a Hammer, and ſo he is as dead as a Door-
, ha, ha!

. And do you laugh, Wretch?

Laugh! ha, ha, ha! let me ſee e'er a younger
in *England* that won't laugh at ſuch a Jeſt.

You appear'd a very ſober pious Gentleman ſome
ago.

Pſhaw, I was a Fool then: But now, Madam,
Wit; I can rake now.—As for your Part, Madam,
ght have had me once!—But now, Madam, if you
fall to eating Chalk, or gnawing the Sheets, it is
none

none of my Fault.—Now, Madam—I have got an Eſta
and I muſt go to the *Jubilee.*

Enter Clincher ſenior *in a Blanket.*

Clin. ſen. Muſt you ſo, Rogue, muſt ye? You will
to the *Jubilee,* will you?

Clin. jun. A Ghoſt, a Ghoſt!—Send for the Dean a
Chapter preſently.

Clin. ſen. A Ghoſt! No, no, Sirrah, I'm an elder Br
ther, Rogue.

Clin. jun. I don't care a Farthing for that; I'm ſt
you're dead in Law.

Clin. ſen. Why ſo, Sirrah; why ſo?

Clin. jun. Becauſe, Sir, I can get a Fellow to ſwear
knock'd out your Brains.

Wild. An odd Way of ſwearing a Man out of his Lift

Clin. jun. Smell him, Gentlemen, he has a deadly Sce
about him.———

Clin. ſen. Truly the Apprehenſions of Death may ha
made me ſavour a little—O Lord,—the Colonel! T
Apprehenſion of him may make the Savour worſe, I
afraid.

Clin. jun. In ſhort, Sir, were you a Ghoſt, or Brother,
Devil, I will go to the *Jubilee,* by *Jupiter Ammon.*

Stand. Go to the *Jubilee,* go the *Bear-Garden,*——t
Travel of ſuch Fools as you doubly injures our Countr
you expoſe our Native Follies, which ridicule us amo
Strangers, and return fraught only with their Vice
which you vend here for faſhionable Gallantry; a trav
ling Fool is as dangerous as a home-bred Villain—G
you to your native Plough and Cart, converſe with Ar
mals like yourſelves, Sheep and Oxen; Men are Cre
tures you don't underſtand.

Wild. Let 'em alone, Colonel, their Folly will be no
diverting. Come, Gentlemen, we'll diſpute this Poi
ſome other time; I hear ſome Fiddles tuning, let's he
how they can entertain us.

A Servant enters and whiſpers Wildair.

Wild. Madam, ſhall I beg you to entertain the Cor
pany in the next Room for a Moment: [*To* Darlin

Darl. With all my Heart—Come, Gentlemen.

[*Exeunt omnes but* Wildair.

Wi

V. A Lady to enquire for me! Who can this be?
Enter Lurewell.

Madam, this Favour is beyond my Expectation,
ıe uninvited to dance at my Wedding—What d'ye
t, Madam?

ı. A monster—if thou'rt marry'd, thou'rt the most
'd Wretch that e'er avouch'd Deceit.

d. Hey dey! Why, Madam, i'm sure I never fwore
rry you: I made indeed a flight Promife, upon
tion of your granting me a fmall Favour, but you
not confent you know.

ı. How he upbraids me with my Shame.—Can you
rour binding Vows when this appears a Witnefs
your Falfhood. [*Shews a Ring.*] Methinks the
of this facred Pledge fhou'd flafh Confufion in
ruilty Face—Read, read here the binding Words of
nd Honour, Words not unknown to your perfidious
ıe,—tho' utter Strangers to your treacherous Heart.

d. The Woman's ftark ftaring mad, that's certain.

ı. Was it malicioufly defign'd to let me find my
ı when paft Redrefs; to let me know you, only to
you falfe?—Had not curfed Chance fhew'd me the
zing Motto, I had been happy—The firft Knowledge
of you was fatal to me, and this fecond worfe.

d. What the Devil is all this!—Madam, I'm not at
: for Raillery at prefent, I have weighty Affairs
my Hands; the Bufinefs of Pleafure, Madam; any
time———   [*Going.*

e. Stay, I conjure you ftay.

d. Faith I can't, my Bride expects me; but hark'e,
the Honey-Moon is over, about a Month or two
, I may do you a fmall Favour.   [*Exit.*

ı. Grant me fome wild Expreffions, Heavens, or
burft—Woman's Weaknefs, Man's Falfhood, my
Shame, and Love's Difdain, at once fwell up my
——Words, Words, or I fhall burft.   [*Going.*
Enter Standard.

d. Stay, Madam, you need not fhun my Sight; for
are perfect Woman, you have Confidence to outface
ne; and bear the Charge of Guilt without a Blufh.

e. The Charge of Guilt! What? Making a Fool of
I've don't, and glory in the Act; the Height of

L. I.   M   Female

Female Juftice were to make you all hang or dro
fembling to the prejudice of Men is Virtue; and ev
or Sign, or Smile, or Tear that can deceive, is me

Stand. Very pretty Principles truly—if there
in Woman, 'tis now in thee—Come, Madam, j
that you're difcovered, and being fenfible you
cape, you wou'd now turn to Bay.

That Ring, Madam, proclaims you guilty.

Lure. O Monfter, Villain, perfidious Villain
told you?

Stand. I'll tell it you, and loudly too.

Lure. O name it not—yet, fpeak it out, 'tis
Punifhment for putting Faith in Man, that I wi
all; and let credulous Maids, that truft their H
the Tongues of Men, thus hear their Shame procl
Speak now, what his bufy Scandal, and your in
Malice both dare utter.

Stand. Your Falfhood can't be reach'd by M
by Satire; your Actions are the jufteft Libel
Fame—your Words, your Looks, your Tears,
lieve in fpite of common Fame. Nay, 'gainft r
Eyes, I ftill maintain'd your Truth. I imagin
dair's boafting of your Favours to be the pure
his own Vanity: At laft he urg'd your taking
of him, as a convincing Proof of which you
from him receiv'd that Ring, which Ring, that
be fure he gave it, I lent it him for that Purpo

Lure. Ha! You lent it him for that Purpofe!

Stand. Yes, yes, Madam, I lent it him for that
——no denying it——I know it well, for I hav
long, and defire you now, Madam, to reftore
juft Owner.

Lure. The juft Owner! Think, Sir, think
what Importance 'tis to own it; if you have I
Honour in your Soul, 'tis then moft juftly y
not, you are a Robber, and have ftol'n it bafelj

Stand. Ha!—your Words, like meeting Flin
ftruck a Light to fhew me fomething ftrange—
me inftantly, is not your real Name *Manly?*

Lure. Anfwer me firft; did not you receive t
about twelve Years ago?

Stand. I did.

. And were not you about that time entertain'd
ghts at the Houſe of Sir *Oliver Manly* in *Oxfordſhire?*
d. I was, I was; [*Runs to her and embraces her*]
left Remembrance fires my Soul with Tranſport——
v the reſt——you are the charming She, and I the
Man.

. How has blind Fortune ſtumbled on the right!
iere have you wander'd ſince?—'twas cruel to for-
ie.

d. The Particulars of my Fortune are too tedious
But to diſcharge myſelf from the Stain of Diſho-
I muſt tell you, that immediately upon my Return
Univerſity, my elder Brother and I quarrell'd: My
, to prevent farther Miſchief, poſts me away to
l: I writ to you from *London,* but fear the Letter
iot to your Hands.

. I never had the leaſt Account of you by Letter
erwiſe.

d. Three Years I liv'd abroad, and at my return,
you were gone out of the Kingdom, tho' none
tell me whither: Miſſing you thus, I went to
rs, ſerv'd my King till the Peace commenced; then
ately going on Board at *Amſterdam,* one Ship tranſ-
us both to *England.* At the firſt Sight I lov'd,
;norant of the hidden Cauſe—You may remember,
n, that talking once of Marriage, I told you I
igaged; to your dear ſelf I meant.

. Then Men are ſtill moſt generous and brave——
reward your Truth, an Eſtate of Three Thouſand
s a Year waits your Acceptance; and if I can ſa-
ou in my paſt Conduct, and the Reaſons that en-
me to deceive all Men, I ſhall expect the honour-
Performance of your Promiſe, and that you will
ith me in *England.*

d. Stay! nor Fame, nor Glory, e'er ſhall part us
.My Honour can be nowhere more concerned
iere.

Enter Wildair, Angelica, *both* Clinchers.

! Sir *Harry,* Fortune has acted Miracles to Day;
ory's ſtrange and tedious, but all amounts to this,
Voman's Mind is charming as her Perſon, and I
ade a Convert too to Beauty.

Wild.

Wild. I wanted only this to make my Pleaſure perfec
And now, Madam, we may dance and ſing, and lo
and kiſs in good Earneſt. ——

A Dance here. After the Dance, enter Smuggler.

Smug. So, Gentlemen and Ladies, I'm glad to fi
you ſo merry ; is my gracious Nephew among ye ?

Wild. Sir, he dares not ſhew his Face among ſuch h
nourable Company, for your gracious Nephew is——

Smug. What, Sir ? Have a care what you ſay.

Wild. A Villain, Sir.

Smug. With all my Heart—I'll pardon you the beatii
me for that very Word. And pray, Sir *Harry*, wh
you ſee him next, tell him this News from me, that
have diſinherited him, that I will leave him as poor as
diſbanded Quarter-maſter. And this is the poſitive and fi
Reſolution of Threeſcore and Ten ; an Age that ſticks
obſtinately to its Purpoſe, as to the old Faſhion of i
Cloak.

Wild. You ſee, Madam, [*To* Angel.] how induſtriouſ
Fortune has puniſh'd his Offence to you.

Angel. I can ſcarcely, Sir, reckon it an Offence, coi
ſidering the happy Conſequence of it.

Smug. O ! Sir *Harry*, he is as hypocritical ——

Lure. As yourſelf, Mr. Alderman. How fares n
go‑d old Nurſe, pray Sir ?

Smug. O Madam, I ſhall be even with you before I pa
with your Writings and Money, that I have in my Hanc

Stand. A Word with you, Mr. Alderman ; do y(
know this Pocket-Book ?

Smug. O Lord, it contains an Account of all my ſecr
Practices in Trading. [*Aſide.*] How came you by it, Si

Stand. Sir *Harry* here duſted it out of your Pocket,
this Lady's Houſe Yeſterday ; It contains an Account
ſome ſecret Practices in your Merchandizing ; among tl
reſt, the Counterpart of an Agreement with a Correſpo
dent at *Bourdeaux*, about tranſporting *French* Wine
Spaniſh Caſks—Firſt return this Lady all her Writing
then I ſhall conſider whether I ſhall lay your Proceedin;
before the Parliament or not, whoſe Juſtice will nev
ſuffer your Smuggling to go unpuniſh'd.

Smug. O my poor Ship and Cargo !

Clin. ſen. Hark'e, Maſter, you had as good come aloi
with me to the *Jubilee* now.

Ang

l. Come, Mr. Alderman, for once let a Woman
: Wou'd you be thought an honeſt Man, baniſh
uſneſs, that worſt Gout of Age : Avarice is a poor
ɡ Quality of the Soul, and will as certainly cheat,
ɪief wou'd ſteal——Wou'd you be thought a Re-
of the Times, be leſs ſevere in your Cenſures, leſs
ɪ your Precepts, and more ſtrict in your Example.
ʼ. Right, Madam, Virtue flows freer from Imita-
han Compulſion ; of which, Colonel, your Con-
ɔn and miné are juſt Examples.

ain are muſty Morals taught in Schools,
ɡid Teachers, and as rigid Rules,
ʹe Virtue with a frowning Aſpect ſtands,
frights the Pupil from its rough Commands.
Woman ————
ming Woman can true Converts make,
ɪve the Precepts for the Teacher's Sake.
ɪe in them appears ſo bright, ſo gay,
ear with Tranſport, and with Pride obey.

The End of the Fifth Act.

XXXXXXXXXXXXXX X XXXXXXXXX

EPILOGU

Spoken by Mr. WILKS.

NOW all depart each his respective Way,
  To spend an Evening's Chat upon the Play ;
Some to Hippolito's *; one homeward goes,*
And one with loving she retires to th' Rose.
The am'rous Pair in all Things frank and free,
Perhaps may save the Play in Number Three.
The tearing Spark, if Phyllis *ought gainsays,*
Breaks th' Drawer's *Head, kicks her, and murders* Bay.
To Coffee *some retreat to save their Pockets,*
Others, more generous, damn the Play at Locket's *;*
But there, I hope, the Author's Fears are vain,
Malice ne'er spoke in generous Champaign.
That Poet merits an ignoble Death,
Who fears to fall over a brave Monteth.
The Privilege of Wine we only ask,
You'll taste again, before you damn the Flask.
Our Author fears not you ; but those he may,
Who in cold Blood murder a Man in Tea.
Those Men of Spleen, who fond the World should know it
Sit down, and for their Two-pence *damn a Poet.*
Their Criticism's good, that we can say for't,
They understand a Play—too well to pay for't.
From Box to Stage, from Stage to Box they run,
First steal the Play, then damn it when they've done.
But now, to know what Fate *may us betide,*
Among our Friends in Cornhill *and* Cheapside.
But those I think, have but one Rule for Plays ;
They'll say they're good, if so the World but says.
If it should please them, and their Spouses know it,
They strait enquire what Kind of Man's the Poet.
But from Side-box we dread a fearful Doom,
All the good-natur'd Beaux are gone to Rome.

EPILOGUE

The Ladies Cenſure I'd almoſt forgot,
Then for a Line or two t'engage their Vote:
But that Way's odd, below our Author's Aim,
No leſs than his whole Play is Compliment to them.
For their Sakes then the Play can't miſs ſucceeding,
Tho' Critics may want Wit, they have good Breeding;
They won't, I'm ſure, forfeit the Ladies Graces,
By ſhewing their Ill-nature to their Faces;
Our Buſineſs with good Manners may be done,
Flatter us here, and damn us when you're gone.

M 4

HARRY WILDAIR.

Being the SEQUEL of the

Trip to the Jubilee.

A

OMEDY,

As it is Acted at the

[EATRE-ROYAL

I N

)RURY-LANE.

LONDON:

for T. LOWNDES, T. CASLON, W. NICOLL, and S. BLADON.

M. DCC. LXXII.

ROLOGUE.

U R *Authors have, in most their late Essays,*
Prologu'd their own, by damning other Plays;
le great Harangues to teach you what was fit
ass for Humour, and go down for Wit.
enian Rules must form an English *Piece,*
' Drury-Lane *comply with ancient* Greece.
ctness only, such as Terence *writ,*
t please our masqu'd Lucretias *in the Pit.*
youthful Author swears he cares not a Pin'
Vossius, Scaliger, Hedelin, *or* Rapin:
leaves to learned Pens such labour'd Lays,
are the Rules by which he writes his Plays.
n musty Books let others take their View,
bates dull Reading, but he studies You.
t, from you Beaux, *his Lesson is Formality;*
t in your Footmen there——most nice Morality;
pleasure them his Pegasus *must fly,*
use they judge, and lodge, three Stories high.
n the Front-Boxes he has pick'd his Stile,
' learns, without a Blush, to make 'em Smile;
esson only taught us by the Fair;
raggish Action——but a modest Air.
ng his Friends here in the Pit, he reads
t Rules that every modish Writer needs.
learns from ev'ry Covent-Garden *Critic's Face,*
modern Forms of Action, Time, *and* Place,
Action he's asham'd to name,——d'ye see,
Time *is* Seven, *the* Place *is* Number Three.
Masques *he only reads by passant Looks,*
dares not venture far into their Books.
s then the Pit *and* Boxes *are his Schools,*
r Air, your Humour, his Dramatic Rules.
Critics *censure then, and hiss like Snakes,*
gains his Ends, if his light Fancy takes
James's *Beaux, and* Covent-Garden *Rakes.*

M 6

Dramatis Personæ.

MEN.

Sir *Harry Wildair*, - - - Mr. *Wilks.*

Col. *Standard*, - - - Mr. *Mills.*

Fireball, a Sea Captain, - - Mr. *Johnson.*

Monf. *Marquis*, a fharping Refugee, Mr. *Cibber.*

Beau Banter, - - - Mrs. *Rogers.*

Clincher the Jubilee-Beau. turn'd } Mr. *Pinkethman.*
  Politician, - - - }

Dicky, Servant to *Wildair*, - - Mr. *Norris.*

Shark, Servant to *Fireball*, - - Mr. *Fairbank.*

Ghoft, - - - - Mrs. *Rogers.*

Lord *Bellamy*, - - - Mr. *Simpfon.*

WOMEN.

Lady *Lurewell*, - - - Mrs. *Verbruggen.*

Angelica, - - - Mrs. *Rogers.*

Parly, - - - - Mrs. *Lucas.*

Servants and Attendants.

SCENE, St. *JAMES*'s.

T H

THE
SECOND PART
OF THE
CONSTANT COUPLE:
OR, A
Trip to the Jubilee.

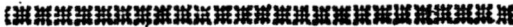

ACT I.

SCENE, *The Park.*

Enter Standard *and* Fireball *meeting.*

AH! Brother *Fireball!* Welcome ashore, What!
Heart whole? Limbs firm, and Frigate safe?
Fire. All, all, as my Fortune and Friends
wish.

Stand. And what News from the *Baltic?*

Fire. Why, yonder are three or four young Boys i'th'
that have got Globes and Sceptres to play with:
fell to Loggerheads about their Playthings; the
came in like *Robin Good-Fellow*, cry'd *Bob*, and
'em quiet.

Stand.

Stand. In the next Place then, you're to congratu
my Succeſs: You have heard, I ſuppoſe, that I've
ry'd a fine Lady with a great Fortune.

Fire. Ay, ay, 'twas my firſt News upon my Land
that Colónel *Standard* had marry'd the fine Lady Lur
—A fine Lady indeed! A very fine Lady!—But F
Brother, I had rather turn Skipper to an *Indian C.*
than manage the Veſſel you're Maſter of.

Stand. Why ſo, Sir?

Fire. Becauſe ſhe'll run adrift with every Wind
blows: She's all Sail and no Ballaſt—Shall I tell you
Character I have heard of a fine Lady? A fine Lady
laugh at the Death of her Huſband, and cry for the
of her Lap-Dog. A fine Lady is angry without a C
and pleas'd without a Reaſon. A fine Lady has the
pours all the Morning, and the Cholic all the Aftern
The Pride of a fine Lady is above the Merit of an un
ſtanding Head; yet her Vanity will ſtoop to the Ad
tion of a Peruke. And in fine, a fine Lady goe
Church for Faſhion's Sake, and to the Baſſet-Table
Devotion; and her Paſſion for Gaming exceeds her
nity of being thought virtuous, or the Deſire of at
the contrary.——We Seamen ſpeak plain, Brother.

Stand. You Seamen are like your Element, always
peſtuous, too ruffling to handle a fine Lady.

Fire. Say you ſo? Why then give me thy Hand,
neſt *Frank,* and let the World talk on and be damn'

Stand. The World talk, ſay you? What does the W
talk?

Fire. Nothing, nothing at all—They only ſay w
uſual upon ſuch Occaſions: That your Wife's the gre
Coquet about the Court, and your Worſhip the gre
Cuckold about the City: That's all.

Stand. How, how, Sir?

Fire. That ſhe's a Coquet, and you a Cuckold.

Stand. She's an Angel in herſelf, and a Paradiſe to

Fire. She's an *Eve* in herſelf, and a Devil to you.

Stand. She's all Truth, and the World a Liar.

Fire. Why then, I gad, Brother, it ſhall be ſo:
back again to *White's,* and whoever dares mutter Sca
of my Brother and Siſter, I'll daſh his Ratifia in's 1
'd call him a Liar.   [G
                                              S

Stand. Hold, hold, Sir. The World is too ftrong for us. Were Scandal and Detraction to be thoroughly re-eng'd, we muft murder all the Beaux, and poifon half the Ladies: Thofe that have nothing elfe to fay, muft tell Stories; Fools over *Burgundy*, and Ladies over *Tea,* muft have fomething that's fharp to relifh their Liquor; Malice is the piquant Sauce of fuch Converfation; and without it, their Entertainment wou'd prove mighty in-fipid—Now, Brother, why fhould we pretend to quarrel with all Mankind?

Fire. Becaufe all Mankind quarrel with us.

Stand. The worft Reafon in the World.—Wou'd you pretend to devour a Lion, becaufe a Lion wou'd devour you?

Fire. Yes, if I cou'd.

Stand. Ay, that's right; if you cou'd: But fince you have neither Teeth nor Paws for fuch an Encounter, lie quietly down, and perhaps the furious Beaft may run over you.

Fire. 'Sdeath, Sir! But I fay, that whoever abufes my Brother's Wife, tho' at the Back of the King's Chair, he's a Villain.

Stand. No, no, Brother, that's a Contradiction; there's no fuch Thing as Villainy at Court. Indeed, if the Prac-ice of Courts were found in a fingle Perfon, he might be til'd Villain with a Vengeance; but Number and Power nthorizes every Thing, and turns the Villain upon their accufers. In fhort, Sir, every Man's Morals, like his Religion now-a-days, pleads Liberty of Confcience; every Man's Confcience is his Convenience, and we know no Convenience but Preferment—As for Inftance, who would be fo complaifant as to thank an Officer for his Courage, when that's the Condition of his Pay? And who can be fo ill-natur'd, as to blame a Courtier for ef-poufing that which is the very Tenure of his Livelihood?

Fire. A very good Argument in a very damnable Caufe: —But, Sir, my Bus'nefs is not with the Court, but with you: I defire you, Sir, to open your Eyes; at leaft, be pleas'd to lend an Ear to what I heard juft now at the Chocolate-Houfe.

Stand. Brother——

Fire. Well, Sir.

Stand. Did the Scandal pleafe you when you heard it?

Fire. No.

Stand. Then why fhou'd you think it fhou'd pleafe me? Be not more uncharitable to your Friends than to your-felf, fweet Sir: If it made you uneafy, there's no queftion but it will torment me, who am fo much nearer concern'd.

Fire. But wou'd you not be glad to know your Enemies?

Stand. Pfhaw! If they abus'd me they are my Friends, my intimate Friends, my Table-Company, and Bottle-Companions.

Fire. Why then, Brother, the Devil take all your Ac-quaintance. You were fo rally'd, fo torn! there was a hundred Ranks of fneering white Teeth drawn upon your Misfortunes at once, which fo mangled your Wife's Re-putation, that fhe can never patch up her Honour while fhe lives.

Stand. And their Teeth were very white, you fay?

Fire. Very white; Blood, Sir, I fay they mangled your Wife's Reputation.

Stand. And I fay, that if they touch my Wife's Repu-tation with nothing but their Teeth, her Honour will be fafe enough.

Fire. Then you won't hear it.

Stand. Not a Syllable. Lift'ning after Slander is lay-ing Nets for Serpents, which, when you have caught, will fting you to Death: Let 'em fpit their Venom among themfelves, and it hurts nobody.

Fire. Lord! Lord! How Cuckoldom and Contentment go together! Fie, fie, Sir! confider you have been a Sol-dier, dignify'd by a noble Poft; diftinguifh'd by brave Actions, an Honour to your Nation, and a Terror to your Enemies.—Hell! that a Man who has ftorm'd *Namur* fhou'd become the Jeft of a Coffee-Table.—The whole Houfe was clearly taken up with the two important Quef-tions, whether the Colonel was a Cuckold? or *Kid* a Pirate?

Stand. This I can't bear. [*Afide.*

Fire. Ay, (fays a fneering Coxcomb) the Colonel has made his Fortune with a Witnefs; he has fecur'd himfelf a good Eftate in this Life, and a Reverfion in the World to come. Then (replies another) I prefume he's oblig'd to your Lordfhip's Bounty for the latter Part of the Set-tlement.

ement. There are others (fays a Third) that have play'd
rith my Lady *Lurewell* at Piquet, befides my Lord; I
ave capotted her myfelf two or three Times in an Even-
ng.

Stand. O Matrimonial Patience, affift me!

Fire. Matrimonial Patience! Matrimonial Peftilence!
—Shake off thefe drowzy Chains that fetter your Refent-
nents. If your Wife has wrong'd ye, pack her off, and
et her Perfon be as public as her Character: If fhe be
honeft, revenge her Quarrel.—I can ftay no longer:
This is my Hour of Attendance at the *Navy-Office*; I'll
some and dine with you; in the mean Time, Revenge I
think on't.   [*Exit* Fireball.

Stand. [*Solus.*] How eafy is it to give Advice, and how
difficult to obferve it! *If your Wife has wrong'd ye, pack
her off.* A·, but how? The Gofpel drives the Matrimonial Nail, and the Law clinches it fo very hard, that
to draw it again wou'd tear the Work to Pieces.—That
her Intentions have wrong'd me here's a young Bawd can
witnefs.

Enter Parly, *running acrofs the Stage.*

Here, here, Mrs. *Parly*, whither fo faft?

Par. Oh Lord! my Mafter!—Sir, I was running to
Madamoifelle *Furbello*, the *French* Milliner, for a new
Burgundy for my Lady's Head.

Stand. No, Child, you're employ'd about an old
afhion'd Garniture for your Mafter's Head, if I miftake
not your Errand.

Par. Oh, Sir! there's the prettieft Fafhion lately come
ver! fo airy, fo *French*, and all that!—The Pinners
re double ruffled with twelve Plaits of a Side, and open
ll from the Face; the Hair is frizzled all up round the
Head, and ftands as ftiff as a Bodkin. Then the Favou-
ites hang loofe upon the Temples with a languifhing
ock in the Middle. Then the Caule is extremely wide,
nd over all is a Cornet rais'd very high, and all the Lap-
ets behind—I muft fetch it prefently.

Stand. Hold a little, Child, I muft talk with you.

Par. Another Time, Sir, my Lady ftays for it.

Stand. One Queftion firft: What Wages does my Wife
give you?

Par. Ten Pounds a Year, Sir, which God knows i
tle enough, confidering how I flave from Place to
upon her Occafions. But then, Sir, my Perquifite
confiderable ; I make above Two Hundred Pounds a
by her old Cloaths.

Stand. Two Hundred Pounds a Year of her old Clo
What then muft her new ones coft ?—But what do yo
by vifiting Gallants, and Picquet ?

Par. About a Hundred Pounds more.

Stand. A Hundred Pounds more ! Now who can e:
to find a Lady's Woman honeft, when fhe gets fo i
by being a Jade ?—What Religion are you of, Mrs. P

Par. Religion, Sir ! I can't tell.

Stand. What was your Father ?

Par. A Mountebank.

Stand. Where was you born ?

Par. In Holland.

Stand. Were you ever Chriften'd ?

Par. No.

Stand. How came that ?

Par. My Parents were Anabaptifts; they dy'd bel
was dipt ; I then forfook their Religion, and ha' got
a new one fince.

Stand. I'm very forry, Madam, that I had not the
nour to know the Worth of your Extraction fooner
I might have paid you the Refpect due to your Qua

Par. Sir, your humble Servant.

Stand. Have you any Principles ?

Par. Five Hundred.

Stand. Have you loft your Maidenhead ?—[*She p
her Mafque, and nods.*] Do you love Money ?

Par. Yaw, Mijn Heer.

Stand. Well, Mrs. *Parly*, now you have been fo
with me, I tell you what you muft truft to in Re
Never to come near my Houfe again. Be gone,
fter, fly.—Hell and Furies ! never Chriften'd ! He
ther a Mountebank !

Par. Lord, Sir, you need not be fo furious. I
Chriften'd ! What then ? I may be a very good Chi
for all that, I fuppofe. Turn me off ! Sir, you f
Meddle with your Fellows ; 'tis my Lady's Bufine
order her Women.

Stand. Here's a young Whore for you now! A sweet Companion for my Wife! Where there's such a hellish Confident, there must be damnable Secrets.—Be gone, I say.—My Wife shall turn you away.

Par. Sir, she won't turn me away, she sha'n't turn me away, nor she can't turn me away. Sir, I say, she dare not turn me away.

Stand. Why, you Jade? Why?

Par. Because I'm the Mistress, not she.

Stand. You the Mistress!

Par. Yes, I know all her Secrets; and let her offer to turn me off if she dares.

Stand. What Secrets do you know?

Par. Humph!—Tell a Wife's Secrets to her Husband! —Very pretty, faith! Sure, Sir, you don't think me such a *Jew*: Tho' I was never Christen'd, I have more Religion than that comes to.

Stand. Are you faithful to your Lady for Affection, or Interest?

Par. Shall I tell you a Christian Lie, or a Pagan Truth?

Stand. Come, Truth for once.

Par. Why then, Interest, Interest! I have a great Soul, which nothing can gain but a great Bribe.

Stand. Well, tho' thou art a Devil, thou art a very honest one—Give me thy Hand, Wench. Should not Interest make you faithful to me, as much as to others?

Par. Honest to you! Marry for what? you gave me indeed two pitiful Pieces the Day you were marry'd, but not a Stiver since. One Gallant gives me ten Guineas, another a Watch, another a Pair of Pendants, a fourth a Diamond Ring; and my noble Master gives me—his Linen to mend.—Faugh!—I'll tell you a Secret, Sir: stinginess to Servants makes more Cuckolds, than Literature to Wives.

Stand. And am I a Cuckold, *Parly!*

Par. No, faith, not yet; tho' in a very fair Way of having the Dignity conferr'd upon you very suddenly.

Stand. Come, Girl, you shall be my Pensioner; you shall have a glorious Revenue; for every Guinea that you get for keeping a Secret, I'll give you two for revealing it: You shall find a Husband once in your Life out-do all your Gallants in Generosity. Take their Money, Child,

Child, take all their Bribes: give 'em Hopes, make
Affignations ; ferve your Lady faithfully, but tell all to
By which means, fhe will be kept chafte, you will grow r
and I fhall preferve my Honour.

Par. But what Security fhall I have for Performance
Articles ?

Stand. Ready Payment, Child.

Par. Then give me Earneft.

Stand. Five Guineas.   [*Giving her M*

Par. Are they right ? No *Gray's-Inn* Pieces amo
'em——All right as my Leg——Now, Sir, I'll give yo
Earneft of my Service. Who d'ye think is come to Tov

Stand. Who ?

Par. Your old Friend, Sir *Harry Willair.*

Stand. Impoffible !

Par. Yes, faith, and as gay as ever.

Stand. And has he forgot his Wife fo foon ?

Par. Why, fhe has been dead now above a Year——
appear'd in the Ring laft Night with fuch Splendor
Equipage, that he eclips'd the Beaux, dazzled the Lac
and made your Wife dream all Night of fix *Flanders* Ma
feven *French* Liveries, a Wig like a Cloak, and a Hat lil
Shuttlecock.

Stand. What are a Woman's Promifes and Oaths ?

Par. Wind, Wind, Sir.

Stand. When I marry'd her, how heartily did fhe (
demn her light preceding Conduct, and for the future vo
herfelf a perfect Pattern of Conjugal Fidelity !

Par. She might as fafely fwear, Sir, That this l
fe'nnight, at Four o'Clock, the Wind will blow fair
Flanders. 'Tis prefuming for any of us all to promife
our Inclinations a whole Week. Befides, Sir, my Lady
got the Knack of coquetting it ; and when once a Wo
has got that in her Head, fhe will have a touch on't e
where elfe.

Stand. An Oracle, Child. But now I muft make the
of a bad Bargain ; and fince I have got you on my Sidi
have fome Hopes, that by conftant Difappointment
Croffes in her Defigns, I may at laft tire her into good
haviour.

Par. Well, Sir, the Condition of the Articles being d
performed, I ftand to the Obligation ; and will tell
           fart

arther, That by and by Sir *Harry Wildair* is to come to ur House to Cards, and that there is a Defign laid to cheat him of his Money.

Stand. What Company will there be befides?

Par. Why, the old Set at the Baffet Table; my Lady *Lovecards*, and the ufual Company: They have made up a Bank of fifteen Hundred *Louis d'Ors* among 'em; the whole Defign lies upon Sir *Harry*'s Purfe, and the *French* Marquis, you know, conftantly *Taillés.*

Stand. Ay, the *French* Marquis; that's one of your Be-nefactors, *Parly*;—the Perfecution of *Buffet* in *Paris* furnifh'd us with that *Refugee*, but the Character of fuch a Fellow ought not to reflect on thofe who have been real Sufferers for their Religion. ——But take no Notice. Be fure only to inform me of all that paffes.——There's more Earneft for you : Be rich and faithful.   [*Exit* Standard.

Par. [*Solus.*] I am now not only *Woman* to the Lady *Lurewell*, but *Steward* to her Hufband, in my double Ca-pacity of knowing *her* Secrets, and commanding his *Purfe.* A very pretty Office in a Family: *For every Guinea that I get for keeping a Secret, he'll give me two for revealing it.——* My Comings-in, at this Rate, will be worth a Mafter in *Chancery*'s Place, and many a poor *Templer* will be glad to marry me with half my Fortune.

Enter Dicky, *meeting her.*

Dick. Here's a Man much fitter for your Purpofes.

Par. Blefs me! Mr. *Dicky* !

Dick. The very fame in Longitude and Latitude! not a Bit diminifh'd, nor a Hair's Breadth increas'd.—Dear Mrs. *Parly*, give me a Bufs, for I'm almoft ftarv'd.

Par. Why fo hungry, Mr. *Dicky* ?

Dick. Why I ha'n't tafted a Bit this Year and half, Wo-man. I have been wandring about all over the World, follow'ng my Mafter, and come home to dear *London* but two Days ago. Now the Devil take me, if I had not rather kifs an *Englifh* Pair of Pattins, than the fineft Lady in *France.*

Par. Then you're over-joy'd to fee *London* again?

Dick. Oh! I was juft dead of a Confumption, till the fweet Smoke of *Cheapfide*, and the dear Perfume of *Fleet-ditch*, made me a Man again.

Par. But how came you to live with Sir *Harry Wildair* ?

Dick.

Dick. Why, feeing me a handfome perfonable Fe
and well qualify'd for a Livery, he took a Fancy t
Figure, that was all.

Par. And what's become of your old Mafter?

Dick. O! hang him, he was a Blockhead, and I t
him off; I turn'd him away.

Par. And were not you very forry for the Lofs of
Miftrefs, Sir Harry's Lady? They fay, fhe was a very
Woman.

Dick. Oh! the fweeteft Woman that ever the Sun
upon. I cou'd almoft weep when I think of her.

[*Wiping his*

Par. How did fhe die, pray? I could never hea
'twas.

Dick. Give me a Bufs then, and I'll tell ye.

Par. You fhall have your Wages when your W
done.

Dick. Well then—Courage!—Now for a doleful T
You know that my Mafter took a Freak to go fee
foolifh *Jubilee* that made fuch a Noife among us here;
no fooner faid than done; away he went; he took hi
French Servants to wait on him, and left me, the poor E
Puppy, to wait upon his Lady at home here.——Wel
far fo good—But fcarce was my Mafter's Back tu
when my Lady fell to fighing, and pouting, and whi
and crying; and in fhort fell fick upon't.

Par. Well, well, I know all this already; and th
pluck'd up her Spirits at laft, and went to follow him.

Dick. Very well: Follow him we did, far and far,
farther than I can tell, till we came to a Place call'd
pellier in *France*; a goodly Place truly.—But Sir Harry
gone to *Rome*; there was our Labour loft.——But,
fhort, my poor Lady, with the Tirefomenefs of Travel
fell fick—and dy'd.

Par. Poor Woman!

Dick. Ay, but that was not all. Here comes the wo
the Story.——Thofe curfed barbarous Devils, the Fr
wou'd not let us bury her.

Par. Not bury her!

Dick. No, fhe was a Heretic Woman, and they w
not let her Corps be put in their Holy Ground —
damn their holy Ground for me.

Par. Now had not I better be an honeſt Pagan, as I am, an ſuch a Chriſtian as one of theſe?——But how did you ſpoſe the Body?

Dick. Why, there was one charitable Gentlewoman that 'd to viſit my Lady in her Sickneſs: She contriv'd the latter ſo, that ſhe had her bury'd in her own private hapel. This Lady and myſelf carried her out upon our wn Shoulders, through a Back-door at the Hour of Mid-'ght, and laid her in a Grave that I dug for her with my wn Hands; and if we had been catch'd by the Prieſts, we id gone to the Gallows without the Benefit of Clergy.

Par. Oh! the Devil take 'em. But what did they mean y a Heretic Woman?

Dick. I don't know; ſome Sort of *Canibal*, I believe. I now there are ſome *Canibal* Woman here in *England*, that ome to the Play-houſes in Maſques; but let them have a are how they go to *France*. (For they are all Heretics, believe.) But I'm ſure my good Lady was none of ieſe.

Par. But how did Sir *Harry* bear the News?

Dick. Why, you muſt know, that my Lady, after ſhe was ury'd, ſent me——

Par. How! after ſhe was bury'd!

Dick. Pſhaw! Why Lord, Miſtreſs, you know what I iean; I went to Sir *Harry* all the Way to *Rome*; and 'here d'ye think I found him?

Par. Where?

Dick. Why, in the Middle of a Monaſtery among a undred and fifty Nuns, 'playing at Hot-cockles. He was irpriz'd to ſee honeſt *Dicky*, you may be ſure. But when told him the ſad Story, he roar'd out a whole Volley of *:ngliſh* Oaths upon the Spot, and ſwore that he would ſet ire on the Pope's Palace for the Injury done to his Wife. le then flew away to his Chamber, lock'd himſelf up for iree Days; we thought to have found him dead; but in-ead of that, he call'd for his beſt Linen, fine W'   ·''. 'oach; and laughing very heartily, ſwore a e reveng'd, and bid them drive to the N' as revenged to ſome Purpoſe.

Par. How, how, dear Mr. *Dicky*?

Dick. Why, in a Matter of five Days h ith Child, and left 'em to prov

Baftards—Ah Plague on 'em, they hate a dead Hereti
they love a piping-hot warm Heretic with all their Hea
So away we came; and thus did he jog on, reve
himfelf at this Rate through all the Catholic Countrie
we pafs'd, till we came home; and now, Mrs. P
fancy he has fome Defigns of Revenge too upon
Lady.

Par. Who cou'd have thought that a Man of his
airy Temper wou'd have been fo revengeful?

Dick. Why, faith, I'm a little malicious too: W
the Bufs you promis'd me, you Jade?

Par. Follow me, you Rogue. {Ru
Dick. Allons. [F*a*

The End of the Firft Aᘓ.

XXXXXXXXXXXXXXXXXXXX

ACT II.

SCENE, *A Lady's Apartment.*

Enter two Chamber-maids.

1ſt Cham. ARE all Things fet in Order? The
fix'd, the Bottles and Combs put in
and the Chocolate ready?

2d Cham. 'Tis no great matter whether they be ri
not; for right or wrong we fhall be fure of our Left
with for my Part that my Time were out.

1ſt Cham. Nay, 'tis a Hundred to one but we m
away before our Time be half expir'd; and fhe's wor
Morning than ever.—Here fhe comes.

Enter Lurewell.

Lure. Ay, there's a Couple of you indeed! Bu
how in the Name of Negligence cou'd you two cont
make a Bed as mine was laft Night; a Wrinkle on on
and a Rumple on t'other; the Pillows awry, and the
afkew.—I did nothing but tumble about, and fence w
Sheets all Night long.—Oh!—my Bones ake this Mo

if I had lain all Night on a Pair of *Dutch* Stairs—Go, ring Chocolate.—And, d'ye hear? Be fure to ftay an Iour or two at leaft.—Well! Thefe *Englifh* Animals are unpolifh'd! I wifh the Perfecution would rage a little arder, that we might have more of thefe *French Refugees* mong us.

Enter the Maids with Chocolate.

Thefe Wenches are gone to *Smyrna* for this Chocolate.— And what made you ftay fo long?

Cham. I thought we did not ftay at all, Madam.

Lure. Only an Hour and a half by the floweft Clock in *Chriftendom*—And fuch Salvers and Difhes too! The Lard be merciful to me! what have I committed, to be plagu'd with fuch Animals?—Where are my new *Japan* Salvers?— Broke, o'my Confcience! All to Pieces, I'll lay my Life on't.

Cham. No, indeed, Madam, but your Hufband——

Lure. How? Hufband, Impudence! I'll teach you Man- ners [*Gives her a Box on the Ear*] Hufband! Is that your *Welfh* Breeding? Hin't the Col. a Name of his own?

Cham. Well then, the Col. He us'd 'em this Morning, and we ha'n't got 'em fince.

Lure. How! the Col. ufe my Things! How dare the Col. ufe any Thing of mine?—But his Campaign Educa- tion muft be pardon'd—And I warrant they were filled about among his dirty Levee of Difbanded Officers?—— Faugh! The very Thoughts of them Fellows with their eager Looks, Iron Swords, ty'd-up Wigs, and tuck'd-in Cravats, make me fick as Death—Come, let me fee.—[*Goes 'o take the Chocolate, and ftarts back.*] Heav'ns protect me from fuch a Sight! Lord, Girl! When did you wafh your Hands laft? And have you been pawing me all this Morn- ing with them dirty Fifts of yours? [*Runs to the Glaf.*] I muft drefs all over again—Go, take it away, I elfe.—Here, Mrs. Monfter, call up my Tav hear? You, Mrs. Hobbyhorfe, fee if my Com to Cards yet.

Enter the Taylor.

Oh, Mr. *Remnant!* I don t know what you have made me; but fomething is like 'em

Rem. I am very forry for that, does your Ladyfhip find?

VOL. I.   N

Lure. I don't know where the Fault lies ; but in fhc don't like 'em ; I can't tell how ; the Things are ' enough made, but I don't like 'em.

Rem. Are they too wide, Madam ?

Lure. No.

Rem. Too ftraight, perhaps ?

Lure. Not at all I they fit me very well ; but—I blefs me ! Can't you tell where the Fault lies ?

Rem. Why truly, Madam, I can't tell.—But your La fhip, I think, is a little too flender for the Fafhion.

Lure. How ! too flender for the Fafhion, fay you ?

Rem. Yes, Madam ; there's no fuch Thing as a g Shape worn among the Quality : Your fine Waifts are c out, Madam.

Lure. And why did not you plump up my Stays to fafhionable Size ?

Rem. I made 'em to fit you, Madam.

Lure. Fit me I fit my Monkey—What d'ye think I w Cloaths to pleafe myfelf I Fit me ! fit the Fafhion, pray ; matter for me—I thought fomething was the Matter, I wan Quality-air.—Pray, Mr. *Remnant*, let me have a Bulk Quality, a fpreading Counter. I do remember now, Ladies in the Apartments, the Birth Night, were moft 'em two Yards about——Indeed, Sir, if you contrive Things any more with your fcanty Chamber-maid's *A* you fhall work no more for me.

Rem. I fhall take Care to pleafe your Ladyfhip for ' future.　　　　　　　　　　　　　　　　　　　　[*E*

Enter a Servant.

Ser. Madam, my Mafter defires——

Lure. Hold, hold, Fellow ; for Gad's Sake hold : thou touch my Cloaths with that Tobacco Breath of thi. I fhall poifon the whole Drawing-Room. Stand at ' Door pray, and fpeak.　　　[*Ser. goes to the Door and fpea*

Ser. My Mafter, Madam, defires——

Lure. Oh hideous ! Now the Rafcal bellows fo loud, tl he tears my Head to Pieces.—Here, Aukwardnefs, go ta the Booby's Meffage, and bring it to me. [*Maid goes to*
　　　　　　　　　　　　　　　　　　[*Door, whifpers and retur*

Cham. My Mafter defires to know how your Ladyf refted laft Night, and if you are pleas'd to admit of a Vi this Morning ?

　　　　　　　　　　　　　　　　　　　　　　Lu

Lure. Ay——Why this is civil. ——'Tis an infupportable Toil tho' for Women of Quality to model their Hufbands to good Breeding.

Enter Standard.

Stand. Good morrow, deareſt Angel.   How have you reſted laſt Night?

Lure. Lard, Lard, Col! What a Room have you made me here with your dirty Feet! Blefs me, Sir! Will you never be reclaim'd from your ſlovenly Campaign Airs ? 'Tis the moſt unmannerly Thing in Nature to make a ſliding Bow in a Lady's Chamber with dirty Shoes; it writes Rudenefs upon the Boards.

Stand. A very odd Kind of Reception this, truly!—I'm very forry, Madam, that the Offences of my Feet ſhould treate an Averſion to my Company: But for the future I ſhall honour your Ladyſhip's Apartment as the Sepulchre at *Jeruſalem,* and always come in bare-foot.

Lure. Sepulchre at *Jeruſalem!* Your Compliment, Sir, is very far-fetch'd: But your Feet indeed have a very travelling Air.

Stand. Come, come, my Dear, no ferious Difputes upon Trifles, ſince you know I never contend with you in Matters of Confequence: You are ſill Miſtrefs of your Fortune, and Marriage has only made you more abfolute in your Pleaſure, by adding one faithful Servant to your Deſires.—— Come, clear your Brow of that uneafy Chagrin, and let that pleaſing Air take Place that firſt enfnar'd my Heart. I have invited ſome Gentlemen to Dinner, whofe Friendſhips deferve a welcome Look.   Let their Entertainment ſhew how blefs'd you have made me by a plentiful Fortune, and the Love of fo agreeable a Creature.

Lure. Your Friends, I fuppofe, are all Men of Quality ?

Stand. Madam, they are Officers, and Men of Honour.

Lure. Officers, and Men of Honour! That is, they will daub the Stairs with their Feet, ſtain all the Rooms with their Wine, talk Bawdy to my Woman, rail at the Parliament, then at one another, fall to cutting of Throats, and break all my China.

Stand. Admitting that I keep fuch Company, 'tis unkind in you, Madam, to talk fo feverely of my Friends.——But my Brother, my Dear, is juſt come from his Voyage, and will be here to-pay his Refpeſts to you.

Lure.

Lure. Sir, I fhall not be at Leifure to entertain a Perfon of his *Wapping* Education, I can affure you.

Enter Parly, *and whifpers her.*

Sir, I have fome Bufinefs with my Woman; you may entertain your Sea-monfter by yourfelf; you may command a Difh of Pork and Peafe, with a Bowl of Punch, I fuppofe; and fo, Sir, much good may do you.—Come, *Parly.*

[*Exeunt* Lure. *and* Par.

Stand. Hell and Furies!

Enter Fireball.

Fire. With all my Heart—Where's your Wife, Brother? —Ho' now Man, what's the Matter?—Is Dinner ready?

Stand. No—I don't know—Hang it, I'm forry that I invited you:—For you muft know that my Wife is very much out of Order; taken dangerous ill of a fudden— So that——

Fire. Pfhaw! Nothing, nothing but a Marriage Qualm; breeding Children, or breeding Mifchief. Where is fhe, Man? Prithee let me fee her; I long to fee this fine Lady you have got.

Stand. Upon my Word fhe's very ill, and can't fee any Body.

Fire. So ill that fhe can't fee any Body! What, fhe's not in Labour fure! I tell you, I will fee her. Where is fhe?

[*Looking about.*

Stand. No, no, Brother; fhe's gone abroad to take the Air.

Fire. What the Devil! dangerous fick, and gone out! So fick, that fhe'll fee nobody within, yet gone abroad to fee all the World!—Ah, you have made your Fortune with a Vengeance!—Then, Brother, you fhall dine with me at *Locket*'s; I hate thefe Family Dinners, where a Man's oblig'd to, O Lard, Madam; no Apology, dear Sir——'Tis very good indeed, Madam.——For yourfelf, dear Madam.—Where between the rubb'd Floor under-foot, the China in one Corner, and the Glaffes in another, a Man can't make two Strides without Hazard of his Life. Commend me to a Boy and a Bell; Coming, coming, Sir. Much Noife, no Attendance, and a dirty Room, where I may eat like a Horfe, drink like a Fifh, and fwear like a Devil. Hang your Family Dinners; come along with me.

As they are going out, enter Banter; *who feeing them feems to retire.*

Stand. Who's that? Come in, Sir. Your Bufinefs, pray Sir?

Ban.

m. Perhaps, Sir, it may not be fo proper to inform you;
ou appear to be as great a Stranger here as myfelf.

r. Come, come away, Brother ; he has fome Bufinefs
your Wife.

m. His Wife! Gad fo! A pretty Fellow, a very pretty
w, a likely Fellow, and a handfome Fellow; I find
ng like a Monfter about him : I wou'd fain fee his
nead tho'—— Sir, your humble Servant.

2nd. Your's S'r —But why d'ye ftare fo in my Face ?

m. I was told, Sir, that the Lady *Lurewell*'s Hufband
omething very remarkable over his Eyes, by which he
t be known.

re. Mark that, Brother.   *[In his Ear.*

2nd. Your Information, Sir, was right ; I have a crofs
over my left Eye that's very remarkable—But pray, Sir,
hat Marks are you to be known ?

m. Sir, I am dignify'd and diftinguifh'd by the Name
Title of *Beau Banter*; I'm younger Brother to Sir
y Wildair; and I hope to inherit his Eftate with his
our, for his Wife, I'm told, is dead, and has left no
l.

2nd. Oh, Sir! I'm your very humble Servant; you're
unlike your Brother in the Face; but methinks, Sir,
don't become his Humour altogether fo well ; for
's Nature in him, looks like Affectation in you.

m. Oh Lard, Sir! 'tis rather Nature in me, what is
ir'd by him; he's beholding to his Education for his
Now where d'ye think my Humour was eftablifh'd ?

2nd. Where ?

m. At *Oxford.*

2nd.
re. } At *Oxford!*

m. Ay: There have I been fucking my dear *Alma*
r thefe feven Years : Yet in Defiance to Legs of Mutton,
Beer, crabbed Books, and four-fac'd Doctors, I can
e a Minuet, court a Miftrefs, play at Piquet, or make
oli, with any *Wildair* in *Chriftendom.* In fhort, Sir, in
of the Univerfity, I'm a pretty Gentleman.—Colonel,
e's your Wife ?

re. [*Mimicking him.*] *In fpite of the Univerfity, I'm a*
Gentleman.——Then, *Colonel, where is your Wife ?*——

Hark ye, young *Plato*, Whether wou'd you have your Nose flit, or your Ears cut?

Ban. Firft tell me, Sir, which would you chufe, to be run through the Body, or fhot through the Head?

Fire. Follow me, and I'll tell ye.

Ban. Sir, my Servants fhall attend ye, if you have no Equipage of your own.

Fire. Blood, Sir!

Stand. Hold, Brother, hold; he's a Boy.

Ban. Look ye, Sir, I keep half a dozen Footmen that have no Bufinefs upon Earth but to anfwer impertinent Queftions: Now, Sir, if your fighting Stomach can digeft thefe fix brawny Fellows for a Breakfaft, their Mafter, perhaps, may do you the Favour to run you through the Body for a Dinner.

Fire. Sirrah, will you fight me? I received juft now fix Month's Pay, and by this Light, I'll give you the half on't for one fair Blow at your Skull.

Ban. Down with your Money, Sir.

Stand. No, no, Brother; if you are fo free of your Pay, get into the next Room; there you'll find fome Company at Cards, I fuppofe; you may find Opportunity for your Revenge; my Houfe protects him now.

Fire. Well, Sir, the Time will come. [*Exit.*

Ban. Well faid, Brazen-head.

Stand. I hope, Sir, you'll excufe the Freedom of this Gentleman; his Education has been among the boifterous Elements, the Winds and Waves.

Ban. Sir, I value neither him, nor his Wind and Waves neither; I'm privileg'd to be very impertinent, being an *Oxonian*, and oblig'd to fight no Man, being a *Beau*.

Stand. Sir, I admire the Freedom of your Condition.— But pray, Sir, have you feen your Brother fince he came laft over?

Ban. I ha'nt feen my Brother thefe feven Years, and fcarcely heard from him but by Report of others. About a Month ago he was pleas'd to honour me with a Letter from *Paris*, importing his Defign of being in *London* very foon, with a Defire of meeting me here. Upon this, I chang'd my Cap and Gown for a long Wig and Sword, came up to *London* to attend him, and went to his Houfe; but that was all in Sable for the Death of his Wife; there I

was

vas told that he defign'd to change his Habitation, becaufe
he wou'd avoid all Remembrances that might difturb his
Quiet.   You are the firft Perfon that has told me of his Arrival, and I expect that you may likewife inform me where
to wait on him.

  Stand. And I fuppofe, Sir, this was the Bus'nefs that oc-
tafion'd me the Honour of this Vifit.

  Ban. Partly this, and partly an Affair of greater Confequence.   You muft know, Sir, that tho' I have read ten
thoufand Lies in the Univerfity, yet I have learn'd to fpeak
the Truth myfelf; and to deal plainly with you, the Honour of this Vifit, as you were pleas'd to term it, was defign'd to the Lady *Lurewell.*

  Stand. My Wife, Sir !

  Ban. My Lady *Lurewell,* I fay, Sir.

  Stand. But I fay, my Wife, Sir—What !

  Ban. Why, look ye, Sir ; you may have the Honour of
being called the Lady *Lurewell's* Hufband ; but you will
never find in any Author, either antient or modern, that
he's called Mr. *Standard's* Wife. 'Tis true, you're a handfome young Fellow ; fhe lik'd you, fhe marry'd you; and
tho' the Prieft made you both one Flefh, yet there's no
fmall Diftinction in your Blood.   You are ftill a difbanded
Colonel, and fhe is ftill a Woman of Quality, I take it.

  Stand. And you are the moft impudent young Fellow I
ever met with in my Life, I take it.

  Ban. Sir, I'm a Mafter of Arts, and I plead the Privilege
of my Standing.

  Enter a Servant, and whifpers Banter.

  Ser. Sir, the Gentleman in the Coach below, fays, he'll
be gone unlefs you come prefently.

  Ban. I had forgot———Col. your humble Servant.
                                                    [*Exit.*

  Stand. Sir, you muft excufe me for not waiting on you
down Stairs.——An impudent young Dog.
                                      [Exit *another Way.*

SCENE changes to another Apartment in the fame Houfe.
Enter Lurewell, Ladies, Monf. Marquis *and* Fireball, *as
  lofing Gamefters, one after another, tearing their Cards, and
  flinging 'em about the Rooms.*

  Lure. Ruin'd ! Undone ! Deftroy'd !
                              N 4   *1ſt La.*

1st La. Oh Fortune! Fortune! Fortune!

2d. La. What will my Husband say?

Monf. Oh *malheur! malheur! malheur!*

Fire. Blood and Fire, I have lost Six Months Pay.

Monf. A hundred and ten Pistoles, sink me.

Fire. Sink you? sink me, that have lost two hundred and ten Pistoles.—Sink you indeed!

Lure. But why wou'd you hazard the Bank upon one Card?

Monf. Becaufe me had lofe by de Card tree Times before —Look, dere Madam, de very next Card had been put. Oh *Morbleu! qui fa?*

Lure. I rely'd altogether on your fetting the Cards; you us'd to *Tailée* with Succefs.

Monf. Morbleu, Madam, me never lofe before: But dat Monfieur Sir *Arry*, dat Chevalier *Wildair* is de Devil —— Vere is de Chevalier?

Lure. Counting our Money within yonder.—Go, go, be gone; and bethink yourfelf of fome Revenge.——Here he comes.

Enter Wildair.

Wild. Fifteen' hundred and feventy *Louis d'Ors?*——Tall dall de rall. [*Sings.*] Look ye, Gentlemen, any Body may dance to this Tune;——Tall dall de rall. I dance to the Tune of fifteen hundred Pounds, the moft elevated Piece of Mufic that ever I heard in my Life; they are the prettieft Caftagnets in the World. [*Chinks the Money.*] Here, Waiters, there's Cards and Candles for you. [*Gives the Servants Money.*] Mrs. *Parly*——here's Hoods and Scarfs for you: [*Gives her Money.*] And here's fine Coaches, fplendid Equipage, lovely Women, and victorious *Burgundy* for me. —— Oh ye charming Angels! the Lofers Sorrow, and the Gainer's Joy: Get ye into my Pocket.—Now, Gentlemen and Ladies, I am your humble Servant——You'll excufe me, I hope, the fmall Devotion here that I pay to my good Fortune—Ho'now! Mute!—Why, Ladies, I know that Lofers have Leave to fpeak; but I don't find that they're privileg'd to be dumb.——*Monfieur!* Ladies! Captain!

[*Claps the Captain on the Shoulder.*

Fire. Death and Hell! Why d'ye ftrike me, Sir?

[*Drawing.*
Wild.

Wild. To comfort you, Sir.——Your Ear, Capt.——The King of *Spain* is dead!

Fire. The King of *Spain* dead!

Wild. Dead as *Julius Cefar*; I had a Letter on't juft now.

Fire. Tall dall de rall. [*Sings.*] Look ye, Sir, pray ftrike me again if you pleafe.——See here, Sir, you have left me but one folitary Guinea in the World. [*Puts it in his Mouth.* Down it goes i'faith.——A lons for the *Thatch'd Houfe* and the *Mediterranean.*——Tall dall de rall.　　　[*Exit.*

Wild. Ha, ha, ha!——Bravely refolv'd, Captain.

Lure. Blefs me, Sir *Harry*! I was afraid of a Quarrel. I'm fo much concern'd!

Wild. At the Lofs of your Money, Madam. But why, why fhould the Fair be afflicted? your Eyes, your Eyes, Ladies, much brighter than the Sun, have equal Power with him, and can transform to Gold whate'er they pleafe. The Lawyer's Tongue, the Soldier's Sword, the Courtier's Flattery, and the Merchant's Trade, are Slaves that dig the Golden Mines for you. Your Eyes unty the Mifer's knotted Purfe. [*To one Lady*] Melt into Coin the Magiftrate's maffy Chain.——Youth mints for you Hereditary Lands. [*To another.*——And Gamefters only win when they can lofe to you. [*To Lurewell.*]——This Luck is the moft rhetorical Thing in Nature.

Lure. I have a great Mind to forfwear Cards as long as I live.

1ft La. And I.　　　　　　　　　　　　　[*Exit.*

2d La. And I.　　　　　　　　　[*Crying, and Exit.*

Wild. What, forfwear Cards! Why, Madam, you'll ruin our Trade.——I'd maintain, that the Money at Court circulates more by the Baffet-Bank, than the Wealth of the Merchants by the Bank of the City. Cards! the great Minifters of Fortune's Power, that blindly fhuffle out her thoughtlefs Favours, and make a Knave more pow'rful than a King.——What Adoration do thefe Pow'rs receive [*Lifting up a Card.*] from the bright Hands and Fingers of the Fair, always lift up to pay Devotion here! And the pleafing Fears, the anxious Hopes, and dubious Joy that entertain our Mind! The Capot at Piquet, the Paroli at Baffet;—— And then Ombre! who can refift the Charms of Mattadors?

Lure. Ay, Sir *Harry*; and then the *Sept le Va, Quinze la Va, & Trante le Va!*

N 5　　　　　　　　　　　　　　　　　*Wild.*

Wild. Right, right, Madam.

Lure. Then the Nine of Diamonds at Comet, three Fives at Cribbidge, and Pam in Lanteraloo, Sir *Harry* !

Wild. Ay, Madam, thefe are Charms indeed. ——Then the Pleafure of picking our Hufband's Pocket over night, to play at Baffet next Day! Then the Advantage a fine Gentleman may make of a Lady's Neceffity, by gaining a Favour for fifty Piftoles, which a hundred Years Courtfhip cou'd never have produc'd.

Lure. Nay, nay, Sir *Harry*, that's foul Play.

Wild. Nay, nay, Madam, it is nothing but the Game; and I have play'd it fo in *France* a hundred Times.

Lure. Come, come, Sir, no more on't. I'll tell you in three Words, that rather than forego my Cards, I'll forfwear my Vifits, Fafhions, my Monkey, Friends and Relations.

Wild. There fpoke the Spirit of true-born *Englifh* Women of Quality, with a true *French* Education.

Lure. Look ye, Sir *Harry*, I am well born, and I was well bred; I brought my Hufband a large Fortune; he fhall mortgage, or I will elope.

Wild. No, no, Madam! there's no Occafion for that: See here, Madam!

Lure. What, the finging Birds! Sir *Harry*, let me fee.

Wild. Pugh, Madam, thefe are but a few.--But I cou'd wifh, *de tout mon cœur, fort quelque Commodite*, where I might be handfomely plunder'd of 'em.

Lure. *Ah! Chevalier! tous jour obligeant, engageant, &* *tout fa* ———

Wild. *Allons, Allons, Madam, tout à votre fervice.*
[*Pulls her.*

Lure. No, no, Sir *Harry*, not at this Time o'day; you fhall hear from me in the Evening.

Wild. Then, Madam, I'll leave you fomething to entertain you the while. 'Tis a *French* Pocket-book, with fome Remarks of my own upon the new Way of making Love. Pleafe to perufe it, and give me your Opinion in the Evening. [*Exit.*

Lure. [*Opening the Book*] A *French* Pocket-book, with Remarks upon the new Way of making Love! Then Sir *Harry* is turning Author I find.—What's here?—Hi, hi, hi! A Bank Bill for a hundred Pounds.—The new Way of
making

making Love!—*Pardie cét fort Gallant*—One of the prettiest Remarks that ever I saw in my Life! Well now, that *Wildair's* a charming Fellow;—Hi, hi, hi!—He has such an Air, and such a Turn in what he does! I warrant now there's a Hundred home-bred Blockheads won'd come,—Madam, I'll give you a Hundred Guineas if you'll let me ——Faugh! hang their naufeous immodeft Proceedings.— Here's a Hundred Pounds now, and he never names the Thing; I love an impudent Action with an Air of Modefty with all my Heart. -   -   [*Exit.*

The End of the Second Act.

M M M M M M M M M M M M M M M M M M M M M M M

A C T III.

S C E N E *continues.*

Enter Lurewell *and* Monfieur Marquis.

Lure. WELL, *Monfieur,* and have you thought how to retaliate your ill Fortune?

Monf. Madam, I have tought dat Fortune be one blind Bitch. Why fhou'd Fortune be kinder to de Anglis Chevalier dan to de France Marquis? Ave I not de bon Grace? Ave not I de Perfonage? Ave I not Underftanding? Can de Anglis Chevalier dance better dan I? Can de Anglis Chevalier fence better dan I? Can de Anglis Chevalier play Baffet better dan I? Den why fhould Fortune be kinder to de Anglis Chevalier dan de France Marquis?

Lure. Why? Becaufe Fortune is blind.

Monf. Blind! Yes begar, and dum and deaf too.—Vell den, Fortune give de Anglis Man de Riches, but Nature gave de France Man de Politique to correct de unequal Diftribution.

Lure. But how can you correct it, Monfieur!

Monf. Ecoute, Madam. Sir *Arry Wildair* his Vife be dead.

Lure. And what Advantage can you make of that?

Monf. Begar, Madam.—Hi, hi, hi!—De Anglis Man's dead Vife fall Cuckold her Ufband!

Lure. How, how, Sir, a dead Woman cuckold her Hufband!

Monf. Mark! Madam: We France-men make de Diftinction between de Defign and de Term of de Treaty.— She canno touch his Head, but fhe can Cuckold his Pocket of ten toufan Livres.

N 6   *Lure.*

Lure. Pray explain yourfelf, Sir.

Monf. I ave Sir *Arry Wildair* his Vife in my Pocket.

Lure. How! Sir *Harry's* Wife in your Pocket!

Monf. Hold, Madam, dére is an autre Diftinction between de Defign and dé Term of de Treaty.

Lure. Pray, Sir, no more of your Diftinctions, but fpeak plain.

Monf. Wen de France-man's Politique is in his Head, dere is noting but Diftinction upon his Tongue.—See here, Madam! I ave de Picture of Sir *Harry's* Vife in my Pocket.

Lure. Is it poffible?

Monf. Voyez.

Lure. The very fame, and finely drawn. Pray, Monfieur, how did you purchafe it?

Monf. As me did purchafe de Picture, fo me did gain de Subftance, de dear, dear Subftance, by de bon mien, de France Air, chatant, charmant, de Politique à la Tête, and dançant à la Pie.

Lure. Lard blefs me! How cunningly fome Women can play the Rogue! Ah! have I found it out! Now, as I hope for Mercy, I am glad on't. I hate to have any Woman more virtuous than myfelf.——Here was fuch a work with my Lady *Wildair's* Piety! my Lady *Wildair's* Conduct! and my Lady *Wildair's* Fidelity, forfooth! Now, dear Monfieur, you have infallibly told me the beft News that I ever heard in my Life. Well, and fhe was but one of us! heh!

Monf. Oh, Madam! me no tell Tale, me no fcandalize de Dead; de Picture be dumb, de Picture fay noting.

Lure. Come, come, Sir, no more Diftinctions; I'm fure it was fo. I wou'd have given the World for fuch a Story of her while fhe was living. She was charitable, forfooth! and fhe was devout, forfooth! and every Body was twitted i'th' Teeth with my Lady *Wildair's* Reputation: And why don't you mark her Behaviour, and her Difcretion? She goes to Church twice a Day.—Ah! I hate thefe Congregation-Women. There's fuch a Fufs, and fuch a Clutter about their Devotion, that it makes more Noife than all the Bells in the Parifh. — Well, but what Advantage can you make now of the Picture?

Monf. De Advantage of ten toufan Livres, parde. —— *Attendez vous,* Madam. Dis Lady fhe die at *Montpellier* in *France*; I ave de Broder in dat City dat write me one Account dat fhe die in dat City, and dat fhe fend me dis Picture

ture as a Legacy, wid a'tonfan bafe mains to de dear Marquis, de charmant Marquis, mon cœur le Marquis.

Lure. Ay, here was Devotion! here was Difcretion!
here was Fidelity! Mon cœur le Marquis! Ha, ha, ha!——
Well, but how will this procure the Money?

Monf. Now, Madam, for de France Politique.

Lure. Ay, what is the *French* Politic?

Monf. Never to tell a Secret to a Voman. —— Madam,
je fui votre ferviteur.   [*Runs off.*

Lure. Hold, hold, Sir, we fha'n't part fo; I will have
it.   [*Follows.*

Enter Standard *and* Fireball.

Fire. Hah! Look! look! look you there, Brother!
See how they coquet it! Oh! there's a Look! there's a
Simper! there's a Squeeze for you! ay, now the Marquis is
at it. *Mon cœur, ma foy, pardie, allons:* Don't you fee how
the *French* Rogue has the Head, and the Feet, and the
Hands, and the Tongue, all going together?

Stand. [*Walking in Diforder.*] Where's my Reafon?
Where's my Philofophy? Where's my Religion now?

Fire. I'll tell you where they are, in your Forehead, Sir.
——Blood! I fay Revenge.

Stand. But how, dear Brother?

Fire. Why ftab him, ftab him now.——*Italian* him, *Spani-*
ard him, I fay.

Stand. Stab him! Why Cuckoldom's a Hydra that bears
a thoufand Heads; and tho' I fhou'd cut this one off, the
Monfter ftill wou'd fprout. Muft I murder all the Fops in
the Nation; and to fave my Head from Horns, expofe my
Neck to the Halter?

Fire. 'Sdeath, Sir, can't you kick and cuff? Kick one.

Stand. Cane another.

Fire. Cut off the Ears of a third.

Stand. Slit the Nofe of a fourth.

Fire. Tear Cravats.

Stand. Burn Perukes.

Fire. Shoot their Coach-horfes.

Stand. A noble Plot.——But now 'tis laid, how fhall we
put it in Execution? for not one of thefe *Fellows* ftirs about
without his Guard du Corps. Then they're ftout as Heroes;
for I can affure you, that a Beau with fix Footmen fhall
fight you any Gentleman in *Chriftendom.*

                                            Enter

Enter Servant.

Ser. Sir, here's Mr. *Clincher* below, who begs the Honour to kiss your Hand.

Stand. Ay, why here's another Beau.

Fire. Let him come, let him come; I'll shew you how to manage a Beau presently.

Stand. Hold, hold, Sir; this is a simple inoffensive Fellow, that will rather make us Diversion.

Fire. Diversion! Ay. Why, I'll knock him down for Diversion.

Stand. No, no: prithee be quiet; I gave him a Surfeit of Intriguing some Months ago before I was marry'd.——Here, bid him come up. He's worth your Acquaintance, Brother.

Fire. My Acquaintance! What is he!

Stand. A Fellow of a strange Weathercock Head, very hard, but as light as the Wind; constantly full of the Times, and never fails to pick up some Humour or other out of the public Revolutions, that proves diverting enough. Some Time ago he had got the Travelling Maggot in his Head, and was going to the *Jubilee* upon all Occasions; but lately, since the new Revolution in *Europe*, another Spirit has possess'd him, and he runs stark mad after News and Politics.

Enter Clincher.

Clinch. News, News, Col. great—Eh! what's this Fellow? Methinks he has a Kind of suspicious Air.——Your Ear, Col.—The Pope's dead.

Stand. Where did you hear it?

Clinch. I read it in the public News.   [*Whispering.*

Stand. Ha, ha, ha!——And why d'ye whisper it for a Secret?

Clinch. Odso! Faith that's true—But that Fellow there; what is he?

Stand. My Brother *Fireball,* just come home from the *Baltick.*

Clinch. Odso! Noble Captain, I'm your most humble and obedient Servant, from the Poop to the Forecastle. —— Nay, a Kiss o't'other Side, pray.——Now, dear Captain, tell us the News.——Odso! I'm so pleas'd I have met you! Well, the News, dear Captain — You sail'd a brave Squadron of Men of War to the *Baltick.*——Well, and what then? eh!

Fire.

Fire. Why then——we came back again.

Clinch. Did you, faith!—Foolish! foolish! very foolish! a right Sea Captain——But what did you do? How did you fight? What Storms did you meet? and what 'Whales did you see?

Fire. We had a violent Storm off the Coast of *Jutland.*

Clinch. Jutland! Ay, that's Part of *Portugal.*——Well, and so,——you enter'd the *Sound*;——and you maul'd *Copenhagen,* 'faith.—And then that pretty, dear, sweet, pretty King of *Sweden!*—What Sort of Man is he, pray?

Fire. Why, tall and slender.

Clinch. Tall and slender! Much about my Pitch? Heh!

Fire. Not so gross, not altogether so low.

Clinch. No! I'm sorry for't; very sorry, indeed.——
[*Here* Parly *enters and stands at the Door;* Clincher *beckons her with his Hands behind, going backwards, and speaking to her and the Gentlemen by Turns.*] Well, and what more? And so you bombarded '*Copenhagen.*—[Mrs. *Parly.*]—Whiz, slap went the Bombs. [Mrs. *Parly.*] And so—Well, not altogether so gross, you say—[Here's a Letter, you Jade.] Very tall, you say? Is the King very tall?——[Here's a Guinea, you Jade.]—*She takes the Letter, and the Col. observes him.*]—Hem! hem! Col. I'm mightily troubled with the Ptysic of late. —— Hem! hem! a strange Stoppage of my Breast here. Hem! but now it is off again.——Well, but Captain, you tell us no News at all.

Fire. I tell you once Piece that all the World knows, and still you are a Stranger to it.

Clinch. Bless me! What can this be?

Fire. That you are a Fool.

Clinch. Eh! Witty, witty Sea Captain. Odso! and I wonder, Captain, that your Understanding did not split your Ship to Pieces.

Fire. Why so, Sir?

Clinch. Because, Sir, it is so very shallow, very *shallow,* There's Wit for you, Sir——

    Enter Parly, *who gives the Col. a Letter.*

Odso! A Letter! Then there's News.—What, is it the foreign Post? What News, dear Col. what News? Hark ye, Mrs. *Parly.*

    [*He talks with* Parly *while the Col. reads the Letter.*

Stand. The Son of a Whore! Is it he? [*Looks at* Clincher.
                      [*Reads.*]

[*Reads.*] Dear Madam,

I Was afraid to break open the Seal of your Letter, left I
    fhou'd violate the Work of your fair Hands —— (Oh ! ful-
fome Fop !) *I therefore with the Warmth of my Kiffes thaw'd
it afunder.* (Ay, here's fuch a Turn of Stile, as takes a
fine Lady !) *I have no News, but that the Pope's dead, and
I have fome Pacquets upon that Affair to fend my Correfpon-
dent in Wales ; but I fhall waeve all Bufinefs, and haften to
wait on you at the Hour appointed, with the Wings of a
Flying-Poft.* *Yours,*

Toby Clincher.

Very well, Mr. *Toby*——Hark'e, Brother, this Fellow's a Rogue.

Fire. A damn'd Rogue.

Stand. See here ! a Letter to my Wife !

Fire. S'death ! let me tear him to Pieces.

Stand. No, no, we'll manage him to more Advantage. Take him with you to *Locket's,* and invent fome
Way or other to fuddle him.—Here, Mr. *Clincher,* I
have prevail'd on my Brother here to give you a particular Account of the whole Voyage to the *Sound* by his
own Journal, if you pleafe to honour him with your
Company at *Locket's.*

Clin. His own Journal ! Odfo, let me fee it.

Stand. Shew it him.

Fire. Here, Sir.

Clin. Now for News—[*Reads.*] Thurfday, Auguft *the
17th, from the 6th at Noon to this Day Noon Winds va-
riable, Courfes* per *Traverfe, true Courfe protracted, with
all Impediments allow'd, is North* 45 *Degrees, Weft* 60
Miles, Difference of Latitude 42 *Miles, Departure Weft* 40
Miles, Latitude per *Judgment* 54 *Degrees* 13 *Minutes, Me-
ridian Diftance current from the Bearing of the Land, and the
Latitude is* 88 *Miles.*—Odfo ! Great News, faith.—Let
me fee. *At Noon broke our Main-Top-Sail Yard, being rotten
in the Sling ; two Whales Southward,*—Odfo ! A Whale !
Great News, faith. Come, come along, Captain. But,
d'ye hear ? with this Provifo, Gentlemen, that I won't
drink ; for, hark'e, Captain, between you and I, there's
a fine Lady in the Wind, and I fhall have the Longitude
and Latitude of a fine Lady, and the———

Fire.

Fire. A fine Lady! Ah the Rogue!   [*Aside.*

Clin. Yes, a fine Lady, Colonel, a very fine Lady. Come, no Ceremony, good Captain.

   [*Exeunt* Fireball *and* Clincher.

Stand. Well, Mrs. *Parly*, how go the reft of our Affairs?

Par. Why, worfe and worfe, Sir; here's more Mifchief ftill, more Branches a fprouting.

Stand. Of whofe planting, pray?

Par. Why, that impudent young Rogue, Sir *Harry Wildair*'s Brother, has commenc'd his Suit, and feed Counfel already.—Look here, Sir, two Pieces, for which, by Article, I am to receive four.

Stand. 'Tis a hard Cafe now, that a Man muft give four Guineas for the good News of his Difhonour. Some Men throw away their Money in debauching other Men's Wives, and I lay out mine to keep my own honeft: But this is making a Man's Fortune!—Well, Child, there's your Pay; and I expect, when I come back, a true Account how the Bufinefs goes on.

Par. But fuppofe the Bus'nefs be done before you come back?

Stand. No, no; fhe ha'nt feen him yet; and her Pride will preferve her againft the firft Affaults. Befides, I fha'n't ftay.   [*Exeunt* Col. *and* Par.

SCENE *changes to another Room in the fame Houfe.*

Enter Wildair *and* Lurewell.

Lure. Well now, Sir *Harry*, this Book you gave me! As I hope to breathe, I think 'tis the beft penn'd Piece I have feen a great while; I don't know any of our Authors have wrote in fo florid and genteel a Stile.

Wild. Upon the Subject, Madam, I dare affirm there is nothing extant more moving.—Look ye, Madam; I am an Author rich in Expreffions; the needy Poets of the Age may fill their Works with Rhapfodies of Flames and Darts, and barren Sighs and Tears, their fpeaking Looks and amorous Vows, that might in *Chaucer's* Time, perhaps, have pafs'd for Love; but now, 'tis only fuch as I can touch that noble Paffion, and by the true, perfuafive Eloquence, turn'd in the moving Stile of *Louis d'Ors*, can raife the ravifh'd Female to a Rapture.—In

fhort,

fhort, Madam, I'll match *Cowly* in Softnefs, o'ertop *Milton* in Sublime, banter *Cicero* in Eloquence, and Dr. *Swan* in Quibbling, by the Help of that moft ingenious Society, call'd the Bank of *England.*

Lure. Ay, Sir *Harry,* I begin to hate that old Thing call'd Love; they fay 'tis clear out in *France.*

Wild, Clear out, clear out, nobody wears it: And here too, Honefty went out with the flafh'd Doublets, and Love with the clofe-body'd Gowns. Love! 'tis fo obfolete, fo mean, and out of Fafhion, that I can compare it to nothing but the miferable Picture of *Patient Grixzel* at the Head of an old Ballad——Faugh!

Lure. Ha, ha! ha!—The beft Emblem in the World. —Come, Sir *Harry,* faith we'll run it down.—Love!— Ay, methinks I fee the mournful *Melpomene* with her Handkerchief at her Eye, her Heart full of Fire, her Eyes full of Water, her Head full of Madnefs, and her Mouth full of Nonfenfe.—Oh! hang it.

Wild. Ay, Madam. Then the doleful Ditties, piteous Plaints, the Daggers, the Poifons!

Lure. Oh the Vapours!

Wild. Then a Man muft kneel, and a Man muft fwear. —There is a Repofe, I fee, in the next Room. [*Afide.*

Lure. Unnatural Stuff.

Wild. Oh, Madam, the moft unnatural Thing in the World; as fulfome as a Sack-Poffet, [*Pulling her towards the Door.*] ungenteel as a Wedding-Ring, and as impudent as the naked Statue was in the Park. [*Pulls her again.*

Lure. Ay, Sir *Harry;* I hate Love that's impudent. Thefe Poets drefs it up fo in their Tragedies, that no modeft Woman can bear it. Your Way is much the more tolerable, I muft confefs.

Wild. Ay, ay, Madam; I hate your rude Whining and Sighing; it puts a Lady out of Countenance.

[*Pulling her.*

Lure. Truly fo it does—Hang their Impudence. But where are we going?

Wild. Only to rail at Love, Madam. [*Pulls her in.*

Enter Banter.

Ban. Hey! Who's here? [*Lurewell comes back.* *Lure.*

Lure. Pshaw, preferred to a Stranger too—Had I been my Husband now—Pshaw—very familiar Sir. [*Banter takes up Wildair's Hat and views it as Bam.*

Ban. Madam, you have dropt your Hat.

Lure. Discover'd me to a Stranger —What shall I do?

Wild. [*From within.*]—Madam, you have got the most confounded Pens here. Can't you get the Colonel to write the Superscriptions of your Letters for you?

Lure. Bless me, Sir Harry Don't you know that the Colonel can't write French? Your Time is so precious!

Wild. Shall I direct my way of Rule to Paris?

Lure. Which you will.

Ban. Madam, I very much applaud your Choice of a Secretary; he understands the Intrigues of all the Courts in *Europe* they say.

Enter Wildair *with a Letter.*

Wild. Here, Madam, I perfume, is right—This Gentleman a Relation of yours, Madam? Damn him.—[*Aside.*

Ban. Brother, your humble Servant.

Wild. Brother! By what Relation, Sir?

Ban. Begotten by the same Father, born of the same Mother, Brother Kindred, and Brother Beau.

Wild. Hey-day! How the Fellow strings his Genealogy! —Look ye, Sir, you may be Brother to *Tom Thumb* for aught I know; but if you are my Brother—I cou'd have wish'd you in your Mother's Womb for an Hour or two longer. [*Aside.*

Ban. Sir, I receiv'd your Letter at *Oxford*, with your Commands to meet you at *London*; and if you can remember your own Hand, there it is. [*Gives a Letter.*

Wild. [*Looking over the Letter.*] Oh! Pray, Sir, let me consider you a little.——By *Jupiter* a very pretty Boy; a handsome Face, good Shape, [*Walks about and views him.*] well dress'd—The Rogue has got a Leg too.— Come kiss me, Child.—Ay, he kisses like one of the Family, the right Velvet Lip.—Can'st thou dance, Child?

Ban. Ouy, Monsieur.

Lure. Hey-day! *French* too: Why sure, Sir, you cou'd never be bred at *Oxford!*

Ban. No, Madam, my Cloaths were made in *London*— Brother, I have some Affairs of Consequence to communicate, which require a little Privacy.

Lure.

Lure. Oh, Sir! I beg your Pardon, I'll leave you. Sir *Harry*, you'll ftay Supper?

Wild. Affurement, Madam.

Ban. Yes, Madam, we'll both ftay.

Wild. Both!—Sir, I'll fend you back to your Mutton-Commons again. How now?

Ban. No, no; I fhall find better Mutton-Commons by meffing with you, Brother—Come, Sir *Harry*; if you ftay, I ftay; if you go, allons.

Wild. Why, the Devil's in this young Fellow.—Why, Sirrah, haft thou any Thoughts of being my Heir? Why, you Dog, you ought to pimp for me; you fhou'd keep a Pack of Wenches o'purpofe to hunt down Matrimony. Don't you know, Sir, that lawful Wedlock in me is certain Poverty to you? Look ye, Sirrah, come along; and for my Difappointment juft now, if you don't get me a new Miftrefs To-night, I'll marry To-morrow, and won't leave you a Groat—Go, Pimp, like a dutiful Brother.   [*Pufhes him out, and* Exit.

The End of the Third Act.

✕✕✕✕✕✕✕✕✕✕✕✕✕✕✕✕ ✕✕✕✕✕✕✕ ✕✕✕✕✕✕✕✕

ACT IV.

SCENE, *A Tavern.*

Enter Fireball, *hauling in* Clincher.

Fire. COme, Sir; not drink the King's Health!

Clin. Pray now, good Captain, excufe me. Look here, Sir; the [*Pulling out his Watch.*] critical Minute, the critical Minute, faith.

Fire. What d'ye mean, Sir?

Clin. The Lady's critical Minute, Sir.—Sir, your humble Servant.

Fire. Well! the Death of this *Spanifh* King will—

Clin. [*Returning.*] Eh! What's that of the *Spanifh* King? Tell me, dear Captain, tell me.

Fire. Sir, if you pleafe to fit down, I'll tell you that old Don *Carlos* is dead.

Clin. Dead! Nay, then [*Sits down.*]—Here, Pen and Ink, Boy; Pen and Ink prefently; I muft write to my
                                        Corre-

Correspondent in *Wales* ſtrait—Dead! [*Riſes and walks*
   Fire. What's the Matter, Sir?   [*about in Diſorder.*
   Clin. Politics, Politics, ſtark mad with Politics.
   Fire. 'Sdeath, Sir, what have ſuch Fools as you to do
with Politics?
   Clin. What, Sir? The Succeſſion.—Not mind the
Succeſſion!
   Fire. Nay, that's minded already; 'tis ſettled upon
a Prince of *France.*
   Clin. What, ſettled already!—The beſt News that
ever came into *England.*—Come, Captain, faith and
troth, Captain, here's a Health to the Succeſſion.
   Fire. Burn the Succeſſion, Sir. I won't drink it.—What,
drink Confuſion to our Trade, Religion, and Liberties!
   Clinch. Ay, by all Means.—As for Trade, d'ye ſee, I'm
a Gentleman, and hate it mortally. Theſe Tradeſmen are
the moſt impudent Fellows we have, and ſpoil all our good
Manners. What have we to do with Trade?
   Fire. A trim Politician, truly!—And what do you think
of our Religion, pray?
   Clinch. Hi, hi, hi!—Religion!—And what has a Gen-
tleman to do with Religion, pray?—And to hear a Sea
Captain talk of Religion! That's pleaſant, faith.
   Fire. And have you no Regard to our Liberties, Sir?
   Clinch. Pſhaw! Liberties! that's a Jeſt. We Beaux
ſhall have Liberty to whore and drink in any Government,
and that's all we care for.—
                Enter Standard.
Dear Colonel, the rareſt News!
   Stand. Damn your News, Sir; why are you not drunk
by this?
   Clinch. A very civil Queſtion, truly!
   Stand. Here, Boy, bring in the Brandy——Fill.
   Clinch. This is a Piece of Politics that I don't ſo well
comprehend.
   Stand. Here, Sir; now drink it off, or [*Draws.*] ex-
pect your Throat cut.
   Clinch. Ay, this comes o'th' Succeſſion; Fire and Sword
already.
   Stand. Come, Sir, off with it.
   Clinch. Pray, Colonel, what have I done to be burnt
alive?
                              Stand.

Stand. Drink, Sir, I fay—Brother, manage him, I muſt be gone.   [*Aſide to* Fireball, *and Exit.*

Fire. Ay, drink, Sir.

Clinch. Eh! What the Devil, attack'd both by Sea and Land!—Look ye, Gentlemen, if I muſt be poiſon'd, pray let me chuſe my own Doſe—Were I a Lord now, I ſhou'd have the Privilege of the Block; and as I'm a Gentleman, pray ſtifle me with Claret at leaſt! don't let me die like a Bawd, with Brandy.

Fire. Brandy, you Dog! abuſe Brandy! Flat Treaſon againſt the Navy Royal.—Sirrah, I'll teach you to abuſe the Fleet—Here, *Shark*—

Enter Shark.

Get three or four of the Ship's Crew, and preſs this Fellow aboard the *Belzebub.*

Sha. Ay, Maſter.   [*Exit.*

Clinch. What! aboard the *Belzebub!*—Nay, nay, dear Captain, I'll chuſe to go to the Devil this Way. Here, Sir, your good Health;—and my own Confuſion, I'm afraid. [*Drinks it off.*] Oh! Fire! Fire! Flames! Brimſtone! and Tobacco!   [*Beats his Stomach.*

Fire. Here, quench it, quench it then.—Take the Glaſs, Sir.

Clinch. What, another Broadſide! nay then, I'm ſunk downright.—Dear Captain, give me Quarter, conſider the preſent Juncture of Affairs; you'll ſpoil my Head, ruin my Politics; faith you will.

Fire. Here, *Shark.*

Clinch. Well, well, I will drink——The Devil take *Shark* for me. [*Drinks.*] Whiz, Buz—Don't you hear it? Put your Ear to my Breaſt, and hear how it whizzes like a hot Iron.—Eh! Bleſs me, how the Ship rolls!—I can't ſtand upon my Legs, faith.—Dear Captain, give me a Kiſs.—Ay, burn the Succeſſion.—Look ye, Captain, I ſhall be Sea-ſick preſently.   [*Falls into* Fireball's *Arms.*

Enter Shark, *and another with a Chair.*

Fire. Here; in with him.

Sha. Ay, ay, Sir——Avaſt, avaſt—Here, Boy.—No Nants left.——   [*Tops the Glaſs.*

Fire. Bring him along.

Clinch. Politics, Politics, Brandy, Politics!

SCENE

SCENE *changes to* Lurewell's *Apartment.*

Enter Lurewell *and* Parly.

Lure. Did you ever fee fuch an impudent young Rogue as that *Bauter?* He follow'd his Brother up and down from Place to Place fo very clofe, that we cou'd not fo much as whifper.

Par. I reckon Sir *Harry* will difpofe him now, Madam, where he may be fecur'd.——But I wonder, Madam, why *Clincher* comes not according to his Letter! it is near the Hour.

Lure. I wifh, *Parly*, that no Harm may befal me to day; for I had a moft frightful Dream laft Night; I dreamt of a Moufe.

Par. 'Tis ftrange, Madam, you fhou'd be fo much afraid of that little Creature that can do you no Harm!

Lure. Look ye, Girl, we Women of Quality have each of us fome darling Fright.——I now hate a Moufe; my Lady *Lovecards* abhors a Cat; Mrs. *Fiddlefan* can't bear a Squirrel; the Countefs of *Piquet* abominates a Frog, and my Lady *Swimair* hates a Man.

Enter Marquis *running.*

Mar. Madam! Madam! Madam! Pardie voyez.—— L'Argent! L'Argent!　　　　　　[*Shews a Bag of Money.*

Lure. As I hope to breathe, he has got it—Well, but how? How, dear Monfieur?

Mar. Ah, Madam! Begar, Monfieur Sir *Arry* be one Pigeaneau—Voyez, Madam! me did tell him dat my Broder in *Montpelier* did furnife his Lady wid ten toufan Livres for de Expence of her Travaille; and dat fhe not being able to wiite when fhe was dying, did give him de Picture for de Certificate and de Credential to receive de Money from her Hufband. Mark ye!

Lure. The beft Plot in the World.—You told him, that your Brother lent her the Money in *France*, when her Bills, I fuppofe, were delay'd.—You put in that, I prefume.

Mar. Ouy, ouy, Madam.

Lure. And that upon her Death-bed fhe gave your Brother the Picture, as a Certificate to Sir *Harry* that fhe had receiv'd the Money, which Picture your Brother fent over to you, with Commiffion to receive the Debt!

Mar. Affurement.—Dere was de Politique, de France Politique!—See, Madam, what he can do, de France Marquis!

quis! He did make de Anglife Lady cuckle her Hufband when fhe was living, and fheat him when fhe was dead, Begar: Ha, ha, ha!—Oh! Pardie, cet bon.

Lure. Ah! But what did Sir *Harry* fay?

Mar. Oh! begar Monfieur Chevalier he love his Vife; he fay, dat if fhe takes up a Hundre Toufan Livres, he weu'd repay it; he knew de Picture, he fay, and order me de Money from his Stewar—Oh, Notre Dame, Monfieur Sir *Arry* be one Dupe.

Lure. Well but, Monfieur, I long to know one Thing. Was the Conqueft you made of his Lady fo eafy? What Affaults did you make? And what Refiftance did fhe fhew?

Mar. Refiftance againft de France Marquis! Voyez! Madam; dere was tree Deux-yeux, one Serenade, and two Capre; dat was all, begar.

Lure. Chatillionte! There's nothing in Nature fo fweet to a longing Woman, as a malicious Story.— Well, Monfieur! 'tis about a Thoufand Pounds; we go Snacks.

Mar. Snacke! Pardie. for what? why Snacke, Madam? Me vill give you de Prefent of Fifty *Louis d'Ors*; dat is ver' good Snacke for you.

Lute. And you'll give me no more? Very well!

Mar. Ver' well! Yes begar, 'tis ver' well.—Confidre, Madam, me be de poor *Refugee,* me ave noting but de religious Charite, and de *France* Politique, de Fruit of my own Addrefs; dat is all.

Lure. Ay, an Object of Charity, with a thoufand Pounds in his Fift! Emh! Oh Monfieur; that's my Hufband, I know his knock. [*Knocking below.*] He muft not fee you. Get into the Clofet till by and by, [*Hurries him in.*] and if I don't be reveng'd upon *France* Politique, then have I no *Englifh* Politique——Hang the Money! I wou'd not for twice a thoufand Pounds forbear abufing this virtuous Woman to her Hufband.

Enter Parly.

Par. 'Tis Sir *Harry,* Madam.

Lure. As I cou'd wifh. Chairs!

Enter Wildair.

Wild. Here, Mrs. *Parly,* in the firft Place I facrifice a *Louis a'Or* to thee for good Luck.

Par. A Guinea, Sir, will do as well.

Wild

Wild. No, no, Child; *French* Money is always moft fuccefsful in Bribes, and very much in Fashion, Child.

Enter Dicky, *and runs to Sir* Harry.

- *Dick.* Sir, wilt you pleafe to have your own Night-caps?

Wild. Sirrah!

Dick. Sir, Sir! fhall I order your Chair to the Back-door by Five o'Clock in the Morning?

Wild. The Devil's in the Fellow. Get you gone.——[Dicky *runs out.*] Now, dear Madam, I have fecur'd my Brother, you have difpos'd of the Colonel, and we'll rail at Love till we ha'n't a Word more to fay.

Lure. Ay, Sir *Harry*—Pleafe to fit a little, Sir.—You muft know I'm in a ftrange Humour of afking you fome Queftions.—How did you like your Lady, pray, Sir?

Wild. Like her! Ha, ha, ha!—So very well, faith, that for her very Sake I'm in Love with every Woman I meet.

Lure. And did Matrimony pleafe you extremely?

Wild. So very much, that if Polygamy were allowed, I wou'd have a new Wife every Day.

Lure. Oh, Sir *Harry*! this is Raillery. But your ferious Thoughts upon the Matter, pray.

Wild. Why then, Madam, to give you my true Sentiments of Wedlock: I had a Lady that I marry'd by Chance, fhe was virtuous by Chance, and I lov'd her by great Chance. Nature gave her Beauty, Education and Air, and Fortune threw a young Fellow of five and twenty in her Lap.—I courted her all Day, lov'd her all Night; fhe was my Miftrefs one Day, and my Wife another: I found in one the Variety of a Thoufand, and the very Confinement of Marriage gave me the Pleafure of Change.

Lure. And fhe was very virtuous?

Wild. Look ye, Madam, you know fhe was beautiful. She had Good-nature about her Mouth, the Smile of Beauty in her Cheeks, fparkling Wit in her Forehead, and fprightly Love in her Eyes.

Lure. Pfhaw! I knew her very well; the Woman was well enough. But you don't anfwer my Queftion, Sir.

Wild. So, Madam, as I told you before, fhe was young and beautiful, I was rich and vigorous; my Eftate gave me a Luftre to my Love, and a Swing to our Enjoyment; round, like the Ring that made us one, our golden Pleafures circled without End.

Lure. Golden Pleasures! Golden Fiddlesticks!—What d'ye tell me of your canting Stuff? Was she virtuous, I say?

Wild. Ready to burst with Envy; but I will torment thee a little. [*Aside.*] So, Madam, I powder'd to please her, she dress'd to engage me; we toy'd away the Morning in amorous Nonsense, loll'd away the Evening in the Park, or the Play-house, and all the Night——Hem!

Lure. Look ye, Sir, answer my Question, or I shall take it ill.

Wild. Then, Madam, there was never such a Pattern of Unity.—Her Wants were still prevented by my Supplies; my own Heart whisper'd me her Desires, 'cause she herself was there; no Contention ever rose, but the dear strife of who shou'd most oblige; no Noise about Authority; for neither would stoop to command, 'cause both thought it Glory to obey.

Lure. Stuff! Stuff! Stuff!—I won't believe a Word on't.

Wild. Ha, ha, ha! Then, Madam, we never felt the Yoke of Matrimony, because our Inclinations made us one; a Power superior to the Forms of Wedlock. The Marriage Torch had lost its weaker Light in the bright Flame of mutual Love that join'd our Hearts before. Then——

Lure. Hold, hold, Sir; I cannot bear it; Sir *Harry*, I'm affronted.

Wild. Ha, ha, ha! Affronted!

Lure. Yes, Sir; it is an Affront to any Woman to hear another commended; and I will resent it.——In short, Sir *Harry*, your Wife was a————

Wild. Buz, Madam—No Detraction—I'll tell you what she was.—So much an Angel in her Conduct, that tho' I saw another in her Arms, I shou'd have thought the Devil had rais'd the Phantom, and my more conscious Reason had given my Eyes the Lye.

Lure. Very well! Then I a'n't to be believ'd, it seems.—But d'ye hear, Sir?

Wild. Nay, Madam, do you hear? I tell you, it is not in the Power of Malice to cast a Blot upon her Fame; and tho' the Vanity of our Sex, and the Envy of yours, conspir'd both against her Honour, I wou'd not hear a Syllable. [*Stopping his Ears.*

Lure. Why then, as I hope to breathe, you shall hear it —The Picture! the Picture! the Picture! [*Bawling aloud.*

Wild. Ran, tan, tan. A Pistol-bullet from Ear to Ear.

Lure,

Lure. That Picture which you had just now from the *French* Marquis for a thousand Pounds ; that very Picture did your very virtuous Wife send to the Marquis as a Pledge of her very virtuous and dying Affection. So that you are both robb'd of your Honour, and cheated of your Money.   [*A'oud.*

Wild. Louder, louder, Madam.

Lure. I tell you, Sir, your Wife was a jilt ; I know it, I'll swear it.—She virtuous ! She was a Devil.

Wild. [*Sings.*] Tal, lal, deral.

Lure. Was ever the like seen ! He won't hear me !—— I burst with Malice, and now he won't mind me !—— Won't you hear me yet ?

Wild. No, no, Madam.

Lure. Nay, then I can't bear it. [*Bursts out a crying.*]—— Sir, I must say that you're an unworthy Person, to use a Woman of Quality at this Rate, when she has her Heart full of Malice ; I don't know but it may make me miscarry. Sir, I say again and again, that she was no better than one of us, and I know it ; I have seen it with my Eyes, so I have.

Wild. Good Heav'ns deliver me, I beseech thee. How shall I 'scape ?

Lure. Will you not hear me yet ? Dear, Sir *Harry,* do but hear me ; I'm longing to speak.

Wild. Oh! I have it——Hush, hush, hush !

Lure. Eh ! What's the Matter ?

Wild. A Mouse ! a Mouse ! a Mouse !

Lure. Where ? where ? where ?

Wild. Your Petticoats, your Petticoats, Madam ! [*Lure. shrieks and runs.*] O my Head ! I was never worsted by a Woman before—But I have heard so much as to know the *Marquis* to be a Villain. [*Knocking.*] Nay then, I must run for't. [*Runs out, and returns.*]——The Entry is stopt by a Chair coming in ; and something there is in that Chair that I will discover, if I can find a Place to hide myself. [*Goes to the Closet-door.*] Fast ! I have Keys about me for most Locks about St. *James's*—Let me see—— [*Tries one Key.*]—No, no ; this opens my Lady *Planthorn's* Back-door.—[*Tries another.*]—Nor this ; this is the Key to my Lady *Stakeall's* Garden. [*Tries a Third.*] Ay, ay, this does it, faith.   [*Goes into the Closet, and peeps out.*

O 2   *Enter*

Enter Shark *and another, with* Clincher *in a Chair* ; Parly.

Par. Hold, hold, Friend; who gave you Orders to Jug in your dirty Chair into the House?

Sha. My Mafter, Sweet-heart.

Par. Who is your Mafter, Impudence?

Sha. Every Body, Sauce-box.—And for the prefent here's my Mafter! and if you have any Thing to fay to him, there he is for ye. [*Lugs* Clincher *out of the Chair, and throws him upon the Floor.*] Steer away, Tom.

Wild. What the Devil, Mr. *Jubilee*, is it you?

Par. Blefs me! the Gentleman's dead! Murder! Murder!

Enter Lurewell.

Lure. Proteƈt me! What's the matter, *Clincher?*

Par. Mr. *Clincher*, are you dead, Sir?

Clin. Yes.

Lure Oh! then it is well enough—Are you drunk, Sir?

Clin. No.

Lure. Well! certainly I'm the moft unfortunate Woman living: All my Affairs, all my Défigns, all my Intrigues, mifcarry.—Faugh! the Beaft! But, Sir, what's the matter with you?

Clin. Politics.

Par. Where have you been, Sir?

Clin. Shark!

Lure. What fhall we do with him, *Parly?* If the Colonel fhou'd come home now, we were ruin'd.

Enter Standard.

Oh, inevitable Deftruƈtion!

Wild. Ay, ay; unlefs I relieve her now, all the World can't fave her.

Stand. Blefs me! What's here? Who are you, Sir?

Clin. Brandy.

Stand. See there, Madam!—Behold the Man that you prefer to me! And fuch as He are all thofe Fop-Gallants that daily haunt my Houfe, ruin your Honour, and difturb my Quiet.—I urge not the facred Bond of Marriage; I'll wave your earneft Vows of Truth to me, and only lay the Cafe in equal Balance; and fee whofe Merit bears the greater Weight, his, or mine.

Wild. Well argu'd, Colonel.

Stand.

Stand. Suppose yourself freely difengag'd, unmarry'd, and to make a Choice of him you thought moft worthy of your Love; wou'd you prefer a Brute? a Monkey? one deftin'd only for the Sport of Man?—Yes; take him to your Bed; there let the Beaft difgorge his fulfome Load in your fair, lovely Bofom, fnore out his Paffion in your foft Embrace, and with the Vapours of his fick Debauch, perfume your fweet Apartment.

Lure. Ah naufeous! naufeous! Poifon!

Stand. I ne'er was taught to fet a Value on myfelf: But when compar'd to him, there Modefty muft ftoop, and Indignation give my Words a Loofe, to tell you, Madam, that I am a Man unblemifh'd in my Honour, have nobly ferv'd my King and Country; and for a Lady's Service, I think that Nature has not been defective.

Wild. Egad, I fhou'd think fo too; the Fellow's well made.

Stand. I'm young as he, my Perfon too as fair to outward View; and for my Mind, I thought it cou'd diftinguifh right, and therefore made a Choice of you——Your Sex have blefs'd our Ifle with Beauty, by diftant Nations priz'd; and cou'd they place their Loves aright, their Lovers might acquire the Envy of Mankind, as well as they the Wonder of the World.

Wild. Ah, now he coaxes—He will conquer, unlefs I relieve her in Time; fhe begins to melt already.

Stand. Add to all this, I love you next to Heav'n; and by that Heav'n I fwear, the conftant Study of my Days and Nights have been to pleafe my deareft Wife. Your Pleafure never met Controul from me, nor your Defires a Frown. —I never mention'd my Diftruft before, nor will I now wrong your Difcretion, fo as e'er to think you made him an Appointment.

Lure. Generous, generous Man! [*Weeps.*

Wild. Nay, then 'tis Time for me; I will relieve her.—— [*He fteals out of the Clofet, and coming behind* Standard, *claps him on the Shoulder.*] Colonel, your humble Servant.——

Stand. Sir *Harry,* how came you hither?

Wild. Ah, poor Fellow! Thou haft got thy Load with a Witnefs; but the Wine was humming ftrong; I have got a Touch on't myfelf. [*Reels a little.*

Stand. Wine, Sir *Harry!* What Wine?

Wild. Why, 'twas new *Burgundy*, heady Stuff. But the Dog was soon gone, knock'd under presently.

Stand. What, then Mr. *Clincher* was with you, it seems? Eh!

Wild. Yes faith, we have been together all this Afternoon: 'Tis a pleasant foolish Fellow. He would-needs give me a Welcome to Town, on Pretence of hearing all the News from the *Jubilee*. The Humor was new to me; so to't we went.——But 'tis a weak-headed Coxcomb! two or three Bumpers did his Business.——Ah, Madam! What do I deserve for this? *[Aside to Lurewell.*

Lure. Look ye there, Sir; you see how Sir *Harry* has clear'd my Innocence——I'm oblig'd t'ye, Sir; but I must have you to make it out. *[To Wild. and Ex.*

Stand. Yes, yes; he has clear'd you wonderfully.——But, pray, Sir—I suppose you can inform me how Mr *Clincher* came into my House? Eh!

Wild. Ay: Why you must know that the Fool got presently as drunk as a Drum; so I had him tumbled into a Chair, and ordered the Fellows to carry him home. Now you must know, he lodges but three Doors off; but the Boobies, it seems, mistook the Door, and brought him in here, like a Brace of Loggerheads.

Stand. O yes; sad Loggerheads, to mistake a Door in *James-Street* for a House in *Covent-Garden*——Here——

Enter Servants.

Take away that Brute. *[Servants carry off Clincher.* And you say 'twas new *Burgundy*, Sir *Harry*, very strong.

Wild. Egad, there is some Trick in this Matter, and I shall be discover'd *[Aside]* Ay, Colonel; but I must be gone: I'm engag'd to meet—Colonel, I'm your humble Servant. *[Going.*

Stand. But, Sir *Harry*, where's your Hat, Sir?

Wild. Oh Morbleu! These Hats, Gloves, Canes, and Swords, are the Ruin of all our Designs. *[Aside.*

Stand. But where's you Hat, Sir *Harry?*

Wild. I'll never intrigue again with any Thing about me but what is just bound to my Body. How shall I come off?————Hark ye, Colonel, in your Ear; I would not have your Lady hear it.——You must know, just as I came into the Room here, what shou'd I spy but a great Mouse running across that Closet-door: I took no notice, for fear your Lady should be frighted, but

with

h all my Force (d'ye fee) I flung my Hat at it, and fo
:w it into the Clofet, and there it lies.

tand. And fo, thinking to kill the Moufe, you flung
r Hat into that Clofet.

Vild. Ay, ay; that was all. I'll go fetch it.

tand. No, Sir *Harry,* I'll bring it out.
　　　　　　　　　　　　　[*Goes into the Clofet.*

Vild. Now have I told a Matter of twenty Lies in a
ath.

tand. Sir *Harry!* Is this the Moufe that you threw your
　　at ?　　[*Standard comes in with the Hat in one Hand,
　　　　　　and hawling in the Marquis with the other.*

Vild. I'm amaz'd !

Mar. Pardie, I'm amaze too.

tand. Look'e, Monfieur *Marquis,* as for your Part, I
l cut your Throat, Sir.

Vild. Give me Leave, I muft cut his Throat firft.

Mar. Vat ! Bote cut my Troat ! Begar, Meffieurs, I
but one Troat.

　　　　　Enter Parly, *and runs to* Standard.

Par. Sir, the Monfieur is innocent; he came upon
:her Defign. My Lady begins to be penitent, and,
ou make any Noife, 'twill fpoil all.

tand. Look'e, Gentlemen, I have too great a Confi-
:e in the Virtue of my Wife, to think it in the Power
ou, or you, Sir, to wrong my Honour: But I am
nd to guard her Reputation, fo that no Attempts be
e that may provoke a Scandal. Therefore, Gentle-
, let me tell you, it is Time to defift. '　　[*Exit.*

Vild. Ay, ay; fo it is, faith. Come, Monfieur, I muft
with you, Sir.　　　　　　　　　　　[*Exeunt.*

❦❦❦❦❦❦❦❦❦❦❦❦❦❦❦❦❦❦❦❦❦❦❦❦

A C T V.

SCENE, Standard's *Houfe.*

Enter Standard *and* Fireball.

d. IN fhort, Brother, a Man may talk till Dooms-
　　day of Sin, Hell, and Damnation: But your
toric will ne'er convince a Lady that there's any Thing
Devil in a handfome Fellow with a fine Coat. You
　　　　　　　　O 4　　　　　　　　muft

muſt ſhew the Cloven-foot, expoſe the Brute, as I have done; and tho' her Virtue ſleeps, her Pride will ſurely take th' Alarm.

Fire Ay, but if you had let me cut off one of the Rogue's Ears before you ſent him away—

Stand. No, no; the Fool has ſerv'd my Turn. without the Scandal of a public Reſentment; and the Effect has ſhewn that my Deſign was right: I've touch'd her very Heart, and ſhe relents apace.

Enter Lurewell *running.*

Lure. Oh! my Dear, ſave me! I'm frighted out of my Life.

Fire. Blood and Fire! Madam, who dare touch you?

[*Draws his Sword and ſtands before her.*

Lure. Oh, Sir! a Ghoſt! a Ghoſt! I have ſeen it twice.

Fire. Nay then, we Soldiers have nothing to do with Ghoſts; ſend for the Parſon.   {*Sheaths his Sword.*

Stand. 'Tis Fancy, my Dear, nothing but Fancy.

Lure. Oh dear Colonel! I'll never lie alone again: I'm frighted to Death; I ſaw it twice; twice it ſtalk'd by my Chamber-door, and with a hollow Voice utter'd a piteous Groan.

Stand. This is ſtrange! Ghoſts by Day light!—Come, my Dear, along with me; don't ſhrink, we'll ſee to find this Ghoſt.   [*Exeunt.*

S C E N E *changes to the Street.*

Enter Wildair, Marquis, *and* Dicky.

Wild. Dicky?

Dick. Sir.

Wild. Do you remember any Thing of a Thouſand Pounds lent to my Wife in *Montpelier* by a *French* Gentleman?

Mar. Oyy, Monſieur *Dicky*, you remembre de Gentleman, he was one Marquis.

Dick. Marqui, Sir! I think, for my Part, that all the Men in *France* are Marqui's. We met above a thouſand Marqui's, but the Devil of one of 'em could lend a Thouſand Pence, much leſs a Thouſand Pounds.

Mar. Morbleu, qui dit vous, Bougre le Chien?

Wild. Hold, Sir, pray anſwer me one Queſtion—What made you fly your Country?

Mar.

Mar. My Religion, Monfieur.

Wild. So you fled for your Religion out of *France*; and are a downright Atheiſt in *England?* A very tender Conſcience truly!

Mar. Begar, Monfieur, my Conſcience be de ver' tendre; he no ſuffre his Maſtre to ſtarve, pardie.

Wild. Come, Sir, no Ceremony; refund.

Mar. Refunde! Vat is dat refunde? Parlez *François,* Monfieur?

Wild. No, Sir; I tell you in plain *Engliſh,* return my Money, or I'll lay you by the Heels.

Mar. Oh! Begar dere is de Anglis-man now. Dere is de Law for me. De Law! Ecoute, Monfieur Sir *Airy*— Vóyez ſa—De *France* Marquis ſcorn de Law. My Broder lead your Vife de Money, and here is my Witneſs.

[*Draws.*

Wild. Your Evidence, Sir, is very poſitive, and ſhall be examin'd; but this is no Place to try the Cauſe; we'll croſs the Park into the Fields; you ſhall throw down the Money between us, and the beſt Title, upon a fair Hearing, ſhall take it up —Allons!

Mar. Oh! de tout mon Cœur—Allons! Fient â là Tate, begar.

[*Exit.*

SCENE, Lurewell's *Apartment.*

Enter Lurewell *and* Parly.

Lure. Pſhaw! I'm ſuch a frighted Fool! 'Twas nothing but a Fancy—Come, *Parly,* get me Pen and Ink, I'll divert it. Sir *Harry* ſhall know what a Wife he had, I'm reſolv'd. Tho' he wou'd not hear me ſpeak, he'll read my Letter ſure.

[*Sits down to write.*

Ghoſt, from within.—Hold!

Lure. Proteét me!—*Parly,* don't leave me.—But I won't mind it.

Ghoſt. Hold!

Lure. Defend me! Don't you hear a Voice?

Par. I thought ſo, Madam.

Lure. It call'd, Hold! I'll venture once more.

[*Sits down to write.*

Ghoſt. Diſturb no more the Quiet of the Dead.

Lure. Now it is plain. I heard the Words.

Par.

Par. Deliver us, Madam, and forgive us our Sins! What is it?

Ghost enters, Lurewell *and* Parly *shriek, and run to a Corner of the Stage.*

Ghost. Behold the airy Form of wrong'd *Angelica,*
Forc'd from the Shades below to vindicate her Fame;
Forbear, malicious Woman, thus to load
With scandalous Reproach the Grave of Innocence.
Repent, vain Woman!
Thy Matrimonial Vow is register'd above,
And all the Breaches of that solemn Faith
Are register'd below. I'm sent to warn thee to
repent.
Forbear to wrong thy injur'd Husband's Bed,
Disturb no more the Quiet of the Dead. [*Stalks off.*
                [Lurewell *swoons, and* Parly *supports her.*

Par. Help! help! help!

Enter Standard *and* Fireball.

Stand. Bless us! What, fainting! What's the Matter?

Fire. Breeding, breeding, Sir.

Par. Oh, Sir! we're frighted to Death; here has been the Ghost again.

Stand. Ghost! Why you're mad, sure! What Ghost?

Par. The Ghost of *Angelica,* Sir *Harry Wildair's* Wife.

Stand. *Angelica!*

Par. Yes, Sir; and here it preach'd to us the Lord knows what, and murder'd my Mistress with mere Morals.

Fire. A good Hearing, Sir; 'twill do her good.

Stand. Take her in, *Parly.* [Parly *leads out* Lurewell.] What can this mean, Brother?

Fire. The Meaning's plain. There's a Design of Communication between your Wife and Sir *Harry*; so his Wife is come to forbid the Bans, that's all.

Stand. No, no, Brother. If I may be induc'd to believe the walking of Ghosts, I rather fancy that the rattle-headed Fellow her Husband has broke the poor Lady's Heart; which, together with the Indignity of her Burial, has made her uneasy in her Grave.—But whatever be the Cause, it's fit we immediately find out Sir *Harry,* and inform him.   [*Exeunt.*

SCENE, *the Park.*

Company walking; Wildair *and* Marquis *passing hastily over the Stage, one calls.*

Lord. Sir *Harry.*   *Wild.*

ld. My Lord?—Monfieur, I'll follow you, Sir.

[*Exit.* Marquis.

I muft talk with you, Sir.

ld. Pray, my Lord, let it be very fhort, for I was in more Hafte in my Life.

May I prefume, Sir, to enquire the Caufe that i'd you fo late laft Night at my Houfe?

ld. More Mifchief again!—Perhaps, my Lord, I not prefume to inform you.

Then perhaps, Sir, I may prefume to extort it you.

ld. Look ye, my Lord, don't frown; it fpoils Face.—But if you muft know, your Lady owes me hundred Guineas, and that Sum I will prefume to t from your Lordfhip.

Two hundred Guineas? Have you any Thing to for it?

ld. Ha, ha, ha! Shew for it, my Lord, I fhew'd t and Quatorz for it; and to a Man of Honour, : as firm as a Bond and Judgment.

. Come, Sir, this won't pafs upon me; I'm a Man onour.

ld. Honour! Ha, ha, ha!—'Tis very ftrange that Men, tho' their Education be never fo gallant, ne'er learn Breeding! Look ye, my Lord, when you I were under the Tuition of our Governors, and ers'd only with old *Cicero, Livy, Virgil, Plutarch,* the like; why then fuch a Man was a Villain, and a one was a Man of Honour: But now, that I have rn the Court, a little of what they call the *Beaumonde,* he *Belle efprit,* I find that Honour looks as ridiculous *oman* Bufkins upon your Lordfhip, or my full Pe- upon *Scipio Africanus.*

. Why fhould you think fo, Sir?

ild. Becaufe the World's improv'd, my Lord, and nd that this Honour is a very troublefome and im- nent Thing—Can't we live together like good hbours and Chriftians, as they do in *France?* I you my Coach, I borrow yours; you dine with me, with you; I lie with your Wife, and you lie with .—Honour! That's fuch an Impertinence!—Pray, .ord, hear me. What does your Honour think of lering your Friend's Reputation; making a Jeft of

O 6　　　　　　　　　　 his

his Misfortunes ; cheating him at Cards; debauching
his Bed ; or the like ?

Lo. Why rank Villainy.

Wild. Pish! Pish! Nothing but good Manners; Excess
of good Manners.   Why you ha'n't been at Court lately.
There 'tis the only Practice to shew our Wit and Breeding—
As for Instance : Your Friend reflects upon you when absent,
because 'tis good Manners ; rallies you when present, because 'tis witty ; cheats you at Piquet, to shew he has been
in *France* ; and lies with your Wife, to shew he's a Man
of Quality.

Lo. Very well, Sir.

Wild. In short, my Lord, you have a wrong Notion of
Things.   Shou'd a Man with a handsome Wife revenge all
Affronts done to his Honour, poor *White, Chaves, Morris,
Locket, Pawlet* and *Pontack*, were utterly ruin'd.

Lo. How so, Sir ?

Wild. Because, my Lord, you must run all their Customers
quite through the Body.   Were it not for abusing your
Men of Honour, Taverns and Chocolate-Houses cou'd not
subsist; and were there but a round Tax laid upon Scandal
and false Politics, we Men of Figure wou'd find it much
heavier than four Shillings in the Pound.——Come, come,
my Lord, no more on't, for Shame ; your Honour is safe
enough, for I have the Key of its Back-door in my Pocket.
                                                    [*Runs off.*

Lo. Sir, I shall meet you another Time.   [*Exit.*

         S C E N E, *the Fields.*

Enter Marquis *with a Servant carrying his fighting Equipage,*
  Pumps, *Cap,* &c. *He dresses himself accordingly, and*
  flourishes about the Stage.

Mar. Sa, sa, sa, fient à la Tate. Sa, Embaracade : Quart
for redouble.   Hey !

         Enter Wildair.

Wild. Ha, ha, ha! the Devil! Must I fight with a
Tumbler ? These *French* are as great Fops in their Quarrels,
as in their Amours.

Mar. Allons! Allons! Stripe, stripe!

Wild. No, no, Sir, I never strip to engage a Man ; I fight
as I dance.——Come, Sir, down with the Money.

Mar. Dere it is, pardie.
                         [*Lays down the Bag between 'em.*
Allons!

                                                    Enter

Enter Dicky, *and gives* Wildair *a Gun.*

Morbleu! que fa?

Wild. Now, Monfieur, if you offer to ftir, I'll fhoot you through the Head.—*Dicky,* take up the Money, and carry it home.

Dick. Here it is, faith: And if my Mafter be kill'd, the Money's my own.

Mar. Oh Morbleu! de Anglis-man be one Coward.

Wild. Ha, ha, ha! Where is your *French* Politique, now? Come, Monfieur, you muft know I fcorn to fight any Man for my own; but now we're upon the Level; and fince you have been at the Trouble of putting on your Habiliments, I muft requite your Pains. So come on, Sir.
[*Lays down the Gun, and ufes his Sword.*

Mar. Come on! For war, wen de Money is gone! De *France-man* fight were dere is no Profit! Pardonnez moy, pardie.   [*Sits down to pull off his Pumps.*

Wild. Hold, hold, Sir; you muft fight. Tell me how you came by this Picture?

Mar. [*Starting up.*] Wy den, begar, Monfieur Chevalier, fince de Money be gone, me will fpeak de veritie:—Pardie, Monfieur, me did make de Cuckle of you, and your Vife fend me de Picture for my Pain.

Wild. Look ye, Sir, if I thought you had Merit enough to gain a Lady's Heart from me, I wou'd fhake Hands immediately, and be Friends: But as I believe you to be a vain fcandalous Liar, I'll cut your Throat.   [*They fight.*

Enter Standard *and* Fireball, *who part 'em.*

Stand. Hold, hold, Gentlemen.——Brother, fecure the Marquis——Come, Sir *Harry,* put up; I have fomething to fay to you very ferious.

Wild. Say it quickly then; for I am a little out of Humour, and want fomething to make me laugh.
[*As they talk,* Marquis *dreffes, and* Fireball *helps him.*

Stand. Will what's very ferious make you laugh?

Wild. Moft of all.

Stand. Pfhaw! Pray, Sir *Harry,* tell me what made you leave your Wife?

Wild. Ha, ha, ha! I knew it——Pray, Colonel, what makes you ftay with your Wife?

Stand. Nay, but pray anfwer me directly; I beg it as a Favour.

                                                                Wild.

Wild. Why then, Colonel, you muſt khow we were a Pair of the moſt happy, toying, fooliſh People in the World, till ſhe got, I don't know how, a Crotchet of Jealouſy in her Head. This made her frumpiſh; but we had ne'er an angry Word: She only fell a crying over Night, and I went for *Italy* next Morning.——But pray no more on't.—— Are you hurt, Monſieur?

Stand. But, Sir *Harry*, you'll be ſerious when I tell you that her Ghoſt appears.

Wild. Her Ghoſt! Ha, ha, ha! That's pleaſant, faith.

Stand. As ſure as Fate, it walks in my Houſe.

Wild. In your Houſe! Come along, Colonel; by the Lard I'll kiſs it.   [*Exeunt* Wild. *and* Stand.

Mar. Monſieur le Captain, Adieu.

Fire. Adieu! No, Sir, you ſhall follow Sir *Harry.*

Mar. For wat?

Fire. For, what! Why d'ye think I'm ſuch a Rogue as to part a Couple of Gentlemen when they're fighting, and not ſee 'em make an End on't:——I think it a leſs Sin to part Man and Wife,——Come along, Sir.

[Exit, *pulling Monſieur.*

SCENE, Standard's *Houſe.*

Enter Wildair *and* Standard.

Wild. Well then; this, it ſeems, is the inchanted Chamber. The Ghoſt has pitch'd upon a handſome Apartment however.—Well, Colonel, when do you intend to begin?

Stand. What, Sir?

Wild. To laugh at me; I know you deſign it.

Stand. Ha! By all that's powerful, there it is.

Ghoſt walks croſs the Stage.

Wild. The Devil it is——Emh! Blood, I'll ſpeak to't.—— Vous, Mademoiſelle Ghoſt, parlez vous François?—No! Hark ye, Mrs Ghoſt, will your Ladyſhip be pleas'd to inform us who you are, that we may pay you the Reſpect due to your Quality.   [*Ghoſt returns.*

Ghoſt. I am the Spirit of thy departed Wife.

Wild. Are you, faith! Why then here's the Body of thy living Huſband, and ſtand me if you dare. [*Runs to her, and embraces her.*]—Ha! 'tis Subſtance, I'm ſure.—But hold,

Lady

Lady Ghoft, ftand off a little, and tell me in good Earneft now, whether you are alive or dead.

Ang. [*Throwing-off her Shroud.*]——Alive! alive! [*Runs and throws her Arms about his Neck.*] and never liv'd fo much as in this Moment.

Wild. What d'ye think of the Ghoft now, Colonel? [*She hangs upon him.*] Is it not a very loving Ghoft?

Stand. Amazement!

Wild. Ay, 'tis Amazement, truly.——Look ye, Madam, I hate to converfe fo familiarly with Spirits: Pray keep your Diftance.

Ang. I am alive, indeed I am.

Wild. I don't believe a Word on't.   [*Moving away.*

Stand. Sir *Harry*, you're more afraid now.than before.

Wild. Ay, moft Men are more afraid of a living Wife than a dead one.

Stand. 'Tis good Manners to leave you together however.   [*Exit.*

Ang. 'Tis unkind, my Dear, after fo long and tedious an Abfence, to act the Stranger fo.   I now fhall die in earneft, and muft for ever vanifh from your Sight.

[*Weeping and going.*

Wild. Hold, hold, Madam.   Don't be angry, my Dear; you took me unprovided: Had you but fent me Word of your coming, I had got three or four Speeches out of *Oroonoko* and the *Mourning-Bride* upon this Occafion, that wou'd have charm'd your very Heart.   But we'll do as well as we can; I'll have the Mufic from both Houfes; *Pawlet* and *Locket* fhall contrive for our Tafte; we'll charm ours with *Abel's* Voice; feaft our Eyes with one another; and thus, with all our Senfes tun'd to Love, we'll hurl off our Cloaths, leap into Bed, and there—Look ye, Madam, if I don't welcome you home with Raptures more natural, and more moving, than all the Plays in *Chriftendom*——I'll fay no more.

Ang. As mad as ever.

Wild. But eafe my Wonder firft, and let me know the Riddle of your Death.

Ang. Your unkind Departure hence, and your avoiding me abroad, made me refolve, fince I cou'd not live with you, to die to all the World befides: I fancy'd, that tho' it exceeded the Force of Love, yet the Power of Grief perhaps
                                           might

might change your Humour, and therefore had it given out that I dy'd in *France*; my Sickness at *Montpelier*, which indeed was next to Death, and the Affront offer'd to the Body of our Ambassador's Chaplain at *Paris* conduc'd to have my Burial private. This deceiv'd my Retinue; and by the Assistance of my Woman, and your faithful Servant, I got into Man's Cloaths, came home into *England*, and sent him to observe your Motions abroad, with Orders not to undeceive you till your Return—Here I met you in the Quality of Beau *Banter*, your busy Brother, under which Disguise I have disappointed your Design upon my Lady *Lurewell*; and, in the Form of a Ghost, have reveng'd the Scandal she this Day threw upon me, and have frighted her sufficiently from lying alone. I did resolve to have frighted you likewise, but you were too hard for me.

Wild. How weak, how squeamish, and how fearful are Women, when they want to be humour'd! and how extravagant, how daring, and how provoking, when they get the impertinent Maggot in their Head!——But by what Means, my Dear, could you purchase this double Disguise? How came you by my Letter to my Brother?

' *Ang.* By intercepting all your Letters since I came home. But for my ghostly Contrivance, good Mrs. *Parly* (mov'd by the Justness of my Cause, and a Bribe) was my chief Engineer.

Enter Fireball *and* Marquis.

Fire. Sir *Harry*, if you have a Mind to fight it out, there's your Man; if not, I have discharg'd my Trust.

Wild. Oh, Monsieur! Won't you salute your Mistress, Sir?

Mar. Oh, Morblea! Begar me must run to some oder Country now for my Religion.

Ang. Oh! what the *French* Marquis! I know him.

Wild. Ay, ay, my Dear, you do know him, and I can't be angry, because 'tis the Fashion for Ladies to know every Body: But methinks, Madam, that Picture now! Hang it, considering 'twas my Gift, you might have kept it—But no matter; my Neighbours shall pay for't.

Ang. Picture, my Dear! Cou'd you think I e'er wou'd part with that? No; of all my Jewels, this alone I kept, 'cause 'twas given by you.   [*Shews the Picture.*

Wild.

Wild. Eh ! Wonderful !—And what's this ?

　　　　　　　　　　　[Pulling out t'other Picture.

Ang. They're very much alike.

Wild. So alike, that one might fairly pass for t'other. —
Monsieur Marquis, *ecouté* —You did lie wid my Vise, and
she did give you de Picture for your Pain. Eh ! Come, Sir,
add to your *France* Politique a little of your Native Impudence, and tell us plainly how you came by't.

Mar. Begar, Monsieur Chevalier, wen de *France-man* can
tell no more Lie, den vill he tell Trute. — I was acquaint
wid de Paintre dat draw your Lady's Picture, an I give him
ten Pistole for de Copy.—An so me ave de Picture of all de
Beauty in *London* ; and by dis Politique, me ave de Reputation to lie wid dem all.

Wild. When perhaps your Pleasure never reach'd above a
Pit-Masque in your Life.

Mar. Au begar, for dat Matre, de Natre of Women, a
Pit-Masque is as good as de best. De Pleasure is noting,
de Glory is all, Alamode de France.　　　　*[Struts out.*

Wild. Go thy ways for a true Pattern of the Vanity, Impertinence, Subtlety, and the Ostentation of thy Country.
—Look ye, Captain, give me thy Hand ; once I was a
Friend to *France* ; but henceforth I promise to sacrifice my
Fashions, Coaches, Wigs, and Vanity, to Horses, Arms,
and Equipage, and serve my King *in propria Persona,* to pro-
mote a vigorous War, if there be Occasion.

Fire. Bravely said, Sir *Harry:* And if all the Beaux in
the Side-boxes were of your Mind, we would send 'em back
their *L'Abbe,* and *Balon,* and shew 'em a new Dance, to the
Tune of *Harry* the Fifth.

　　　　Enter Standard, Lurewell, Dicky *and* Parly.

Wild. Oh Colonel ! Such Discoveries !

Stand. Sir, I have heard all from your Servant ; honest
Dicky has told me the whole Story.

Wild. Why then let *Dicky* run for the Fiddles immediately.

Dick. Oh, Sir ; I knew what it would come to ; they're
here already, Sir.

Wild. Then, Colonel, we'll have a new Wedding, and
begin it with a Dance—Strike up.　　　　*[A Dance here.*

Stand. Now, Sir *Harry,* we have retriev'd our Wives ;
yours from Death, and mine from the Devil ; and they are,
at present very honest. But how shall she keep 'em so ?

　　　　　　　　　　　　　　　　　　Ang.

Ang. By being good Husbands, Sir ; and the great Secret for keeping Matters right in Wedlock, is never to quarrel with your Wives for Trifles : For we are but Babies at best, and must have our Play things, our Longings, our Vapours, our Frights, our Monkies, our China, our Fashions, our Washes, our Patches, our Waters, our Tattle and Impertinence; therefore, I say, 'tis better to let a Woman play the Fool, than provoke her to play the Devil.

Lure. And another Rule, Gentleman, let me advise you to observe ; never to be jealous ; or if you shou'd, be sure never to let your Wife think you suspect her ; for we are more restrain'd by the Scandal of the Lewdness, than by the Wickedness of the Fact ; when once a Woman has borne the Shame of a Whore, she'll dispatch you the Sin in a Moment.

Wild We're oblig'd to you Ladies, for your Advice; and in Return, give me Leave to give you the Definition of a good Wife, in the Character of my own.

The Wit of her Conversation never out-strips the Conduct of her Behaviour : She's affable to all Men, free with no Man, and only kind to me : Often chearful, sometimes gay, and always pleas'd, but when I am angry ; then sorry, not sullen : The Park, Play-house, and Cards, she frequents in Compliance with Custom ; but her Diversions of Inclination are at home ; She's more cautious of a remarkable Woman, than of a noted Wit, well knowing that the Infect on of her own Sex is more catching than the Temptation of ours : To all this, she is beautiful to a Wonder, scorns all Devices that engage a Gallant, and uses all Arts to please her Husband.

> *So, spite of Satire 'gainst a marry'd Life,*
> *A Man is truly blest with such a Wife.*

EPILOGUE.

By a FRIEND.

Ventre bleu! vere is dis dam Poet? vere
  Garzoon! me vil cut off ail his two Ear:
Je suis Enrage——— now he is not here.
He has affront de French! Le vilainé Béte!
De French! your best Friend!———you suffre dat?
Parbleu! Messieurs a serait fort Ingrate!
Vat have you English dat you can call your own?
Vat have you of grand Pleasure in dis Town,
Vidout it come from France, dat vil go down!
Picquet. Basset; your Vin, your Dress, your Dance;
'Tis all, you see, tout Alamode de France.
De Beau dere buy a hondre Knick-knack;
He carry out Wit, but seldom bring it back:
But den he bring a Snuff-box Hinge, so small
De Joint, you canno see de Vark at all,
Cost him five Pistoles, dat is sheap enough,
In tre Year it sall save half an Ounce of Snuffe.
De Coquet, she ave her Ratasia dere,
Her Gown, her Complexion, Deux yeux, her Lovere.
As for de Cuckold——— dat indeed you can make here,
De French it is dat teach de Lady wear
De short Muff, wit her vite Elbow bare;
De Beaux de large Muff, wit his Sleeve down dere. *
Ve teach your Vifes to ope dere Husbands Purses,
To put de Furbelo round dere Coach, and dere Horses.
Garzoon! ve teach you every Ting de Varle;
For vy den your damn Poet dare to snarle?
Begar, me vil be revenge upon his Play,
Tre toufan Refugee (Parbleu c'est vray)
Sall ail come here, and damn him upon his tird Day.

* Pointing to his Fingers.

FINIS.

FARCES,

FARCES, &c. 8vo. lately printed, 1s each.

Amintas, an Opera
Author, by Mr. Foote
Boarding-School, with Music, by Coffey
Britons Strike Home, with Music, by W. Philips, Esq.
Beggar's Wedding
Chambermaid, with Music
Coffee-House, by Miller
Citizen, by Mr. Murphy
Devil of a Duke
Damon and Phyllida, by C. Cibber
Edgar and Emmeline, by Dr. Hawkesworth
Fatal Extravagance, by A. Hill
Generous Free-mason, by Mr. Chetwood, with Music

King Lear, altered by Mr. Colman
Hospital for Fools, by Mr. Miller
Livery Rake, by Mr. Philips, with Music
Muses in Mourning, to which is added Merlin in Love, by A. Hill
Merry Cobbler, or Second Part of Devil to pay, with Music, by Coffey
Oroonoko, altered by Dr. Hawkesworth
Quakers Opera, with Music, by Mr. Walker
Rover, by Mrs. Behn
Spirit of Contradiction
Stratford Jubilee, by Mr. Gentleman
Taste, by Mr. Foote
Thomas and Sally, by Bickerstaff

PLAYS, 12mo. 6d each.

Æsop, by Vanbrugh
Albion and Albianus
Albion Queens, by Bankes
Alcibiades, by Otway
All for Love, by Dryden
Ambitious Step-mother
Amboyna, by Dryden
Amorous Widow
Amphytrion, by Dryden
Anatomist, by Ravenscroft

Anna Bullen, by Bankes
Artful Husband
Artifice, by Centlivre
Athalia, by Duncomb
Aurengzebe, by Dryden
Basset Table, by Centlivre
Beggars Opera, by Gay
Bold Stroke for a Wife
Busiris, by Dr. Young
Busy Body, by Centlivre

Caius

PLAYS, 12mo. 6d. each.

Marius
ves, by Gay
:fs Hufband
by Addifon
:es
et, by Mr. Mendez
iittee, by Howard
ieft of Granada
dy of Errors
ious Lovers
ivances, by Carey
:ry Laffes
eline, by Shakefpeare
eline, altered by Mr.
rrick
in and Phillida, by Mr.
iden
to Pay, by Coffey
ffed Mother
Carlos, by Otway
Sebaftian
le Dealer
le Gallant
mer, by Addifon
of Guife
and no Duke
if Effex, by Bankes
ng's Love
Man in his Humour,
red by Mr. Garrick
Quaker of Deal
'enitent, by Rowe
Secret
or Hob in the Well
lfhip in Fafhion
al, by Sir R. Steele
fter, by Mrs. Cent-
e
ge Barnwell, by Lillo
iwich Park

Hamlet, by Shakefpeare
Henry V. by Shakefpeare
Henry V. by A. Hill
Heroic Daughter
Honeft Yorkfhireman
Inconftant, by Farquhar
Indian Emperor, by Dryden
Indian Queen, by ditto
Ifland Princefs
Jane Gray, by Mr. Rowe
Jane Shore, by ditto
King Arthur, by Dryden
King Lear, by Shakefpeare
Ditto, by Tate
King John, by Shakefpeare
Ladies Laft Stake
Love for Love
Love in a Riddle
Love's Laft Shift
Love makes a Man
Lying Lover, by Steele
Macbeth
Mourning Bride
Nonjurer
Old Bachelor
Oroonoko, by Southern
Orphan, by Otway
Othello, by Shakefpeare
Phædra and Hippolitus
Polly, by Mr. Gay
Provoked Hufband, by
Cibber
Provoked Wife
Recruiting Officer
Refufal, by Cibber
Rehearfal, by D. of Bucks
Relapfe, by Vanbrugh
Revenge, by Dr. Young
Richard III. altered by
Cibber

Rival

PILOGUE.

By a FRIEND.

tre bleu! vere is dis dam Poet? vere
Garzoon! me vil cut off all his two Ear:
us Enrage——now he is not here.
is affront de French! Le vilaine Bête!
rench! your best Friend!——you suffre dat?
eu! Messieurs a serait fort Ingrate!
ave you English dat you can call your own?
ave you of grand Pleasure in dis Town,
t it come from France, dat vil go down!
et, Basset; your Vin, your Dress, your Dance;
ill, you see, tout Alamode de France.
eau dere buy a bondre Knick-knack;
rry out Wit, but seldom bring it back:
en be bring a Snuff-box Hinge, so small
cint, you canno see de Vark at all,
him five Pistoles, dat is sheap enough,
t Year it sall save half an Ounce of Snuffe.
cquet, she ave her Ratafia dere,
own, her Complexion, Deux yeux, her Lovere.
r de Cuckold——dat indeed you can make here,
ench it is dat teach de Lady wear
urt Muff, wit her vite Elbow bare;
eaux de large Muff, wit his Sleeve down dere. *
ch your Vifes to ope dere Husbands Purses,
t de Furbelo round dere Coach, and dere Horses.
oon! ve teach you every Ting de Varle;
y den your damn Poet dare to snarle?
r, me vil be revenge upon his Play,
ulan Refugee (Parbleu c'est vray)
ll come here, and damn him upon his tird Day.

---

* Pointing to his Fingers.

F I N I S.

PLAYS, 12mo. 6d. each.

Rival Queens, by Lee
Romeo and Juliet, altered by Mr. Garrick
Schoolboy, by Cibber
She would and she would not, by Cibber
Siege of Damascus
Sir Courtly Nice, by Crown
Sir Harry Wildair
Sir Walter Raleigh
'Squire of Alfatia
Stage Coach, by Farquhar
Suspicious Husband
Tamerlane, by Rowe

Tender Husband, by Ste
Theodosius, by Lee
Timon of Athens
Tunbridge Walks
Twin Rivals, by Farqu
Venice Preserved, by (
    way
Way of the World
What d'ye call it?
Wild Gallant
Wit without Money
Woman's a Riddle
Wonder, by Centlivre
Zara, by A Hill, Esq.

H. M.

CPSIA information can be obtained at www.ICGtesting.com
Printed in the USA
LVOW061529120612

285781LV00004B/44/P